Discourse Grammar
of the Greek
New Testament

Discourse Grammar of the Greek New Testament

A Practical Introduction for Teaching and Exegesis

Lexham Bible Reference Series

STEVEN E. RUNGE

HENDRICKSON PUBLISHERS

Discourse Grammar of the Greek New Testament
by Steven E. Runge

Hendrickson Publishers Marketing, LLC
P. O. Box 3473
Peabody, Massachusetts 01961-3473

ISBN 978-1-59856-583-6

Published by arrangement with Logos Research Systems, Inc.,
1313 Commercial Street, Bellingham, WA 98225.

Printed in the United States of America

First Printing—December 2010

Hendrickson Publishers is strongly committed to environmentally respon-sible printing practices. The pages of this book were printed using only soy or vegetable content inks.

Library of Congress Cataloging-in-Publication Data

Runge, Steven E., 1967–
    Discourse grammar of the Greek New Testament : a practical
    introduction for teaching & exegesis / Steven E. Runge.
        p. cm.
    Text in English and Greek.
    Includes bibliographical references.
    ISBN 978-1-59856-583-6 (alk. paper)
    1. Greek language, Biblical—Study and teaching. 2. Greek language,
Biblical—Grammar. 3. Greek language, Biblical—Discourse analysis.
    4. Bible. N.T.—Language, style. I. Title.
    PA817.R68 2010
    487′.4—dc22
                                            2010041842

CONTENTS

Part 3 Information Structuring Devices

CREDITS

ABBREVIATIONS

General

B.C.E.	before the common era
c.	century
cf.	*confer*, compare
DA	Discourse Analysis
e.g.	*exempli gratia*, for example
esp.	especially
FG	Functional Grammar
HP	historical present
i.e.	*id est*, that is
no.	number
NT	New Testament
OT	Old Testament
RRG	Role and Reference Grammar
RT	Relevance Theory
SFL	Systemic Functional Linguistics

Biblical Books

Gen	Genesis
Exod	Exodus
Deut	Deuteronomy
Josh	Joshua
Ps	Psalm
Isa	Isaiah
Hab	Habakkuk
Matt	Matthew
Rom	Romans
1–2 Cor	1–2 Corinthians
Gal	Galatians
Eph	Ephesians
Phil	Philippians
Col	Colossians
1–2 Thess	1–2 Thessalonians
1–2 Tim	1–2 Timothy

Phlm   Philemon
Heb   Hebrews
Jas   James
1–2 Pet   1–2 Peter
Rev   Revelation

Bible Editions and Versions

ESV   English Standard Version
KJV   Authorized (King James) Version
LDGNT   *Lexham Discourse Greek New Testament*
LEB   Lexham English Bible
LXX   Septuagint Greek Old Testament
NA²⁷   *Novum Testamentum Graece*, Nestle-Aland, 27th edition
NASB   New American Standard Version
NIV   New International Version
NKJV   New King James Version
NRSV   New Revised Standard Version
RSV   Revised Standard Version
UBS⁴   *Greek New Testament*, United Bible Societies, 4th edition

Apostolic Fathers

2 Clem.   *Second Clement*
Ign. *Eph.*   Ignatius, *To the Ephesians*
Ign. *Phld.* Ignatius, *To the Philadelphians*
Ign. *Pol.*   Ignatius, *To Polycarp*
Ign. *Rom.*   Ignatius, *To the Romans*
Ign. *Trall.* Ignatius, *To the Trallians*
Pol. *Phil.* Polycarp, *To the Philippians*

Secondary Sources

BDAG   Bauer, W., F. W. Danker, W. F. Arndt, and F. W. Gingrich.
              *Greek-English Lexicon of the New Testament and Other Early
              Christian Literature*. 3rd ed. Chicago, 1999
BDF   Blass, F., A. Debrunner, and R. W. Funk. *A Greek Grammar
              of the New Testament and Other Early Christian Literature*.
              Chicago, 1961
BLS   Bible and Literature Series
CCC   Crossway Classic Commentaries
CLLT   *Corpus Linguistics and Linguistic Theory*
CSL   Cambridge Studies in Linguistics
FGS   Functional Grammar Series

FilNeot	*Filología Neotestamentaria*
FL	*Foundations of Language*
HSM	Harvard Semitic Monographs
IBC	Interpretation: A Bible Commentary for Teaching and Preaching
ICC	International Critical Commentary
IVPNTC	IVP New Testament Commentary
JBL	*Journal of Biblical Literature*
JGChJ	*Journal of Greco-Roman Christianity and Judaism*
JL	*Journal of Linguistics*
JLIABG	*Journal of the Linguistics Institute of Ancient and Biblical Greek*
JSNTSup	Journal for the Study of the New Testament Supplement Series
JSOTSup	Journal for the Study of the Old Testament Supplement Series
JSS	*Journal of Semitic Studies*
LABC	Life Application Biblical Commentary
LNTS	Library of New Testament Studies
LSAWS	Linguistic Studies in Ancient West Semitic
MHT	Moulton, Howard, and Turner, *A Grammar of New Testament Greek*
NAC	New American Commentary
NIGTC	New International Greek Testament Commentary
Notes	*Notes on Translation*
NovT	*Novum Testamentum*
NTC	New Testament Commentary
OThM	Oxford Theological Monographs
PNTC	Pillar New Testament Commentary
RBL	*Review of Biblical Literature*
RR	*Rhetoric Review*
SBG	Studies in Biblical Greek
SBJT	*Southern Baptist Journal of Theology*
SBLSBS	Society of Biblical Literature Sources for Biblcal Study
SFSL	Studies in Functional and Structural Linguistics
SNTG	Studies in New Testament Greek
TCQ	*Technical Communication Quarterly*
TSL	Typological Studies in Language
VT	*Vetus Testamentum*
WBC	Word Biblical Commentary
WPL	Working Papers in Linguistics

FOREWORD

This volume is long overdue. Students of the New Testament have been barraged for decades with linguists touting the value of discourse analysis, but few works have demonstrated its importance for exegesis. The esoteric vocabulary, minimal illustrations (especially of any substantial exegetical significance), and conflicting linguistic models have all contributed to massive inertia on the part of exegetes to dive into the material. In 2001, the theme of the annual convention of the Institute for Biblical Research was on the exegetical pay-off of grammar and linguistics. The very theme showed the nervousness of biblical scholars: they wanted to see the value of linguistic studies for the Greek and Hebrew texts, but the general sense was that there had been, to date, more bluster than substance.

Stanley Porter, Stephen Levinsohn, and others have been working tirelessly to show New Testament students that they need to learn about linguistics if they are to be accurate exegetes. They stand on good, solid shoulders. For biblical studies, the clarion call came with James Barr's *Semantics of Biblical Language*. His tome, produced fifty years ago, introduced students of the Bible to the fascinating work of Ferdinand de Saussure's *Cours de linguistique générale* (1916), which was translated into English in 1959. But it largely focused on lexical rather than grammatical linguistics. Still, Barr's *Semantics* stimulated many biblical scholars to investigate more thoroughly the realm of linguistics and to wrestle with its implications for exegesis. The ball was rolling, but it has taken decades to capture the imagination and interests of exegetes along the way.

What Runge has done is to focus on the exegetical significance of discourse grammar for *Neutestamenters*. He has gathered together several strands of linguistic insights (he calls his approach 'cross-linguistic' and 'function-based') that are often treated in isolation and sometimes without much more than lip service for exegesis. In short, Runge has made discourse analysis accessible, systematic, comprehensive, and meaningful to students of the New Testament. His presentation is clear, straightforward, and well researched.

At every turn, he offers linguistic insights into phenomena that are either only touched on in traditional grammars or dealt with too simplistically or even inaccurately. Plenty of examples from the New Testament are presented, along with detailed explanations. Traditional descriptions of various features of the Greek New Testament are compared with those of discourse analysis. At all points Runge is concerned to show that "if there is more than one way of accomplishing a discourse task, there is most likely a meaning associated with each choice" (148).

Discourse Grammar is a complement to traditional grammars, rather than in competition with them, although there are times when Runge chastises traditional grammarians (including me) for missing the forest for the trees. It almost goes without saying that not all grammarians or linguists will agree with every one of Runge's points. Yet even on those issues over which one might disagree, there is much food for thought here. I have learned a great deal from this volume and will continue to do so for many years. To students of the New Testament, I say, "The time has come. *Tolle lege!*"

Daniel B. Wallace
Professor of New Testament Studies
Dallas Theological Seminary

Executive Director
Center for the Study of New Testament Manuscripts

PREFACE

Linguistics has been touted by some in NT studies as the solution to a host of problems left unaddressed by traditional approaches to grammar. Unfortunately, linguistic practitioners often do little more than reshape the problem using complex jargon. Although there have been some breakthroughs, many believe that linguistics and discourse studies have overpromised and underdelivered. Wallace's statement is representative of this sentiment:

> Contrary to the current trend, this work has no chapter on discourse analysis (DA). The rationale for this lacuna is fourfold: (1) DA is still in its infant stages of development, in which the methods, terminology, and results tend to be unstable and overly subjective. (2) DA's methods, as shifting as they are, tend not to start from the ground up (i.e., they do not begin with the word, nor even with the sentence). This by no means invalidates DA; but it does make its approach quite different from that of syntactical investigation. (3) Along these lines, since this is explicitly a work on syntax, DA by definition only plays at the perimeter of that topic and hence is not to be included.[1]

The goal of this project is to fill in this lacuna, providing practical solutions to grammatical problems with minimal jargon. I do not seek to reinvent Greek grammar or to supplant previous work. I intentionally begin each chapter by reviewing how the particular issue has been treated by NT grammarians. It quickly becomes apparent that many contradictory claims have been made over the years, with little effort to reconcile them. My approach

---

1. Daniel B. Wallace, *Greek Grammar beyond the Basics: An Exegetical Syntax of the New Testament* (Grand Rapids: Zondervan, 1999), xv.

is to provide a unified description of each of the discourse features treated. The general result is to affirm most of the divergent claims, helping the reader synthesize a holistic understanding of the feature rather than just seeing the discrete parts.

Much of the grammatical discussion can be compared to trying to use only one adjective to describe a plastic drinking straw. Some might argue it is long, others might say it is round, while still others might insist it is hollow. Each viewpoint looks at only one aspect and thus fails to capture an accurate representation of the whole. In similar ways, this grammar seeks to unify what look like contradictory or divergent claims about a discourse feature.

The linguistic approach used here is *cross-linguistic,* meaning that it looks at how languages tend to operate rather than just focusing on Greek. Failure to look more broadly at language has led to implausible claims being made about Greek. Languages tend to operate in certain ways, following cross-linguistic patterns. Knowing this can greatly simplify the analytical process, leading to a more accurate description. It also allows for easier reference to other languages such as English or Hebrew.

The approach is also *function-based,* meaning that primary attention will be given to describing the task accomplished by each discourse feature. This function-based approach helps one to conceptualize what is happening in Greek by understanding how the comparable task is accomplished in another language. There are many mismatches between Greek and English, where the two languages use different devices to accomplish the same discourse task. Traditional approaches typically do not lend themselves to adequate explanations of such mismatches.

I will not ask you to throw out all that you have known to be true about Koiné Greek in favor of a brand new linguistic analysis. On the contrary, I endeavor to clear a pathway from the traditional field of NT studies to the field of functional linguistics for each of the features discussed. The goal is to bridge the chasm that has too long existed between traditional and linguistic approaches.

This text is designed to function as part of a larger suite of discourse resources I have developed over the last three years. Although I attempt to be thorough in my descriptions of devices, certain portions (chapters 9–14) are too complex to adequately equip the reader to do their own analysis after reading only this volume. For this reason I created the *Lexham Discourse Greek New Testament (LDGNT),*[2] which annotates all occurrences of the

---

2. Steve Runge, *The Lexham Discourse Greek New Testament* (Bellingham, Wash.: Logos Bible Software, 2007).

devices discussed below, using the same identifying symbols as I use in this volume.

I have found that even first-year Greek students can productively interact with the *LDGNT* after providing a basic introduction to the concepts. The *LDGNT* database is designed to function as a specialized discourse commentary, identifying exegetically significant features for consideration. The reader still bears the responsibility of synthesizing and interpreting the analysis and can choose to reject a claim just as one might with most any other scholarly resource. There is also an accompanying English edition bundled with the Greek analysis called the *Lexham High Definition New Testament* (*HDNT*).[3] It features most of the same Greek-based analysis overlaid on the ESV text.

The grammatical descriptions that follow are not based on carefully chosen selections designed to prove my point. Rather, the *LDGNT* project required me to rigorously apply my model to the entire Greek New Testament. So far as I know, no other scholar has completed such a comprehensive discourse-based description and application. Completing the analysis before writing the grammar had a number of benefits. First, it forced me to engage and address problematic counterexamples that challenged and improved my descriptions. Second, the *LDGNT* database enabled me to efficiently find illustrative examples for this resource as well as to verify the accuracy of the database.

The greatest single benefit derived from this research project, in my opinion, is the democratization of discourse studies for the nonspecialist. Gaining the kinds of insights to be found in the *LDGNT* required me to invest more than a decade of study to prepare and three years of work to complete. If you can grasp the concepts that follow, you will benefit from a more extensive interaction with *LDGNT* analysis. In a perfect world, everyone would develop sufficient competency in each exegetical specialization to conduct their own analysis. In reality, this is rarely attainable. We regularly rely upon the specialization of others to conduct exegesis, whether the analysis of text-critical scholars for critical editions of biblical texts, or the research of specialists in sociocultural, archaeological, or rhetorical studies for commentaries and monographs. In each case, we expect to gain a working knowledge of the principles governing the discipline, and then we critically interact with the scholarly works.

This volume provides the requisite overview of the needed principles and concepts. The *LDGNT* analysis permits you to quickly integrate discourse grammar into your ongoing study and research. The *HDNT* facilitates com-

---

3. Steve Runge, *The Lexham High Definition New Testament* (Bellingham, Wash.: Logos Bible Software, 2008).

munication of the same concepts to English-based audiences. There has been a method to my madness. I have invested my academic career in promoting a field that I believe can sharpen exegesis and help turn the receding tide of interest in biblical languages. However, all of these benefits are of little value if they are not readily transferable to others (besides my own students) and clearly explained with a view to practical application. This is the rationale for developing a suite of resources instead of just a monograph or database.

This work has benefited from research and interaction with numerous individuals over the years, most notably Stephen Levinsohn, Christo Van der Merwe, Randall Buth, Stan Porter, Carl Conrad, Rick Brannan, and many others. It will not be the final word on the matter. It is my hope that students and colleagues will develop an interest in these discourse features and will in turn provide more thorough and complete descriptions than are possible here. This is the intention for including the "suggested reading" sections at the end of each chapter. I want to get you interested and then get out of your way. I have painted in very broad strokes, likely too broad at some points. It is my hope that people who are more detail-oriented will come behind and tidy the messes that I have inevitably left behind. I alone bear responsibility for the shortcomings of this volume. I dedicate this volume to my father, the other Dr. Runge, who was teaching me how to think and problem-solve far before I ever figured out what he was up to.

PART 1   FOUNDATIONS

This section introduces some key concepts and covers the discourse function of Greek conjunctions.

INTRODUCTION

The purpose of this book is to introduce a function-based approach to language using discourse grammar.[1] I describe grammatical conventions based upon the discourse functions they accomplish, not based on their translation. Traditional approaches to grammar have focused primarily on word-level or sentence-level phenomenon. This has left a large body of usage poorly explained. Some attribute the remaining usage to "stylistic variation" or simply "optional usage" that has little significance. Although there are stylistic differences among writers, "to cite 'stylistic variation' as an explanation for the presence versus the absence of features in texts by a *single* storyteller is a cop-out."[2]

The difficulty that formal, structural approaches have experienced in describing the discourse phenomenon has led to the widespread belief that "discourse is too complex, too messy, too ill defined to be treated in a rigorous manner."[3] Although discourse is indeed messy and complex, one need

---

1. Dooley, cited by Levinsohn, describes it as "an attempt to discover and describe what linguistic structures are used for: the functions they serve, the factors that condition their use" (Stephen H. Levinsohn, *Discourse Features of New Testament Greek: A Coursebook on the Information Structure of New Testament Greek* [2nd ed.; Dallas: SIL International], vii). Levinsohn elsewhere states, "*Text-linguistics* (discourse analysis) does not draw its explanations from within the sentence or word (in other words, the factors involved are not syntactic or morphological). Rather, its explanations are *extra-sentential* (from the linguistic and wider context of the utterance). A significant part of text-linguistics involves the study of *information structure*, which concerns 'the interaction of sentences and their contexts' (Lambrecht 1994:9)" (Stephen H. Levinsohn, *Self-Instruction Materials on Narrative Discourse Analysis* [Dallas: SIL International, 2007], 1).

2. Levinsohn, *Narrative Discourse Analysis,* 3.

3. Livia Polyani, *The Linguistic Structure of Discourse* (Technical Report CSLI-96-200; Stanford, Calif.: CSLI Publications, 1996), 2.

not give up hope. The problems have more to do with the inadequacies of the descriptive framework used than they do with the incomprehensibility of language. After all, languages form a system, and meaning is tied to the operations within this system. The existence of a system implies that there are indeed describable patterns of usage.

Researchers have found that there is far greater consistency and intentionality in language usage than formal approaches would lead us to believe. What is needed is a descriptive framework functional and adaptable enough to "roll with the punches" of discourse, robust enough to handle the "mess." The framework also needs to be cross-linguistic in nature, informed by the kinds of tasks that every language needs to accomplish and by how all languages tend to operate.

Many of the devices described below involve the use of some grammatical feature in a context where it does not formally belong, one that essentially "breaks" the grammatical rules. Using devices in the "wrong" place to accomplish a discourse task contributes to the apparent messiness of the discourse devices: they do not play by the rules. Consider the kinds of descriptions one finds in NT Greek grammars. We traditionally label a present-tense verb used in a context where a past-tense verb is expected in English as a "historical present." We label an adverbial participle used in a context where we would expect an imperative in English as an "imperatival participle." Although such labeling does describe the usage to some extent, it tells us little about why the Greek writer would use such a form or about the specific effect that it achieves. Traditional descriptive frameworks often tell us more about how Greek and English differ than they do about Greek *as Greek*. Discourse grammar provides principles for understanding why a writer would use a historical present (see chapter 6) or an imperatival participle (see chapter 12). It provides a descriptive framework that is flexible and robust enough to elegantly capture the complexity of discourse phenomenon in a concise and practical description.

As compelling as the insights from discourse grammar might be, Levinsohn outlines two pitfalls to be avoided when analyzing texts. The first is "that we can become so enamoured with text-linguistic explanations that we fail to realise that a perfectly good syntactic rule or semantic definition accounts for the feature being analysed."[4] If there are semantic or grammatical constraints that require a certain usage in a certain context, there is little to be learned from discourse grammar. Although "some linguistic features can only

---

4. Levinsohn, *Narrative Discourse Analysis*, 2.

be explained with reference to extra-sentential factors," others are constrained "from a syntactic rule or semantic definition."[5]

The second pitfall is "*not relating* text-linguistic observations to a valid syntactic rule or semantic definition."[6] For example, it is common in Greek to see demonstrative pronouns discussed under several different sections of a grammar, leading to disparate comments that lack unity. Chapter 18 describes how Greek writers utilize demonstratives to signal or create near/far distinctions. This principle informs the function of demonstratives regardless of whether they function as personal pronouns, as demonstrative pronouns, or as modifiers. Discourse grammar can offer a unified explanation.

Discourse grammar does not replace formal approaches; it complements them. The description of optional usage is primarily where discourse grammar can make the greatest contribution. Remembering this helps us to avoid the first pitfall. Discourse grammar often provides more of a unified description of usage than is typically found in traditional approaches, and it can help us to avoid the second pitfall.

My approach presupposes three core principles:

- Choice implies meaning (§1.1).
- Semantic or inherent meaning should be differentiated from pragmatic effect (§1.2).
- Default patterns of usage should be distinguished from marked ones (§1.3).

These principles provide a framework for understanding and interpreting the decisions made regarding language usage. They have less to do with the specifics of a particular language and more to do with how humans are wired to process language. They are part of a cross-linguistic approach to language that applies just as much to Greek or English as to other languages. You will see this claim substantiated as the effects achieved by the discourse features are described. Examples are provided from both English and Greek, but there is no shortage of comparable examples that could be documented from other unrelated languages.

1.1   Choice Implies Meaning

One of the key presuppositions of discourse grammar is that *choice implies meaning*. All of us make choices as we communicate: what to include, how to prioritize and order events, how to represent what we want to say. The choices

---

5. Ibid.
6. Ibid.

we make are directed by the goals and objectives of our communication. The implication is that if a choice is made, then there is meaning associated with the choice. Let's unpack this idea a bit.

If I choose to do X when Y and Z are also available options, this means that I have at the same time chosen not to do Y or Z. Most of these decisions are made without conscious thought. As speakers of the language, we just do what fits best in the context based on what we want to communicate. Although we may not think consciously about these decisions, we are making them nonetheless.[7]

The same principle holds true for the writers of the NT. If a writer chose to use a participle to describe an action, he has at the same time chosen not to use an indicative or other finite verb form. This implies that there is some meaning associated with this decision. Representing the action using a participle communicates something that using a different mood would not have communicated. Defining the meaning associated with the choice is different from assigning a syntactic force or from determining an appropriate translation. It requires understanding what discourse task is performed by the participle that would not have been accomplished by another verb form.

Although there is tremendous diversity among languages, every language has to accomplish certain basic tasks. For instance, if I want to tell you a story about the first time I went rock climbing, I need to accomplish several tasks, such as:

- introduce the people involved in the story;
- set the time, place, and situation;
- provide background information that I think you might need (e.g., I have a fear of heights).

Once the scene is set and the story is underway, I need to do other things, such as:

- help you track who is doing what to whom;
- clearly communicate changes in time, place, or participants;
- provide some indication of how the events relate to one another;
- decide what information I want to group together in a single sentence and what I want to break into separate sentences;
- decide which part of the story is the climax and use the appropriate signals to communicate this to you;

---

7. This holds true whether we are skilled speakers of the language or not. Even illiterate speakers will vary their usage based on their communication objectives. It is an issue not of competency, but of choice.

- choose when to attract extra attention to significant details along the way.

Regardless of whether I am speaking or writing, I need some means of accomplishing these tasks. Since there is a common set of tasks that need to be accomplished across all languages, the task list can inform our description of what the different grammatical choices accomplish. The tasks provide an organizational framework to help us understand the meaningful difference between choosing X versus Y or Z.

This book is organized by task, not by morphology or syntax. Part 1 introduces some foundational concepts, including the discourse function of Greek conjunctions; part 2 describes forward-pointing devices; part 3 covers information structuring devices (emphasis and framing); part 4 covers thematic highlighting devices. Although there are several forward-pointing devices, each one accomplishes a slightly different task than do other grammatical devices, or they are differentiated by their use in narrative versus nonnarrative genres. Some devices use particles, others use pronouns. However, they all accomplish the same basic function. The objective here is to provide a unified description of these devices that complements traditional grammatical approaches.

Greek and English differ in a number of ways, making it difficult to understand Greek using English as your framework. At times, it can be like putting the proverbial square peg in a round hole. Using a task-based, cross-linguistic framework allows us to make apples-to-apples comparisons between Greek and English, even where they differ significantly. This is accomplished by talking about how the comparable task is accomplished in English, German, Hebrew, and so on. It enables us to understand Greek on its own terms *as Greek*, as well as to understand what the same task looks like in another language.

1.2   Semantic Meaning versus Pragmatic Effect

It is very important to distinguish between the inherent meaning of something (its semantic meaning) and the effect achieved by using it in a particular context (its pragmatic effect). For instance, the phrase "your children" is straightforward in its inherent meaning and typically is used to refer to kids that are not *mine*, but *yours*. If used in the right context however, a very different pragmatic effect can be achieved, one that is not part of its inherent meaning.

Imagine that my wife asked me how our kids behaved while she was out. If I began my answer with "Your children…," it would have a specific pragmatic effect, based on the context. This effect is not some hidden semantic meaning underlying the phrase, just an effect of using it in the right way in the right context. The pragmatic effect is achieved by using a more distant relational expression (*your*) in a context where a less distant one holds true (*my*). The expected norm is that I would use the closest relational expression possible. After all, they are my kids too! Calling them *my kids* or *the kids* is the expected norm. When I depart from this norm, a specific pragmatic effect of "distancing" is achieved, even though what I said was completely truthful.

Levinsohn offers another example:

> The progressive construction has a semantic meaning of incompleteness, as in "It's raining." However, in certain contexts it carries an overtone of insincerity, as in "John is being polite," in contrast to "John is polite." ... Insincerity is not part of the semantic meaning of the progressive; it is a pragmatic effect that is achieved by the use of the progressive in certain specific contexts.[8]

The unstated expectation is that qualities a person possesses should be expressed as a state ("he is polite"), not as a progressive action ("he is being polite"). The effect of using the progressive is to imply that the current state of affairs does not always hold true but is a passing thing.

Many jokes employ this principle of semantic meaning versus pragmatic effect to achieve humor. Often the joke establishes a state of affairs in preparation for the punch line, whose semantic meaning has a specific pragmatic effect in the context. In the movie *Airplane*, they repeatedly used the rhetorical question "What is it?" to create laughs. For example:

Speaker A: "We need to get to the airport."
Speaker B: "The airport, what is it?"
Speaker A: "It's a big place where airplanes land, but that's not important right now. What is important is...."

Speaker B is asking a rhetorical question, essentially "what is wrong?" Speaker A purposefully misconstrues the rhetorical question as though it were a content question asking for a definition for "airport." The context makes the listener expect one thing, but the expectation is unmet by the response as though it were a content question. The humor that comes about is a pragmatic effect of the usage in the context, not some hidden semantic meaning of the question.

This distinction between semantic meaning and pragmatic effect applies to ancient languages as well, such as Koiné Greek. Present-tense verbs typically are used to convey ongoing, continuous action that is occurring.[9] We

---

8. Levinsohn, *Discourse Features*, ix.
9. There is ongoing debate in Greek whether verbs convey tense, aspect, or both. Set-

could identify this as its semantic meaning. However, present-tense verbs are often used in the Gospels of Mark and John to encode past action in the narrative. This usage is traditionally called the "historical present," but this description provides little insight into why a Greek writer would use it. So what is the pragmatic effect of using a historical present in the Gospels?

The historical present (see chapter 6) stands out in the context because the expected pattern of usage is broken. Rather than changing the basic semantic meaning of the verb form or considering it to be incorrect usage, the historical present is a good example of taking an established pattern of usage and breaking it in order to achieve a specific pragmatic effect. Describing the effect of the historical present in Mark and John, Callow says that it

> does *not* draw attention to the event which the [historical present] verb itself refers to, as those events, in themselves, are not particularly important—*to go, to say, to gather together, to see, etc.*... [I]t has a *cataphoric* function; that is, it points on beyond itself into the narrative, it draws attention to what is following.[10]

The pragmatic effect of the historical present is to attract extra attention to the speech or event that follows, not to the historical present itself. The present tense does not have the inherent semantic meaning of "highlighting." The "historical" usage has the pragmatic effect of drawing extra attention to what follows, since it breaks the expected pattern of usage.

Most languages do not have specialized devices that are singularly devoted to prominence marking. It is far more common to find a nonstandard usage achieving specific pragmatic effects. Greek is no exception. The use of the historical present for forward-pointing highlighting exemplifies this. Using a grammatical construction in an ostensibly wrong or unexpected way has the effect of making something stand out. The pragmatic effect achieved is dependent upon the discourse context in which it occurs. The devices described in the chapters that follow exploit some departure from an expected norm to achieve a specific pragmatic effect. Distinguishing semantic meaning from pragmatic effect is critical to providing a coherent and accurate description of the device and its function within the discourse. Neglecting this distinction leaves you with "messy discourse"!

---

ting the debate aside, I maintain that the imperfective aspect (imperfect and present) is the most likely candidate for grammaticalizing some kind of tense information, since there are two options for conveying the same aspect. My interest here is not to settle the "tense versus aspect" debate, but to illustrate a text-linguistic principle with a well-attested usage.

10. John Callow, "The Historic Present in Mark" (seminar handout, 1996), 2, cited in Levinsohn, *Discourse Features*, 202.

1.3   Default versus Marked Framework

We have already noted several ways that speakers' choices inform grammatical usage. Another aspect of discourse grammar is the arrangement of the available choices for a given task into an organized system. It is useful to consider the various options available for a given task as comprising an asymmetrical set based upon *markedness theory*.[11]

This approach to markedness is quantitative in nature, seeking to differentiate a set of similar items from one another based on the unique quality that each member brings to bear. The members are similar but not the same, so there must be something that sets each apart from the other. Asymmetrical markedness provides this differentiation qualitatively, describing the set of characteristics that make each member of the set unique.

Consider English personal pronouns as an example. We could divide them up by number, obtaining one group of singular ones, and another of plural. Alternatively, we could divide them up by person, arriving at three groups—first, second and third person:

	Singular	Plural
1st Person	I	We
2nd Person	You	You
3rd Person	He/She/It	They

By combining the two qualities of number and person, we could uniquely differentiate each pronoun using a plus/minus system with the symbol S representing the singular quality. For instance, "I" would be singular (+S) and first person, and "they" would be plural (-S) and third person. The pronoun "you" provides something of a challenge, since it can be used in both singular and plural contexts.

---

11. See Edna Andrews, *Markedness Theory: The Union of Asymmetry and Semiosis in Language* (Durham, N.C.: Duke University Press, 1990). An asymmetrical approach to markedness views each member of a given set as uniquely marking the presence of some discrete feature. In other words, there is not symmetry among the members; each differs in some way from the other. In contrast, a symmetrical approach to markedness views the members of the set as being differentiated on the basis of frequency of occurrence and distribution. See Stanley E. Porter and Matthew Brook O'Donnell, "The Greek Verbal Network Viewed from a Probabilistic Standpoint: An Exercise in Hallidayan Linguistics," *FilNeot* 14 (2001): 3–41.

	PERSON	NUMBER
I	1st	+S
WE	1st	-S
THEY	3rd	-S
YOU	2nd	?

Markedness is fundamentally the study of "markers," those things that signal the presence of some quality or linguistic feature. In the case of "you," the person is clearly signaled (second person), but the number is not. It could be singular or plural. We could say that "you" is *unmarked* for number. There is no marker present to tell us whether it is singular or plural; we would have to rely on context.

Believe it or not, this kind of ambiguity happens quite a bit in language, with one form wearing multiple hats. It may seem strange to an outsider, but to the native speaker it is "normal." In English, we have no concern for insuring that the listener knows which "you" we mean, except perhaps in the southern United States, where the form "y'all" is used to disambiguate second person plural from singular (though I have heard this form used for a singular person–me!). Similary, Old English used the distinct forms *thou* and *ye* to differentiate singular from plural. Pressure for efficiency and other factors in the historical development of the language led to a streamlining of the forms until the two finally came to share a single form.

To summarize, markedness theory presupposes that one member of a set is the most basic or simple member, called the "default" member. All of the other members signal or "mark" the presence of some unique quality, one that would not have been marked if the default option were used. The marked options are described based on how they uniquely differ both from the default and from one another.

Consider the aforementioned example of "my" children compared to "your" children. I could organize the various options for referring to my kids into a qualitative set. When I have no special task to accomplish, I most typically use "the kids" as a referring expression. Taking this expression as the default, using expressions such as "your kids," "my kids," or "Ruth and her sister" would be expected to signal the presence of some quality or discourse feature that "the kids" would not have signaled. Using "the kids" does not explicitly signal whether I am distancing myself from them or not, whereas "your kids" does.

The default option is considered "unmarked" for the qualities found in the other members of the set. The quality may or may not be present. The choice to use a marked form represents the choice to explicitly signal the presence of a quality that would only have been implicit if the default were used.

Since the default or unmarked option is the most basic, it is often the one that occurs most frequently. Caution is called for when appealing to statistics, since the objective of markedness is to find the most basic option, the one that carries the least freight with it. It is not simply the most frequently occurring one.[12] The more complex a set of items becomes (beyond a binary opposition), the more misleading and unrepresentative the insights from statistics become.[13] Factors such as genre and content can skew frequency, so care must be taken in selecting the default.[14] Once the default is selected, the marked forms are then described based on the unique quality that each one signals is present. Think of the default as the foil against which the marked forms are contrasted and described.[15]

Chapter 2 describes the unique discourse constraints communicated by each of the most frequently occurring connectives found in the Greek NT. Theoretically, one of them is the most basic or default conjunction, the one the writer uses when there is no particular quality to be signaled. This implies that each of the other connectives brings some specific constraint to bear in the context that the other members do not. Compare this approach to a more traditional description provided by Wallace, summarized here:

- Ascensive (*even*): καί, δέ, and μηδέ;
- Connective (*and, also*): καί and δέ;
- Contrastive (*but, rather, however*): ἀλλά, πλήν, sometimes καί and δέ;
- Correlative: μέν ... δέ (*on the one hand ... on the other hand*); καί ... καί (*both ... and*);

---

12. Andrews devotes a chapter to the "Myths about Markedness," debunking some commonly held notions regarding the use of statistics in distinguishing default and marked forms. She states, "The purpose of markedness theory is to explain properties of meaning that are invariant, not to justify a system based upon statistical frequency, which, by definition, is a context-specific phenomenon" (*Markedness Theory*, 137).

13. Ibid., 138–39.

14. Certain discourse contexts may make the occurrence of marked forms inordinately high. Paul's heated defenses exhibit a very different distribution of discourse devices compared to a narrative. Discontinuity of time, place, action, or participants will result in the use of different forms compared to a context of relative continuity.

15. For an overview of the default-marked approach to language description, see Robert A. Dooley and Stephen H. Levinsohn, *Analyzing Discourse: A Manual of Basic Concepts* (Dallas: SIL International, 2001), 64–68; Steven E. Runge, "A Discourse-Functional Description of Participant Reference in Biblical Hebrew Narrative" (D.Litt. diss., University of Stellenbosch, 2007), 20–25.

- Disjunctive (*or*): ἤ;
- Emphatic (*certainly*, *indeed*): ἀλλά, οὐ μή, οὖν, γέ, δή, μενοῦνγε, μέντοι, ναί, and νή;
- Explanatory (*for, you see*, or *that is, namely*): γάρ, δέ, εἰ, καί;
- Inferential (*therefore*): ἄρα, γάρ, διό, διότι, οὖν, πλήν, τοιγαροῦν, τοινῦν, and ὥστε;
- Transitional (*now, then*): οὖν and especially δέ.[16]

Of the various logical functions that Wallace recognizes, note how many times καί and δέ are listed together. In fact, there are only two logical functions that δέ does not possess. Although these logical relations may work well for differentiating English conjunctions, the amount of cross-listing suggests that these relations are not well-suited for differentiating Greek connectives. Mapping the connectives to an English counterpart highlights the mismatches in function between the English and Greek conjunctions but offers little help for differentiating the distinctive functions of καί and δέ.[17]

Languages tend to be very efficient, dropping elements that do not serve some unique purpose. Wallace's description leaves the impression that καί and δέ share significant semantic overlap. Chapter 2 demonstrates that δέ marks a discourse feature that is most often signaled in English using adverbs, not conjunctions. Furthermore, some English conjunctions distinguish semantic continuity versus semantic discontinuity (*and* versus *but*). The conjunctions καί and δέ do not encode this semantic constraint, leading them to be listed under both connective and contrastive relations. The messiness of this overlap is caused by the mismatch of the feature to the framework used, not by the overlapping features that are marked. Καί and δέ are unmarked for the feature of semantic continuity or discontinuity.

1.4   Prominence and Contrast

1.4.1   Prominence

It is now time to synthesize the implications of pragmatic choices and their effects. This is where the notion of prominence comes in. The primary objec-

---

16. Daniel B. Wallace, *Greek Grammar beyond the Basics: An Exegetical Syntax of the New Testament* (Grand Rapids: Zondervan, 1999), 761.

17. Wallace is not the only one wrestling with this issue. Dana and Mantey seem to regard English as something of an anomaly in that its conjunctions only have one meaning, whereas this is not the case in other languages. They state, "In Greek, as in Hebrew and Latin, but unlike the English use, a conjunction may have several meanings, each requiring separate and careful study" (H. E. Dana and Julius R. Mantey, *A Manual Grammar of the Greek New Testament* [New York: Macmillan, 1968], 240).

tive of using the various discourse devices is to attract extra attention to certain parts or aspects of the discourse—that is, to mark them as prominent. Callow introduces prominence by stating,

> A story in which every character was equally important and every event equally significant can hardly be imagined. Even the simplest story has at least a central character and a plot, and this means one character is more important than the others, and certain events likewise. Human beings cannot observe events simply as happenings; they observe them as related and significant happenings, and they report them as such.[18]

She later defines prominence as "any device whatsoever which gives certain events, participants, or objects more significance than others in the same context."[19] Regardless of whether we are looking at a scenic view, a piece of visual art, or even listening to music, we are constantly making judgments about what is "normal" and what is "prominent" based on the devices used to signal prominence.

So what exactly are the signals? What is it that makes some things blend into the scenery and other things jump out? In visual art there are all kinds of choices available regarding how to portray a subject.

Mount Shuksan is one of the most photographed landmarks around the city I live in. A favorite shot is to frame the mountain with tall evergreens on either side, with a small mountain lake in the lower foreground, as in A and B in example 1.

Example 1 :: Framing and prominence

A   B   C

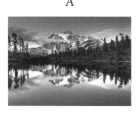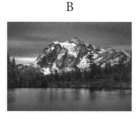

The effect of this photographic framing is to provide a sharp contrast of color between the vibrant green of the evergreen trees, the deep blue of the lake, and the dull white and gray of the snow and glaciers on the mountain.

---

18. Kathleen Callow, *Discourse Considerations in Translating the Word of God* (Grand Rapids: Zondervan, 1974), 49.

19. Ibid., 50.

(Of course, a bit of imagination will be required to visualize the colorful contrasts I describe from the black-and-white photos reproduced in this print edition.) In B, the sky is overcast and the mountain appears larger since less of the foreground lake scene is included. In C, the picture is taken on the hillside beyond the lake, with a valley and ski lodge in the foreground. This change in foreground effectively shows more of the mountain, making it seem more imposing. Although the pictures are only two-dimensional, changing the proportions can affect the sense of depth in the work.

The weather conditions also make a difference. Pictures A and C are taken on relatively clear days, providing bright lighting. There is far less light due to the cloud cover in B, highlighting different details than the other two. Having the lake in the foreground provides another kind of contrast, but it also provides the added bonus of reflecting the object of interest.

Finally, the placement of the mountain in the picture gives some indication of the artist's main interest. It figures prominently in B, less so in C. In A, even though the mountain appears smaller, the artist's use of the reflection in the lake effectively doubles its size. In terms of scale, A seems to be the standard view, the one used most frequently by visitors. Option B is more specialized, using a zoom and choosing a specific kind of day to create a contrast. Option C represents an entirely different portrayal by omitting the lake. The subject is the same, but the decisions about prominence, framing, point of view, and contrast make a huge difference in the presentation.

1.4.2   Contrast

The writers of the NT used different devices to communicate prominence and to create contrast. Longacre observes, "Discourse without prominence would be like pointing to a piece of black cardboard and insisting that it was a picture of black camels crossing black sands at midnight."[20] Using the analogy of the picture above, a writer can make something stand out by "pulling" it to the foreground, comparable to taking a close-up photo. The same task can be accomplished also by pushing everything else into the background in order to leave just a few prominent elements by themselves in the foreground. This would be like taking a photo of two people who are fairly close to the camera against the backdrop of distant mountains. The things that appear to be close would attract our attention more than the things in the background. Although

---

20. Robert E. Longacre, "Discourse Peak as Zone of Turbulence," in *Beyond the Sentence: Discourse and Sentential Form* (ed. Jessica R. Wirth; Ann Arbor, Mich.: Karoma, 1985), 83.

both of these methods accomplish the task of directing our attention, each choice brings about a different effect.

Another way of making something stand out exploits patterns and expectations. Humans are wired to recognize patterns. When patterns are broken or expectations are unmet, the standard response is to associate some kind of meaning with the change. Let's take a look at how breaking an established pattern can make something stand out.

Imagine a co-worker who regularly dresses in jeans and T-shirts arriving for work one day dressed in a suit. The break in the pattern attracts attention, perhaps prompting questions about what it meant. Did this person have an interview or a presentation? Was there a special event after work? What was the motivation for wearing the suit?

Similarly, musicians and songwriters employ patterns to do all kinds of things. Devices such as refrains or repetition of a theme often function to segment a piece of music into movements or verses—smaller chunks. The repetition of the same notes (such as a refrain or a theme) can let us know where these transitions are. Increasing or decreasing the volume can also function as an indicator of prominence, such as building to a loud crescendo for a climax.

Since prominence is fundamentally about making something stand out in its context, marking prominence typically involves creating contrast with other things in the context. Contrast, in turn, presupposes that a person recognizes the underlying pattern. Even if we cannot verbalize the pattern, we can still perceive contrast. I do not need a music theory class to pick out a refrain; I do not need an art class to pick out the center of interest in most paintings.

We constantly make choices about how and what to communicate. Although languages have their differences, they all have a common set of tasks to be accomplished. The choices we make have meaning associated with them. The choice to break the expected pattern implies that there was some reason not to follow the pattern. The choice implies meaning. These same devices also allow us to make some things more prominent, others less prominent.

Suggested Reading

Callow, Kathleen. *Discourse Considerations in Translating the Word of God.* 9–18, 49–53.

Dooley, Robert A., and Stephen H. Levinsohn. *Analyzing Discourse: A Manual of Basic Concepts.* 64–68.

Levinsohn, Stephen H. *Self-Instruction Materials on Narrative Discourse Analysis.* 1–7.

———. "The Relevance of Greek Discourse Studies to Exegesis."

CONNECTING PROPOSITIONS

This chapter provides a very basic overview of the different sorts of relations that can be communicated by the most commonly used NT Greek connectives. The term "connective" is used here in place of the more specific "conjunction" because languages commonly use forms other than conjunctions to perform the task of connecting clause elements. Adverbs often serve as connectives, both in Greek and in English. Understanding the discourse function of these words is foundational for properly understanding the devices that follow.[1] Greek has a much more diverse set of connectives than we have in English, resulting in some significant mismatches between the languages. In English, most of our clauses are joined without using an explicit connector—that is, asyndeton.

In contrast, Greek has a much more sophisticated system, which Robertson describes:

> The Greeks, especially in the literary style, felt the propriety of indicating the inner relation of the various independent sentences that composed a paragraph. This was not merely an artistic device, but a logical expression of coherence of thought. Particles like καί, δέ, ἀλλά, γάρ, οὖν, δή, etc., were

---

1. I encourage you to read this chapter closely and then to read it again, along with the introduction, after you have finished the rest of the book. When you assemble a bicycle or a lawnmower, the instructions advocate using it for a bit after the initial assembly but then to go back and retighten what may have loosened up. I expect that some items will not be completely secure after a first read through this chapter, as is to be expected. Much of what follows will be brand new to some readers. Do your best to assimilate it with what you have previously learned, but again, I strongly urge you to read this chapter and the introduction after completing the rest of the book.

very common in this connection. Demonstrative pronouns, adverbs, and even relative pronouns were also used for this purpose.[2]

Greek connectives play a functional role in discourse by indicating how the writer intended one clause to relate to another, based on the connective used.

Although the diversity of connectives provides valuable exegetical information about the writer's intentions, it often has caused a good deal of confusion regarding exactly how each one differs from the other. Conjunctions traditionally have been defined based upon their translation, mapping them to an English counterpart. Consider the following summary from Wallace, with particular attention to how many times καί and δέ are listed together, and how many different ways they can be translated into English.

Logical Functions:

- Ascensive: *even* ... καί, δέ, and μηδέ
- Connective (continuative, coordinate): *and, also* ... καί and δέ
- Contrastive (adversative): *but, rather, however* ... ἀλλά, πλήν, sometimes καί and δέ
- Correlative: e.g., μέν ... δέ (*on the one hand ... on the other hand*); καί ... καί (*both ... and*)
- Disjunctive (Alternative): *or* ... ἤ
- Emphatic: *certainly, indeed* ... ἀλλά (*certainly*), οὐ μή (*certainly not* or *by no means*), οὖν (*certainly*); true emphatic conjunctions include γέ, δή, μενοῦνγε, μέντοι, ναί, and νή
- Explanatory: *for, you see,* or *that is, namely* ... γάρ, δέ, εἰ (after verbs of emotion), and καί
- Inferential: *therefore* ... ἄρα, γάρ, διό, διότι, οὖν, πλήν, τοιγαροῦν, τοινῦν, and ὥστε
- Transitional: *now, then* ... οὖν and especially δέ[3]

Wallace's approach helps us understand how each Greek conjunction maps to an English counterpart, but there are some drawbacks. Listing καί and δέ together as ascensive, connective, contrastive, and correlative raises questions. What exactly do these conjunctions do *in Greek*? Does each do a

---

2. A. T. Robertson, *A Grammar of the Greek New Testament in the Light of Historical Research* (1919; repr., Bellingham, Wash.: Logos, 2006), 443.

3. Daniel B. Wallace, *Greek Grammar beyond the Basics: An Exegetical Syntax of the New Testament* (Grand Rapids: Zondervan, 1999), 761. These functions were first mentioned in chapter 1.

bunch of different things, or is there one unifying function that it performs? What is the meaningful difference between them if they can be translated by the same English conjunctions in so many instances? Problems such as these illustrate the need for finding a different way of understanding Greek that is not so dependent upon English.

Each Greek connective brings to bear a unique constraint upon the connected elements. This is true even where there is a series of connectives in a row, as in Phil 3:8 (ἀλλὰ μενοῦνγε καὶ). Each connective plays a specific role, bringing its unique constraint to bear in the context. The objective is not to know how to translate the connective, but to understand how each one uniquely differs from another based on the function that it accomplishes in Greek.

Exegesis and exposition are all about understanding the original and drawing out the meaning. Translation is often an ill-suited medium for this, even though it is the one most commonly used. One may have a very clear understanding of something and still find it troublesome to capture all of the information in a translation. Do not worry: exposition gives you the opportunity to elaborate aspects of a passage that cannot be well-captured in translation.

Dooley and Levinsohn highlight a principle that provides the basis for the following discussion:

> A general principle in human language is Behaghel's Law, which states that "items that belong together mentally are grouped together syntactically" (MacWhinney 1991:276). One application of Behaghel's Law is that, when two sentences are adjacent, or two clauses are adjacent within a sentence, then, other things being equal, the propositions they embody should be interpreted as being in a close conceptual relation.[4]

This principle helps us understand a reader's default expectation when seeing adjacent elements: they share a conceptual relationship *of some kind*. Blakemore describes the role of a connective, saying that "it encodes information about the inferential process that the hearer should use" in connecting what follows the connective to what precedes.[5] Connectives play the role of specifying what kind of relationship the writer intended. Each provides a unique constraint on how to process the discourse that follows.

---

4. Robert A. Dooley and Stephen H. Levinsohn, *Analyzing Discourse: A Manual of Basic Concepts* (Dallas: SIL International, 2001), 15.

5. Diane Blakemore, *Relevance and Linguistic Meaning: The Semantics and Pragmatics of Discourse Markers* (CSL 99; Cambridge: Cambridge University Press, 2002), 90.

2.1 Asyndeton (Ø)

Asyndeton refers to the linking of clauses or clause components without the use of a conjunction. This concept will be abbreviated using the Ø symbol. If you look at my writing in this chapter, you will note that most of the main clauses are not linked with any conjunction. Asyndeton is the default means of connecting clauses in English, the option that one chooses when there is no specific relationship to explicitly signal. It is the option used when the writer judges that the implicit relation between the clauses is sufficiently clear.

Example 2 :: Asyndeton in English

A "I went to the store. Ø I bought some milk."
B "I went to the store **and** bought some milk."
C "I went to the store **but only** bought some milk."
D "I went to the store **in order to** buy some milk."

Each of these options constrains the two clauses to be related to one another in different ways. In A, the use of asyndeton does not bring any particular constraint upon how these clauses are to be related to one another. Since each clause describes an action, the default expectation is that second action followed the first. There may be other specific relations, but they are not made explicit.

In B the two actions are explicitly connected using *and*. It makes constrains a closer connection to be drawn between the actions that may or may not be present using Ø. The use of *but only* in option C implies that there was an unmet expectation of some kind, as though something more than "just milk" was to be purchased. Finally, option D specifies a cause-and-effect relationship between the two actions. This same purpose of buying milk may have been the cause of going to the store in A, but the use of Ø leaves this unspecified.

To summarize, the use of asyndeton indicates that the writer did not feel the need to specify any kind of relationship between the clauses. The relation might be causative, it might be contrary to expectation, or it might simply be continuity. Asyndeton means that the writer did not feel compelled to specify a relation. If they had wanted to constrain a specific relation, there are plenty of conjunctions to make the intended relation explicit. The choice to use asyndeton represents the choice not to specify a relation.

In Koiné Greek, asyndeton is the default means of connecting clauses in the Epistles and in speeches reported within narrative. It is also used in the narrative of the Gospel of John. Recall that default does not mean that it is the most commonly occurring option, but that it is the most basic ("unmarked") option. It is the option chosen when there is no particular reason to signal that some feature is present. Here are some examples.

Example 3 :: John 1:1–8

¹ Ø Ἐν ἀρχῇ ἦν ὁ λόγος, **καὶ** ὁ λόγος ἦν πρὸς τὸν θεόν, **καὶ** θεὸς ἦν ὁ λόγος.

[1] Ø In the beginning was the Word, **and** the Word was with God, **and** the Word was God.

² Ø οὗτος ἦν ἐν ἀρχῇ πρὸς τὸν θεόν.

[2] Ø This one was in the beginning with God.

³ Ø πάντα δι᾽ αὐτοῦ ἐγένετο, **καὶ** χωρὶς αὐτοῦ ἐγένετο οὐδὲ ἕν. ὃ γέγονεν

[3] Ø All things came into being through him, **and** apart from him not one thing came into being that has come into being.

⁴ Ø ἐν αὐτῷ ζωὴ ἦν, **καὶ** ἡ ζωὴ ἦν τὸ φῶς τῶν ἀνθρώπων· ⁵ **καὶ** τὸ φῶς ἐν τῇ σκοτίᾳ φαίνει, **καὶ** ἡ σκοτία αὐτὸ οὐ κατέλαβεν.

[4] Ø In him was life, **and** the life was the light of humanity. [5] **And** the light shines in the darkness, **and** the darkness did not overcome it.

⁶ Ø Ἐγένετο ἄνθρωπος, ἀπεσταλμένος παρὰ θεοῦ,

[6] Ø A man came, sent from God,

Ø ὄνομα αὐτῷ Ἰωάννης·

Ø whose name was John.

⁷ Ø οὗτος ἦλθεν εἰς μαρτυρίαν ἵνα μαρτυρήσῃ περὶ τοῦ φωτός, ἵνα πάντες πιστεύσωσιν δι᾽ αὐτοῦ.

[7] Ø This one came for a witness, in order that he could testify about the light, so that all would believe through him.

⁸ Ø οὐκ ἦν ἐκεῖνος τὸ φῶς, **ἀλλ᾽** ἵνα μαρτυρήσῃ περὶ τοῦ φωτός.

[8] Ø That one was not the light, **but** came in order that he could testify about the light.[6]

As indicated by the boldface type, most of the conjunctions from this passage translate quite naturally in the English translation. Asyndeton is used at the beginning of a new thought, or simply where the relation between clauses is clear. *And* is used to create a tighter connection between clauses that only would have been implicit using Ø.

---

6. Unless otherwise noted, all quotations of the NT in English translation are taken from the *Lexham English Bible* (LEB).

There is a similar use of Ø in the speeches reported within narratives, as in the Gospel of Matthew.

Example 4 :: Matthew 6:24–26

[24] Ø Οὐδεὶς δύναται δυσὶ κυρίοις δουλεύειν· ἢ **γὰρ** τὸν ἕνα μισήσει καὶ τὸν ἕτερον ἀγαπήσει, **ἢ** ἑνὸς ἀνθέξεται καὶ τοῦ ἑτέρου καταφρονήσει.	[24] Ø "No one is able to serve two masters. **For** either he will hate the one and love the other, **or** he will be devoted to one and despise the other.
Ø οὐ δύνασθε θεῷ δουλεύειν καὶ μαμωνᾷ.	Ø You are not able to serve God and money.
Ø οὐχὶ ἡ ψυχὴ πλεῖόν ἐστιν τῆς τροφῆς καὶ τὸ σῶμα τοῦ ἐνδύματος;	Ø Is your life not more than food and your body more than clothing?
[25] **Διὰ τοῦτο**[7] λέγω ὑμῖν,	[25] **For this reason** I say to you,
Ø μὴ μεριμνᾶτε τῇ ψυχῇ ὑμῶν τί φάγητε [ἢ τί πίητε], **μηδὲ** τῷ σώματι ὑμῶν τί ἐνδύσησθε.	Ø do not be anxious for your life, what you will eat or what you will drink, **and not** for your body, what you will wear.
[26] Ø ἐμβλέψατε εἰς τὰ πετεινὰ τοῦ οὐρανοῦ ὅτι οὐ σπείρουσιν οὐδὲ θερίζουσιν οὐδὲ συνάγουσιν εἰς ἀποθήκας, **καὶ** ὁ πατὴρ ὑμῶν ὁ οὐράνιος τρέφει αὐτά·	[26] Ø Consider the birds of the sky, that they do not sow or reap or gather produce into barns, **and** your heavenly Father feeds them.
Ø οὐχ ὑμεῖς μᾶλλον διαφέρετε αὐτῶν;	Ø Are you not worth more than they are?"

Many of the clauses above are joined using Ø. Those using conjunctions provide an explicit relation. The use of asyndeton indicates that the writer chose not to make a relation explicit. The relation must be gleaned from the context. Note that Ø is used at the beginning of a new thought (e.g., "No one is able to serve two masters," "Consider the birds of the air").

Asyndeton can be used at points of discontinuity, as at the beginning of a new thought or topic. Levinsohn summarizes the use of asyndeton in non-narrative by stating that since explicit connectives are used to indicate clause

---

7. For a description of the discourse function of διὰ τοῦτο, see §2.6.

relationships such as strengthening, developmental, associative, or inferential, "the use of asyndeton tends to imply '*not* strengthening, *not* developmental, *not* associative, *not* inferential, *etc.*'"[8] It is not only used in contexts where there is a change in topic (e.g., at the beginning of a new paragraph). Levinsohn notes that it may also be used in contexts of close connection, such as moving from *generic* to *specific*.

2.2   Καί

One of the significant mismatches between English and Greek conjunctions is clearly seen in the different senses ascribed to καί. The primary senses are *connective* ("and") and *adversative* ("but"). These two English conjunctions, however, mark an inherent semantic quality that is not marked by either καί or δέ. This quality is captured in the labels *connective* and *adversative*, and it can be described more generally as *semantic continuity* versus *semantic discontinuity*. This semantic quality that distinguishes *and* from *but* is not marked by καί. It may or may not be present. The same is true with δέ. To ascribe this semantic quality to these Greek connectives is to force them into the descriptive box of English, whether it fits well or not. The labels *adversative* and *connective* may be helpful in determining an English translation, but they cause confusion when it comes to understanding the function of καί in Greek.

Καί is a coordinating conjunction that may join individual words, phrases, clauses or paragraphs.

Example 5 :: James 1:21–24

[21] διὸ ἀποθέμενοι πᾶσαν ῥυπαρίαν **καὶ** περισσείαν κακίας ἐν πραΰτητι,	[21] Therefore, putting aside all moral uncleanness **and** wicked excess,
Ø δέξασθε τὸν ἔμφυτον λόγον τὸν δυνάμενον σῶσαι τὰς ψυχὰς ὑμῶν.	Ø welcome with humility the implanted message which is able to save your souls.
[22] Γίνεσθε δὲ ποιηταὶ λόγου **καὶ** μὴ μόνον ἀκροαταὶ παραλογιζόμενοι ἑαυτούς.	[22] But be doers of the message **and** not only hearers, deceiving yourselves,

---

8. Stephen H. Levinsohn, *Discourse Features of New Testament Greek: A Coursebook on the Information Structure of New Testament Greek* (2nd ed.; Dallas: SIL International), 119.

\

^{23} ὅτι εἴ τις ἀκροατὴς λόγου ἐστὶν ^{23} because if anyone is a hearer of
καὶ οὐ ποιητής, οὗτος ἔοικεν ἀνδρὶ   the message **and** not a doer, this
κατανοοῦντι τὸ πρόσωπον τῆς   one is like someone staring at his
γενέσεως αὐτοῦ ἐν ἐσόπτρῳ·   own face in a mirror,

^{24} κατενόησεν γὰρ ἑαυτὸν **καὶ** ^{24} for he looks at himself **and** goes
ἀπελήλυθεν **καὶ** εὐθέως ἐπελάθετο   away **and** immediately forgets
ὁποῖος ἦν.   what sort of person he was.

In v. 21 two noun phrases are linked, describing the two things that are to be put away. In vv. 22 and 23, two more objects are linked using καί even though they are opposites. The conjunction does not mark the presence or absence of semantic continuity; it simply "is used to link items of equal status."[9] Verse 24 illustrates the joining of three main clauses closely together instead of using asyndeton. Adding one to another to another creates the impression that these actions take place in close succession, or that one leads to the next. This close connection is expressed in the LEB through the omission of the subject *he* in the second and third clauses, making the latter two dependent on the first for a subject.

Καί does not mark a distinction of semantic continuity or discontinuity; it connects two items of equal status, constraining them to be closely related to one another. Consider the "adversative" usage in 1 Thess 2:18.

Example 6 :: 1 Thessalonians 2:18

διότι ἠθελήσαμεν ἐλθεῖν πρὸς   because we wanted to come to
ὑμᾶς, ἐγὼ μὲν Παῦλος καὶ ἅπαξ   you—I, Paul, on more than one
καὶ δίς, **καὶ** ἐνέκοψεν ἡμᾶς ὁ   occasion—**and** Satan hindered us.
σατανᾶς.

The use of καί here simply links two items of equal status, without any judgment regarding semantic continuity or discontinuity. This semantic distinction is not marked by καί. Even though the associated clauses are clearly contrastive, καί simply signals that they are to be added together. Contrast is a quality that is dependent upon the semantics of the context. It is either there or it is not, depending upon the discourse content.[10] Other connectives and various syntactic devices can make the contrast more pronounced.

---

9. Stanley E. Porter, *Idioms of the Greek New Testament* (2nd ed.; Sheffield: Sheffield Academic, 1999), 211.

10. Compare Rev 3:1: οἶδά σου τὰ ἔργα ὅτι ὄνομα ἔχεις ὅτι ζῇς, **καὶ** νεκρὸς εἶ.

In contexts where asyndeton is the default means of coordination, Levinsohn claims that καί "constrains the material it introduces to be processed as being added to and associated with previous material."[11] In comparison to asyndeton, coordination with καί signals to the reader to more closely associate the connected elements. The use of the connective represents the writer's choice to "add" the one element to the other.[12] Let's revisit example 3, repeated below for convenience.

Example 3 :: John 1:1–8

¹ Ø Ἐν ἀρχῇ ἦν ὁ λόγος, **καὶ** ὁ λόγος ἦν πρὸς τὸν θεόν, **καὶ** θεὸς ἦν ὁ λόγος.

¹ Ø In the beginning was the Word, **and** the Word was with God, **and** the Word was God.

² Ø οὗτος ἦν ἐν ἀρχῇ πρὸς τὸν θεόν.

² Ø This one was in the beginning with God.

³ Ø πάντα δι᾽ αὐτοῦ ἐγένετο, **καὶ** χωρὶς αὐτοῦ ἐγένετο οὐδὲ ἕν. ὃ γέγονεν

³ Ø All things came into being through him, **and** apart from him not one thing came into being that has come into being.

⁴ Ø ἐν αὐτῷ ζωὴ ἦν, **καὶ** ἡ ζωὴ ἦν τὸ φῶς τῶν ἀνθρώπων· ⁵ **καὶ** τὸ φῶς ἐν τῇ σκοτίᾳ φαίνει, **καὶ** ἡ σκοτία αὐτὸ οὐ κατέλαβεν.

⁴ Ø In him was life, **and** the life was the light of humanity. ⁵ **And** the light shines in the darkness, **and** the darkness did not overcome it.

⁶ Ø Ἐγένετο ἄνθρωπος, ἀπεσταλμένος παρὰ θεοῦ,

⁶ Ø A man came, sent from God,

Ø ὄνομα αὐτῷ Ἰωάννης·

Ø whose name was John.

⁷ Ø οὗτος ἦλθεν εἰς μαρτυρίαν ἵνα μαρτυρήσῃ περὶ τοῦ φωτός, ἵνα πάντες πιστεύσωσιν δι᾽ αὐτοῦ.

⁷ Ø This one came for a witness, in order that he could testify about the light, so that all would believe through him.

---

11. Levinsohn, *Discourse Features*, 125.

12. Compare chapter 16 on thematic addition, where clausal elements are "added" to one another. In many cases the added elements are from different clauses, not simple coordination. Although the proximity of the added elements is different in thematic addition compared to simple coordination, καί still brings to bear the same constraint on the elements—that is, constraining "the material it introduces to be processed as being added to and associated with previous material" (ibid.).

⁸ Ø οὐκ ἦν ἐκεῖνος τὸ φῶς, ἀλλ'   ⁸ Ø That one was not the light, but
ἵνα μαρτυρήσῃ περὶ τοῦ φωτός.   came in order that he could testify
                                     about the light.

Look at the clauses that are joined by καί, compared to those joined by Ø. The
use of καί constrains these elements to be more closely related to one another
than those joined by Ø. Beginning new thoughts with Ø makes good sense,
in that using καί would constrain the elements to be processed as though they
were part of the same thought or topic. Using καί to associate clauses within
the same main thought also makes sense, since it helps the reader to understand the flow of the discourse.

In most narrative contexts καί functions as the default means of coordination. Levinsohn describes the situation:

> It is possible to relate a whole episode of a narrative in New Testament Greek
> using a single sentence conjunction, viz., καί. Such passages are comparable
> to narratives in Hebrew in which the single conjunction *waw* is used. You
> can think of such passages as "straight narrative."[13]

Based on the definition that καί links items of equal status, the implication
is that the narrative events that are added one to another are judged by the
writer to be of equal status. This means that narrative events are linked using
καί unless there is some break or discontinuity in the discourse. The most
common reasons for switching from the default καί in narrative are to mark *a
new development* or to mark the transition to or from *background information*
(see §2.3).

To summarize, the use of καί constrains the connected element to be
closely associated with what comes before, regardless of whether there is
semantic continuity or not. The implication is that the elements joined by
καί are of equal status. In contexts where asyndeton is the default means of
coordination, as in most of the Epistles and reported speeches, the use of καί
signals a closer connection of the elements than using Ø. In most narrative
contexts (except John's gospel), the narrative events that are connected by καί
are judged by the writer to be of equal status and are portrayed as "straight"
narrative. Consider the use of καί in the healing of the Gerasene demoniac in
Mark 5:14–19.

---

13. Ibid., 71.

Example 7 :: Mark 5:14–19

¹⁴ **καὶ** οἱ βόσκοντες αὐτοὺς ἔφυγον	¹⁴ **And** their herdsmen fled
καὶ ἀπήγγειλαν εἰς τὴν πόλιν καὶ εἰς τοὺς ἀγρούς·	**and** reported it in the town and in the countryside,
καὶ ἦλθον ἰδεῖν τί ἐστιν τὸ γεγονὸς	**and** they came to see what it was that had happened.
¹⁵ **καὶ** ἔρχονται πρὸς τὸν Ἰησοῦν	¹⁵ **And** they came to Jesus
καὶ θεωροῦσιν τὸν δαιμονιζόμενον καθήμενον ἱματισμένον καὶ σωφρονοῦντα, τὸν ἐσχηκότα τὸν λεγιῶνα,	**and** saw the demon-possessed man sitting there clothed and in his right mind—the one who had had the legion—
καὶ ἐφοβήθησαν.	**and** they were afraid.
¹⁶ **καὶ** διηγήσαντο αὐτοῖς οἱ ἰδόντες πῶς ἐγένετο τῷ δαιμονιζομένῳ καὶ περὶ τῶν χοίρων.	¹⁶ **And** those who had seen it described to them what had happened to the demon-possessed man, and about the pigs.
¹⁷ **καὶ** ἤρξαντο παρακαλεῖν αὐτὸν ἀπελθεῖν ἀπὸ τῶν ὁρίων αὐτῶν	¹⁷ **And** they began to urge him to depart from their region.
¹⁸ **καὶ** ἐμβαίνοντος αὐτοῦ εἰς τὸ πλοῖον παρεκάλει αὐτὸν ὁ δαιμονισθεὶς ἵνα μετ᾽ αὐτοῦ ᾖ.	¹⁸ **And** as he was getting into the boat, the man who had been demon-possessed began to implore him that he could go with him.
¹⁹ **καὶ** οὐκ ἀφῆκεν αὐτόν, ἀλλὰ λέγει αὐτῷ, Ὕπαγε εἰς τὸν οἶκόν σου …	¹⁹ **And** he did not permit him, but said to him, "Go to your home …"

The LEB translator rendered the connections established by καί using "and" in English. Markers other than connectives are used to indicate a minor break in the development of the discourse.[14]

---

14. Verse 14a uses a topical frame to signal the minor discontinuity as the story shifts from the interaction between the demons and Jesus to the response of the herders (see chapters 9–11). In v. 18, a genitive absolute may signal the same kind of low-level break in the discourse (for its use with asyndeton at breaks in the discourse, see Levinsohn, *Discourse Features*, 84).

2.3   Δέ

2.3.1   Introduction to Development Markers

According to BDAG, δέ is

> used to connect one clause to another, either to express contrast or simple
> continuation. When it is felt that there is some contrast betw. clauses—though
> the contrast is oft. scarcely discernible—the most common translation is
> 'but.' When a simple connective is desired, without contrast being clearly
> implied, 'and' will suffice, and in certain occurrences the marker may be left
> untranslated.[15]

Recall the discussion above regarding English *and* and *but* marking the
semantic distinction of continuity versus discontinuity, respectively. On the
other hand, καί does not encode this distinction. It may or may not be present. The presence of this distinction in the English conjunctions has led to the
assumption that it is present in their Greek counterparts.

As with καί, the connective δέ does not mark the presence of semantic
discontinuity, as BDAG claims. The fact that semantic discontinuity or continuity may be present is indicated by their reference to "contrast or simple
continuation," respectively. Either may be present, δέ does not mark its presence or absence. This is not to say that contrast is not present in many contexts
where δέ occurs; I claim only that the presence of the connective is not what
brings it about. Contrast has everything to do with the semantics of the elements present in the context. This explains why δέ is sometimes said to be
contrastive and sometimes not. Grammarians have worked diligently to make
καί correspond to "and," and δέ to "but," which has led to great confusion
regarding the unique grammatical role that each plays.

One very important discourse task that every language needs to accomplish is to mark where to break the discourse into smaller chunks. There is a
limit to how much information we can take in without breaking it down into
smaller pieces. Think about trying to listen to a run-on sentence, or trying to
memorize a long list of items. You probably would have difficulty taking it all
in. But if the run-on were properly formed into smaller clauses, and if the list
of items were broken down into several smaller lists of several items each, the
task of processing and retaining the information would become much easier.

Languages use various devices for this task of "chunking" or segmenting
the discourse into smaller bits for easier processing. The most obvious one

---

15. BDAG, 213.

is thematic breaks or *discontinuities* in the discourse. Typically, such breaks entail a change of time, location, participant/topic, or kind of action. Such changes represent *natural* discontinuities based on the discourse content. We are most likely to segment texts at junctures like these. But what happens in contexts of relative continuity, where there are no natural breaks? How are decisions made about chunking here?

The *Concise Oxford English Dictionary* defines continuity as "a connection or line of development with no sharp breaks."[16] Think about what is meant by "line of development." If you are explaining a process to someone or formulating an argument of some kind, there will most likely be steps or stages in that line of development. So too in stories, which are made up of a series of events or scenes. The events themselves often are composed of distinct actions or reactions. Linguists refer to these distinct stages or steps as *developments*. Languages use various markers to signal new developments, particularly in contexts of relative continuity. Development markers guide the reader in breaking the discourse into meaningful chunks, based upon how the writer conceived of the action or argument.

Returning to the other part of the BDAG definition, we note that it states that δέ expresses "simple continuation." Some of the English glosses that BDAG provides for this sense are "now," "then," and "so." All three of these words are English adverbs. They are frequently used in English to accomplish the same kind of development-marking tasks accomplished by Greek connectives. Here is how Dooley and Levinsohn describe it:

> Whereas connectives like *and* and some additives instruct the hearer to associate information together, some conjunctions convey the opposite and constrain the reader to *move on to the next point*. We will call these connectives "DEVELOPMENTAL MARKERS" because they indicate that the material so marked represents a new development in the story or argument, as far as the author's purpose is concerned.[17]

We frequently use temporal expressions such as *then* or *now* to mark developments in English. Read Example 8 and consider the difference that development markers can play in how you process and structure what you are reading.

---

16. Catherine Soanes and Angus Stevenson, eds., *Concise Oxford English Dictionary* (electronic ed.; 11th ed.; Oxford: Oxford University Press, 2004), n.p.

17. Dooley and Levinsohn, *Analyzing Discourse*, 93.

Example 8 :: Marking development in English

No Developments	With Developments I	With Developments II
I woke up early this morning. I read for a while. I ate breakfast. I showered and got dressed. I went to the office. I checked email. I began working on the next chapter of my project. I ate lunch with a friend.	I woke up early this morning and read for a while. **Then** I ate breakfast, showered, and got dressed. **After that**, I went to the office and checked email. **Then** I began working on the next chapter of my project. I ate lunch with a friend.	I woke up early this morning, read for a while, and ate breakfast. I showered, got dressed, and went to the office. **At the office**, I checked email and began working on the next chapter of my project. **After that**, I ate lunch with a friend.

Notice the difference that adding temporal ("then," "after that," etc.) or spatial markers ("at the office") makes in how you process the discourse. The first column lacks any specific markers about where to segment the text. It is left to the reader to make these decisions based on the content. For instance, one might chose to break the text at the change in location from "home" to the "office." Dropping some of the "I" subject pronouns and joining the sentences with "and" would also give some indication, as seen in the examples with καί in §2.2.

Look at the difference that the location of the development markers makes in the second and third columns. The second column portrays the events as four distinct developments: getting up, getting ready, getting settled at work, doing work. The third column uses two developments to express the same information, but both of them are in different places than in the second column.

This example illustrates the latitude available to writers in how they organize a discourse. To be sure, there are natural places in a discourse for beginning new developments, such as changes of time, place, participants, or kind of action. Even with these constraints, however, great flexibility is available to the writer as to where to segment the discourse and how frequently to segment it.

Dooley and Levinsohn make a significant point about the relationship of the flexibility of where to chunk the text and the author's intention: "the material so marked represents a new development in the story or argument, *as far as the author's purpose is concerned.*"[18] Since there is typically flexibility about how to chunk the text into developments, closely attending to these authorial decisions should inform our exegesis. The shaping and organization of the content provide exegetical clues about the writer's conceptualization of the content and purposes.

So far, we have looked at how English uses adverbials such as *then* and *now* to mark new developments. Greek uses its rich set of connectives to mark development, resulting in a mismatch between the function of some conjunctions in Greek and that of their English counterparts. The most commonly used development markers in the Greek NT are δέ and οὖν.

Not only do the particles δέ and οὖν serve as conjunctions, but also they serve as development markers in the discourse in ways comparable to temporal adverbs in English. This raises the question of how best to translate them. Should we translate οὖν as "therefore," "then," or "now"? This quandary illustrates the problem of needing to express all grammatical information in translation. There may not be an easy translation solution. This is where exegesis and exposition come in. Even if we cannot capture everything in a single English word, we can still understand the function of the Greek word. We can understand what it signals in the discourse and find other ways of capturing or communicating its function.

2.3.2   Function of Δέ

Now we can come back to our consideration of δέ and provide a more complete description of its function in the Greek NT. Δέ is a coordinating conjunction like καί, but it includes the added constraint of signaling a new development (notated "+ development"). Καί, on the other hand, is unmarked for development ("- development"). The use of δέ represents the writer's choice to explicitly signal that what follows is a new, distinct development in the story or argument, based on how the writer conceived of it.[19] If the exegete is seek-

---

18. Ibid (italics added).

19. When I talk about a writer's "choice," I am not conceiving of stopping and laboring over whether to signal a development or not. Rather, I have in mind the kinds of intentional yet unconscious decisions that speakers of a language are constantly making, choosing what "fits best" or is most appropriate, based on their communication objectives. In English, we do not stop to consider the placement of "then" to segment a story. We simply do it without conscious thought. The grammatical marker is telltale evidence of how the writer or speaker conceived of the action, how it broke down in his or her mental picture of it.

ing to understand the author's intent, devices such as development markers are worthy of attention.

Example 9 illustrates the meaningful difference that attention to development markers can make in understanding how the writer conceived of the discourse. In the example, the reported speeches have been abbreviated.

Example 9 :: Matthew 2:1–10

¹ Τοῦ δὲ Ἰησοῦ γεννηθέντος ἐν Βηθλέεμ τῆς Ἰουδαίας ἐν ἡμέραις Ἡρῴδου τοῦ βασιλέως, ἰδοὺ μάγοι ἀπὸ ἀνατολῶν παρεγένοντο εἰς Ἱεροσόλυμα ² λέγοντες, Ποῦ ἐστιν ὁ τεχθεὶς βασιλεὺς.…

¹ Now after Jesus was born in Bethlehem of Judea in the days of Herod the king, behold, wise men from the east came to Jerusalem, ² saying, "Where is the one who has been born king.…"

³ ἀκούσας **δὲ** ὁ βασιλεὺς Ἡρῴδης ἐταράχθη καὶ πᾶσα Ἱεροσόλυμα μετ᾽ αὐτοῦ, καὶ συναγαγὼν πάντας τοὺς ἀρχιερεῖς καὶ γραμματεῖς τοῦ λαοῦ ἐπυνθάνετο παρ᾽ αὐτῶν ποῦ ὁ Χριστὸς γεννᾶται.

³ **And** when King Herod heard it, he was troubled, and all Jerusalem with him, ⁴ and after calling together all the chief priests and scribes of the people, he inquired from them where the Christ was to be born.

⁵ οἱ **δὲ** εἶπαν αὐτῷ, Ἐν Βηθλέεμ.…

⁵ **So** they said to him, "In Bethlehem.…"

⁷ **Τότε** Ἡρῴδης λάθρᾳ καλέσας τοὺς μάγους ἠκρίβωσεν παρ᾽ αὐτῶν τὸν χρόνον τοῦ φαινομένου ἀστέρος, ⁸ καὶ πέμψας αὐτοὺς εἰς Βηθλέεμ εἶπεν, Πορευθέντες ἐξετάσατε ἀκριβῶς περὶ τοῦ παιδίου.…

⁷ **Then** Herod secretly summoned the wise men and determined precisely from them the time when the star appeared. ⁸ And he sent them to Bethlehem and said, "Go, inquire carefully concerning the child.…"

⁹ οἱ **δὲ** ἀκούσαντες τοῦ βασιλέως ἐπορεύθησαν καὶ ἰδοὺ ὁ ἀστήρ, ὃν εἶδον ἐν τῇ ἀνατολῇ, προῆγεν αὐτούς, ἕως ἐλθὼν ἐστάθη ἐπάνω οὗ ἦν τὸ παιδίον.

⁹ **After** they listened to the king, they went out, and behold, the star which they had seen at its rising led them until it came and stood above the place where the child was.

¹⁰ ἰδόντες **δὲ** τὸν ἀστέρα ἐχάρησαν χαρὰν μεγάλην σφόδρα.

¹⁰ **Now** when they saw the star, they rejoiced with very great joy.

According to the use of development markers, this excerpt is organized into six developments. The first development unit (vv. 1–2) sets the stage for the story that follows, introducing the complicating incident around which the story unfolds: Herod learning from the wise men that there is a newborn king. The next development recounts Herod's response to the situation (vv. 3–4). He becomes troubled and seeks to find where the new king was born. The answer to Herod's inquiry in vv. 5–6 is framed as the next development, followed by his summoning of the wise men to search for the king. The response of the wise men is segmented as the next development (v. 9), followed by their response to seeing the star (vv. 10).

Notice that there are only three explicit development markers in the LEB: "now" in v. 1 and "so" in v. 5 to render δέ, and "then" that translates the "narrative τότε" in v. 7. The ESV text appears only to recognize the two developments in the story based on the paragraphing: at vv. 1 and 7.

The preferred length of development units seems to vary from language to language. Even within Greek, it seems that Mark has a much higher threshold for what he considers to warrant a development marker compared to Matthew or Luke. This is illustrated in example 10. In the LEB, "**DM**" represents the presence of a development marker in the Greek text.

Example 10 :: Narrative development in parallel texts

Matthew 14:22–27	Mark 6:45–50
22 Καὶ εὐθέως ἠνάγκασεν τοὺς μαθητὰς ἐμβῆναι εἰς τὸ πλοῖον καὶ προάγειν αὐτὸν εἰς τὸ πέραν, ἕως οὗ ἀπολύσῃ τοὺς ὄχλους. 23 καὶ ἀπολύσας τοὺς ὄχλους ἀνέβη εἰς τὸ ὄρος κατ᾽ ἰδίαν προσεύξασθαι.	45 Καὶ εὐθὺς ἠνάγκασεν τοὺς μαθητὰς αὐτοῦ ἐμβῆναι εἰς τὸ πλοῖον καὶ προάγειν εἰς τὸ πέραν πρὸς Βηθσαϊδάν, ἕως αὐτὸς ἀπολύει τὸν ὄχλον. 46 καὶ ἀποταξάμενος αὐτοῖς ἀπῆλθεν εἰς τὸ ὄρος προσεύξασθαι
ὀψίας **δὲ** γενομένης μόνος ἦν ἐκεῖ.	47 **καὶ** ὀψίας γενομένης ἦν τὸ πλοῖον ἐν μέσῳ τῆς θαλάσσης, **καὶ** αὐτὸς μόνος ἐπὶ τῆς γῆς.
24 τὸ **δὲ** πλοῖον ἤδη σταδίους πολλοὺς ἀπὸ τῆς γῆς ἀπεῖχεν βασανιζόμενον ὑπὸ τῶν κυμάτων, ἦν γὰρ ἐναντίος ὁ ἄνεμος.	48 **καὶ** ἰδὼν αὐτοὺς βασανιζομένους ἐν τῷ ἐλαύνειν, ἦν γὰρ ὁ ἄνεμος ἐναντίος αὐτοῖς,

²⁵ τετάρτη **δὲ** φυλακῇ τῆς νυκτὸς ἦλθεν πρὸς αὐτοὺς περιπατῶν ἐπὶ τὴν θάλασσαν.

²⁶ οἱ **δὲ** μαθηταὶ ἰδόντες αὐτὸν ἐπὶ τῆς θαλάσσης περιπατοῦντα ἐταράχθησαν λέγοντες ὅτι Φάντασμά ἐστιν, καὶ ἀπὸ τοῦ φόβου ἔκραξαν.

²⁷ εὐθὺς **δὲ** ἐλάλησεν [ὁ Ἰησοῦς] αὐτοῖς λέγων, Θαρσεῖτε, ἐγώ εἰμι· μὴ φοβεῖσθε.

περὶ τετάρτην φυλακὴν τῆς νυκτὸς ἔρχεται πρὸς αὐτοὺς περιπατῶν ἐπὶ τῆς θαλάσσης **καὶ** ἤθελεν παρελθεῖν αὐτούς.

⁴⁹ οἱ **δὲ** ἰδόντες αὐτὸν ἐπὶ τῆς θαλάσσης περιπατοῦντα ἔδοξαν ὅτι φάντασμά ἐστιν, καὶ ἀνέκραξαν· ⁵⁰ πάντες γὰρ αὐτὸν εἶδον καὶ ἐταράχθησαν.

ὁ **δὲ** εὐθὺς ἐλάλησεν μετ᾽ αὐτῶν, καὶ λέγει αὐτοῖς, Θαρσεῖτε, ἐγώ εἰμι· μὴ φοβεῖσθε.

²² And immediately he made the disciples get into the boat and go ahead of him to the other side, while he sent away the crowds. ²³ And after he sent away the crowds, he went up on the mountain by himself to pray.

DM So when evening came, he was there alone.

²⁴ **DM** But the boat was already many stadia distant from the land, being beaten by the waves, because the wind was against it.

²⁵ **DM** And in the fourth watch of the night he came to them, walking on the sea.

²⁶ **DM** But the disciples, when they saw him walking on the sea, were terrified, saying, "It is a ghost!" and they cried out in fear.

⁴⁵ And immediately he made his disciples get into the boat and go on ahead to the other side, to Bethsaida, while he himself dismissed the crowd. ⁴⁶ And after he had said farewell to them, he went away to the mountain to pray.

⁴⁷ **And** when evening came, the boat was in the middle of the sea and he was alone on the land.

⁴⁸ **And** he saw them being beaten in their rowing because the wind was against them.

Ø Around the fourth watch of the night he came to them, walking on the sea, and he was wanting to pass by them.

⁴⁹ **DM** But when they saw him walking on the sea, they thought that it was a ghost, and they cried out. ⁵⁰ For they all saw him and were terrified.

²⁷ **DM** But immediately Jesus spoke to them, saying, "Have courage, I am he! Do not be afraid!"

DM But immediately he spoke with them and said to them, "Have courage, I am he! Do not be afraid!"

The two accounts begin similarly regarding the grouping of the background information in the first few verses. Matthew segments as distinct developments the statements about Jesus being alone, the boat already being a long way from shore, and Jesus coming to the boat during the fourth watch. This has the effect of making each of these elements stand out more than in Mark's version, since each is portrayed as a distinct development or change.

For Mark, vv. 45–48 lead up to two significant events: the disciples seeing Jesus (v. 49) and his encouragement to them to take heart (v. 50c). Both versions convey virtually the same content. They differ in the amount of attention that they draw to various events. By virtue of the fact that Mark signals fewer developments, those that he does signal would likely receive more attention than those in Matthew. On the other hand, segmenting the text into more distinct developments can also have the effect of "picking up the pace" of the narrative. In Matthew's account, the text is segmented into smaller and smaller chunks the closer one gets to the climax of the story. This is true of Mark's account as well, in that he only signals developments near the climax. Shortening the length of the developments has the effect of making them "pass by" more quickly, in a sense picking up the pace of the story.

One final example of the difference between καί and δέ is taken from 1 Corinthians.

Example 11 :: 1 Corinthians 12:3b–7

³ᵇ καὶ οὐδεὶς δύναται εἰπεῖν, Κύριος Ἰησοῦς, εἰ μὴ ἐν πνεύματι ἁγίῳ.

³ᵇ and no one is able to say "Jesus is Lord" except by the Holy Spirit.

⁴ Διαιρέσεις **δὲ** χαρισμάτων εἰσίν, τὸ **δὲ** αὐτὸ πνεῦμα·

⁴ **Now** there are varieties of gifts, **but** the same Spirit,

⁵ καὶ διαιρέσεις διακονιῶν εἰσιν, καὶ ὁ αὐτὸς κύριος·

⁵ and there are varieties of ministries, and the same Lord,

⁶ καὶ διαιρέσεις ἐνεργημάτων εἰσίν, ὁ **δὲ** αὐτὸς θεὸς ὁ ἐνεργῶν τὰ πάντα ἐν πᾶσιν.

⁶ and there are varieties of activities, **but** the same God, who works all things in all people.

⁷ ἑκάστῳ **δὲ** δίδοται ἡ φανέρωσις τοῦ πνεύματος πρὸς τὸ συμφέρον.

⁷ **But** to each one is given the manifestation of the Spirit for what is beneficial to all.

Like καί, δέ can join words, phrases, clauses, or paragraphs. The first δέ in v. 4 (translated "now") signals that the clause that follows represents the next distinct step in the argument. Paul returns to the initial proposition from v. 1 regarding spiritual gifts following his comment in v. 3 about evidence of the Spirit's work in a believer's life.

Within v. 4 itself there is a development from v. 4a to v. 4b, signaled by the second δέ. Paul's goal is not simply to lay out two things side by side (e.g., "there are varieties of gifts and the same Spirit"). This would have indicated that there is a single, two-part thought. The use of the development marker signals that one thing builds on top of another, constraining the reader to process the two things as distinct elements that move toward the same goal. Since they are semantically different (many/one) and yet related (gifts of the Spirit/ the Spirit himself), the natural contrast that was already present in the context is drawn out by the development constraint of δέ.

Note that v. 5 is added to v. 4 by the use of καί. This indicates that it is part of the same step of Paul's argument. He establishes a similar contrast to the one found in v. 4 (variety/same), but the two elements are linked here using καί instead of δέ. There is not a different spirit behind each of the gifts, but rather the same one.

The development in v. 6 reiterates what we probably expected to be a development in v. 5. By simply joining the elements in v. 5 through the use of καί and moving on to the next comparison, Paul is able to build suspense about his primary point. He is not arguing just for a unified view of the Spirit or God, but for a unified understanding of the diverse manifestations of the Spirit. Regardless of appearances, God is using the varied elements to accomplish a single, unified result for the common good. The development of v. 7 builds upon this idea of singularity, switching to the individual who receives one of the diverse gifts.

For speakers of English, development is a very difficult concept to grasp. It is natural to conceive of *temporal* development, as in a sequence of events, but challenging to conceptualize *logical* development when it does not involve sequence. It can sometimes be helpful to think about what was not used when trying to understand the significance of a development marker in a particular context.

2.4   Narrative Τότε

In the introduction to development markers, I made the point that temporal adverbs are often used in English to mark new developments, segmenting the text into smaller chunks in contexts of relative continuity. Temporal adverbs are used as development markers in the Greek NT as well,[20] particularly in Matthew and Acts. The adverb τότε ("then") can fulfill the same role as a connective in contexts where none are present. This usage has been referred to as "narrative τότε" based on its distribution.[21]

It is important to keep in mind some qualities of narrative. First, Longacre has observed that it possesses two significant parameters: + contingent temporal succession and + agent orientation.[22] In other words, narratives typically are composed of sequentially ordered events, and they focus primarily upon the agents performing the action. This means that the default expectation of the reader is that

- one event or action follows the next sequentially, and
- there is a consistent passage of time as these events unfold.

These are the expectations unless the writer indicates otherwise (e.g., "before these things" or "three years later"). Consider the use of *then* in the following example:

I got up, *then* I got dressed, *then* I ate breakfast.

Based on the assumption of sequential ordering of events, using *then* tells me nothing specific about how much time passed. I could have used asyndeton to link these clauses and relied upon the assumption that one thing followed the next.

The use of *then* in this context is unnecessary for semantic reasons, yet it still serves a discourse function: segmenting the text into developments. The same holds true in the Greek NT. Τότε conveys the same sequential constraint as *then*. Since it is assumed that one narrative event follows the next in a sequence, the pragmatic effect of using it in a context of relative continuity

---

20. Similarly, one finds וְעַתָּה ("and now") frequently used in biblical Hebrew reported speeches or exhortations to signal the transition from some state of affairs to what is to be done in response. It may serve as a development marker.

21. Levinsohn (*Discourse Features*, 95) states, "It is often used, especially in Matthew and Acts, as 'a connective particle' (BDF §459(2)), perhaps because of Semitic influence (Turner 1963:341)." BDF's description is consistent with the definition of "development" that I use above.

22. Robert E. Longacre, *The Grammar of Discourse* (Topics in Language and Linguistics; New York: Plenum, 1996), 8–9.

is to instruct the reader to segment the text into a new chunk. Τότε indicates that the primary basis for relating what follows to what precedes is as the next discrete step or development in the discourse, based on how the writer conceived of the action.

Since both δέ and τότε mark new developments, the question arises of how they differ from one another. Based on the idea of default versus marked, δέ should be viewed as the default development marker, the one used when there is no desire to specify the exact nature of the development. Due to the semantic nature of τότε, it makes explicit that the development that follows is *temporal* in nature. At times this may end up being a generic transition in time, but it is still temporal in nature.

Narrative τότε is often found at the margins of the paragraphs created in the critical Greek texts by modern editors. In Matt 18:15–20, Jesus provides instruction about what to do if someone sins against you. Peter then asks a question related to Jesus' teaching. The use of τότε here has the effect of segmenting Peter's question as a distinct yet related part of the discourse.

Example 12 :: Matthew 18:2

Τότε προσελθὼν ὁ Πέτρος εἶπεν αὐτῷ, Κύριε, ποσάκις ἁμαρτήσει εἰς ἐμὲ ὁ ἀδελφός μου καὶ ἀφήσω αὐτῷ; ἕως ἑπτάκις;	**Then** Peter came up and said to him, "Lord, how many times will my brother sin against me and I will forgive him? Up to seven times?"

Then simply signals a low-level break in the text, yet not so great as to make the reader think that a whole new topic follows. Both NA[27] and UBS[4] make v. 21 the beginning of a new paragraph. Other paragraph-initial instances of τότε are Matt 2:7, 16; 4:1, 5; 15:12; 16:24.

There are also a number of instances where τότε is not paragraph-initial but rather is found in the middle of a paragraph. In all but two of these instances (Matt 13:43; 24:40) τότε is found at natural transition points, just before a speech, in response to a speech, or both. Here too τότε indicates that what follows is the next development of the discourse. It can operate at various levels of the discourse.

In the following example, τότε occurs twice in the middle of what NA[27] and UBS[4] consider to be a single paragraph. Each occurrence is found at a potential transition in the story.

Example 13 :: Matthew 12:43–45

⁴³Ὅταν **δὲ** τὸ ἀκάθαρτον πνεῦμα ἐξέλθῃ ἀπὸ τοῦ ἀνθρώπου, διέρχεται δι᾽ ἀνύδρων τόπων ζητοῦν ἀνάπαυσιν καὶ οὐχ εὑρίσκει.	⁴³ "**Now** whenever an unclean spirit has gone out of a person, it travels through waterless places searching for rest, and does not find it.
⁴⁴ **τότε** λέγει, Εἰς τὸν οἶκόν μου ἐπιστρέψω ὅθεν ἐξῆλθον· **καὶ** ἐλθὸν εὑρίσκει σχολάζοντα σεσαρωμένον καὶ κεκοσμημένον.	⁴⁴ **Then** it says, 'I will return to my house from which I came out.' **And** when it arrives it finds the house unoccupied and swept and put in order.
⁴⁵ **τότε** πορεύεται καὶ παραλαμβάνει μεθ᾽ ἑαυτοῦ ἑπτὰ ἕτερα πνεύματα πονηρότερα ἑαυτοῦ **καὶ** εἰσελθόντα κατοικεῖ ἐκεῖ· καὶ γίνεται τὰ ἔσχατα τοῦ ἀνθρώπου ἐκείνου χείρονα τῶν πρώτων. οὕτως ἔσται καὶ τῇ γενεᾷ ταύτῃ τῇ πονηρᾷ.	⁴⁵ **Then** it goes and brings along with itself seven other spirits more evil than itself, **and** they go in and live there. And the last state of that person becomes worse than the first. So it will be for this evil generation also!"

One could have potentially made what happens upon the spirit's return into a distinct development; so too with the different clauses of v. 45. The use of τότε gives insight into how the writer/speaker construed the structure of the discourse, based on the connectives used.

There are two instances of δέ in example 14. The first introduces Jesus' speech; the second marks the development from the affirmation that Elijah will come first to the declaration that he already has come. Τότε is used to mark the development that resulted from Jesus' speech.

Example 14 :: Matthew 17:10–13

¹⁰ καὶ ἐπηρώτησαν αὐτὸν οἱ μαθηταὶ λέγοντες, Τί οὖν οἱ γραμματεῖς λέγουσιν ὅτι Ἠλίαν δεῖ ἐλθεῖν πρῶτον;	¹⁰ And the disciples asked him, "Then why do the scribes say that first Elijah must come?"
¹¹ ὁ **δὲ** ἀποκριθεὶς εἶπεν, Ἠλίας μὲν ἔρχεται καὶ ἀποκαταστήσει πάντα·	¹¹ **DM** He answered, "Elijah does come, and he will restore all things.

¹² λέγω **δὲ** ὑμῖν ὅτι Ἡλίας ἤδη ἦλθεν, καὶ οὐκ ἐπέγνωσαν αὐτὸν ἀλλὰ ἐποίησαν ἐν αὐτῷ ὅσα ἠθέλησαν· οὕτως καὶ ὁ υἱὸς τοῦ ἀνθρώπου μέλλει πάσχειν ὑπ᾽ αὐτῶν.

¹² **But** I tell you that Elijah has already come, and they did not recognize him, but did to him whatever they pleased. So also the Son of Man will certainly suffer at their hands."

¹³ **τότε** συνῆκαν οἱ μαθηταὶ ὅτι περὶ Ἰωάννου τοῦ βαπτιστοῦ εἶπεν αὐτοῖς.

¹³ **Then** the disciples understood that he was speaking to them of John the Baptist.

Whereas the disciples did not understand whom Jesus was talking about in the beginning, they understood as a result of the speech that he was talking about John the Baptist. Generally speaking, segmenting something off as a distinct development attracts more attention to it than if it were just another part of the preceding unit. Using τότε here has the effect of making v. 13 a distinct step, thereby making it stand out.

The usage in example 15 is not found at the transition to or from a speech. It simply marks the result that follows from a preceding action as the next development in the story. In this case, τότε introduces the conclusion the sequence.[23]

Example 15 :: Matthew 4:9–11

⁹ καὶ εἶπεν αὐτῷ, Ταῦτά σοι πάντα δώσω, ἐὰν πεσὼν προσκυνήσῃς μοι.

⁹ And he said to him, "All these I will give you, if you will fall down and worship me."

¹⁰ **τότε** λέγει αὐτῷ ὁ Ἰησοῦς, Ὕπαγε, Σατανᾶ· γέγραπται γάρ....

¹⁰ **Then** Jesus said to him, "Be gone, Satan! For it is written...."

¹¹ **Τότε** ἀφίησιν αὐτὸν ὁ διάβολος, καὶ ἰδοὺ ἄγγελοι προσῆλθον καὶ διηκόνουν αὐτῷ.

¹¹ **Then** the devil left him, and behold, angels came and were ministering to him.

Τότε in v. 10 is used at the transition in a speech where Jesus responds to the devil. It is used again in v. 11 to introduce the devil's response to Jesus. Sequentiality would have been assumed even without the use of τότε. The use of the development marker τότε indicates that they were viewed by the writer

---

23. Levinsohn (*Discourse Features*, 98) states, "Typically, conclusions introduced with τότε attain the goal sought or predicted in earlier events."

as distinct steps. The use of *then* in translation captures this segmentation very naturally in English. NA[27], UBS[4], and the LEB render v. 11 as a new paragraph despite its connection to what precedes.

In example 16, τότε segments the part of the discourse that returns to describe what happens to the righteous, those signified by the "good seed" in the parable. This development also represents the goal that is sought in the parable.

Example 16 :: Matthew 13:41–43

[41] Ø ἀποστελεῖ ὁ υἱὸς τοῦ ἀνθρώπου τοὺς ἀγγέλους αὐτοῦ, καὶ συλλέξουσιν ἐκ τῆς βασιλείας αὐτοῦ πάντα τὰ σκάνδαλα καὶ τοὺς ποιοῦντας τὴν ἀνομίαν

[41] Ø "The Son of Man will send his angels, and they will gather out of his kingdom all causes of sin and all law-breakers,

[42] καὶ βαλοῦσιν αὐτοὺς εἰς τὴν κάμινον τοῦ πυρός· Ø ἐκεῖ ἔσται ὁ κλαυθμὸς καὶ ὁ βρυγμὸς τῶν ὀδόντων.

[42] and throw them into the fiery furnace. Ø In that place there will be weeping and gnashing of teeth.

[43] **Τότε** οἱ δίκαιοι ἐκλάμψουσιν ὡς ὁ ἥλιος ἐν τῇ βασιλείᾳ τοῦ πατρὸς αὐτῶν. ὁ ἔχων ὦτα ἀκουέτω.

[43] **Then** the righteous will shine like the sun in the kingdom of their Father. He who has ears, let him hear."

The enemy is seeking to prevent the good seed from being safely harvested. Segmenting v. 43 has the effect of attracting more attention to this conclusion, compared to simply linking it to the preceding one by using καί.

Τότε serves the same basic function as δέ in that both signal that what follows is the next development in the story or discourse. Τότε is used as a connective primarily in Matthew and Acts in contexts where there is no switch in time from some other point to *then*. Such a switch would be a construed as a temporal frame of reference.[24] The primary basis for relating it to what precedes is as a passage of time. However, since the default expectation in narrative is that the events are sequentially ordered and temporally related, τότε indicates that the writer chose to mark what follows as a distinct development that is temporal in nature.

The chart below summarizes what has been claimed so far about Greek connectives, focusing on how they differ from one another rather than how

---

24. See §10.2.

they should be translated. Development markers serve to attract attention to a transition or discontinuity in the context for the sake of breaking it into smaller chunks for easier processing. Developments reflect the writer's conception of the action or argument, so there are no hard-and-fast rules about when and where these markers must be used. I have shown how they are found at thematic transitions, such as changes in time, location, participants, and kind of action. I have also shown that different writers can have different conceptions of the same action, based on their use of development markers.

Whereas καί signals a close continuity, development markers highlight some level of discontinuity, in particular the segmentation of discourse in contexts of relative continuity. Narrative τότε is the first connective covered that carries a specific semantic constraint, based on its temporal meaning. It indicates that the change or development is portrayed as temporal in nature. In contrast, δέ is the default development marker and is unmarked for such semantic constraints.

Table 1 :: Function of connectives καί, δέ, τότε

	Continuity	Development	Semantic Constraint
Ø	-	-	-
Καί	+	-	-
Δέ	-	+	-
Τότε	-	+	Temporal

So far we have looked at two kinds of connective relationships: indicating the continuity of two joined elements (Ø versus καί), and signaling whether what follows represents the next step or development of what precedes (δέ and τότε). In §2.4 we were introduced to the idea of a connective conveying a semantic constraint besides continuity and development, with narrative τότε marking an explicitly temporal development, something that is unmarked by δέ. All the connectives that follow carry some additional semantic constraint that differentiates them from the connectives already discussed. We begin with οὖν.

2.5   Οὖν

BDAG attributes two primary functions to οὖν. The first is as an "inferential" connective, which BDAG describes as "denoting that what it introduces is the result of or an inference fr. what precedes."[25] In this sense, οὖν is backward-pointing like καί and δέ, but it carries additional constraints. Viewing οὖν as simply a logical, inferential particle fails to capture its broader function outside the NT Epistles. This is where the second sense from BDAG comes in.

BDAG also claims that οὖν is a "marker of continuation in a narrative," to be glossed using "so," "now," or "then."[26] BDAG cites Robertson, who speaks of οὖν as "a transitional particle relating clauses or sentences loosely together by way of confirmation."[27] As with δέ and τότε, it seems clear that the traditional grammarians recognized the function of οὖν as a development marker, based on the attribution of "continuation," "transitional," and the English adverbial glosses.

Οὖν differs from the other development markers by adding the constraint of close continuity with what precedes. In this sense, it resembles καί by closely linking discourse elements together, but with the added constraint of a new development. In the NT Epistles, it is regularly translated as "therefore" to indicate that what follows the particle is either inferentially drawn or concluded from what precedes, hence + continuity. One often finds οὖν at high-level boundaries in the discourse, where the next major topic is drawn from and builds upon what precedes. In this way, it signals + development. This is illustrated from Rom 5:1, where Paul transitions from the means of justification to a discussion of the results that it brings about.

Example 17 :: Romans 4:23–5:1

[23] Οὐκ ἐγράφη δὲ δι' αὐτὸν μόνον ὅτι ἐλογίσθη αὐτῷ [24] ἀλλὰ καὶ δι' ἡμᾶς, οἷς μέλλει λογίζεσθαι, τοῖς πιστεύουσιν ἐπὶ τὸν ἐγείραντα Ἰησοῦν τὸν κύριον ἡμῶν ἐκ νεκρῶν, [25] ὃς παρεδόθη διὰ τὰ παραπτώματα ἡμῶν καὶ ἠγέρθη διὰ τὴν δικαίωσιν ἡμῶν.	[23] But it was not written for the sake of him alone that it was credited to him, [24] but also for the sake of us to whom it is going to be credited, to those who believe in the one who raised Jesus our Lord from the dead, [25] who was handed over on account of our trespasses, and was raised up in the interest of our justification.

---

25. BDAG, 736.
26. Ibid.
27. Robertson, *Grammar*, 1191.

^{5:1} Δικαιωθέντες **οὖν** ἐκ πίστεως εἰρήνην ἔχομεν πρὸς τὸν θεὸν διὰ τοῦ κυρίου ἡμῶν Ἰησοῦ Χριστοῦ.…

^{5:1} **Therefore**, because we have been declared righteous by faith, we have peace with God through our Lord Jesus Christ.…

The circumstantial participial clause of Rom 5:1 reiterates the conclusion reached in the preceding context. The particle οὖν constrains what follows to be understood as building closely upon what precedes, yet as a distinct new development in the argument.

Οὖν can be used to mark lower-level developments in the discourse as well. This usage is often found in the reported speeches of the Gospels. Consider the use in John the Baptist's speech to the Pharisees and Sadducees who come to him as people are being baptized and confessing their sins.

Example 18 :: Matthew 3:7–8

⁷ Ἰδὼν δὲ πολλοὺς τῶν Φαρισαίων καὶ Σαδδουκαίων ἐρχομένους ἐπὶ τὸ βάπτισμα αὐτοῦ εἶπεν αὐτοῖς· γεννήματα ἐχιδνῶν, τίς ὑπέδειξεν ὑμῖν φυγεῖν ἀπὸ τῆς μελλούσης ὀργῆς;

⁷ But when he saw many of the Pharisees and Sadducees coming to his baptism, he said to them, "Offspring of vipers! Who warned you to flee from the coming wrath?

⁸ ποιήσατε **οὖν** καρπὸν ἄξιον τῆς μετανοίας

⁸ **Therefore** produce fruit worthy of repentance!

Based on the fact that he addresses them as a brood of vipers, it would seem that John views them as in need of repentance. This is confirmed by his casting their journey as flight from the coming wrath. Flight itself is insufficient to deliver them; something more is needed. Verse 8 introduces a command to produce fruit worthy of repentance, with οὖν constraining the statement to be read as a closely related next step. The NIV, ESV and NRSV provide no indication of οὖν. John's exhortation does not come out of thin air; it is directly related to the preceding context. The use of οὖν makes this explicit in Greek, whereas the nature of the relationship is left implicit or unmarked in these translations through the use of asyndeton. It may or may not be present. Regardless of whether one translates οὖν or not, it is crucial to recognize the function that it plays in the exegesis of this discourse.

Another sense attributed to οὖν by BDAG is "resuming a discourse that has been interrupted."[28] In other words, it signals the resumption of the main

---

28. BDAG, 213.

discourse following a digression, whether in narrative proper[29] or in the Epistles.[30] Levinsohn notes that this usage highlights a distinction between οὖν and
δέ: "Whether the amount of intervening material is short or long, the presence
of οὖν only constrains what follows to be interpreted as further development
of the topic that has been resumed."[31] In contrast to continuing or resuming
the same main topic, δέ "permits a change of topic."[32] In other words, if the
event line of a narrative is interrupted by background material, it is common
to find the resumption of the mainline marked by οὖν. The + development
signals the transition from background to mainline; the + continuity indicates
that the same event line will be resumed. In contrast, resumption using δέ
would indicate a new line of development.

In Matthew's account of Jesus' trial, background information is provided
by way of imperfect and pluperfect indicative verbs. These tense-forms typically are used in narrative to describe introductory states of affairs rather than
main events.[33]

Example 19 :: Matthew 27:14–17

[14] καὶ οὐκ ἀπεκρίθη αὐτῷ πρὸς οὐδὲ ἓν ῥῆμα, ὥστε θαυμάζειν τὸν ἡγεμόνα λίαν.	[14] And he did not reply to him, not even with reference to one state- ment, so that the governor was very astonished.

---

29. See Levinsohn, *Discourse Features*, 85, 128–29.

30. Jacob K. Heckert, *Discourse Function of Conjoiners in the Pastoral Epistles* (Dallas:
SIL International, 1996), 98.

31. Levinsohn, *Discourse Features*, 129.

32. Ibid., 85.

33. Levinsohn (ibid., 174) quotes Foley and Van Valin regarding "an inherent correlation between perfective versus imperfective aspect and foreground versus background":
"[T]he perfective aspect is the primary aspectual category found in the temporal structure of narrative discourse in a number of languages and imperfective aspect is primary in
durational/descriptive structure. (op. cit. 373) This finding [the statement on p. 373] is not
surprising, since perfective aspect codes completed actions and events and imperfective
incomplete events and actions and the former fit more naturally into the temporal structure of narrative, the latter into durational/descriptive structure. (op. cit. 397)." Levinsohn
concludes, "Thus, it is natural in a narrative in Greek for a clause with the verb in the
imperfect (which has imperfective aspect) to be conveying information of less importance
than one with the verb in the aorist (perfective aspect); this is due to the nature of the
respective aspects."

¹⁵ Κατὰ **δὲ** ἑορτὴν εἰώθει ὁ ἡγεμὼν ἀπολύειν ἕνα τῷ ὄχλῳ δέσμιον ὃν ἤθελον.

¹⁵ **Now** at each feast, the governor was accustomed to release one prisoner to the crowd—the one whom they wanted.

¹⁶ εἶχον **δὲ** τότε³⁴ δέσμιον ἐπίσημον λεγόμενον [Ἰησοῦν] Βαραββᾶν.

¹⁶ **DM** And at that time they had a notorious prisoner named Jesus Barabbas.

¹⁷ συνηγμένων **οὖν** αὐτῶν εἶπεν αὐτοῖς ὁ Πιλᾶτος· τίνα θέλετε ἀπολύσω ὑμῖν, [Ἰησοῦν τὸν] ραββᾶν ἢ Ἰησοῦν τὸν λεγόμενον χριστόν;

¹⁷ **So** after they had assembled, Pilate said to them, "Whom do you want me to release for you— Jesus Barabbas or Jesus who is called Christ?"

The verbs εἰώθει, ἤθελον, and εἶχον are all imperfective aspect, associated with offline background material. This does not mean that the material of vv. 15–17 is unimportant; on the contrary, it is crucial to understanding Pilate's motivation in v. 17. Background material does not advance the narrative plot but fleshes out some aspect of it before moving forward. The οὖν in v. 17 simply signals a resumption of the event line suspended in v. 14. The + development marks the transition from offline back to the mainline, whereas the + continuity signals the resumption of the same event line that was suspended in v. 14. Using δέ here would have left the door open for moving on to a new development of some kind, as in example 20. ³⁵

In this case, Jesus has dismissed the crowds and gone off to pray after sending the disciples to cross the lake without him. Verses 23b–24 use imperfect-tense forms and a verbless clause to describe the offline information regarding the situation of the disciples, without reference to Jesus.

Example 20 :: Matthew 14:23–25

²³ καὶ ἀπολύσας τοὺς ὄχλους ἀνέβη εἰς τὸ ὄρος κατ᾽ ἰδίαν προσεύξασθαι. ὀψίας **δὲ** γενομένης μόνος ἦν ἐκεῖ.

²³ And after he sent away the crowds, he went up on the mountain by himself to pray. **So** when evening came, he was there alone.

---

34. Τότε functions here as a simple adverb, based on the presence of the connective δέ.

35. Compare the discussion of this passage to Stephanie Black, *Sentence Conjunctions in the Gospel of Matthew* (JSNTSup 216; Sheffield: Sheffield Academic, 2002), 275–76. She does not draw a meaningful distinction between continuity and development.

^{24} τὸ **δὲ** πλοῖον ἤδη σταδίους πολλοὺς ἀπὸ τῆς γῆς ἀπεῖχεν βασανιζόμενον ὑπὸ τῶν κυμάτων, ἦν γὰρ ἐναντίος ὁ ἄνεμος.	^{24} **But** the boat was already many stadia distant from the land, being beaten by the waves, because the wind was against it.
^{25} τετάρτη **δὲ** φυλακῇ τῆς νυκτὸς ἦλθεν πρὸς αὐτοὺς περιπατῶν ἐπὶ τὴν θάλασσαν.	^{25} **DM** And in the fourth watch of the night he came to them, walking on the sea.

The arrival of Jesus is not directly related to some preceding line that was interrupted; it is a new development that builds on what precedes. It lacks the close connection observed with οὖν.

A comment is in order concerning the use of οὖν in John's gospel. In many respects, John uses οὖν to mark new developments in the same way that Matthew and Luke use δέ, though there are some distinctions. Levinsohn states,

> Οὖν may be thought of as a marked developmental conjunction, employed in specific contexts in which δέ would have been used in the Synoptics. It is used in John's Gospel in two specific contexts (see also sec. 7.4):
>   1.   in connection with a return to the storyline (i.e., as a *resumptive*), provided the event concerned represents a new development, as far as the author's purpose is concerned
>   2.   when an *inferential* (logical) relation with the preceding event is to the fore.[36]

In other words, οὖν bears the same constraints in John as it does in the Epistles and some reported speeches of narrative.

Οὖν marks development in the same way as the other development markers that we have considered, but with the added constraint of + continuity to differentiate it. It traditionally had been described as inferential or continuative/resumptive. These "senses" are consistent with the linguistic constraints of continuity and development. The English gloss *therefore* most closely matches the inferential sense of οὖν, whereas *thus* often captures the resumptive sense well. However, these English glosses fail to represent the semantic constraints that οὖν brings about in Greek. Understanding what each connective uniquely signals is the key to overcoming the mismatches between English and Greek. Each connective constrains a slightly different relation than the others, regardless of the English glosses that we might use to represent it in translation. Attempting to understand the constraints that a

---

36. Levinsohn, *Discourse Features*, 85.

connective signals based upon one or two English glosses will only obscure the issue.

2.6   Διὰ Τοῦτο

Διὰ τοῦτο is not a conjunction from the standpoint of morphology, yet as a set expression it has come to function as a connective in Koiné Greek. In Robertson's description of "connection between separate sentences," he cites the use of διὰ τοῦτο in Matt 24:44, where it "answers as a link of union" comparable to δέ, γάρ, and ἄρα.[37] Similarly, Wallace refers to this idiom as a "formulaic phrase" that refers back to the previous argument, though he does not treat it as a connective.[38] In a later section describing the classification of independent clauses, he notes that certain prepositional phrases may determine the function of independent clauses, ostensibly in lieu of a coordinating conjunction. Διὰ τοῦτο is one of the seven listed and one of four that he lists using some form of τοῦτο.[39] Titrud also lists it alongside the conjunctions διό, ἄρα, and ἄρα οὖν that may introduce a paragraph.[40]

The specific context that I will focus on here is the use of διὰ τοῦτο in the absence of any other coordinating conjunction (i.e., asyndeton).[41] To Wallace's point, in the absence of a full morphological conjunction, διὰ τοῦτο plays the same functional role of indicating how the independent clause that follows is to be related to what precedes. The preposition διά contributes a causal sense in most cases, "the reason why someth[ing] happens, results, exists: *because of, for the sake of.*"[42] The demonstrative pronoun τοῦτο reiterates a proposition from the preceding context.[43] Thus, the clause introduced by διὰ τοῦτο is constrained to have a causal relation with the preceding discourse. It is similar to οὖν in that both indicate + development and + continuity, but διὰ τοῦτο

---

37. Robertson, *Grammar*, 443.

38. Wallace, *Greek Grammar*, 333.

39. Ibid., 658.

40. Kermit Titrud, "The Function of καί in the Greek New Testament and an Application to 2 Peter," in *Linguistics and New Testament Interpretation: Essays on Discourse Analysis* (ed. David Alan Black, Katharine Barnwell, and Stephen Levinsohn; Nashville: Broadman, 1992), 251.

41. I include those instances where καί is functioning adverbially and not as a connective (e.g., Luke 11:49). In such cases καί will not occur at the beginning of the clause.

42. BDAG, 225.

43. There are a few instances where διὰ τοῦτο is forward-pointing (e.g., John 8:47), but there are coordinating conjunctions present, indicating that it is not functioning as a connective.

offers a narrower semantic constraint than οὖν does.[44] In this way, there is significant overlap in semantic meaning between the two, with the meaningful distinction being the narrower *causal* constraint in the case of διὰ τοῦτο. This overlap is analogous to that between δέ and τότε, with the latter having the narrower *temporal* constraint.

Διὰ τοῦτο is often used in the Gospels within reported speeches to introduce a key proposition, co-occurring with various highlighting devices.[45] Example 21 illustrates this. Διὰ τοῦτο comes in the midst of a speech at the conclusion of the parable of the rich fool and serves as the introduction to the teaching on anxiety. It functions as a hinge between the two pericopes, closely linking them yet indicating a distinct new step in the discourse.[46] The reintroduction of Jesus midspeech at the beginning of v. 22 provides further segmentation of the speech.[47]

Example 21 :: Luke 12:22

[20] "But God said to him, 'Fool! This night your life is demanded from you, and the things which you have prepared—whose will they be?' [21] So is the one who stores up treasure for himself, and who is not rich toward God!"

[22] Εἶπεν δὲ πρὸς τοὺς μαθητὰς [αὐτοῦ]· **διὰ τοῦτο** λέγω ὑμῖν· μὴ μεριμνᾶτε τῇ ψυχῇ τί φάγητε, μηδὲ τῷ σώματι τί ἐνδύσησθε.	[22] **DM** And he said to his disciples, "**For this reason** I tell you, do not be anxious for your life, what you will eat, or for your body, what you will wear."

Διὰ τοῦτο indicates that what follows is closely related to what precedes. It constrains what follows to be viewed as a response to some situation in the preceding context. In this case, v. 22 introduces how one ought to handle anxiety associated with wealth (or its lack). It also signals that what follows is a new development or step in the argument. In this case, it comes at the transition between the story of the rich fool and the teaching about avoiding anxiety. It is distinct from what precedes (i.e., a new pericope or teaching) yet closely

---

44. BDAG provides the gloss *therefore* for διὰ τοῦτο in section B.2.b.

45. In some instances it co-occurs with forward-pointing devices such as metacomments (e.g., Matt 6:25; 12:31; 21:43; Mark 11:24; Luke 12:22 [see chapter 5]) or attention-getters (e.g., Matt 23:34 [see §5.4.2]).

46. The NASB is the only English translation that does not begin a new paragraph at v. 22.

47. On the midspeech use of quotative frames, see §7.2.2.

related. There is also a metacomment (λέγω ὑμῖν, "I tell you"), a forward-pointing device that attracts attention to the proposition that it introduces.[48]

Διὰ τοῦτο here serves to signal a distinct new development in the discourse yet to closely link it with what precedes. It also constrains a narrower relationship between the two parts than does οὖν. The story of the rich fool teaches what not to do; διὰ τοῦτο introduces what is to be done instead, in response to the preceding story.

In the parallel of this story in Matt 6:25, διὰ τοῦτο plays a similar "hinge" role, connecting two discrete sections that are closely related.[49] However, in Matthew's account the preceding teaching concerns serving two masters instead of the parable of the rich fool. The response to the situation is the same in both cases: do not worry. Matthew also uses a metacomment to highlight the main proposition.

Example 22 illustrates διὰ τοῦτο in a context of relative continuity in a series of commands.

Example 22 :: Ephesians 5:15–17

[15] Βλέπετε **οὖν** ἀκριβῶς πῶς περιπατεῖτε μὴ ὡς ἄσοφοι ἀλλ' ὡς σοφοί, [16] ἐξαγοραζόμενοι τὸν καιρόν, ὅτι αἱ ἡμέραι πονηραί εἰσιν.	[15] **Therefore**, consider carefully how you live, not as unwise but as wise, [16] making the most of the time because the days are evil.
[17] **διὰ τοῦτο** μὴ γίνεσθε ἄφρονες, ἀλλὰ συνίετε τί τὸ θέλημα τοῦ κυρίου.	[17] **Because of this** do not become foolish, but understand what the will of the Lord is.

Verse 15 begins with οὖν to indicate that it provides a summary or conclusion drawn from the preceding context and is thus closely connected. Verse 16 uses an adverbial clause to elaborate on this verse. Verse 17 introduces the next command in the series, one that is related to what precedes using διὰ τοῦτο. This indicates that what follows represents a distinct development that is closely related to v. 15. It also provides a causative constraint, indicating that the command not to be foolish bears a causal relation to what precedes (vv. 15–16). The days being evil and the need for walking wisely are cast as the reason why we ought not be foolish. Οὖν would have implicitly allowed for this semantic relation, but διὰ τοῦτο makes it explicit.

---

48. See chapter 5.

49. The NKJV is the only English version that does not begin a new paragraph at v. 25.

Not every instance of διὰ τοῦτο functions as a connective. In the absence of any coordinating conjunction, this phrase provides guidance in how to relate what follows to the preceding context. When it functions as a connective, it signals + continuity, + development, as well as adding a causal constraint to the relationship between the two parts.[50]

Table 2 :: Function of connectives καί, δέ, τότε, οὖν, διὰ τοῦτο

	Continuity	Development	Semantic Constraint
Ø	-	-	-
Καί	+	-	-
Δέ	-	+	-
Τότε	-	+	Temporal
Οὖν	+	+	-
Διὰ τοῦτο	+	+	Causal

The rest of the connectives covered in this chapter are related to one another only in that none of them mark development. Each of them brings to bear a unique semantic constraint to the relationship of the clause that follows with some other portion of the discourse.

2.7   Γάρ

The diverse usage of γάρ has resulted in a wide variety of claims being made about it. Both Wallace and Young contend that it functions as both a coordinating and subordinating conjunction.[51] BDAG describes it as expressing

---

50. Other examples include Matt 12:27, 31; 13:13, 52; 18:23; 21:43; 23:34; 24:44; Mark 11:24; Luke 11:19, 49; John 1:31; 6:65; 7:22; 8:47; 9:23; 10:17; 12:18, 39; 13:11; 15:19; 16:15; 19:11; Acts 2:26; Rom 1:26; 4:16; 5:12; 15:9; 1 Cor 4:17; 11:10, 30; 2 Cor 4:1; 7:13; 13:10; Eph 1:15–16; 6:13; Col 1:9; 1 Thess 3:5, 7; 2 Tim 2:10; Heb 1:9; 2:1; 1 John 3:1; 4:5; 3 John 10; Rev 7:15; 12:12; 18:8. John 5:18 is another possible instance, where many textual witnesses omit οὖν.

51. Wallace, *Greek Grammar*, 669; Richard A. Young, *Intermediate New Testament Greek: A Linguistic and Exegetical Approach* (Nashville: Broadman & Holman, 1994), 182.

cause, clarification, or inference.[52] Robertson advocates that it is best viewed as explanatory in nature, before making an appeal for other senses.[53]

Robertson's "explanatory" assertion has largely been confirmed as the core constraint of γάρ in modern linguistic treatments. Heckert concludes that it introduces material that strengthens or confirms a previous proposition.[54] Levinsohn states,

> Background material introduced by γάρ provides explanations or expositions of the previous assertion (see Winer 1882:566–67, Robertson 1919:1190, Harbeck 1970:12). The presence of γάρ constrains the material that it introduces to be interpreted as *strengthening* some aspect of the previous assertion, rather than as distinctive information.[55]

In other words, the information introduced does not advance the discourse but adds background information that strengthens or supports what precedes. Black also correlates the use of γάρ with background information, noting a tendency for it to be used with forms of εἰμί and imperfect-tense forms.[56] She states, "Γάρ is used to direct the audience to strengthen a preceding proposition, confirming it as part of the mental representation they construct of the discourse."[57]

In terms of the constraints assigned to the other connectives discussed thus far, γάρ, like καί, οὖν, and διὰ τοῦτο, signals close continuity with what precedes. However, it differs from the latter two in that it does not mark development. It differs from καί by adding the semantic constraint of strengthening/support. It does not advance the mainline of the discourse but rather introduces offline material that strengthens or supports what precedes. Γάρ can introduce a single clause that strengthens, or it may introduce an entire paragraph. Of the 1,041 instances in the Greek NT, only 10 percent of them are found in narrative proper, compared to usage in reported speeches and the Epistles. The books of Romans and Hebrews have the greatest concentration of usage, followed closely by 1–2 Corinthians and Galatians.[58]

Where it occurs in narrative proper, the proposition introduced by γάρ fleshes out some aspect of what precedes. It may be in the form of background

---

52. BDAG, 189.
53. Robertson, *Grammar*, 1190.
54. Heckert, *Discourse Function*, 31, 36.
55. Levinsohn, *Discourse Features*, 91.
56. Black, *Sentence Conjunctions*, 280.
57. Ibid.
58. This statement is based on the number of occurrences normalized per thousand words in the book.

information; it may introduce the reason or rationale for some preceding action or state. For instance, six of the thirty-three narrative occurrences in Mark introduce verbs of speaking, describing what people were saying in response to or to precipitate the preceding action.[59] Twelve more narrative instances introduce "being" verbs, while eleven others introduce states of being or perception (e.g., knowing, fearing, understanding, seeing). The remaining narrative instances introduce states of affair (e.g., Mark 3:10: πολλοὺς γὰρ ἐθεράπευσεν, "for he had healed many").

The first illustration comes from Matt 10, where Jesus warns his disciples about a day when they will be arrested and handed over to the authorities for following him.

Example 23 :: Matthew 10:19–20

¹⁹ ὅταν **δὲ** παραδῶσιν ὑμᾶς, μὴ μεριμνήσητε πῶς ἢ τί λαλήσητε· δοθήσεται.	¹⁹ **DM** But whenever they hand you over, do not be anxious how to speak or what you should say,
γὰρ ὑμῖν ἐν ἐκείνῃ τῇ ὥρᾳ τί λαλήσητε	**for** what you should say will be given to you at that hour.
²⁰ οὐ **γὰρ** ὑμεῖς ἐστε οἱ λαλοῦντες ἀλλὰ τὸ πνεῦμα τοῦ πατρὸς ὑμῶν τὸ λαλοῦν ἐν ὑμῖν.	²⁰ **For** you are not the ones who are speaking, but the Spirit of your Father who is speaking through you.

In light of the circumstances Jesus describes, it seems counterintuitive not to be anxious. Verse 19b provides support for his assertion by stating that what they need to say will be given to them, they will not be left on their own. This statement is in turn supported by v. 20, stating that it is not just a matter of being given the words, but of who is speaking the words. In this case, the Spirit of their Father will be the one speaking.

The information introduced by γάρ is important to the discourse, but it does not advance the main description of how they are to respond when arrested. Instead, it introduces propositions that strengthen and support what precedes. The main flow of the discourse is resumed in v. 21, introduced by δέ because it is a new point rather than the resumption of one that was interrupted.

Galatians 5 opens with the statement that it was for freedom that Christ has set us free, not to be reenslaved to a keeping of the law. In v. 12, Paul

---

59. See Mark 3:21; 5:8, 28; 6:18; 14:2, 56.

expresses his wish that those who had distracted the Galatians with the need for circumcision would mutilate themselves. This verse is followed by what is considered to be a new section, introduced in v. 13 with γάρ.

Example 24 :: Galatians 5:13–14

¹³ Ὑμεῖς **γὰρ** ἐπ᾽ ἐλευθερίᾳ ἐκλήθητε, ἀδελφοί· μόνον μὴ τὴν ἐλευθερίαν εἰς ἀφορμὴν τῇ σαρκί, ἀλλὰ διὰ τῆς ἀγάπης δουλεύετε ἀλλήλοις.	¹³ **For** you were called to freedom, brothers. Only do not let your freedom become an opportunity for the flesh, but through love serve one another.
¹⁴ ὁ **γὰρ** πᾶς νόμος ἐν ἑνὶ λόγῳ πεπλήρωται, ἐν τῷ· ἀγαπήσεις τὸν πλησίον σου ὡς σεαυτόν.	¹⁴ **For** the whole law is fulfilled in one statement, namely, "You shall love your neighbor as yourself."

The paragraph introduced in v. 13 strengthens the preceding section of vv. 1–12 rather than advancing the argument with a new point. Rather than using their freedom as a license for the fight among themselves and with Paul, they were to be using it as an opportunity to serve. Verse 14 in turn strengthens the assertion of v. 13, adding support to the significance of serving one another through love. This section reiterates what the freedom they received was intended to bring about. Verses 13–15 provide supporting material that is important but does not advance the argument. The next major step is introduced in v. 16 by δέ.

Γάρ introduces explanatory material that strengthens or supports what precedes. This may consist of a single clause, or it may be a longer digression. Although the strengthening material is important to the discourse, it does not advance the argument or story. Instead, it supports what precedes by providing background or detail that is needed to understand what follows. Plots or arguments that are resumed after the supporting material are typically introduced using οὖν, whereas new lines of argument are signaled by δέ.

2.8   Μέν

The use of the connective μέν is described in detail in §4.1 in the discussion of point/counterpoint sets. The discussion here is limited to a basic overview. BDAG construes μέν primarily as a marker of correlation working in conjunction with other connectives, "introducing a concessive clause, followed by another clause w[ith] an adversative particle: *to be sure … but, on the one hand*

... on the other hand." [60] It serves primarily to correlate the clause that it introduces with some corresponding element that follows, typically introduced by δέ. In contrast to the other connectives considered so far, μέν is *forward-pointing*. Its sole function is to create the expectation that some related element will follow.

In many cases, the element introduced by μέν functions as a concession, just as the use in English of *although, inasmuch as, on the one hand,* or, more colloquially, *while*. Levinsohn states,

> The presence of μέν not only anticipates a corresponding sentence containing δέ but frequently, in narrative, it also downgrades the importance of the sentence containing μέν. In particular, the information introduced with μέν is often of a secondary importance in comparison with that introduced with δέ.[61]

There are other instances where μέν simply serves to explicitly correlate two elements that otherwise would only have an implicit relation. In such cases, there is simply a connection made between the two rather than the downgrading described by Levinsohn.

The use of μέν ... δέ to create correlated sets in Koiné Greek is found far more frequently than is observed in English using corresponding particles. This difference in usage might be related to the difference between the rather cumbersome *inasmuch as* and *on the one hand* in comparison to the tiny particle μέν. The mismatch in usage leads BDAG to state that a direct equivalence translation of μέν is often impossible.[62] The fact that we do not use forward-pointing correlatives nearly as frequently in English means that in many cases μέν is left untranslated in English versions.

In terms of linguistic constraints, μέν expresses + continuity. More specifically, it signals a forward-pointing correlation with an element introduced by δέ in most cases. It does not mark development. This connective will be covered in more detail in the discussion of point/counterpoint sets.

2.9 Ἀλλά

Ἀλλά is primarily used in the creation of point/counterpoint and is therefore treated more fully in §4.3. The purpose here is to discuss the semantic constraints that it brings to bear on the element that it introduces. BDAG

---

60. BDAG, 628. Cf. Wallace, *Greek Grammar*, 672; Robertson, *Grammar*, 1151–52.

61. Levinsohn, *Discourse Features*, 170.

62. BDAG, 628.

describes it as an adversative particle "indicating a difference with or contrast to what precedes, in the case of individual clauses as well as whole sentences."[63] Recall the comments made earlier about contrast being context-dependent, not a quality of the connective. Ἀλλά is often used following a negated clause to introduce a positive alternative. On this basis, ἀλλά is nearly always used in the context of contrast, serving to sharpen it.[64]

Heckert is able to reach more specific conclusions than "adversative" in his description of ἀλλά. He describes ἀλλά as a "global marker of contrast," one that "introduces a correction of the expectation created by the first conjunct; an incorrect expectation is cancelled and a proper expectation is put in its place."[65] It provides a corrective to whatever it stands in contrast with in the preceding context, even if it is positive rather than negative.[66] Levinsohn adds, "When ἀλλά links a negative characteristic or proposition with a following positive one, the negative proposition usually retains its relevance."[67]

In terms of the semantic constraints that we have discussed so far, ἀλλά is unmarked for continuity. It is also unmarked for development. It is a correlator of items of equal status, like καί and μέν, but differs from καί by being unmarked for continuity (– continuity), and it differs from μέν by not being forward-pointing. The constraint that it brings to bear is "correction" of some aspect in the preceding context. This is summarized in the chart on the following page.

---

63. BDAG, 44.
64. See Robertson, *Grammar*, 1187; Porter, *Idioms*, 205; Wallace, *Greek Grammar*, 671.
65. Heckert, *Discourse Function,* 23.
66. Levinsohn, *Discourse Features*, 115.
67. Ibid.

Table 3 :: Function of Greek connectives

	Continuity	Development	Correlation	Forward-pointing	Semantic Constraint
Ø	-	-	-	-	-
Καί	+	-	+	-	-
Δέ	-	+	-	-	-
Τότε	-	+	-	-	Temporal
Οὖν	+	+	-	-	-
Διὰ τοῦτο	+	+	-	-	Causal
Γάρ	+	-	-	-	Support
Μέν	+	-	+	+	Expectation
Ἀλλά	-	-	+	-	Correction

Suggested Reading

Blass, F., A. Debrunner, and R. W. Funk. *A Greek Grammar of the New Testament and Other Early Christian Literature.* §§442–52, 459(2).

Black, Stephanie. *Sentence Conjunctions in the Gospel of Matthew.* 202–53.

Dooley, Robert A., and Stephen H. Levinsohn. *Analyzing Discourse: A Manual of Basic Concepts.* 48–49.

Heckert, Jacob K. *Discourse Function of Conjoiners in the Pastoral Epistles.*

Levinsohn, Stephen H. *Discourse Features of New Testament Greek: A Coursebook on the Information Structure of New Testament Greek.* 71–91, 118–26, 170–73.

Porter, Stanley E. *Idioms of the Greek New Testament.* 205–17.

Robertson, A. T. *A Grammar of the Greek New Testament in the Light of Historical Research.* 1177–92.

Wallace, Daniel B. *Greek Grammar beyond the Basics: An Exegetical Syntax of the New Testament.* 670–74.

PART 2   FORWARD-POINTING DEVICES

This section describes a number of conventions used to attract attention to something significant in the discourse, something that would not have garnered the same attention had the prominence-marking device not been used. There are two criteria that qualify these various devices to be classified under one umbrella:

- none of the devices is required to understand the content that follows (i.e., they are semantically redundant);

- the same propositional content could have been conveyed more simply and efficiently without them.

FORWARD-POINTING REFERENCE AND TARGET

We are used to pronouns such as *he, they,* and *this* referring to concepts previously mentioned in the discourse (e.g., "I have a *sister. She* lives in Los Angeles.") The default use of pronouns is to point backward to something that has already been introduced. There is also a nondefault use to point forward to things that have not yet been introduced.

At times we will use *this* or *here* to point forward to some "target" that follows. Such forward-pointing usage stands out, attracting extra attention to the thing to which it refers. The forward-pointing pronoun is the *reference*, indicated by →. The thing to which it points is the *target*, indicated by ⊙. The forward-pointing reference has the effect of attracting extra attention to the target.

We use forward-pointing references a lot more than you might think. Here are some examples taken from everyday American English that illustrate how forward-pointing references are used to attract extra attention to the target they introduce.

- Get *this*!
- Listen to *this*!
- Guess *what*!
- You know *what*?
- *Here's* the deal!
- *This* is my final offer.

Think about the context in which you would use these expressions. I might use "Get this" just before announcing some great news or something shocking that just happened. If I had been trying to negotiate with someone, I might preface my next offer by saying, "Alright, here's the deal."

So why use a forward-pointing reference? Why not just go ahead and say whatever was so important? Generally speaking, expressions like these are a way slowing down the flow of the discourse before something surprising or important. This slowing down disrupts the flow of the discourse. It has the pragmatic effect attracting extra attention to the target of the forward-pointing reference. It would be simpler to skip the additional reference and get on with whatever it is you have to say. The extra reference serves to pique curiosity about the target, in the same way that a drum roll or other dramatic delay has the effect of building suspense when an audience is expecting something to happen.

If the forward-pointing reference had not been used, the information that followed would not have changed in its importance; it simply would not have been marked as important. If it had not been marked, there is a greater chance that its importance might have been overlooked. I might not have assigned the same significance to it as the writer did. By choosing to use a prominence-marking device, the writer increases the likelihood that the reader will assign the same significance to the target. The device explicitly marks the target as significant. If we are trying to establish the author's intent, attention to prominence-marking devices can play a critical role in making such determinations.

3.1 Conventional Explanation

Most grammarians provide some discussion about the forward-pointing use of pronouns, but they say little about why a writer might use this device. BDF states, "οὗτος (τοιοῦτος likewise) is seldom used to point to a following clause…; only τοῦτο is somewhat more frequently used as preparation for a subordinate clause with ὅτι, ἵνα etc. or for an infinitive or substantive."[1] Wallace likewise notes that although most pronouns refer backward and thus have "antecedents," there are instances where pronouns point forward and have what he calls "postcedents."[2] He notes that forward-pointing pronouns can refer to a ὅτι clause:

> This usage is normally in apposition to the demonstrative τοῦτο in such expressions as "I say *this* to you, *namely, that* …" and the like. As such, the pronoun is kataphoric or proleptic, in that its content is revealed by what follows rather than by what precedes.[3]

He does not discuss why a writer would use a proleptic construction. Similar comments may be made about Robertson and Porter. Robertson

---

1. BDF §290.

2. Daniel B. Wallace, *Greek Grammar beyond the Basics: An Exegetical Syntax of the New Testament* (Grand Rapids: Zondervan, 1999), 318.

3. Ibid., 459.

describes the forward-pointing use of demonstratives as "in apposition" and lists a number of examples to illustrate the usage,[4] and Porter notes that forward-pointing usage is common both in the Greek NT and extrabiblical Greek.[5] However, neither one describes the effect achieved by this marked use of pronouns.

3.2   Discourse Explanation

There are several principles from the introduction that help us better understand the discourse function of forward-pointing references and targets. First, since they represent a nontypical or marked use of pronouns, there must be some meaning associated with the choice to use this construction. As with most other forward-pointing devices, the forward-pointing reference ends up creating a discontinuity just before the target to which it points. This extra reference has the effect of slowing down the flow of the discourse.

The forward-pointing usage contrasts with the more frequent default use of pronouns to point backward to something, and thus it stands out in the context. It is far more common to first introduce a concept before referring to it with a pronoun than vice versa. To point forward to something that has yet to be introduced risks creating confusion. The same concept could have been introduced much more easily and unambiguously by omitting the unneeded reference. The forward-pointing reference signals the presence of some discourse feature. The choice to use a marked form also implies that there is a meaning associated with the choice.[6]

---

4. A. T. Robertson, *A Grammar of the Greek New Testament in the Light of Historical Research* (1919; repr., Bellingham, Wash.: Logos, 2006), 698–99.

5. Stanley E. Porter, *Idioms of the Greek New Testament* (2nd ed.; Sheffield: Sheffield Academic, 1999), 136.

6. A more technical explanation of why forward-pointing references add prominence to their target is provided by Smith based upon "mental space" theory: "The cataphor's evocation of special emphasis in these situations is likely due to the fact that overt designation of the mental space set up by the matrix verb draws more attention to the proposition contained in and characterized specifically by the knowledge structures inherent in that space than if the pronoun were absent. Also, by momentarily delaying mention of the subordinate clause by the use of the pronoun the speaker creates an air of anticipation in the flow of the discourse about what is to follow which can heighten the hearer's interest in the subsequent information (again evoking another kind of conceptual distance). Related to this is that the use of the cataphor in effect results in a kind of double-mention in which the space designated by the pronoun metonymically relates to the proposition located conceptually within that space by prefiguring the space grammatically" (Michael B. Smith, "Cataphoric Pronouns as Mental Space Designators: Their Conceptual Import and Discourse Function," in *Cognitive and Communicative Approaches to Linguistic Analysis* [ed. Ellen

3.3 Application

There are three different ways of creating a forward-pointing reference:

- use of a forward-pointing interrogatives (i.e., question words such as *what* or *who*) to create rhetorical questions that are then answered by the same speaker;
- use of demonstrative pronouns (e.g., *this* or *those*) to point forward to a person or concept;
- use of adverbs as substitutes (i.e., "pro-adverbs") to point forward to an action that describes the manner in which something is done.

Not every pronoun or pro-adverb is forward pointing; most will be anaphoric. The claims that follow apply only to those forms that have no antecedent.

3.3.1 Forward-Pointing Interrogatives

I begin with some examples of interrogative pronouns used for forward-pointing references. In example 25, Jesus asks a series of rhetorical questions. These are construed as intentional forward-pointing references because he proceeds to answer his own questions. Since these are rhetorical rather than interrogative questions, they serve to pique the hearers' (or readers') interest.

Example 25 :: Matthew 11:7b–9

7b ⟨→τί→⟩ ἐξήλθατε εἰς τὴν ἔρημον θεάσασθαι; ⟨⊙κάλαμον ὑπὸ ἀνέμου σαλευόμενον;⊙⟩

8 ἀλλὰ ⟨→τί→⟩ ἐξήλθατε ἰδεῖν; ⟨⊙ἄνθρωπον ἐν μαλακοῖς ἠμφιεσμένον;⊙⟩ ἰδοὺ οἱ τὰ μαλακὰ φοροῦντες ἐν τοῖς οἴκοις τῶν βασιλέων εἰσίν.

7b ⟨→ "What→⟩ did you go out into the wilderness to see? ⟨⊙A reed shaken by the wind?⊙⟩

8 But ⟨→what→⟩ did you go out to see? ⟨⊙A man dressed in soft clothing?⊙⟩ Behold, those who wear soft clothing are in the houses of kings.

Contini-Morava, Robert S. Kirsner, and Betsy Rodríquez-Bachiller; SFSL 51; Amsterdam: John Benjamins, 2004], 81). Forward-pointing references that target subordinate clauses are also referred to as "hypotactic apposition" by Jason M. Brenier and Laura A. Michaelis, "Optimization via Syntactic Amalgam: Syntax-Prosody Mismatch and Copula Doubling," *CLLT* 1 (2005): 45–88.

⁹ ἀλλὰ ‹→τί→› ἐξήλθατε ἰδεῖν;
‹⊙προφήτην;⊙› ναὶ λέγω ὑμῖν,
‹⊙καὶ περισσότερον προφήτου.⊙›

⁹ But ‹→what→› did you go out
to see? ‹⊙A prophet?⊙› Yes, I
tell you, ‹⊙and even more than a
prophet!"⊙›

In each case it would have been simpler to ask, "Did you go out to the wilderness to see X?" (e.g., "a reed shaken by the wind"). The repetition of the
rhetorical question "What did you go out to see" has the effect of increasing
the suspense regarding why the people came to see John the Baptist. The extra
reference causes the reader to try to find the target in order to resolve the
reference. In this case, the correct target is only revealed (v. 9b) after Jesus provides and dismisses two potential answers. The forward-pointing references
function here to highlight Jesus' claim about John the Baptist, the key idea of
the section. Omitting the forward-pointing references would have dramatically reduced the poignancy of Jesus' message.

Another example of an interrogative pronoun used rhetorically for a forward-pointing reference is found in Rom 3:1, where Paul introduces his next
topic of discussion.

Example 26 :: Romans 3:1–2

¹ ‹→Τί→› οὖν τὸ περισσὸν τοῦ
Ἰουδαίου ἢ ‹→τίς→› ἡ ὠφέλεια τῆς
περιτομῆς;

² ‹⊙πολὺ κατὰ πάντα
τρόπον.⊙› πρῶτον μὲν [γὰρ] ὅτι
ἐπιστεύθησαν τὰ λόγια τοῦ θεοῦ.

¹ Therefore, ‹→what→› is the
advantage of the Jew, or ‹→what→›
is the use of circumcision?

² ‹⊙Much in every way.⊙› For
first, that they were entrusted with
the oracles of God.

At the end of Rom 2, Paul makes the claim that only the Jew who is circumcised
in the heart is the true Jew, not those who are only outwardly circumcised.
This raises the question of whether there is any advantage to being a Jew. In
order to highlight the introduction of this new topic, Paul asks two rhetorical questions that he then answers in the balance of Rom 3. Verse 2 provides
a generic answer ("much in every way") that he elaborates in v. 2b (the Jews
were entrusted with the oracles of God). Omitting the forward-pointing references would not have attracted nearly the same attention to this new topic.
The choice to use the forward-pointing references telegraphs Paul's desire to
attract attention to it. He uses it here to highlight the introduction of the next
big idea in the book. Forward-pointing interrogative pronouns are a very
effective rhetorical means of introducing a new topic and drawing attention
to it at the same time.

Paul uses another pair of forward-pointing interrogatives later in Rom 3 to strengthen a point he makes.

Example 27 :: Romans 3:27

⟨→Ποῦ→⟩ οὖν ἡ καύχησις;   Therefore, ⟨→where→⟩ is boast-
⟨⊙ἐξεκλείσθη.⊙⟩ διὰ ⟨→ποίου→⟩   ing? ⟨⊙ It has been excluded.⊙⟩
νόμου; ⟨⊙τῶν ἔργων;⊙⟩ οὐχί,   By ⟨→what kind→⟩ of law? ⟨⊙Of
ἀλλὰ ⟨⊙διὰ νόμου πίστεως.⊙⟩   works?⊙⟩ No, but ⟨⊙by a law of
          faith.⊙⟩

Paul could have made the same point more plainly by stating, ἡ καύχησις οὖν ἐξεκλείσθη διὰ νόμου πίστεως ("Therefore boasting is excluded by the law of faith"), but this would significantly reduce the rhetorical impact compared to using the forward-pointing references. Unpacking this principle in two parts allows each one to sink in. Allowing the reader to think about the questions adds significantly to the power of these statements. It also allows Paul to draw extra attention to exactly what kind of law it is that excludes boasting. He uses a point/counterpoint set (see chapter 4) to further reinforce the answer. The counterpoint provides a possible answer, which is rejected. The point stands out in much greater relief because there is a counterpoint providing a basis of comparison.

3.3.2 Forward-Pointing Demonstratives

In the same way that interrogatives can be used for forward-pointing references, demonstrative pronouns can accomplish the task of attracting extra attention to a target. It is not some special semantic meaning of the part of speech that has the effect of highlighting; it is the fact that it is pointing forward to a yet-to-be-introduced target. Forward-pointing references are most often associated with the writings of John and Paul.[7]

There are six instances in John's first epistle where he uses the phrase ἐν τούτῳ ("in this") as a forward-pointing reference to highlight an important concept.

---

7. For a description of forward-pointing references in Luke's gospel, see Steven E. Runge, "The Exegetical Significance of Prospective Demonstrative Pronouns in Luke's Gospel" (paper presented at the Pacific Northwest regional meeting of the Evangelical Theological Society, Salem, Ore., 24 February 2007).

Example 28 :: 1 John 4:9–10

⁹ ⟨→ἐν τούτῳ→⟩ ἐφανερώθη ἡ ἀγάπη τοῦ θεοῦ ἐν ἡμῖν, ὅτι ⟨⊙τὸν υἱὸν αὐτοῦ τὸν μονογενῆ ἀπέσταλκεν ὁ θεὸς εἰς τὸν κόσμον⊙⟩ ἵνα ⟨⊙ζήσωμεν δ᾽αὐτοῦ.⊙⟩	⁹ ⟨→By this→⟩ the love of God is revealed in us: that ⟨⊙God sent his one and only Son into the world⊙⟩ in order that ⟨⊙we may live through him.⊙⟩
¹⁰ ⟨→ἐν τούτῳ→⟩ ἐστὶν ἡ ἀγάπη, ⟨⊙οὐχ ὅτι ἡμεῖς ἠγαπήκαμεν τὸν θεὸν⊙⟩ ἀλλ᾽ ὅτι ⟨⊙αὐτὸς ἠγάπησεν ἡμᾶς καὶ ἀπέστειλεν τὸν υἱὸν αὐτοῦ ἱλασμὸν περὶ τῶν ἁμαρτιῶν ἡμῶν.⊙⟩	¹⁰ ⟨→In this→⟩ is love: ⟨⊙not that we have loved God,⊙⟩ but that ⟨⊙he loved us and sent his Son to be the propitiation for our sins.⊙⟩

In v. 9, John introduces the means by which the love of God was revealed to us: God sending his one and only Son into the world. The phrase ἐν τούτῳ highlights the target, the subordinate clause introduced by ὅτι. In v. 10 he points forward to a definition of love that consists of a point/counterpoint set. The effect is to doubly highlight the point that is eventually introduced at the end of the verse: God loved us and sent his Son to be the propitiation for our sins. The counterpoint functions as a foil for the two-part point that follows, contrasting what love is not with what it is.

Keep in mind that the same information could have been communicated without using the forward-pointing references (e.g., "The love of God is revealed because he sent his one and only Son…."). Removing the prominence-marking devices would significantly weaken the effect achieved, making it much more likely that the reader would not have assigned the same significance to the highlighted concepts as the writer intended. The combination of prominence markers provides exegetical evidence of the writer's intention to highlight the information.

Another forward-pointing reference is found later in the same chapter. In this case, a generic noun phrase is used to point forward instead of only a pronoun.

Example 29 :: 1 John 4:21

καὶ ⟨→ταύτην τὴν ἐντολὴν→⟩ ἔχομεν ἀπ᾽ αὐτοῦ ἵνα ⟨⊙ὁ ἀγαπῶν τὸν θεὸν ἀγαπᾷ καὶ τὸν ἀδελφὸν αὐτοῦ.⊙⟩	And ⟨→this is the commandment→⟩ we have from him: that ⟨⊙the one who loves God should love his brother also.⊙⟩

Remember, it is not the part of speech used that achieves added prominence, but rather the non-default use of the expression to point forward. The context before v. 21 states that anyone who claims to love God and yet hates his or her brother is a liar. The forward-pointing reference in v. 21 highlights the introduction of the command that applies to this context, which is introduced in the ἵνα-clause. The reference and target attract attention to a proposition that is key to John's argument.

3.3.3 Forward-Pointing Adverbs

Adverbs are another grammatical means used for forward-pointing references.[8] There are a handful of adverbs in Greek that can be used as substitute words just like pronouns. I will refer to them as "pro-adverbs." Adverbs function as modifiers of verbal action, describing either the manner in which an action is done (i.e., in what way) or the degree to which the action is done (i.e., how much). Pro-adverbs stand in the place of the action and can either be backward-pointing ("anaphoric") or forward-pointing ("cataphoric").

The Lord's Prayer is introduced in Matthew's gospel with a forward-pointing reference, highlighting the manner in which the disciples are to pray. The prayer that follows is the target of the forward-pointing reference.

Example 30 :: Matthew 6:9

‹→Οὕτως→› οὖν προσεύχεσθε ὑμεῖς· ‹⊙Πάτερ ἡμῶν ὁ ἐν τοῖς οὐρανοῖς....⊙›	"Therefore you pray ‹→in this way:→› ‹⊙Our Father who is in heaven...."⊙›

In the preceding context Jesus has discussed how not to pray, but he has not provided the positive alternative. The entire prayer is the target of the pro-adverb οὕτως, describing the manner in which they should pray. The pragmatic effect of the forward-pointing reference is to attract extra attention to this significant part of the discourse, making it stand out much more by the extra reference.

---

8. Gundry and Howell make the point that most uses of οὕτως are backward-pointing rather than forward-pointing, though they do leave the door open for the latter (Robert H. Gundry and Russell W. Howell, "The Sense and Syntax of John 3:14–17 with Special Reference to the Use of οὕτως ... ὥστε in John 3:16," *NovT* 41 [1999]: 24–39). BDAG (742) also notes the forward-pointing use in the second part of its definition for οὕτως.

Example 31 illustrates the use of adverbial elements as interrogatives to create rhetorical questions. The same kind of rhetorical effect is achieved because they are pointing forward to something yet to be introduced.

Example 31 :: Mark 4:30–31

30 Καὶ ἔλεγεν· ‹→πῶς→› ὁμοιώσωμεν τὴν βασιλείαν τοῦ θεοῦ ἢ ‹→ἐν τίνι→› αὐτὴν παραβολῇ θῶμεν;	30 And he said, ‹→"With what→› can we compare the kingdom of God, or ‹→by what parable→› can we present it?
31 ‹⊙ὡς κόκκῳ σινάπεως …⊙›	31 ‹⊙It is like a mustard seed …⊙›

Jesus is telling parables in Mark 4 describing the kingdom of God. In v. 30 he uses two adverbs as interrogative pronouns. These adverbs stand in the place of a single target that follows in vv. 31–32, which state that "the kingdom of God is like a mustard seed." Skipping the forward-pointing references would have been more direct, but it would have destroyed the rhetorical effect of the canonical version. Using the twofold reference helps to pique interest, attracting extra attention to the target that follows. The device is used to introduce the next major component of the discourse, not just to highlight a significant proposition.

The same forward-pointing technique is used to introduce the first parable of the kingdom from v. 26, the parable of the seed. It also uses an adverb for the forward reference but not phrased in the form of a question.

Example 32 :: Mark 4:26

Καὶ ἔλεγεν· ‹→οὕτως→› ἐστὶν ἡ βασιλεία τοῦ θεοῦ ‹⊙ὡς ἄνθρωπος βάλῃ τὸν σπόρον ἐπὶ τῆς γῆς⊙›	And he said, "The kingdom of God is ‹→ like this:→› ‹⊙like a man scatters seed on the ground."⊙›

The adverb functions like a pronoun by standing in the place of an entire action—a man scattering seed in the ground. Many of these forward-pointing adverbial references are awkward in English, leading translators to smooth them over by omitting the extra reference. The NASB translates, "The kingdom of God is like a man who casts seed upon the soil"; the ESV translates, "The kingdom of God is as if a man should scatter seed on the ground." In both cases the forward-pointing reference is eliminated. Regardless of the translation, remember that the discourse function of forward-pointing references is to attract extra attention to the target. In these examples from Mark the highlighted targets introduce the next major theme of the discourse. The same kind of attention-getting strategy can be utilized in your teaching or preaching.

Summary

This chapter demonstrated that pronouns, pro-adverbs and other substitute forms can be used to refer ahead to something that is yet to be introduced. The expected norm is that such forms point backward to something that has already been introduced. Referring to some yet-to-be-introduced entity runs the risk of creating confusion for the reader. Because this forward-pointing usage breaks from the expected norm, the target to which it points ends up receiving additional prominence. Forward-pointing references are used to attract attention to significant propositions that they would not otherwise have received, such as conclusions or key ideas of a pericope. They are also used to highlight the introduction of a new pericope, as illustrated by the parables from Mark.

Example 33 pulls together the concepts we have discussed so far. It recounts the parable of the rich fool, told in response to a man who asked Jesus to mediate a dispute over a family inheritance. Jesus makes use of prominence-marking features in order to highlight significant points that he wants to make. Verses 16b–17a set the stage by establishing a state of affair for the rich man.

Example 33 :: Luke 12:16–18

16 Εἶπεν δὲ παραβολὴν πρὸς αὐτοὺς λέγων· ἀνθρώπου τινὸς πλουσίου εὐφόρησεν ἡ χώρα.

16 And he told a parable to them, saying, "The land of a certain rich man yielded an abundant harvest.

17 καὶ διελογίζετο ἐν ἑαυτῷ λέγων· ‹→τί→› ποιήσω, ὅτι οὐκ ἔχω ποῦ συνάξω τοὺς καρπούς μου;

17 And he reasoned to himself, saying, ‹→'What→› should I do? For I do not have anywhere I can gather in my crops.'

18 καὶ εἶπεν· ‹→τοῦτο→› ποιήσω, ‹⊙καθελῶ μου τὰς ἀποθήκας καὶ μείζονας οἰκοδομήσω καὶ συνάξω ἐκεῖ πάντα τὸν σῖτον καὶ τὰ ἀγαθά μου.⊙›

18 And he said, 'I will do ‹→this:→› ‹⊙I will tear down my barns and build larger ones, and I will gather in there all my grain and possessions.'"⊙›

The rich man asks a question in v. 17b: "What should I do?" However, we do not learn why there is a problem until after we read the question: he has more crops than he can currently store in his barns. The question is actually rhetorical, in that he answers it himself. It serves to attract extra attention to the solution to which it points.

The reader is left to ponder what the rich man might do with his excess. Will he give some or all of it to the poor? Will he tithe a portion? If the rhetorical question had not been asked, the reader would not have had as much time to think about these matters. Even more time is given by the insertion of a redundant quotative frame (see chapter 7) at the beginning of v. 18. Since there has been no change of speaker from the rich man to someone else, there is no need to reintroduce the existing speaker. The effect of the redundant frame is to build suspense for what follows by delaying the rich fool's solution.

The suspense continues to build through the use of another forward-pointing reference τοῦτο ("this") following the quotative frame. This reference points to the same target as the rhetorical question: the rich man's proposed solution. More attention is focused on the target by emphasizing τοῦτο using word order (see chapter 13).

It would have been much simpler to skip both forward-pointing references and to proceed to the solution of building bigger barns. The combined effect of these prominence-marking devices is to attract extra attention to the fool's solution. It is this solution that leads Jesus to characterize him as a fool, using thematic address (see chapter 17) in v. 20a. Instead of being able to enjoy his excess, the rich fool ends up forfeiting his soul "this very night." The pro-adverb οὕτως ("so") in v. 21 stands in the place of the action described in the parable, pointing backward anaphorically, as we would normally expect (see example 21).

The choice to use these devices to add prominence to the same part of the parable clearly indicates the importance of the fool's solution to the discourse. Being rich was not the man's problem, but rather hoarding excess far beyond his needs.

Suggested Reading

Blass, F., A. Debrunner, and R. W. Funk. *A Greek Grammar of the New Testament and Other Early Christian Literature.* §290(3).

Robertson, A. T. *A Grammar of the Greek New Testament in the Light of Historical Research.* 698–99.

Runge, Steven E. "The Exegetical Significance of Prospective Demonstrative Pronouns in Luke's Gospel."

Smith, Michael B. "Cataphoric Pronouns as Mental Space Designators: Their Conceptual Import and Discourse Function."

Wallace, Daniel B. *Greek Grammar beyond the Basics: An Exegetical Syntax of the New Testament.* 459–60.

POINT/COUNTERPOINT SETS

Chapter 2 presented an overview of the different kinds of relations that can be created through the use of connectives. The present chapter applies this information to the creation of point/counterpoint relationships between propositions. Counterpoints will be indicated by the ✗ symbol, whereas points are indicated by the ✓ symbol. Recall from chapter 2 that according to Behaghel's Law, the default expectation is that adjacent clauses are assumed to have some kind of relation to one another. Consider the relationships between the following pairs of clauses:

A   I liked the introduction. The conclusion was very poor.
B   I liked the introduction, **but** the conclusion was very poor.
C   **Although** I liked the introduction, the conclusion was very poor.

In A the two clauses are simply juxtaposed by asyndeton, without any explicit markers constraining how the clauses should be related to one another. In B a relationship is signaled by *but,* which we would traditionally call *contrastive.* Note that it follows the first clause. In C the use of the conjunction *although* creates the expectation that something more is coming, and that it is most likely contrastive in nature. Both *but* and *although* constrain a relationship between the clauses, but the latter signals it from the very beginning. It is the proverbial "first shoe to drop," creating the expectation that another related shoe drop will follow. Asyndeton leaves the relationship implicit without an overt marker. *But* signals the nature of the relation after the first part, whereas *although* creates the expectation of a related counterpart from the outset.

The term *point/counterpoint set* describes clauses or clause elements that have been related to one another through one or more grammatical means:

- the prospective use of μέν to create anticipation that some related point will follow;
- the use of an interrogative or negated clause that is restricted using εἰ μή or πλήν;
- the use of ἀλλά to correct or replace something in the preceding context.

In each case, a grammatical device constrains the reader to relate the elements to one another in a particular way. If the grammatical markers had not been used, the connection might have been missed. In terms of the example above, it represents the choice to move from an implicit relation, as with asyndeton in A, to an explicit relation, as in B and C. The grammatical markers represent the writer's intent to create an explicit connection.

4.1   The Use of Μέν

4.1.1   Conventional Explanation

Denniston provides three different senses for μέν: emphatic, adversative, and preparatory, noting that the emphatic usage was being "ousted" by the preparatory sometime early in the fourth century B.C.E.[1] I noted in chapter 2 that it is common for grammarians to assign contrast as a semantic value of conjunctions, whereas contrast is better understood as something that may or may not be inherent in the context. In most cases, it is not a semantic component of the particle.[2] The particle μέν is best understood as unmarked for contrast. Instead, it is anticipatory in nature, creating the expectation that another related point will follow.

The most common usage associated with μέν is to correlate a clause with one that follows introduced by δέ or ἀλλά.[3] The correlated elements can be

---

1. John Dewar Denniston, *The Greek Particles* (2nd ed.; Indianapolis: Hackett, 1996), 359–69. BDAG (630) classifies μέν as an affirmative particle that can be either a marker of correlation or a marker of contrast/continuation without express correlation. Porter considers it either an emphatic or adversative conjunction that often is used for contrast (Stanley E. Porter, *Idioms of the Greek New Testament* [2nd ed.; Sheffield: Sheffield Academic, 1999], 212). Wallace considers the particle to be correlative, pairing with other conjunctions to establish relationships, though it can also be emphatic (Daniel B. Wallace, *Greek Grammar beyond the Basics: An Exegetical Syntax of the New Testament* [Grand Rapids: Zondervan, 1999], 671).

2. Robertson supports this view, stating, "There is no doubt at all that in itself μέν does not mean or imply antithesis" (A. T. Robertson, *A Grammar of the Greek New Testament in the Light of Historical Research* [1919; repr., Bellingham, Wash.: Logos, 2006], 1151).

3. See Denniston, *Greek Particles*, 369–73; Robertson, *Grammar*, 1151; Porter, *Idioms*,

clause components or whole clauses. BDF states that "the inclusion of μέν throws the emphasis on the second member (indicated by δέ)."[4] Besides this standard correlative or preparatory usage, there is a predilection to assign additional senses to μέν when it occurs in a collocation with other particles— e.g., μενοῦν or μενοῦνγε, particularly an "emphatic" sense. Denniston notes that any possible emphatic usage was dropping out of the language during the classical period: "In Attic the use of emphatic μέν is extremely limited. It is often difficult to decide whether μέν is to be taken as purely emphatic, or as suggesting an unexpressed antithesis (the so-called *μέν solitarium*)."[5] Claiming an emphatic usage often stems from multiple other factors, not the presence of the particle. One should expect that each particle retains its core function, even when combined with other particles (see discussion of Phil 3:8 below). For example, the collocation μέν γάρ is sometimes considered to have a different meaning in combination than when occurring individually, par- ticularly when there is no following δέ. I contend that γάρ maintains it core function of introducing strengthening or supporting material, and likewise the prospective function of μέν. In many of these cases, the μέν either com- bines with a lesser-used partner (e.g., ἀλλά in Acts 4:16–17) or is operating at a higher level of the discourse than expected (e.g., Acts 13:36–37).[6]

4.1.2 Discourse Explanation

In spite of the multiplicity of senses claimed, μέν signals the presence of one common constraint: anticipation of a related sentence that follows.[7] Occur-

---

213. It is also found in combination with καί (Denniston, *Greek Particles*, 373–74; Porter, *Idioms*, 213).

4. BDF §447(5).

5. Denniston, *Greek Particles*, 364.

6. Having said this, I acknowledge that there are isolated instances such as Acts 28:22, where the correlated element is not readily apparent. One might argue that the use here is intended to suggest that there is another side to the story, opening the door to accept Paul's premise that he has been falsely accused.

7. My claim here is less specific than Levinsohn's: "The presence of μέν not only antici- pates a corresponding sentence containing δέ. Frequently, in narrative, it also downgrades the importance of the sentence containing μέν" (Stephen H. Levinsohn, *Discourse Features of New Testament Greek: A Coursebook on the Information Structure of New Testament Greek* [2nd ed.; Dallas: SIL International], 170). I contend that μέν simply creates anticipa- tion of a related clause, most often introduced by δέ. Levinsohn's association with down- grading the information results from the use of μέν to create concessions that function as rhetorical counterpoints. The concessions are most often found in reported speeches and the Epistles, not in narrative proper. However, narrative passages such as Mark 16:19; Luke 3:18; 23:33, 56; John 7:12; 11:6; 19:24, 32; 20:30; Acts 2:41; 5:41; 9:7, 31; 12:5; 13:4; 14:3, 4;

rence in collocation with other conjunctions does not change this; the same constraint is brought to bear along with those of the other conjunctions present. Following Levinsohn, I view μέν as always prospective, even in instances where δέ does not follow. I will present a few examples of the standard usage attributed to μέν/δέ sets and then move on to the nontypical usage that has led some to assert a nonprospective sense to μέν.[8]

In the instances cited as evidence of emphatic usage, typically either there is a string of conjunctions (e.g., Phil 3:8) or the correlated element is separated from the μέν clause by several clauses. The core constraint to keep in mind is forward-pointing correlation. The counterexamples cited by the traditional grammars will be used to substantiate the discourse explanation that I am offering here when the "prospective" constraint and the broader context are factored in.

4.1.3   Application

The most common usage of μέν/δέ sets is found in the speeches reported within narratives or in the epistolary literature. Here are some representative examples.

Example 34 :: Matthew 3:1

⟨✗Ἐγὼ μὲν ὑμᾶς βαπτίζω ἐν ὕδατι εἰς μετάνοιαν,✗⟩ ⟨✓ὁ δὲ ὀπίσω μου ἐρχόμενος ἰσχυρότερός μού ἐστιν, οὗ οὐκ εἰμὶ ἱκανὸς τὰ ὑποδήματα βαστάσαι· αὐτὸς ὑμᾶς βαπτίσει ἐν πνεύματι ἁγίῳ καὶ πυρί·✓⟩

⟨✗"I baptize you with water for repentance,✗⟩ ⟨✓but the one who comes after me is more powerful than I am, whose sandals I am not worthy to carry. He will baptize you with the Holy Spirit and fire."✓⟩

15:30; 16:5; 17:12, 17, 32; 23:8, 18, 22; 23:31; 25:4; 27:41, 44; 28:5, 24 illustrate the limit of the downgrading claim. Forty percent of the narrative-proper instances of μέν are found in clauses whose main verb uses the imperfect tense, a factor that Levinsohn attributes to the "natural backgrounding" of the clause based on the tense form (ibid., 173–75). Much of the information introduced by μέν is either introductory or concluding material (i.e., transitional), which is also naturally less important than event-line material. The use of μέν seems intended to stitch otherwise unrelated clauses more tightly together. The downgrading effect that Levinsohn asserts is better explained by the nature of the offline information that it often introduces than by the particle itself.

8. It is important to note that both μέν and δέ are postpositive particles and cannot occur in the initial position in the clause. Both will be placed after the first word rather than after the first constituent (i.e., after the article rather than after the whole noun phrase).

The counterpoint statement from John the Baptist in v. 11a is closely linked to the following clause in several ways. The placement of the subjects in the clause-initial position suggests a juxtaposing of the clauses, with the first fronted subject functioning as a foil or "setup" for the one that follows.[9] There is also a contrast in the means by which the two subjects baptize, due to the repetition of the verb βαπτίζω. Verses 11a and 11b–d are naturally correlated based on their content. The presence of μέν strengthens this connection by creating the expectation that a related clause will follow. Both the contrast and the connection are present even without μέν; these qualities are inherent in the content. Contrast is not a semantic quality of the particle. The presence of μέν only serves to highlight and strengthen what was already present, ensuring that the reader or hearer does not miss the speaker's intended connection. The use of μέν also creates anticipation that a related element will follow, one that is typically more important than the counterpoint.

Example 35 illustrates another case where two clauses are syntactically and semantically connected.

Example 35 :: Mark 14:38b

⟨✗ τὸ μὲν πνεῦμα πρόθυμον✗⟩   ⟨✗"The spirit is willing,✗⟩ but
⟨✓ἡ δὲ σὰρξ ἀσθενής.✓⟩   ⟨✓the flesh is weak!"✓⟩

Both verbless clauses are subject-predicate in order. Both subjects are semantically related, forming a natural contrast between "the spirit" and "the flesh." The presence of μέν simply strengthens the connection already present by creating the expectation that a related clause will follow. In this instance, the μέν clause functions as a counterpoint for a more important point that follows.

The clause related to μέν need not be the next adjacent clause, even though this is the norm. Sometimes the μέν clause is further developed by another clause or two before the related clause is found, as is illustrated by the next few examples. Example 36 is taken from the crucifixion discussion between the criminals in Luke 23:39–43. One was hurling abuse at Jesus, and v. 41 is part of the other man's response, defending Jesus.

---

9. For a discussion of topical frames of reference, see §10.1.

Example 36 :: Luke 23:41

⟨✗καὶ ἡμεῖς μὲν δικαίως,✗⟩ ἄξια γὰρ ὧν ἐπράξαμεν ἀπολαμβάνομεν· ⟨✓οὗτος δὲ οὐδὲν ἄτοπον ἔπραξεν.✓⟩	⟨✗"And we indeed justly,✗⟩ for we are receiving what we deserve for what we have done. ⟨✓But this man has done nothing wrong!"✓⟩

The particle καί links v. 41 to the preceding context. The μέν creates the expectation that another related element will follow. Verse 41a concerns the criminals and how they justly received their punishment based on their wrongdoing. Verse 41b strengthens the assertion of v. 41a. The corresponding point that relates to v. 41a is found in v. 41c, which includes switching topics from the criminals to "this man" Jesus, using a topical frame.[10]

Once again we find several things that naturally relate these verses to one another: us versus him, justly versus unjustly, and the parallel syntax. The μέν creates the expectation that a related clause will follow. The presence of the intervening γάρ makes the connection between v. 41a and v. 41c slightly more difficult to track. The use of μέν constrains the reader to be on the lookout for a related element that follows. It is the writer's way of insuring that the reader makes the intended connection between the clauses by making it much more explicit. The μέν clause establishes a counterpoint that anticipates a related point that follows. The criminal's justification of punishment is not the primary point of the discussion, but rather a foil for what follows.

One finds very sophisticated uses of μέν in Hebrews, at times with significant separation between the counterpoint and the point.[11] One of the most extreme examples is found in chapter 9.

Example 37 :: Hebrews 9:1–11

[1] ⟨✗✗Εἶχε μὲν οὖν καὶ ἡ πρώτη δικαιώματα λατρείας τό τε ἅγιον κοσμικόν.✗✗⟩	[1] ⟨✗✗Now even the first covenant had regulations for worship and the earthly sanctuary.✗✗⟩

[2] For [γάρ] a tent was prepared, the first one, in which were the lamp-stand and the table and the presentation of the loaves, which is called the holy place. [3] And after the second curtain was a tent called the holy of holies, [4] containing the golden incense altar and the ark of

---

10. See §10.1.

11. Where the point/counterpoint sets are complex and include another set nested within one member, the symbols are doubled (e.g., ✗✗) to indicate which set is subordinated within the other.

the covenant covered on all sides with gold, in which were a golden jar containing the manna and the rod of Aaron that budded and the tablets of the covenant. [5] And above it were the cherubim of glory overshadowing the mercy seat, about which it is not now possible to speak in detail.

[6] Now these things having been prepared in this way, the priests enter into the first tent continually as they accomplish their service, [7] but only the high priest enters into the second tent once a year, not without blood, which he offers on behalf of himself and the sins of the people committed in ignorance. [8] The Holy Spirit was making this clear, that the way into the holy place was not yet revealed, while the first tent was still in existence, [9] which was a symbol for the present time, in which both the gifts and sacrifices which were offered were not able to perfect the worshiper with respect to the conscience, [10] concerning instead only food and drink and different washings, regulations of outward things imposed until the time of setting things right.

[11] ‹𝐖Χριστὸς δὲ παραγενόμενος ἀρχιερεὺς τῶν γενομένων ἀγαθῶν διὰ τῆς μείζονος καὶ τελειοτέρας σκηνῆς οὐ χειροποιήτου, τοῦτ' ἔστιν οὐ ταύτης τῆς κτίσεως,

[12] ‹✗οὐδὲ δι' αἵματος τράγων καὶ μόσχων✗› ‹✓διὰ δὲ τοῦ ἰδίου αἵματος✓› εἰσῆλθεν ἐφάπαξ εἰς τὰ ἅγια αἰωνίαν λύτρωσιν εὑράμενος.𝐖›

[11] ‹𝐖But Christ has arrived as a high priest of the good things to come. Through the greater and more perfect tent not made by hands, that is, not of this creation,

[12] ‹✗and not by the blood of goats and calves,✗› ‹✓but by his own blood,✓› he entered once for all into the most holy place, obtaining eternal redemption.𝐖›

Hebrews 9 begins with a discussion of the earthly priesthood, connected to the preceding discourse by the conjunction οὖν. Verses 1–10 provide a description of the work of the high priests and the offering of sacrifices. The presence of μέν constrains the reader to be looking for a related clause that follows. In this case, it is found in v. 11. Note the parallels between the two:

- the use of "first" in v. 1 creates anticipation of a "second," otherwise there would be no need for the distinction;
- the overly specific description of the sanctuary as "earthly" creates the expectation of some other kind of sanctuary to follow, otherwise there would be no need for the distinction;
- the description of Jesus as a high priest correlates with the ministry described in vv. 6–7.

These connections would have been present with or without the use of μέν by virtue of the content.[12] The use here makes what might have been an implicit connection an explicit one through the expectation that some point will relate back to the paragraph-level counterpoint of v. 1. This usage of μέν where the related clause is separated by one or more clauses is likely what has led some grammarians to see this usage as something other than forward-pointing. Ellingworth states, "There is a general contrast between vv. 1–10 and 11–22, but the δέ of v. 1 [sic] is probably too far from the μέν of v. 11 [sic] for them to be directly related."[13] In other words, he sees the connection, but he discounts it on the basis of the distance. I contend that μέν is best understood as always prospective.

Now for some examples that are considered either emphatic or *μέν solitarium*, where there does not appear to be a forward-pointing correlation to what follows. Example 38 illustrates the use of a μέν/δέ set in narrative proper to join two potentially unrelated events together more closely.

Example 38 :: Acts 2:41–42

[41] ⟨✗οἱ μὲν οὖν ἀποδεξάμενοι τὸν λόγον αὐτοῦ ἐβαπτίσθησαν καὶ προσετέθησαν ἐν τῇ ἡμέρᾳ ἐκείνῃ ψυχαὶ ὡσεὶ τρισχίλιαι.✗⟩

[41] ⟨✗So those who accepted his message were baptized, and on that day about three thousand souls were added.✗⟩

[42] ⟨✓ʾΗσαν δὲ προσκαρτεροῦντες τῇ διδαχῇ τῶν ἀποστόλων καὶ τῇ κοινωνίᾳ, τῇ κλάσει τοῦ ἄρτου καὶ ταῖς προσευχαῖς.✓⟩

[42] ⟨✓And they were devoting themselves to the teaching of the apostles and to fellowship, to the breaking of bread and to prayers.✓⟩

---

12. Kistemaker (*Exposition of the Epistle to the Hebrews* [NTC; Grand Rapids: Baker, 1984], 236) and Moffat (*A Critical and Exegetical Commentary on the Epistle to the Hebrews* [ICC; Edinburgh: T & T Clark, 1924], 112) note the connection between v. 1 and v. 11, but not on the basis of μέν. In contrast, Attridge (*The Epistle to the Hebrews: A Commentary on the Epistle to the Hebrews* [Hermeneia; Philadelphia: Fortress, 1989], 231) views the reference to "first" as referring backward to the previous section rather than creating anticipation for another kind of service introduced in v. 11. Lane (*Hebrews 9–13* [WBC 47B; Dallas: Word, 2002], 214) similarly notes a connection backward rather than forward, stating, "The expression μὲν οὖν appears to be transitional, simply denoting continuation (cf. 7:11; 8:4)."

13. Paul Ellingworth, *The Epistle to the Hebrews: A Commentary on the Greek Text* (NIGTC; Grand Rapids: Eerdmans, 1993), 420.

This passage describes the people's response to Peter's sermon on Pentecost in Jerusalem. The particle οὖν constrains the point/counterpoint set to be read as the consequence or conclusion of what precedes. The use of μέν creates the expectation that there is another related element that follows. In this case, the effect is to constrain all of these events as the response to the sermon, rather than just the report in v. 41 of the three thousand accepting the message and being baptized.

The activities described in v. 42 have a thematic correlation to the "making disciples" and "teaching them to obey" portions of the Great Commission of Matt 28:19–20. Although one cannot infer an explicit connection to the Great Commission, it is noteworthy that the writer chose to explicitly link these events together as the response, not just the accepting and baptizing. The point/counterpoint set provides a close grammatical connection between v. 41 and v. 42, one that NA[27] obscures by beginning a new paragraph at v. 42. UBS[4] preserves the connection by beginning the new paragraph at v. 43. The usage here should not be construed as *μέν solitarium*, in that the collocation with δέ is consistent with the writer's thematic objectives in the context. This transition may be better understood as a *janus* verse, one that points in both directions rather than just one.

Robertson cites 2 Cor 11:4 as an example of μέν "where there is no thought of δέ or ἀλλά."[14]

Example 39 :: 2 Corinthians 11:4

εἰ ⟨✗μὲν γὰρ ὁ ἐρχόμενος ἄλλον Ἰησοῦν κηρύσσει ὃν οὐκ ἐκηρύξαμεν,✗⟩ ἢ ⟨✓πνεῦμα ἕτερον λαμβάνετε ὃ οὐκ ἐλάβετε,✓⟩ ἢ ⟨✓εὐαγγέλιον ἕτερον ὃ οὐκ ἐδέξασθε,✓⟩ καλῶς ἀνέχεσθε.	⟨✗For if the one who comes proclaims another Jesus whom we have not proclaimed,✗⟩ or ⟨✓you receive a different spirit which you did not receive,✓⟩ or ⟨✓a different gospel which you did not accept,✓⟩ you put up with it well enough!

In this context, the particle εἰ introduces a three-part conditional clause, referring to a different "Jesus," a different "Spirit," or a different "gospel." The particle γάρ indicates how the entire conditional complex relates to the preceding context. Although this is an uncommon collocation, the standard function of each connective must be taken into account. Harris notes the correlated set but does not strengthen this assertion by noting the presence of μέν:

---

14. Robertson, *Grammar*, 1151.

There is a distinct pattern in Paul's description of the intruders' message and its relation to his own message.

some intruder preaches	Jesus	*we* preached
you receive	Spirit	*you* received
[*you* receive]	gospel	*you* embraced.[15]

Paul states that if any of these things happen, "you bear this beautifully" (NASB).

To summarize, the γάρ looks backward, constraining all of v. 4 to be understood as supporting or strengthening what precedes. The μέν looks forward, performing the very same function that we have seen elsewhere. It creates the expectation that one or more related elements will follow, which Harris has noted. What is different in this context is that neither δέ nor ἀλλά is appropriate for connecting the related conditional elements to the μέν clause. This should not be understood as a new sense of μέν; it simply means that the most common set of paired connectives is not found here, based on the constraints of the context.

Just as in the other examples we have considered, there is a syntactic parallelism in each of the clauses in v. 4a–c. The object occurs before the verb, and each one is elaborated through the use of a relative clause. The only problem with construing μέν here as forward-pointing is the expectation created by grammarians of a following δέ. There are actually three things that Paul wants the Corinthians to look out for, not just "proclaiming another Jesus." The "Spirit" and the "gospel" both relate semantically to "Jesus" by each being "different." These syntactic and lexical connections would have been present even without the use of μέν. Including the connective here creates the expectation that more related elements will follow, and this expectation is met in vv. 4b–c. They do not create a traditional point/counterpoint rhetorical set but simply the anticipation of a correlated set by virtue of the first member being marked by the presence of μέν. One need not appeal to anacoluthon in order to provide a reasonable account of the presence of μέν in this context.

One final example of μέν used without δέ is found in Colossians, where asyndeton is acceptable because of the clarity of the connection. This correlation takes place as part of the elaboration of a main clause.

---

15. Murray J. Harris, *The Second Epistle to the Corinthians: A Commentary on the Greek Text* (NIGTC; Grand Rapids: Eerdmans, 2005), 743.

Example 40 :: Colossians 2:23

ἅτινά ἐστιν ⟨✗λόγον μὲν ἔχοντα σοφίας ἐν ἐθελοθρησκίᾳ καὶ ταπεινοφροσύνῃ καὶ ἀφειδίᾳ σώματος,✗⟩ ⟨✓οὐκ ἐν τιμῇ τινι πρὸς πλησμονὴν τῆς σαρκός.✓⟩

which things ⟨✗although they have, to be sure, an appearance of wisdom in self-made religion and humility and unsparing treatment of the body,✗⟩ ⟨✓do not have any value against the indulgence of the flesh.✓⟩

Paul essentially talks about two sides of the same coin, forecasting this through the forward-pointing use of μέν. It is as if to say that "although these things have the appearance of wisdom, they have no value against indulgence." The presence of μέν here informs the reader that although the current statement sounds very positive, it is not the final word on the matter; more is coming. This correlation has the effect of creating a point/counterpoint set, as indicated above. There still would have been a correlation between these two clauses had the writer not used μέν; however, it would only have been implicit. The use of the particle represents the writer's choice to make the connection explicit by adding the forward-pointing constraint associated with μέν.

4.2   The Use of Exception or Restriction

This section describes the use of negation followed by an excepted or restricted element as a means of drawing extra attention to this element. Example 41 contains a negated clause that is followed by an exception:

Example 41 :: Matthew 12:24

οὗτος ⟨✗οὐκ ἐκβάλλει τὰ δαιμόνια✗⟩ εἰ μὴ ⟨✓ἐν τῷ Βεελζεβοὺλ ἄρχοντι τῶν δαιμονίων.✓⟩

"This man ⟨✗does not expel demons✗⟩ except ⟨✓by Beelzebul the ruler of demons!"✓⟩

The negated statement is not entirely true without the inclusion of the excepted element. Jesus has indeed been casting out demons. In fact, his exorcisms are what lead the religious leaders to make this claim. So why not just state, "This one casts out demons by Beezebul, the ruler of demons"? It communicates the same content, right? The reason for the use of the negative + exception/restriction is the rhetorical impact that it has on the content. The leaders want to do more than just comment about the source of his power; they want to highlight this source. They do so by making a sweeping negative statement that is not actually true. He is able to cast out demons; it is a matter of by what power. The power that they want to highlight is disclosed in the exceptive clause.

This rhetorical process is analogous to having a table full of items, sweeping all of them onto the floor, and then placing the one item you are interested in back onto the table all by itself. You could have simply pointed to the item and said, "This is the one I am interested in." But sweeping every item onto the floor has a dramatic effect, on top of making a mess! Removing everything and then adding back the important item that was already there attracts far more attention to it than just pointing to it on the table. The same holds for negation + exception/restriction. The same propositional content could have been more easily communicated using a positive statement: "This one casts out demons by Beezebul, the ruler of demons." Saying that he does not cast out demons (which by itself is untrue) and then adding the means by which he does do it effectively highlights the excepted element.

4.2.1 Conventional Explanation

Most grammarians give little attention to exceptive/restrictive constructions, as this falls more under the heading of rhetoric than grammar.[16] Besides saying that this collocation οὐκ … εἰ μή is often found in the Synoptics, BDF has little to say about the issue of its rhetorical function.[17] The closest description to what I am claiming is Blass's observation that Paul uses πλήν to single out a main point at the end of an argument, as in 1 Cor 11:11; Eph 5:33; Phil 3:16; 4:14.[18] Robertson builds on this by noting that "εἰ and μή seem to coalesce into one word like πλήν," and that use of negation + exception/restriction in an apodosis "is very common as in classic Greek."[19] Heth provides a helpful application of the rhetorical function of exceptive clauses in his discussion of Jesus' view on divorce.[20]

---

16. Robertson (*Grammar*, 1186) notes the use of εἰ μή to create exceptions, but he does not discuss its rhetorical function. Porter (*Idioms*) and Wallace (*Greek Grammar*) do not discuss restrictive clauses. Powell and Baima ("Εἰ μή Clauses in the NT: Interpretation and Translation" [online: http://bible.org/article/font-facegreekeij-mhvfont-clauses-nt-interpretation-and-translation]) consider the issue in terms of translation to English rather than within a unified Greek explanation.

17. BDF §376.

18. Friedrich Blass, *Grammar of New Testament Greek* (trans. Henry St. John Thackeray; New York: Macmillan, 1898), 269, cited in Robertson, *Grammar*, 1187.

19. Robertson, *Grammar*, 1024.

20. William A. Heth, "Jesus on Divorce: How My Mind Has Changed," *SBJT* 6.1 (2002):

4.2.2   Discourse Explanation

I have claimed elsewhere that there are two distinct functions of exceptive/ restrictive clauses in the NT, depending on their placement in the clause.

> In cases where the exceptive clause *precedes* the main clause (i.e., protasis), it functions to establish a specific "frame of reference" for the clause that follows (e.g., Matthew 24:22; Mark 8:14; 13:20; John 9:33; 15:22; 18:30; Romans 9:29; 1 Corinthians 7:17).
>
> In cases where the exceptive clause *follows* the main clause (i.e., apodosis) and is preceded by either a negated main clause or an interrogative clause, the exceptive clause receives emphasis with respect to the main clause. This is due to the counterpoint-point relation with the negated clause, or by supplying the answer to the rhetorical question posed by the interrogative pronoun in the main clause (e.g., Luke 5:21; Romans 11:15; 1 Corinthians 2:11; 2 Corinthians 2:2; Ephesians 4:9; Hebrews 3:18; 1 John 2:22; 5:5). The few exceptions to this latter point that I found are Acts 26:32; 1 Corinthians 14:5; and 15:2.[21]

The examples that follow have one thing in common: a conceptual set of data is established either by use of a negated or an interrogative clause. The negation serves to remove all possible candidates from the data set, essentially wiping the slate clean by negation (e.g., *no one* can do X = X cannot be done by *anyone*). The interrogative asks a question that expects a negative answer (e.g., "Who can do this?" "No one"). In both cases, this protasis has the effect of predicating a set of items that will be completely removed from consideration. This is where the exceptive/restrictive apodosis comes in. One member

---

4–29 available online at http://www.sbts.edu/media/publications/sbjt/sbjt_2002spring2 .pdf.

21. Steven E. Runge, "Teaching Them What NOT to Do: The Nuances of Negation in the Greek New Testament" (paper presented at the annual meeting of the Evangelical Theology Society, San Diego, Calif., 13–16 November 2007), 8. Diessel recognizes a comparable distinction across languages regarding the factors that influence the placement of conditional clauses. He states, "What this example suggests is that initial conditional clauses do not just provide a thematic ground for the discourse that follows; rather, they describe a contrastive situation that establishes a specific framework—a specific semantic constellation—for the discourse that follows. In other words, conditional clauses predominantly precede the main clause, providing an orientation for interpreting subsequent clauses, because of their meaning (cf. Lehmann 1974; Dancygier and Sweetser 2000). In fact, the meaning of conditional clauses favors initial occurrence so strongly that the occurrence of final conditional clauses requires a particular explanation" (Holger Diessel, "Competing Motivations for the Ordering of Main and Adverbial Clauses," *Linguistics* 43, no. 3 [2005]: 461–62).

from this negated set is presented as the exception. Only after reading the apodosis does the reader realize that the totality of the initial protasis is not the
complete story. There is one item singled out for consideration, as illustrated
in figure 1.

Figure 1

original set	negated set	restricted element added
{ A B C X Y Z }	{ Ø }	{ Y }

The original set contains all of the potential members that could fill in the
blank. Negating this entire set temporarily removes all of the members from
consideration. Finally we reach the exceptive element that adds back one
member (Y) from the original set. This one item could have just as easily been
stated in a simple affirmative statement, as in Matt 12:24 above. The effect of
creating a set, removing all members of the set, and then adding one member
back is to attract additional attention to the excepted item, attention that it
would not otherwise have received.

Remember the idea of having a table full of items, sweeping all of them
onto the floor, and then putting back the one item that you want people to
focus on. The key concept is that the excepted element was a member of the
original set. The use of negation + exception/restriction in Greek is comparable to its use in English. This means that the same technique can be exploited
in explaining the significance of exceptive clauses to an English audience
when teaching or preaching. So in regard to Matt 12:24 you could say, "Is
Jesus really unable to cast out demons? Isn't that why they are upset with him,
because he *is* casting them out? So it is not the fact that he is casting them out
as much as it is the means by which they think he is doing it."

4.2.3   Application

I begin this section by looking at statements where the entire clause is negated
then excepted, followed by examples where an interrogative statement is used
to accomplish the same effect.[22] Consider example 42, from Mark 6.

---

22. I argue elsewhere (Runge, "Teaching Them") that when a negative particle negates
a declarative clause, the entire propositional content of the clause is negated, not just the
element that follows the negative particle. The pragmatic placement of the negative particle
is better understood as a marker of emphasis, rather than as negating a single clause element. This distinction was shown to provide a unified description of negation that recon-

Example 42 :: Mark 6:4–5

⁴ καὶ ἔλεγεν αὐτοῖς ὁ Ἰησοῦς ὅτι ⟨✗οὐκ ἔστιν προφήτης ἄτιμος✗⟩ εἰ μὴ ⟨✓ἐν τῇ πατρίδι αὐτοῦ καὶ ἐν τοῖς συγγενεῦσιν αὐτοῦ καὶ ἐν τῇ οἰκίᾳ αὐτοῦ.✓⟩	⁴ And Jesus said to them, ⟨✗"A prophet is not without honor✗⟩ except ⟨✓in his hometown, and among his relatives, and in his own household."✓⟩
⁵ καὶ ⟨✗οὐκ ἐδύνατο ἐκεῖ ποιῆσαι οὐδεμίαν δύναμιν,✗⟩ εἰ μὴ ⟨✓ὀλίγοις ἀρρώστοις ἐπιθεὶς τὰς χεῖρας ἐθεράπευσεν.✓⟩	⁵ And ⟨✗he was not able to do any miracle in that place✗⟩ except ⟨✓to lay his hands on a few sick people and heal them.✓⟩

The negated statements in v. 4 and v. 5 are not entirely true; exceptions to each statement are added in the apodosis. There actually is a context where a prophet is without honor: in his hometown among his relatives and his household. Jesus actually was able to perform miracles in Nazareth: he laid hands on a few sick people, healing them. The statements are essentially incomplete until one reads the apodoses; it is only then that they are accurate. The incomplete proposition of the negated clause sets the stage to highlight the restricted element that follows.

Note that the same propositional information could have been communicated using only positive statements, thereby avoiding the complexity of the negation and restriction:

- A prophet is without honor in his hometown.
- Jesus was able to lay hands on a few sick people and heal them.

Both of these statements communicate the same information as the negated statements in Mark 6:4–5, but they lack the rhetorical punch. The pragmatic effect of using the negation + exception/restriction is to highlight the restricted element because of its significance to the discourse.

The focus here is not on the fact that Jesus was dishonored but on the location where it takes place. Of all the people who know him and should accept him, it is the hometown crowd. Think of how many small towns tout some native son's achievements as their claim to fame. In the case of Jesus, they reject him. As a result, he apparently was limited in the works he was able to perform there. Using only the positive statements would not have focused

---

cited many of the conflicting claims made by grammarians regarding the exegetical significance of the placement of the negative particle.

the reader's attention on these significant elements in nearly the same way as in the biblical text.

Consider how the command in example 43 is affected by adding an exception.

Example 43 :: 1 Corinthians 7:5

⟨✗μὴ ἀποστερεῖτε ἀλλήλους,✗⟩ εἰ μήτι ἂν ⟨✓ἐκ συμφώνου πρὸς καιρόν,✓⟩ ἵνα σχολάσητε τῇ προσευχῇ καὶ πάλιν ἐπὶ τὸ αὐτὸ ἦτε, ἵνα μὴ πειράζῃ ὑμᾶς ὁ σατανᾶς διὰ τὴν ἀκρασίαν ὑμῶν.

⟨✗Do not deprive each other✗⟩ except ⟨✓by mutual consent and for a time,✓⟩ so that you may devote yourselves to prayer. Then come together again so that Satan will not tempt you because of your lack of self-control. (NIV)

The command not to deprive one another actually contains a loophole. There is a time when it is appropriate: when it is by agreement and only for a time. The same propositional information could have been stated positively: "You may deprive one another by agreement for a time." This positive statement makes the behavior sound much more acceptable than the negated/excepted version.

Stating it as he does, Paul is able to make a nearly blanket statement and draw attention to the very narrow exception at the same time. The only rationale he provides for the mutual depriving is prayer. This removes any room for using sexual deprivation as a bargaining chip in a relationship. Doing so would expose the couple to temptation from Satan because of a lack of self-control. The counterpoint and the point appear to be equally relevant. The negation + exception/restriction creates a very close connection between the two elements, attracting attention to the restriction that it would not otherwise have received.

Example 44 :: 2 Timothy 2:5

⟨✗ἐὰν δὲ καὶ ἀθλῇ τις, οὐ στεφανοῦται✗⟩ ἐὰν μὴ ⟨✓νομίμως ἀθλήσῃ.✓⟩

⟨✗And also if anyone competes he is not crowned✗⟩ unless ⟨✓he competes according to the rules.✓⟩

The grammatical complexity of this verse is rarely captured in English translations. The key idea is that no athlete is crowned unless he competes according to the rules. The ascensive καί (translated as "also") serves to more closely connect this illustration of competing with the previous illustration about soldiering in v. 4. The primary purpose of the counterpoint is to state that one who competes is not crowned, even though this is not completely true. How could one be crowned who did not compete? The apodosis provides the restriction that makes the counterpoint true: the need to compete lawfully.

This same propositional content could have been stated positively, avoiding the complexity: "The one crowned must compete lawfully." Notice how innocuous this statement is in comparison to the more complex combination of negation + exception/restriction. Of course they must compete lawfully. The negated version takes the stated objective of receiving the crown and places it in jeopardy through the use of negation. Fulfilling the constraint of the exceptive clause is the key to qualifying for the goal. Paul's use of the more complex construction reflects the importance he places on this facet of his illustration. Just as the soldier of v. 4 must remain focused by avoiding civilian entanglements, so too the athlete must play by the rules to have any hope of qualifying for the prize.

Example 45 provides another case where one point/counterpoint set can be embedded within another, as in example 37.

Example 45 :: Romans 7:7

⟨✖Τί οὖν ἐροῦμεν; ὁ νόμος ἁμαρτία;✖⟩ μὴ γένοιτο· ἀλλὰ ⟨✔ ⟨✖τὴν ἁμαρτίαν οὐκ ἔγνων✖⟩ εἰ μὴ ⟨✔διὰ νόμου·✔⟩ ✔⟩ ⟨✖τήν τε γὰρ ἐπιθυμίαν οὐκ ᾔδειν✖⟩ εἰ μὴ ⟨✔ὁ νόμος ἔλεγεν· οὐκ ἐπιθυμήσεις.✔⟩

⟨✖What then shall we say? Is the law sin?✖⟩ May it never be! ⟨✔ ⟨✖But I would not have known sin ✖⟩ except ⟨✔through the law,✔⟩ ✔⟩ for ⟨✖I would not have known covetousness✖⟩ if ⟨✔the law had not said, "Do not covet."✔⟩

Paul makes a higher-level point (✔) that consists of an embedded point/counterpoint set that connects back to a corresponding counterpoint (✖) in v. 7a–b. The higher-level counterpoint is replaced by the complex point introduced by ἀλλά. The statement that Paul "did not know sin" is not completely true. He did indeed know sin, and he knew it through of the law. The negated counterpoint sets the stage for the excepted point that follows. In this way, Paul attracts attention to the purpose and value of the law: making sin known to the sinner.

Similarly, his statement about not knowing covetousness is not entirely true apart from the apodosis. He did know not to covet, but it is only in the restriction that we learn why: the law was telling him not to covet. It is this detail that makes the statement complete and true. It is this detail that is key to Paul's argument, hence the use of the rhetorical device to ensure that the reader does not miss it.

The same propositional content could have been conveyed using only positive assertions. "I had known about sin because of the law; I had known about covetousness because the law was saying, 'You shall not covet.'" These positive statements would not have explicitly placed the same emphasis on the role of the law as is found in the statements using negation and exception/restriction. Paul's focus in the context is on the important role that the law plays. Even if it is not a means to righteousness, it still has an important role to play.

In the following two examples, only one element of the clause is negated through the use of a negative pronoun.[23]

Example 46 :: Mark 9:29

καὶ εἶπεν αὐτοῖς· ⟨✗τοῦτο τὸ γένος   And he said to them, ⟨✗"This kind
ἐν οὐδενὶ δύναται ἐξελθεῖν✗⟩ εἰ μὴ   can come out by nothing✗⟩ except
⟨✓ἐν προσευχῇ.✓⟩   ⟨✓by prayer."✓⟩

Only one word is negated, not the entire clause, but the effect is the same. The implication is that nothing is able to cast out this kind of demon, which is not entirely true. There actually is one means that will work, and it is part of the set of all possible means that was negated. It is by prayer. He could have said, "This kind can [only] be cast out by prayer," but it would have not have highlighted the importance of prayer in nearly the same way. Phrasing it as he does, Jesus highlights the significance of prayer in such situations by virtue of his choice to use negation + exception/restriction. Even though this context uses a slightly different form of negation, the effect is the same.

In example 47, extra steps are taken to stress the totality of the negation in order to attract that much more attention to the restricted element.

Example 47 :: Matthew 24:36

Περὶ δὲ τῆς ἡμέρας ἐκείνης καὶ   "But concerning that day and hour
ὥρας ⟨✗οὐδεὶς οἶδεν, οὐδὲ οἱ   ⟨✗no one knows—not even the
ἄγγελοι τῶν οὐρανῶν οὐδὲ ὁ   angels of heaven nor the Son—✗⟩
υἱός,✗⟩ εἰ μὴ ⟨✓ὁ πατὴρ μόνος.✓⟩   except ⟨✓the Father alone."✓⟩

---

23. Porter (*Idioms*, 282) states that the "most common word negation occurs with the negative pronouns οὐδείς and μηδείς."

The negative pronoun οὐδεὶς ("no one") excludes everyone; it totally negates the set. In order to reinforce the totality of this negation, Jesus also dismisses two of the most likely candidates who might know the hour of his coming: the angels and the Son. In doing so, he takes the set that was already empty and shakes it out just to show that there really is nothing else left. It is only then that he introduces the Father as the restricted element: the Father is the one exception. The use of μόνος ("alone") serves to further highlight the singularity of the Father: he alone knows, no one else.

The examples above illustrate the use of negated clauses in combination with exceptions to attract extra attention to the excepted elements. By formulating the positive assertion into a negation + exception/restriction, extra attention can be placed on the excepted element. Rhetorical questions can also be used to create the same effect, where the expected answer to the question is "nothing" or "no one."

Example 48 comes from the scene where Jesus forgives the sins of the paralytic before healing him. The Pharisees' question leads Jesus to respond by asking which is easier, to heal or to forgive sins. Here is the Pharisees' response to Jesus forgiving the man's sins:

Example 48 :: Mark 2:7

τί οὗτος οὕτως λαλεῖ; βλασφημεῖ· ⟨✘τίς δύναται ἀφιέναι ἁμαρτίας✘⟩ εἰ μὴ ⟨✔εἷς ὁ θεός;✔⟩	"Why does this man speak like this? He is blaspheming! ⟨✘Who is able to forgive sins✘⟩ except ⟨✔God alone?"✔⟩

The question "Who?" creates a set of potential candidates who can forgive sins. The implicit answer is that no one can, creating the same effect as the negated clauses or pronouns in the examples above.

The question is also rhetorical in that the speaker provides the answer to his own question. The interrogative pronoun serves as a forward-pointing reference attracting attention to an intended target (see §3.3.1). In this usage with the exceptive clause, the forward-pointing reference has a secondary effect of creating a counterpoint that highlights the more important point that follows in the excepted clause. Other examples of this usage are found in 1 John 2:22; 5:5.

4.3   The Use of Ἀλλά to Correct or Replace

4.3.1   Conventional Explanation

The particle ἀλλά typically is classified as an adversative coordinating conjunction.[24] Robertson notes that if the conjunction is preceded by a negative clause, "the antithesis is sharp," citing as examples Mark 9:7; Luke 1:60; John 6:32.[25]

As far as describing what ἀλλά does, Robertson states that "ἀλλά alone may refer to an interruption in thought not expressed, as in Jo. 12:27."[26] Although ἀλλά and εἰ μή are considered to be adversatives, there is little discussion about the functional difference between them—i.e., the semantic distinction between them.[27] Regarding the difference between ἀλλά and πλήν, BDF seems to view them as rather similar, with πλήν being the stronger of the two.[28] The primary focus of the discussions is on what it means in English, not really on what it does. One significant comment regarding function was made by Blass in regard to Paul's use of πλήν, and this will function as our point of departure into a discourse explanation. He observes "that Paul uses it at the end of an argument to single out the main point."[29] Just as in the case of excepted elements, elements introduced by ἀλλά and πλήν are highlighted for rhetorical purposes and could have been conveyed using more simplified structures.

---

24. See Porter, *Idioms*, 206; Robertson, *Grammar*, 1187–88; BDF §448.

25. Robertson, *Grammar*, 1188.

26. Ibid., 1187.

27. Robertson (ibid., 1188) summarizes the traditional views as follows: "Both Winer and W. F. Moulton (W.-M., p. 566) felt certain that ἀλλά never equalled [*sic*] εἰ μή, not even in Mt. 20:23 and Mk. 4:22. But J. H. Moulton (*Prol.*, p. 241) quotes Tb. P. 104 (i/B.C.), καὶ μὴ ἐξέστω Φιλίσκωι γυναῖκα ἄλλην ἐπαγαγέσθαι ἀλλὰ Ἀπολλωνίαν, where ἀλλά means practically 'except.'" The distinction concerns whether the replacement belonged to the negated set (εἰ μὴ) versus whether it was a brand new item (ἀλλά), and the apparent exception that Robertson sees in Matt 20:23 can be accounted for as standard usage of ἀλλά. Jesus has said it is not his to grant to sit on the right or left. The Father is not included in this set, but replaces "Jesus" as the authority that can grant this request, hence the use of ἀλλά.

28. "(1) ... Πλήν rather than ἀλλά (§448(3)) was evidently the really colloquial word for this idea (Schmid I 133). (2) Πλήν means more nearly 'only, in any case' in Paul, used to conclude a discussion and emphasize what is essential.—Rob[ertson] 1187" (BDF §449).

29. Cited in Robertson, *Grammar*, 1188.

4.3.2   Discourse Explanation

Heckert describes ἀλλά as a "global marker of contrast," one that "introduces a correction of the expectation created by the first conjunct; an incorrect expectation is cancelled and a proper expectation is put in its place."[30] If we take the traditional idea of "adversative," this particle does more than just indicate contrast. This holds true even if the preceding element is positive rather than negative.[31] It provides a corrective to whatever it stands in contrast with. Levinsohn adds, "When ἀλλά links a negative characteristic or proposition with a following positive one, the negative proposition usually retains its relevance."[32]

Although there are several contrastive or adversative particles, ἀλλά adds the unique constraint of correcting some aspect of what precedes. In terms of distinguishing ἀλλά from εἰ μή, the key is the relation of what follows the particle to what precedes. In the case of εἰ μή, the excepted element that replaces what precedes was a potential member of the negated set. In the case of ἀλλά, the correcting member was not a member of the original set; it is a new element.

Figure 2

original set	corrected set	replaced set
{ A B C D E F }	{ A B C Y D E F }	{ Y }

In both cases, the element following these particles receives more attention than if a simple, positive assertion has been used that did not involve exception or restriction.

4.3.3   Application

I begin with some basic examples of how ἀλλά is used to create a correlation with a preceding clause or proposition. In each case, the clause element introduced by ἀλλά either replaces or corrects some aspect of what precedes.

---

30. Jacob K. Heckert, *Discourse Function of Conjoiners in the Pastoral Epistles* (Dallas: SIL International, 1996), 23.

31. Levinsohn, *Discourse Features*, 115.

32. Ibid.

Example 49 :: Matthew 4:4

ὁ δὲ ἀποκριθεὶς εἶπεν· γέγραπται· ⟨✗οὐκ ἐπ' ἄρτῳ μόνῳ ζήσεται ὁ ἄνθρωπος,✗⟩ ἀλλ' ⟨✓ἐπὶ παντὶ ῥήματι ἐκπορευομένῳ διὰ στόματος θεοῦ.✓⟩

But he answered and said, "It is written, ⟨✗'Man will not live on bread alone,✗⟩ but ⟨✓on every word that comes out of the mouth of God.'"✓⟩

The negated clause stating that man will not live on bread alone presupposes that man must live on something else besides just bread. The placement of the prepositional phrase ἐπ' ἄρτῳ μόνῳ ("on bread alone") following the negative particle οὐκ ("not") has the effect of placing emphasis on it. It also sets the stage for this element to be corrected by the element introduced by ἀλλά. Specifying that one does not live on bread alone increases the expectation that something more is coming that will supply the missing element. The clause element introduced by ἀλλά fills in this blank.

One could have more simply stated, "You will live on bread and on every word that proceeds from the mouth of God." Doing so would have placed "bread" and "every word …" on the same plane, without assigning more significance to one or the other. In Matthew's formulation, bread is portrayed as a required element, but the less important of the two. Introducing "every word …" using ἀλλά highlights this concept in ways it would otherwise not have received using a less complex construction. Notice that one prepositional phrase is replaced by an analogous prepositional phrase. There will typically be a close grammatical correspondence between the two elements.

Example 50 contains part of Jesus' instructions for when his disciples bear witness before kings and governors.

Example 50 :: Matthew 10:19–20

[19] ὅταν δὲ παραδῶσιν ὑμᾶς, μὴ μεριμνήσητε πῶς ἢ τί λαλήσητε· δοθήσεται γὰρ ὑμῖν ἐν ἐκείνῃ τῇ ὥρᾳ τί λαλήσητε·

[19] "But whenever they hand you over, do not be anxious how to speak or what you should say, for what you should say will be given to you at that hour.

[20] ⟨✗οὐ γὰρ ὑμεῖς ἐστε οἱ λαλοῦντες✗⟩ ἀλλὰ ⟨✓τὸ πνεῦμα τοῦ πατρὸς ὑμῶν τὸ λαλοῦν ἐν ὑμῖν.✓⟩

[20] ⟨✗For you are not the ones who are speaking,✗⟩ but ⟨✓the Spirit of your Father who is speaking through you."✓⟩

Verse 20 provides support for the command not to be anxious, and it presupposes that someone will be speaking; we know that it will not be "you." This raises the question of who will be speaking if not the disciples. The answer introduced following ἀλλά clarifies that although the disciples will be speaking, it is the Spirit of the Father who will be speaking through them. Note that there is also a close grammatical correspondence between what is replaced and its replacement, just as in Matt 4:4; in this case, the complement of the verb is replaced with an alternate complement.

The counterpoint here addresses the natural inclination to think that we are on our own in such instances. It is countered by stating that we are not the ones speaking; it is the Spirit, who indwells us. Stating "Do not be anxious…, the Spirit of our Father is the one speaking in you" communicates the same basic content, but without explicitly eliminating the thought that we need to go it alone.

Example 51 is a classic "not only … but also" construction that forms a very close connection between the counterpoint and the point. It also affirms Levinsohn's claim that when a negative precedes ἀλλά, the negative proposition generally remains relevant to the discourse.[33]

Example 51 :: Romans 13:5

διὸ ἀνάγκη ὑποτάσσεσθαι, ⟨✗οὐ μόνον διὰ τὴν ὀργὴν✗⟩ ἀλλὰ ⟨✓καὶ διὰ τὴν συνείδησιν.✓⟩	Therefore one must be in subjection, ⟨✗not only to avoid God's wrath✗⟩ but ⟨✓also for the sake of conscience.✓⟩ (RSV)

There is a need to be in subjection; the question is on what basis. It should not simply be on the basis of potential wrath, but on the basis of our conscience as well. Paul could have stated that we should be in subjection based on wrath and conscience, but this would have robbed "conscience" of the prominence that it enjoys in the point/counterpoint set. The element introduced by ἀλλά provides a corrective to a corresponding element and is analogous in terms of morphology (i.e., a prepositional phrase using διά).

In Paul's comparison of tongues to prophecy in example 52, one of the distinctions that he makes concerns the audience—that is, who is being addressed.

---

33. Ibid.

Example 52 :: 1 Corinthians 14:2

ὁ γὰρ λαλῶν γλώσσῃ ⟨✘οὐκ ἀνθρώποις λαλεῖ✘⟩ ἀλλὰ ⟨✔θεῷ·✔⟩ οὐδεὶς γὰρ ἀκούει, πνεύματι δὲ λαλεῖ μυστήρια·

For the one who speaks in a tongue ⟨✘does not speak to people✘⟩ but ⟨✔to God,✔⟩ because no one understands, but by the Spirit he speaks mysteries.

In order to draw out the contrast regarding edification, Paul highlights the one being addressed by speaking in tongues. He could have communicated the same propositional content by skipping the negative counterpoint (i.e., "The one who speaks in a tongue speaks to God"). Using this construction draws attention to what is negated in the counterpoint (see chapter 13) as a backdrop to make the point stand out that much more. Once again there is direct grammatical correspondence between what is replaced and the element introduced by ἀλλά.

Here is another example that uses negation to emphasize the counterpoint element that will be replaced by the point introduced with ἀλλά. There is also an ascensive καί ("also") in the point that further strengthens the connection between the two elements. The use of negation suggests that the counterpoint remains relevant.

Example 53 :: Philippians 2:4

⟨✘μὴ τὰ ἑαυτῶν ἕκαστος σκοποῦντες✘⟩ ἀλλὰ ⟨✔[καὶ] τὰ ἑτέρων ἕκαστοι.✔⟩

⟨✘each one of you not looking out for his own interests,✘⟩ but ⟨✔also each of you looking out for the interests of others.✔⟩

Paul is not asking his readers to forsake their own interests altogether, but rather to not limit their concern to theirs alone. The emphasis of the verse is placed on the point, insuring that the counterintuitive "valuing of other people" receives primary attention. The statement "Look out for your own interests and the interests of others" implies that the two interests are of equal importance. With selfishness naturally inclining us to look out for our own interests, the rhetorical use of the point/counterpoint set ensures that looking out for the interests of others is not overlooked. Note again the morphological correspondence between the correlated elements; both are complements of the verb.

Matthew 20:28 illustrates that more than one element can be replaced or corrected. In this case, two infinitives replace the one that is negated in the first part of the verse, exchanging one purpose for the Son of Man's coming for two other purposes.

Example 54 :: Matthew 20:28

ὥσπερ ‹✗ὁ υἱὸς τοῦ ἀνθρώπου οὐκ ἦλθεν διακονηθῆναι✗› ἀλλὰ ‹✓διακονῆσαι καὶ δοῦναι τὴν ψυχὴν αὐτοῦ λύτρον ἀντὶ πολλῶν.✓›	just as ‹✗the Son of Man did not come to be served,✗› but ‹✓to serve, and to give his life as a ransom for many.✓›

The same information could have been conveyed without using a negative counterpoint, but it would not have attracted the same amount of attention to Jesus' purposes. Stating why he did not come creates the expectation that an alternative reason why he did come will be provided. The fact that the same verb has been used in both parts (διακονέω, "I serve") heightens the contrast even more. The counterpoint uses a passive form of the infinitive ("to be served") compared to the active form ("to serve") in the point. The conjunction καί adds a second purpose to the first: to give his life as a ransom for many. Again, note the morphological parallelism between that which is replaced and the elements introduced by ἀλλά.

In 2 Tim 1:7 we have another instance where a single element is replaced by more than one corresponding element introduced by ἀλλά.

Example 55 :: 2 Timothy 1:7

‹✗οὐ γὰρ ἔδωκεν ἡμῖν ὁ θεὸς πνεῦμα δειλίας✗› ἀλλὰ ‹✓δυνάμεως καὶ ἀγάπης καὶ σωφρονισμοῦ.✓›	‹✗For God has not given us a spirit of cowardice,✗› but ‹✓of power and love and self-discipline.✓›

The fact that God has not given us a spirit of timidity presupposes that he has given us some other kind of spirit; it is just a question of what kind. The conjunction ἀλλά introduces what turns out to be kinds of spirit rather than a single one. The three are coordinated by καί, providing a threefold replacement of the one. Notice that the word πνεῦμα ("spirit") is not repeated; only the modifiers defining "spirit" are mentioned. The net result is to set up the counterpoint as a foil against which the following points introduced by ἀλλά stand out all the more.

So far, all of the examples of ἀλλά have replaced single elements of a clause with one or more corresponding elements. The next examples show

that clauses can be replaced by other clauses, thus maintaining the principle
of corresponding elements replacing one another.

Example 56 :: Ephesians 6:4

Καὶ οἱ πατέρες, ⟨✗μὴ παροργίζετε τὰ τέκνα ὑμῶν✗⟩ ἀλλὰ ⟨✓ἐκτρέφετε αὐτὰ ἐν παιδείᾳ καὶ νουθεσίᾳ κυρίου.✓⟩	And fathers, ⟨✗do not provoke your children to anger,✗⟩ but ⟨✓bring them up in the discipline and instruction of the Lord.✓⟩ (RSV)

The command not to provoke one's children does more than state a rather
obvious principle; it provides a backdrop for the following point. The negative
statement about what not to do raises the question of what should be done.
Even though whole clauses are replaced, note that there is correspondence of
subject and object between them. Both are concerned with the same thing;
they just convey different courses of action.

It is now time to pull together all that has been covered so far in this chapter and to apply it to one of the most complex point/counterpoint sets found
in the NT. The usage in these verses is often considered "emphatic." In spite of
this, I contend that each conjunction in v. 8 is playing a standard role, placing
a single constraint on how to process the proposition.

Example 57 :: Philippians 3:7–9

7 [Ἀλλὰ] ⟨✓ἅτινα ἦν μοι κέρδη, ταῦτα ἥγημαι διὰ τὸν Χριστὸν ζημίαν.✓⟩	7 But ⟨✓whatever things were gain to me, these things I have consid-ered loss because of Christ.✓⟩
8 ἀλλὰ ⟨✗✗ ⟨✓μενοῦνγε καὶ ἡγοῦμαι πάντα ζημίαν εἶναι διὰ τὸ ὑπερέχον τῆς γνώσεως Χριστοῦ Ἰησοῦ τοῦ κυρίου μου,✓⟩ δι' ὃν τὰ πάντα ἐζημιώθην,✗✗⟩ καὶ ⟨Ѡἡγοῦμαι σκύβαλα, ἵνα Χριστὸν κερδήσω	8 More than that, ⟨✗✗ ⟨✓I even consider all things to be loss because of the surpassing great-ness of the knowledge of Christ Jesus my Lord,✓⟩ for the sake of whom I have suffered the loss of all things,✗✗⟩ and ⟨Ѡconsider them dung, in order that I may gain Christ
9 καὶ εὑρεθῶ ἐν αὐτῷ, ⟨✗μὴ ἔχων ἐμὴν δικαιοσύνην τὴν ἐκ νόμου✗⟩ ἀλλὰ ⟨✓τὴν	9 and may be found in him, ⟨✗not having my righteousness which is from the law,✗⟩ but ⟨✓which is

διὰ πίστεως Χριστοῦ,✔⟩ τὴν ἐκ θεοῦ δικαιοσύνην ἐπὶ τῇ πίστει....	through faith in Christ,✔) the righteousness from God on the basis of faith....

Verses 4b–6 describe Paul's potential reasons for boasting. Think of these items as trophies in a case that he could point to if he wanted to boast in the flesh. This may also be the list of items that his listeners most highly regarded about him, their reasons for putting him on a pedestal. Paul uses this section to readjust the reader's view of him, to indicate that he has not arrived, but that he is still in process like the rest of us (see vv. 12–14). These reasons serve as a counterpoint for the point introduced by ἀλλά in v. 7, signaling that what follows replaces his potential reasons for boasting. "Whatever things were gain to me" refers back to this list. Instead of considering them grounds for boasting, he considers them loss because of Christ.

Verse 8 contains another ἀλλά, which has the same constraint to replace or correct some aspect of what precedes. In this case, the correction is a shift from counting just his potential list as loss to counting all things as loss. Since there are back-to-back ἀλλάs, the οὖν of the compound μενοῦνγε instructs the reader to view v. 8 as an inferential development closely connected to v. 7. The μέν has the normal forward-pointing constraint, signaling a counterpoint correlation with some related element that follows (v. 8d). The combination of an ascensive καί with γε strengthens the connection with v. 7 by creating this additional thematic link (see chapter 16). To summarize, v. 8a has three links: one backward-pointing inferential one (οὖν), a backward-pointing thematic addition (γε καί), and a forward-pointing counterpoint relation (μέν). Verses 8b and 8c elaborate the content of 8a.

Verse 8d is the point that correlates with the μέν of v. 8a, introduced by καί. In v. 7 there was a shift from counting Paul's list (vv. 4–6) as loss for the sake of knowing Christ to counting all things as loss in v. 8a. This thought is intensified in the point of v. 8d, which was anticipated by the presence of μέν. He shifts from counting all things as loss to counting them as dung, an even more derisive view of what the world would hold as dear.

The cumulative effect of this continued intensification is to continue to raise the bar on how valuable a thing it is to know Christ and to be found in Him not having a righteousness of his own. It would have been much easier for Paul to skip the intervening steps and simply call his list "dung." Alternatively, he could have skipped the connections and anticipation created by the combination of conjunctions and instead just listed the statements connected by δέ. Using either of these options would have significantly weakened the rhetorical impact of Paul's grammatical buildup to the climactic statement beginning in v. 8d.

Note that vv. 8d–11 comprise a paragraph-level point that correlates to the complex of vv. 8a–8c, and that is syntactically parallel in terms of structure. The conjunctions in v. 8a are generally considered to be an emphatic conglomeration that has some sense other than the basic constraint of each individual particle. As with other compound conjunctions, the μενοῦνγε combination retains the basic sense of each individual part, as opposed to creating an emphatic superparticle. This collocation has been treated as separate words in previous editions of the critical Greek text, with editors making different judgments about how to render the words.[34] Patiently unpacking the role that each particle plays can pay great exegetical dividends. It can also highlight the care and precision that the writers exercised in communicating their intended message.

Suggested Reading

Blass, F., A. Debrunner, and R. W. Funk. *A Greek Grammar of the New Testament and Other Early Christian Literature.* §§447–48.

Brannan, Richard. "The Discourse Function of ALLA."

Denniston, John Dewar. *The Greek Particles.* 369–74.

Diessel, Holger. "Competing Motivations for the Ordering of Main and Adverbial Clauses." 461–62.

Heckert, Jacob K. *Discourse Function of Conjoiners in the Pastoral Epistles.* 13–28.

Levinsohn, Stephen H. *Discourse Features of New Testament Greek: A Course-Book on the Information Structure of New Testament Greek.* 115–19.

Porter, Stanley E. *Idioms of the Greek New Testament.* 206–13.

Robertson, A. T. *A Grammar of the Greek New Testament in the Light of Historical Research.* 1151, 1187–88.

Runge, "Teaching Them What NOT to Do: The Nuances of Negation in the Greek New Testament."

Wallace, Daniel B. *Greek Grammar beyond the Basics: An Exegetical Syntax of the New Testament.* 672.

---

34. Note that through at least the ninth edition of Eberhard Nestle's *Novum Testamentum Graece* (Stuttgart: Privilegierte Württembergische Bibelanstalt, 1912), μενοῦνγε was printed as three distinct words and not as a compound. By the twenty-first edition (1952), it was rendered as μενοῦν γε. In a later edition the editors made the decision to read all three as a single compound conjunction.

METACOMMENTS

When people speak, they spend the majority of their time communicating what they want you to know. However, at times they step back from the content of the topic and make a comment about it, such as:

- "It is very important that you understand that...."
- "I want you to know that...."
- "Don't you know that...."
- "Of all the things that you have learned so far, the most important thing is that...."
- "If you remember nothing else that I say, remember that...."

Each of these statements has the common characteristic of interrupting the speech by making an abstracted statement about what is about to be said.[1] These are English examples of *metacomment*.[2] Here is a working definition:

> **Metacomment**: When speakers stop saying what they are saying in order to comment on what is going to be said, speaking abstractly about it.

---

1. Metacomments are not a form of parenthetical comment, since the latter focus on something off topic, such as background information. Metacomments look forward to what is coming, commenting on it in a way that does not substantially contribute to the propositional content. The verbs tend to be perceptual or volitional in nature.

2. Berlin describes a similar phenomenon in Biblical Hebrew that she calls "frame breaks." This is where "the narrator leaves his story for a moment to make a comment about it," referring to the narrative comment about the practice in Israel from Ruth 4 (Adele Berlin, *Poetics and Interpretation of Biblical Narrative* [BLS 9; Sheffield: Almond, 1983], 99).

Very often in narrative speeches or in the Epistles of the NT, speakers will suspend what they are talking about in order to comment on what they are about to say. Examples of this include:

- "I say to you...."
- "I tell you the truth...."
- "We know that...."
- "I ask that...."
- "I want you to know that...."

These expressions are used to introduce significant propositions, ones to which the writer or speaker wants to attract extra attention. The litmus test for identifying a metacomment is a speaker interrupting what is being talked about in order to comment on what is going to be talked about. This means that the metacomment could be removed from the discourse without substantially altering the propositional content. For instance, consider the metacomment in example 58, delineated by the ⊐ symbol:

Example 58 :: Romans 12:1

⟨⊐Παρακαλῶ οὖν ὑμᾶς,⊐⟩ ἀδελφοί, διὰ τῶν οἰκτιρμῶν τοῦ θεοῦ παραστῆσαι τὰ σώματα ὑμῶν θυσίαν ζῶσαν ἁγίαν εὐάρεστον τῷ θεῷ, τὴν λογικὴν λατρείαν ὑμῶν·

Therefore ⟨⊐I exhort you,⊐⟩ brothers, through the mercies of God, to present your bodies as a living sacrifice, holy and pleasing to God, which is your reasonable service.

Paul could have simply issued the command, "Present your bodies as living sacrifices...." Omitting the metacomment would not change the basic content; it would simply weaken the urgency of it. Metacomments serve only to introduce; they do not convey content needed to understand what follows.

5.1   Conventional Explanation

The phenomenon that I describe as a metacomment is most often discussed in biblical studies under the rubric of form criticism. Form critics seek to understand a text by classifying similarly structured or phrased portions of discourse as "forms," based on the function that they serve.[3] In other words,

---

3. This sounds rather simple in theory, but it is difficult in practice. One often finds disagreement in analyses and classification of forms—for example, "Some analyses identify vv. 13–15 as also belonging to the thanksgiving, but the disclosure formula in v. 13 and the

they focus on the repeated use of a specific collocation of words in a specific structure but not necessarily in a rigid order.[4] Critics then seek to understand the meaning of the text by understanding how the particular form was used. The metacomments of the NT have been variously classified as disclosure formulas,[5] request formulas, hearing forms, petition formulas, and introduction formulas.[6]

According to form critics, it is not the context of usage that makes the form, but rather the formal requirements being met.[7] Sanders states that the disclosure formula "is generally used to introduce new material, to change the subject of discussion, or when the argument takes a new tack."[8] At times the rigidity of strictly defined forms crumbles under the weight of the counterexamples that must be accounted for.[9]

---

content of these verses lead me to the identification of vv. 13–15 as a *narratio* that explains the background and rationale of Paul's forthcoming visit" (Robert Jewett, *Romans: A Commentary* [Hermeneia; Minneapolis: Fortress, 2006], 117).

4. See Terence Y. Mullins, "Disclosure: A Literary Form in the New Testament," *NovT* 7 (1964): 44–50.

5. Jewett (*Romans*, 1016) defines a disclosure formula as "a standardized way of saying, 'I want you to know....'"

6. See John L. White, "Introductory Formulae in the Body of the Pauline Letter," *JBL* 90 (1971): 91–97; J. T. Sanders, "The Transition from Opening Epistolary Thanksgiving to Body in the Letters of the Pauline Corpus," *JBL* 71 (1962): 348–62; Terence Y. Mullins, "Petition as a Literary Form," *NovT* 5 (1962): 46–54; "Formulas in New Testament Epistles," *JBL* 91 (1972): 380–90.

7. Compare the description by Mullins ("Disclosure," 46) of the disclosure form:
There is one peculiar use of θέλω which properly deserves to be recognized as a distinct literary form, for θέλω, when used with a noetic verb in the infinitive, serves as a rhetorical stereotype for the presentation of specific information. Its form follows pretty well the description given of the second type by Sanders. I call this form the Disclosure. Four elements constitute the Disclosure. They are:
   1) θέλω,
   2) *noetic verb* in the infinitive,
   3) person addressed,
   4) information.
Mullins notes that there is the option of adding a vocative of address. "Thus the elements which constitute the Disclosure follow a fairly regular but not a rigid order in the New Testament. It is an order different from that usually occurring in the epistolary papyri, but found in one, P. Oslo. 50" (ibid., 49).

8. Sanders, "Transition," 349.

9. Compare the discussion by Sanders of the use of περί versus ἐπί to introduce the topic of an injunction (ibid., 350), or the use of λέγω as possibly being an acceptable substitute for "the more prevalent παρακαλῶ" (ibid., 353). The same holds true with his discussion of οἴδατε in 1 Thess 2:1 (ibid., 356): "Though the form here is not as precise as in some

There is an important difference between using "I say to you" in a context where it is semantically required to understand what follows and using the same collocation in a context where it is not semantically required. It is the redundant usage that makes the metacomment stand out, not just the collocation itself as a formula.[10] Furthermore, it is not just one specific collocation of words that can function as a metacomment. Anything that satisfies the requirements of a metacomment can serve as one. It is not the semantic meaning of the collocation that makes a metacomment; it is a pragmatic effect of using the unnecessary collocation in a specific context.

Conversely, there is evidence that others found certain collocations accomplishing a similar form-critical function, collocations that had not been properly classified as forms.[11] Although these collocations may be legitimate ancient epistolary forms, the fact that they are used much more broadly in

---

other places, still all the necessary elements are present to justify placing this clause among these opening formulae: the use of αὐτοὶ οἴδατε easily replaces the more prevalent οὐ θέλω ἀγνοεῖν; and the characteristic ὑμᾶς is, of course, out of place with the use of a verb in the second person."

10. Mullins, a form critic who sought to rein in what he considered misapplication of forms, makes the point that not every occurrence of a collocation makes it a form, though he does not specify criteria for making this important distinction. He states, "In order to have clean distinctions, I feel we must restrict forms to pure types. Thus, 2 Cor. xii 8 would not properly be classed as a Petition. And nothing is to be gained by calling it a pseudo-Petition or a quasi-Petition. We may better say simply that sometimes phrases which resemble the form stand in lieu of a form, or that they serve the formal operation of a form" ("Disclosure," 45). This illustrates the importance of distinguishing when something is semantically required from when it is not; the former would not be a metacomment, whereas the latter would be because it could be removed without changing the propositional content. The fact that it is metadiscourse is what achieves the effect; it is not an inherent meaning of the phrase.

11. Sanders makes reference in a footnote that the "word λέγω sometimes is used in place of the more prevalent παρακαλῶ" ("Transition," 353), although he does not apply this claim outside the Pauline corpus. This raises the question of whether this usage is something more widespread than an epistolary form, since they are found in the Gospels as well. Similarly, Longenecker comments, "In most of Paul's letters there is an εὐχαριστῶ ('I am thankful')—παρακαλῶ ('I exhort') structure. In Galatians, however, the verbs θαυμάζω ('I am amazed/astonished') and δέομαι ('I plead') appear and serve a similar function" (Richard N. Longenecker, *Galatians* [WBC 41; Dallas: Word, 1990], 184). Bruce observes that a disclosure formula is found in 1 Thess 2:1, "although here nothing is being disclosed (as in 4:13); an appeal is rather being made to what the Thessalonians already know (as in 1:5)" (F. F. Bruce, *1 and 2 Thessalonians* [WBC 45; Dallas: Word, 1982], 24). Bauckham notes regarding Jude 5, "'I wish to *remind* you that …' is superficially an example of conventional polite style (cf. Rom 15:14–15; 2 Pet 1:12; 1 Clem 53:1) but also makes a serious point" (Richard J. Bauckham, *Jude, 2 Peter* [WBC 50; Dallas: Word, 2002], 48).

ancient Greek discourse than just in letters (as well as in other languages both ancient and modern) calls for a more unified definition and description.

5.2   Discourse Explanation

There has been a growing interest among linguists in studying discourse-related phenomenon loosely referred to as *metadiscourse*. Mao defines metadiscourse as "various kinds of linguistic tokens that an author employs in her text to guide or direct her reader as to how to understand her, her text, and her stance toward it."[12] He argues that metadiscourse plays an integral role in the overall rhetorical shaping of texts.[13] Similar claims have been made within biblical studies, such as this one by Jervis:

> An author's purpose is wedded to the function the communication is meant to perform, and since function is tied closely to the formal features of the text, it is from the formal features that we may find indications of a text's communicative function and thereby of the purpose of the author.[14]

My purpose is to focus on one specific aspect of metadiscourse that I refer to as *metacomment*.[15] Mao's definition makes some significant points. First, metadiscourse guides or directs the reader, which means that it is an indicator of the author's intent. Second, it helps us to understand not only the text, but also the writer's stance toward it. This also speaks to authorial intent. Although metacomments might indeed have a formulaic quality, they also represent the writer's choice to mark the presence of some feature that might otherwise have been overlooked. The claims that I make about their discourse function are consistent with those found within NT studies.

---

12. Luming R. Mao, "I Conclude Not: Toward a Pragmatic Account of Metadiscourse," *RR* 11 (1993): 265.

13. Carl Conrad (in personal correspondence) makes the important point that devices such as metacomments can make just as big an impact on a discourse that is heard as on one that is read because they "are even more standard in speech than they are in ordinary writing." My focus on written discourse should not be understood to negate the comparable function of these devices in oral forms of communication.

14. L. Ann Jervis, *The Purpose of Romans: A Comparative Letter Structure Investigation* (JSNTSup 55; Sheffield: JSOT, 1991), 30, cited in Arthur G. Patzia, review of L. Ann Jervis, *The Purpose of Romans: A Comparative Letter Structure Investigation*, JBL 111 (1992): 729–30.

15. Eric P. Kumpf classifies metacommentary under the heading of "interpersonal" metadiscourse ("Visual Metadiscourse: Designing the Considerate Text," *TCQ* 9, no. 4 [2000]: 403).

Here is a sampling of the claims that NT commentators assign to the function of what I am referring to as metacomments:

- George describes "I want you to know" and its negative counterpart "I do not wish you to be ignorant" as "Paul's way of saying, 'I want to make this perfectly clear.' "[16]
- Longenecker claims that "Paul also uses [a disclosure formula] to introduce somewhat formal and solemn assertions (cf. 1 Cor 12:3; 15:1; 2 Cor 8:1)." [17]
- Burton comments on the significance of the proposition introduced by the disclosure formula of Gal 1:11, "The assertion that follows is in effect the proposition to the proving of which the whole argument of 1:13–2:21 is directed.[18]
- Longenecker notes that clusters of disclosure formulas with vocatives of address tend to signal breaks or turning points in the development of a writer's argument.[19]
- Jewett states that a disclosure formula "prepares the audience for something significant," and that "the formulation θέλω/θέλομεν ὑμᾶς ἀγνοεῖν, ἀδελφοί is uniquely Pauline … and always introduces a point of great importance."[20]
- Cranfield describes the disclosure formula in Rom 11:25 as "a formula which Paul uses when he wishes to bring home to his

---

16. Timothy George, *Galatians* (NAC 30; Nashville: Broadman & Holman, 2001), 107–8.

17. Longenecker, *Galatians*, 22.

18. Ernest De Witt Burton, *A Critical and Exegetical Commentary on the Epistle to the Galatians* (ICC; New York: Charles Scribner's Sons, 1920), 35.

19. Longenecker, *Galatians*, cviii. Longenecker (ibid., 11) later states, "Even the various stages within the development of Paul's rebuke section in Galatians are fairly well set off by certain rather conventional epistolary expressions, which tend to be grouped at the start of each new subsection in the argument or to bring matters to a close. For example, the rebuke formula of 1:6 (θαυμάζω ὅτι, 'I am astonished that') and the reminder of past teaching at 1:9 (ὡς προειρήκαμεν καὶ ἄρτι πάλιν λέγω, 'as we have said before, so now I say again') serve as the epistolary pegs for 1:6–10. Likewise, the disclosure formulae of 1:11 (γνωρίζω δὲ ὑμῖν, 'I want you to know') and 1:13 (ἠκούσατε γὰρ, 'for you have heard') serve as the beginning points for their respective sections, 1:11–12 and 1:13–2:21—with these two subsections being closely related, the first as the thesis for what immediately follows and the second as an autobiographical elaboration in support of that thesis.… Also to be observed is the fact that the disclosure formula of 3:7 (γινώσκετε ἄρα ὅτι, 'you know, then, that'), which draws a conclusion from the quotation of Gen 15:6 in 3:6, provides a transition to the extended argument from Scripture in 3:6–4:10."

20. Jewett, *Romans*, 695, 697.

readers with emphasis something which he regards as of special importance."[21]

- Reed observes that the three most commonly identified formulas primarily serve the same task of disclosing information.[22]

These comments regarding the discourse function of forms like disclosure formulas are the exception rather than the norm. Biblical scholars are more generally interested in their role as structural markers of the various form-critical sections of the epistle than in their rhetorical function to highlight the proposition that they introduce.

The comments above are consistent with what I am claiming to be a more broadly occurring phenomenon than an epistolary form. A writer who desires to attract extra attention to a proposition has the choice to suspend the discourse in order to comment on what is to follow. The writer pauses in what is being said and talks about what is going to be said. Though there is overlap between what I describe as metacomments and what form-critics classify as disclosure, request, introduction, and petition formulas, they cannot be equated, based on the latter's failure to distinguish between semantic meaning and pragmatic effect.[23]

5.3   Application

Metacomments are often used to create a mitigated form of a command, one that makes the point less directly than does an imperative verb form.[24] Recall that there are two identifying criteria:

---

21. C. E. B. Cranfield, *A Critical and Exegetical Commentary on the Epistle to the Romans* (ICC; Edinburgh: T & T Clark, 1979), 573.

22. Jeffrey T. Reed, *A Discourse Analysis of Philippians: Method and Rhetoric in the Debate over Literary Integrity* (JSNTSup 136; Sheffield: Sheffield Academic, 1997), 211.

23. Longenecker (*Galatians*, 26) identifies ἠκούσατε ("you have heard") in Gal 1:13 as a disclosure formula, which it may well be. It indeed orients the reader to the context that follows. However, it does not meet our standard of being redundant. All of v. 13a introduces a new topic that would not have been explicitly identified otherwise. Further research into metacommentary is needed to better understand the relation of disclosure formulas and metacomments. They are distinct concepts even though there is overlap. The same holds true for the claim by Sanders ("Transition," 353) regarding Phil 4:2 being a "personal petition" form.

24. Levinsohn, referring to metacomments as a kind of "orienter," states, "Orienters often introduce exhortations in Greek. The exhortations themselves are most often expressed in infinitival clauses, though they may be encoded as imperatives ... or final clauses. Some orienters act as mitigating expressions. Others provide motivation for obey-

- the suspension of what was being said in order to comment on what is about to be said;
- the ability to remove the metacomment without substantially changing the propositional content.

The first few examples will illustrate this usage to mitigate or soften an exhortation. This will be followed by examples illustrating the use of metacomments to strengthen the force of a command. Let's take a look at Rom 12:1 in closer detail, repeated from above.

Example 59 :: Romans 12:1

⟨◫Παρακαλῶ οὖν ὑμᾶς,◫⟩ ἀδελφοί, διὰ τῶν οἰκτιρμῶν τοῦ θεοῦ παραστῆσαι τὰ σώματα ὑμῶν θυσίαν ζῶσαν ἁγίαν εὐάρεστον τῷ θεῷ, τὴν λογικὴν λατρείαν ὑμῶν·

Therefore ⟨◫I exhort you,◫⟩ brothers, through the mercies of God, to present your bodies as a living sacrifice, holy and pleasing to God, which is your reasonable service.

This verse introduces an inferential principle drawn from the preceding discourse, essentially describing what the audience ought to do in response to what precedes. Paul has suspended his discourse in order to exhort the Romans to do something: present their bodies as living sacrifices. Rather than using the metacomment, Paul could have more easily commanded them, "Present your bodies…," using an imperative or hortatory subjunctive.[25] The pragmatic effect of the metacomment in this context is to highlight the proposition that it introduces. It also serves to mitigate or lessen the severity of the exhortation.[26]

Although form critics have noted that epistolary formulas occur at major seams of a text (e.g., between Rom 9–11 and 12–15), they are not found in such contexts only. Consider the impact that the metacomment a few verses later in v. 3 has on the proposition that follows.

---

ing the exhortations and may even highlight them" (Stephen H. Levinsohn, *Self-instruction Materials on Non-narrative Discourse Analysis* [Dallas: SIL International, 2008], 84).

25. The prepositional phrase διὰ τῶν οἰκτιρμῶν τοῦ θεοῦ ("through the mercies of God") could be construed either as part of the metacomment (i.e., describing the basis on which Paul makes his exhortation) or as a spatial frame of reference for the proposition that it introduces (see §10.3). For this reason, it has been excluded from the metacomment annotation. The analysis of the prepositional phrase does not affect the reading of παρακαλῶ ὑμᾶς as a metacomment in any case.

26. See Levinsohn, *Non-Narrative Discourse Analysis*, 79–89.

Example 60 :: Romans 12:3

⟨🗗Λέγω γὰρ διὰ τῆς χάριτος τῆς δοθείσης μοι παντὶ τῷ ὄντι ἐν ὑμῖν🗗⟩ μὴ ὑπερφρονεῖν παρ' ὃ δεῖ φρονεῖν ἀλλὰ φρονεῖν εἰς τὸ σωφρονεῖν, ἑκάστῳ ὡς ὁ θεὸς ἐμέρισεν μέτρον πίστεως.	⟨🗗For by the grace given to me I say to everyone who is among you🗗⟩ not to think more highly of yourself than what one ought to think, but to think sensibly, as God has apportioned a measure of faith to each one.

Paul has begun the chapter by urging the readers to present themselves as living sacrifices, followed by a point/counterpoint set of commands in v. 2 (i.e., not to be conformed to this age, but [ἀλλά] to be transformed by the renewing of their minds). Verse 3 is introduced by γάρ, indicating that what follows is intended to strengthen or support what precedes. Rather than signaling a significant break in the discourse, the metacomment of v. 3 functions to highlight the complex exhortation that it introduces. Just as Paul bases his appeal of v. 1 on the mercies of God (rather than on his own authority or something else), he makes a comparable appeal here based upon the grace that he has received.

Paul more easily could have commanded them, "Do not think more highly of yourselves…, but rather have sound judgment…." This command could have been simplified even more by omitting the negative counterpoint. In the formulation that Paul actually uses, the metacomments in v. 1 and v. 3 have the effect of highlighting the propositions that they introduce and mitigating the harshness that a simple imperative would have conveyed. The combination of metacomment with basis for the command introduced by διά likely carries more rhetorical force than a simple imperative. At the same time, the combination avoids any sense of harshness or condescension. He makes a more powerful rhetorical impression even while using a mitigated grammatical form.

In contrast to the mitigating effect observed with the use of metacomments in Rom 12:1, 3, the usage in Gal 1:9 has the opposite effect. Instead of toning down the harshness, the metacomment has the effect of intensifying it. Note that the main exhortation is a third-person imperative, not an infinitival form that is dependent upon the metacomment.

Example 61 :: Galatians 1:9

> [6] I am astonished that you are so quickly deserting him who called you in the grace of Christ and are turning to a different gospel— [7] not that there is another one, but there are some who trouble you and want to

distort the gospel of Christ. [8] But even if we or an angel from heaven should preach to you a gospel contrary to the one we preached to you, let him be accursed.

[9] (⌑ὡς προειρήκαμεν καὶ ἄρτι πάλιν λέγω·⌑) εἴ τις ὑμᾶς εὐαγγελίζεται παρ' ὃ παρελάβετε, ἀνάθεμα ἔστω.	[9] (⌑As we said before, so now I say again,⌑) if anyone is proclaiming a gospel to you contrary to what you have received, let him be accursed! (ESV)

Paul wastes no time in getting to his main point in Galatians, making it in vv. 6–8. He utilizes a complex point/counterpoint set (see chapter 4) to state the key idea. Rather than deserting the gospel, they should be holding fast to what Paul has imparted to them. Verse 9 is essentially a repetition of the content of v. 8 and is introduced by a metacomment. Rather than a simple "I say to you" or "I want you to know," the metacomment of v. 9 is much more impassioned. I liken it to saying in English, "I am going to speak slowly and use small words." The metacomment introduces something that should be patently obvious. The main verb following the metacomment is an imperative, and it has the opposite effect of that seen in Rom 12:1. Rather than mitigating the exhortation, the metacomment + imperative has the effect of making the exhortation more potent.

The metacomment lets the reader know that Paul is almost condescendingly repeating what should have been understood without being said. This view fits with his statements in v. 8 that no matter who might try to persuade them otherwise, they should not forsake the gospel that was delivered to them. Notice that the entire metacomment could be removed without affecting the propositional content of v. 9 (i.e., "If anyone should preach to you a gospel …") Paul suspends what he is saying and comments on what he is going to say. Just comparing v. 8 to v. 9 makes it clear that he is repeating what he has already told them. There is no need to overtly state it unless there is some meaning behind the choice to do this.

So far, we have looked at metacomments used with exhortations, both to strengthen them and to mitigate them. They are also used to highlight a new topic at a boundary in the discourse, as illustrated in Gal 1:11. The metacomment enables Paul to highlight the introduction of his topic (the gospel that he has proclaimed) and make a comment about it (this gospel is not from a human source).

Example 62 :: Galatians 1:11

| ⟨ᗡΓνωρίζω γὰρ ὑμῖν,ᗡ⟩ ἀδελφοί, τὸ εὐαγγέλιον τὸ εὐαγγελισθὲν ὑπ' ἐμοῦ ὅτι οὐκ ἔστιν κατὰ ἄνθρωπον· | For ⟨ᗡI make known to you,ᗡ⟩ brothers, the gospel that has been proclaimed by me, that it is not of human origin. |

Paul could have communicated the same content without the metacomment, but it would not have attracted attention to the new topic. In other words, simply stating "The gospel that I proclaimed is not of human origin" conveys the same idea, but without the attaching the same import to it. The metacomment is redundant; the Galatians knew that Paul was the one who had proclaimed the gospel. Making a redundant comment in this context has the effect of suspending the flow of the discourse and highlighting what comes ahead. The highlighting in this case draws attention to a significant transition in the discourse. If the information had not been redundant, it would not have had this effect.

Forward-pointing devices like metacomments are often placed at discourse boundaries in order to help the reader properly track where the writer is going (as illustrated in Rom 12:1 above). The same content could be communicated without the device, but the reader might miss the transition. They function something like speed bumps to "slow" the reader and attract his or her attention. Use of these devices at junctures and transitions illustrates the care that the biblical writers took to ensure their intended message would be clearly tracked and understood.

This next example, from James, illustrates how metacomments are used to stop the discourse and to comment on what follows, highlighting the proposition that it precedes.[27]

Example 63 :: James 1:16–17

| [16] ⟨ᗡΜὴ πλανᾶσθε,ᗡ⟩ ἀδελφοί μου ἀγαπητοί. [17] πᾶσα δόσις ἀγαθὴ καὶ πᾶν δώρημα τέλειον | [16] ⟨ᗡDo not be deceived,ᗡ⟩ my dear brothers. [17] Every good gift and every perfect gift is from |

---

27. Ropes comments that μὴ πλανᾶσθε is "used to introduce a pointed utterance … as in 1 Cor. 6:9, 15:33, Gal. 6:7" (James Hardy Ropes, *A Critical and Exegetical Commentary on the Epistle of St. James* [ICC; Edinburgh: T & T Clark, 1916], 158); Moo remarks that James "does not want his readers to make any mistake about what he is about to say about God as the source of all good gifts" (Douglas J. Moo, *The Letter of James* [PNTC; Grand Rapids: Eerdmans, 2000], 76).

ἄνωθέν ἐστιν καταβαῖνον ἀπὸ τοῦ   above, coming down from the
πατρὸς τῶν φώτων, παρ᾽ ᾧ οὐκ ἔνι   Father of lights, with whom there
παραλλαγὴ ἢ τροπῆς ἀποσκίασμα.   is no variation or shadow of
change.

Dibelius and Greeven note that the same formula is used to introduce another significant maxim in 1 Cor 15:33: "Do not be deceived! Bad company corrupts good morals."[28] The principle that "every good gift comes down from above" provides a corollary to what was claimed in vv. 13–15, that God does not tempt and is not tempted. Verse 16 provides an important corrective to close out this section; introducing it with a metacomment ensures that the reader assigns the same importance to it as the writer does. Verse 16 does not introduce a new unit, but highlights the principle that concludes the unit of vv. 13–18.

So far, all the examples considered have come from the epistolary literature. Nearly half of the metacomments in the NT are found in the Gospels and Acts;[29] only one of them is found outside of reported speeches. In the midst of Jesus' description of the temple's future destruction in Mark 13 there is a metacomment inserted that addresses the reader rather than the hearer. Interestingly, there are no textual variants attesting the exclusion of the metacomment in NA[27].

Example 64 :: Mark 13:14

Ὅταν δὲ ἴδητε τὸ βδέλυγμα τῆς   "But when you see the abomina-
ἐρημώσεως ἑστηκότα ὅπου οὐ δεῖ,   tion of desolation standing where
‹🔲 ὁ ἀναγινώσκων νοείτω,🔲› τότε   it should not be" ‹🔲(let the one
οἱ ἐν τῇ Ἰουδαίᾳ φευγέτωσαν εἰς   who reads understand),🔲› "then
τὰ ὄρη,   those in Judea must flee to the
mountains!"

The pragmatic effect of inserting the metacomment here is to create a dramatic pause by addressing the reader directly regarding the apocalyptic events being described. The LEB translates the metacomment as a parenthetical insertion. It is placed just before the instructions regarding how to respond when

---

28. Martin Dibelius and Heinrich Greeven, *James: A Commentary on the Epistle of James* (Hermeneia; Philadelphia: Fortress, 1976), 100.

29. Based on the current *LDGNT* analysis, there are 174 metacomments in the Epistles and Revelation versus 165 in the Gospels and Acts.

the antichrist desecrates the holy of holies. Note also that the temporal frame (see §10.2) itself is interrupted: "*when* this event happens..., *then* flee to the mountains." Separating the time when something will happen from what is to be done at that time effectively builds the suspense. The interruption is such that the temporal information is reiterated using τότε, thereby creating a left-dislocation (see chapter 14). The entire proposition could have more simply been stated, "Flee to the mountains when you see the abomination that causes desolation standing where he ought not be." Predicating the time and then delaying the disclosure of what should happen then has a cumulative effect of significantly highlighting what follows. The break from addressing the hearer to addressing the reader intensifies this.

Jesus concludes the teaching in Mark 13 with one main exhortation in v. 37 to be alert, introduced with a metacomment.[30] In v. 33, he gives two commands, "Watch out" and "Be alert," followed by the parable of the master who goes away on a journey. Verse 37 provides the summary conclusion for both the parable and the chapter.

Example 65 :: Mark 13:37

[33] "Watch out! Be alert, because you do not know when the time is! [34] It is like a man away on a journey, who left his house and gave his slaves authority—to each one his work—and to the doorkeeper he gave orders that he should be on the alert. [35] Therefore be on the alert, for you do not know when the master of the house is coming—whether in the evening, or at midnight, or when the rooster crows, or early in the morning— [36] lest he arrive suddenly and find you sleeping."

[37] ⟨❑ὃ δὲ ὑμῖν λέγω πᾶσιν λέγω,❑⟩ γρηγορεῖτε.	[37] "And ⟨❑what I say to you, I say to everyone:❑⟩ Be on the alert!"

The exhortation to be alert summarizes how Jesus wants people to respond to the coming doom. He has already stated this in v. 33 and then illustrated it in a parable. He could have more easily skipped the repetition of γρηγορεῖτε in v. 37, or repeated it alone without the metacomment: "Be on the alert!" The metacomment creates a break in the flow of the discourse just before something significant. The comment also redirects what Jesus is saying to others besides his disciples. It is doubtful that the hearers were wondering to whom

---

30. Edwards states, "'Watch!' is the final and most important word of the Olivet discourse. The point of Mark 13 is not so much to inform as to admonish; not to provide knowledge of arcane matters but to instill obedience in believers" (James R. Edwards, *The Gospel According to Mark* [PNTC; Grand Rapids: Eerdmans, 2002], 409).

this teaching would have applied, especially since no one had been excluded previously in the discourse. The plural command anticipates broad application.

Commentators agree that the conclusion of v. 37 is very emphatic, but they do so without discussing the pragmatic factors that lead them to this conclusion, such as the inclusion of a metacomment. Simple repetition of the imperative alone would not have brought about this effect.

Luke 4 recounts Jesus identifying himself as the one fulfilling the prophecy from Isa 61. He made this claim in the synagogue of his hometown, Nazareth. However, the people responded by questioning Jesus' claim, leading him to make the statement of v. 24, which references the OT stories about Elijah.

Example 66 :: Luke 4:24–25

²⁴ εἶπεν δέ· ἀμὴν ‹◻λέγω ὑμῖν◻› ὅτι οὐδεὶς προφήτης δεκτός ἐστιν ἐν τῇ πατρίδι αὐτοῦ.

²⁴ And he said, "Truly ‹◻I say to you◻› that no prophet is acceptable in his own hometown.

²⁵ ‹◻ἐπ' ἀληθείας δὲ λέγω ὑμῖν,◻› πολλαὶ χῆραι ἦσαν ἐν ταῖς ἡμέραις Ἠλίου ἐν τῷ Ἰσραήλ, ὅτε ἐκλείσθη ὁ οὐρανὸς ἐπὶ ἔτη τρία καὶ μῆνας ἕξ, ὡς ἐγένετο λιμὸς μέγας ἐπὶ πᾶσαν τὴν γῆν,

²⁵ But ‹◻in truth I say to you,◻› there were many widows in Israel in the days of Elijah, when the sky was shut for three years and six months while a great famine took place over all the land."

The combined use of the attention-getter ἀμήν and the metacomment in v. 24 has the effect of attracting extra attention to the proposition introduced in the subordinate clause. It is not an exhortation or prohibition, but a principle that explains the people's difficulty in accepting his testimony. He follows this proverbial statement about the lot of a prophet by relating it to story of Elijah. Here too he uses a metacomment to attract extra attention to the introduction of the illustration. The phrase ἐπ' ἀληθείας most likely serves a comparable attention-getting role as ἀμήν,[31] evincing an effort to mark the significance of vv. 25–27 as much as the proverb of v. 24.

In Matt 15, Jesus responds to a question from the Pharisees and scribes regarding why his disciples do not wash their hands when they eat bread.

---

31. Marshall states, "ἐπ' ἀληθείας (20:21; 22:59; Acts 4:27; 10:34; Mk. 12:14, 32) may here be a substitute for an original ἀμήν, laying stress on the following saying. (If so, this would confirm the genuineness of the saying, but also suggest that originally it did not follow v. 24.)" (I. Howard Marshall, *The Gospel of Luke: A Commentary on the Greek Text* [NIGTC; Grand Rapids: Eerdmans, 1978], 189).

Jesus addresses the broader problems associated with the Pharisaic laws in vv. 3–9 before returning to the specific issue of washing in v. 10. His response is in the form of a complex principle consisting of a point/counterpoint set and is introduced with a metacomment.

Example 67 :: Matthew 15:10–11

[10] καὶ προσκαλεσάμενος τὸν ὄχλον εἶπεν αὐτοῖς· ⟨🖵ἀκούετε καὶ συνίετε·🖵⟩	[10] And summoning the crowd, he said to them, ⟨🖵"Hear and understand:🖵⟩
[11] ⟨✗οὐ τὸ εἰσερχόμενον εἰς τὸ στόμα κοινοῖ τὸν ἄνθρωπον,✗⟩ ἀλλὰ ⟨✓τὸ ἐκπορευόμενον ἐκ τοῦ στόματος τοῦτο κοινοῖ τὸν ἄνθρωπον.✓⟩	[11] ⟨✗It is not what goes into the mouth that defiles a person,✗⟩ but ⟨✓what comes out of the mouth— this defiles a person."✓⟩

The commands to hear and understand are not needed for semantic reasons. It is comparable to someone in English saying, "Listen up!" or "Pay attention!" The metacomment ensures that the gravity of what follows is not missed. Jesus reinforces the principle by using a point/counterpoint set to state it both positively and negatively for clarity and rhetorical impact (see chapter 4).

One final group of examples is taken from Matthew, where "to him who has ears, let him hear" is used to punctuate the conclusion of a discourse rather than the introduction.

Example 68 :: Matthew 11:14–15

[14] καὶ εἰ θέλετε δέξασθαι, αὐτός ἐστιν Ἠλίας ὁ μέλλων ἔρχεσθαι. [15] ⟨🖵ὁ ἔχων ὦτα ἀκουέτω.🖵⟩	[14] "and if you are willing to accept it, he is Elijah, the one who is going to come. [15] ⟨🖵The one who has ears, let him hear!"🖵⟩

Note that asyndeton is used to connect v. 15 to what precedes, indicating that there is no clear guidance as to whether this relates to what precedes or whether it begins a new, unrelated section. However, the use of δέ in v. 16 provides some guidance, indicating that what follows is a new development built upon the preceding discourse. Since it cannot just be building upon the content of v. 15, it must be building upon the preceding pericope.[32] This implies

---

32. Hagner comments, "The closing exhortation points to the unusual and difficult

that the metacomment relates to what precedes, signaling the conclusion of the section and adding some solemnity to the final proposition—that is, the statement in v. 14 that John the Baptist is the Elijah who was expected to come.

This same idiom is used twice more as a metacomment in Matt 13 to punctuate the close of a section. In the next example, it concludes the parable of the sower, marking the transition to the disciples asking why Jesus teaches in parables.

Example 69 :: Matthew 13:8–9

[8] ἄλλα δὲ ἔπεσεν ἐπὶ τὴν γῆν τὴν καλὴν καὶ ἐδίδου καρπόν, ὃ μὲν ἑκατόν, ὃ δὲ ἑξήκοντα, ὃ δὲ τριάκοντα. [9] ⟨🖰ὁ ἔχων ὦτα ἀκουέτω.🖰⟩	[8] "But other seed fell on the good soil and produced grain, this one a hundred times as much and this one sixty and this one thirty. [9] ⟨🖰The one who has ears, let him hear!"🖰⟩

A bit later in the same chapter, the metacomment marks the conclusion of the explanation of the parable of the tares, creating a clear division between this parable and the parable of the hidden treasure, which immediately follows.

Example 70 :: Matthew 13:43

τότε οἱ δίκαιοι ἐκλάμψουσιν ὡς ὁ ἥλιος ἐν τῇ βασιλείᾳ τοῦ πατρὸς αὐτῶν. ⟨🖰ὁ ἔχων ὦτα ἀκουέτω.🖰⟩	"Then the righteous will shine like the sun in the kingdom of their Father. ⟨🖰The one who has ears, let him hear!"🖰⟩

Just as in the other examples, it punctuates the concluding proposition of the preceding discourse.

---

character of the preceding section. The formula, or one very similar to it, is often used in contexts where difficult content is present (e.g., 13:9, 43; Mark 4:9, 23; Luke 8:8; 14:35; cf. Rev 2:7, 11, 17, etc.)" (Donald A. Hagner, *Matthew 1–13* [WBC 33A; Dallas: Word, 1993], 308). Davies and Allison similarly comment, "It typically functions as a hermeneutical warning and/or to mark the conclusion of a paragraph or other literary unit" (W. D. Davies and Dale C. Allison, *A Critical and Exegetical Commentary on the Gospel According to Saint Matthew*, vol. 2 [ICC; Edinburgh: T & T Clark, 2004], 259).

5.4   Forward-Pointing Devices Associated with Metacomments

So far, I have discussed only metacomments on their own, but many of the examples have also included either attention-getters (such as ἀμήν ["truly"] and ἐπ᾽ ἀληθείας ["in truth"] in example 66) or redundant forms of address (such as ἀδελφοί ["brothers"] in examples 58, 62, 63). Both of these devices are annotated in the *LDGNT* and often co-occur with metacomments. This section provides a brief introduction to each of these devices along with a few illustrations where they occur by themselves.

5.4.1   Redundant Vocatives as Forward-Pointing Devices

Vocatives and nominatives of address generally are used to identify the "addressee," the one to whom the writer or speaker is addressing the communication. They typically are used either to identify the intended audience or to signal a switch to a new addressee. The vocatives or nominatives of address are indicated by the ⚓ symbol. In Eph 6, the forms of address are needed to clearly identify Paul's intended audiences as he moves from topic to topic.

Example 71 :: Ephesians 6:1, 4–5

¹ ‹⚓Τὰ τέκνα,⚓› ὑπακούετε τοῖς γονεῦσιν ὑμῶν [ἐν κυρίῳ]· τοῦτο γάρ ἐστιν δίκαιον.

¹ ‹⚓Children,⚓› obey your parents in the Lord, for this is right.

⁴ Καὶ ‹⚓οἱ πατέρες,⚓› μὴ παροργίζετε τὰ τέκνα ὑμῶν ἀλλὰ ἐκτρέφετε αὐτὰ ἐν παιδείᾳ καὶ νουθεσίᾳ κυρίου.

⁴ And ‹⚓fathers,⚓› do not make your children angry, but bring them up in the discipline and instruction of the Lord.

⁵ ‹⚓Οἱ δοῦλοι,⚓› ὑπακούετε τοῖς κατὰ σάρκα κυρίοις μετὰ φόβου καὶ τρόμου ἐν ἁπλότητι τῆς καρδίας ὑμῶν ὡς τῷ Χριστῷ....

⁵ ‹⚓Slaves,⚓› obey your earthly masters with fear and trembling, in the sincerity of your heart, as to Christ....

Paul is addressing different groups of listeners, and the forms of address are used to signal these switches and to alert a new group of addressees that what follows is directed to them. However, I have demonstrated elsewhere that this explanation can only account for 31 percent of the usage found in the NT Epistles.[33] One portion of the remaining data can be accounted for

---

33. See Steven E. Runge and Sean Boisen, "'So, Brothers': Pauline Use of the Vocative"

as "thematic address" (see chapter 17). The remaining redundant references normally are attributed to establishing warm ties with the readers through the use of familial terms such as "brothers." Although this might explain the usage of this term, it does little to explain the syntax of vocatives and nominatives of address. Why do they sometimes come at the beginning of a clause, sometimes in the middle, and sometimes at the end? Is it stylistic variation?

One of the core presuppositions of my approach to discourse grammar is that "choice implies meaning." The redundant use of generic vocatives such as "brothers" provides a great example of the explanatory power of this principle. If the writer made the choice to include some unnecessary element and chose where to put it in the clause, then there is bound to be some meaning associated with it. These redundant terms of address operate just like the other forward-pointing devices that we have looked at. They prototypically create a break in the discourse just before something surprising or important. I will present some examples of redundant vocatives functioning without other forward-pointing devices and then return to their use with metacomments.

Example 72 :: 1 Corinthians 7:24

²³ You were bought at a price; do not become slaves of men.

²⁴ ἕκαστος ἐν ᾧ ἐκλήθη, ⟨☛ἀδελφοί,☚⟩ ἐν τούτῳ μενέτω παρὰ θεῷ.

²⁴ Each one in the situation in which he was called, ⟨☛brothers☚⟩—in this he should remain with God.

Paul tells the Corinthians in v. 23 that they were bought with a price and should not become slaves of human masters. Verse 24 uses two framing devices to establish specific bits of information in order to be able to strongly make his point. The subject ἕκαστος ("each") provides a topical frame of reference (see chapter 10) for the proposition; what follows applies to each of them. A second frame of reference describes a situation, established through the use of a left-dislocation or *pendens* construction (see chapter 14). So each of them are to do something regarding the situation they are in; the only question is what that something is.

Although the insertion of "brothers" here may indeed create warm, fuzzy feelings, its placement also has the effect of delaying the disclosure of what they must do. It is similar to how the metacomment "I want you to know" has

(paper presented at the annual meeting of the Society of Biblical Literature, San Diego, Calif., 17–20 November 2007).

the effect of delaying learning exactly what it is that the author wants them to know.[34] The usage and placement of "brothers" in this context has a specific effect, interrupting the flow of the discourse to build up anticipation. Paul wants them to remain where they are as opposed to changing to some other situation, such as slavery.

In the context preceding example 73, Paul provided an illustration of how death sets a limitation on the enforcement of law, noting the meaningful difference between a woman marrying another man while her husband is alive versus doing so after he is dead.

Example 73 :: Romans 7:4

ὥστε, ⟨☛ἀδελφοί μου,☚⟩ καὶ ὑμεῖς ἐθανατώθητε τῷ νόμῳ διὰ τοῦ σώματος τοῦ Χριστοῦ, εἰς τὸ γενέσθαι ὑμᾶς ἑτέρῳ, τῷ ἐκ νεκρῶν ἐγερθέντι, ἵνα καρποφορήσωμεν τῷ θεῷ.	So then, ⟨☛my brothers,☚⟩ you also were brought to death with respect to the law through the body of Christ, so that you may belong to another, to the one who was raised from the dead, in order that we may bear fruit for God.

Paul's primary interest is not in marriage but rather in sin. He is also not as interested in how this principle of death applies to the wife as he is in how it applies to us. In v. 4, Paul switches from his illustration to the point that he draws from it, hence the presence of ὥστε. The use of the redundant vocative helps to signal the transition by creating a break. He could have accomplished this without a signal, but doing so would have increased the likelihood of readers not properly following this transition. Right after the break, Paul uses an ascensive καί (see chapter 16) to strengthen the thematic connection back to the illustration, adding "you" to the wife; both are freed from the law because of death.[35]

---

34. For a description of how the quotative frame "says the Lord" in Acts 2:17 has the effect of delaying learning exactly what will "come about in that day," see Steven E. Runge, "Joel 3:1–5 in Acts 2:17–21: The Discourse and Text-Critical Implications of Quotation and Variation from the LXX," in *Exegetical Studies* (vol. 2 of *Early Christian Literature and Intertextuality*; ed. Craig A. Evans and Danny Zacharias; LNTS; New York: T & T Clark, 2009), 103–13. This kind of grammatical delay tactic is found in many languages besides Greek.

35. Note that τῷ νόμῳ clarifies what kind of death Paul is referring to, death from the standpoint of the law as opposed to physical death.

We find another redundant vocative at a similar transition in the discourse, but at the break between larger units of the text rather than within a unit.

Example 74 :: Romans 8:12

⁹ But you are not in the flesh but in the Spirit, if indeed the Spirit of God lives in you. But if anyone does not have the Spirit of Christ, this person does not belong to him. ¹⁰ But if Christ is in you, the body is dead because of sin, but the Spirit is life because of righteousness. ¹¹ And if the Spirit of the one who raised Jesus from the dead lives in you, the one who raised Christ from the dead will also make alive your mortal bodies through his Spirit who lives in you.

¹² Ἄρα οὖν, ⟨✒ἀδελφοί,✒⟩ ὀφειλέται ἐσμὲν οὐ τῇ σαρκὶ τοῦ κατὰ σάρκα ζῆν,	¹² So then, ⟨✒brothers,✒⟩ we are obligated not to the flesh, to live according to the flesh.

The content of v. 12 resumes the thought introduced in v. 9a and elaborated in vv. 9b–11, with the inferential particles ἄρα and οὖν corroborating the relation of v. 12 with what precedes. Interruptions in the discourse like those created by redundant forms of address always draw attention to something. It might be something important or surprising, it might be a discontinuity in the text such as the transition to a new point or topic. Adding forward-pointing devices like redundant forms of address helps ensure that the reader slows down and pays closer attention to such things.

In Gal 4, Paul compares the descendants of Sarah with those of Hagar as an illustration of what it means to be free. The transition from the illustration back to the point that he wants to make is marked by the development connective δέ, in combination with the discontinuities created by the topical frame ὑμεῖς and the redundant form of address ἀδελφοί.

Example 75 :: Galatians 4:28

Ὑμεῖς δέ, ⟨✒ἀδελφοί,✒⟩ κατὰ Ἰσαὰκ ἐπαγγελίας τέκνα ἐστέ.	But you, ⟨✒brothers,✒⟩ are children of the promise, just as Isaac.

Paul is not disambiguating whom he is addressing by using "brothers." The verb ἐστέ grammaticalizes the subject, so there is no need for the explicit pronoun ὑμεῖς. The form of address and what traditionally is called a "contrastive pronoun" mark a discontinuity in the text to help the reader make the transition from the illustration to the point associated with it. The discontinuity in the text would have existed by virtue of the content alone. The topical frame and redundant address create a speed bump to make sure that nothing is missed.

When redundant forms of address occur with metacomments, the address prototypically comes between the metacomment and the proposition that it introduces.[36] Even operating in tandem with the metacomment, redundant address has the same effect of creating some measure of suspense by delaying the introduction of the proposition that follows (see examples 59, 62, 63). This combination is found almost exclusively in the Epistles, whereas in narrative speeches metacomments combine with attention-getters to achieve a similar effect (see §5.4.2).

Consider the case of Phil 1:12 below. One of the main concerns that Paul addresses in this letter is the impact of his present situation in jail on the advancement of the gospel. Verse 12 fits the form-critical mold of a disclosure formula, but now we can more fully understand how this formula achieves the effects that have been attributed to it.

Example 76 :: Philippians 1:12

⟨❏Γινώσκειν δὲ ὑμᾶς βούλομαι,❏⟩ ⟨🖘ἀδελφοί,🖘⟩ ὅτι τὰ κατ᾽ ἐμὲ μᾶλλον εἰς προκοπὴν τοῦ εὐαγγελίου ἐλήλυθεν.…

Now ⟨❏I want you to know,❏⟩ ⟨🖘brothers,🖘⟩ that my circumstances have happened instead for the progress of the gospel.…

The readers would have expected that Paul wanted them to know all that he wrote; otherwise he would not have included it. As in the previous examples, the redundant address intervenes between the metacomment and what it introduces. In this case, it is the surprising claim that these seemingly negative things actually had a positive impact regarding the advancement of the gospel. This point is highly significant for understanding what follows, so it should be no surprise that Paul highlights it as he does.

---

36. Mullins states, "Usually the *vocative address* comes between the *noetic verb* and the *information*. Only two of the eight occurrences of the Disclosure in the New Testament lack the *vocative address*, but one which has it, 1 Cor. 12:1b, has the entire order of the elements scrambled and the *vocative address* comes between the *information* and θέλω" ("Disclosure," 48). Sanders ("Transition," 349–53) cites as examples Rom 11:25; 12:1; 15:30; 16:17; 1 Cor 1:10; 10:1; 11:3; 12:1–3; 15:1–3; 16:15; 2 Cor 2:8; 6:1; 10:1; 12:8; Phil 1:12; 4:2, 15; 2 Thess 2:1, 9; 3:2, 7; 4:10, 13; 5:1, 12; in the deuteropauline corpus, Eph 4:17; 5:5, 32; Col. 2:1–4; 2 Thess 3:7, 12; 1 Tim 2:1; 4:11; 5:7; 6:3, 13, 17; 2 Tim 3:1; 1 Pet 2:11; 5:1, 12; in the Apostolic Fathers, *2 Clem.* 14:2; Ign. *Eph.* 2:1; 3:2; Ign. *Trall.* 6:1; 12:2; Ign. *Rom.* 4:1; Ign. *Phld.* 8:2; Ign. *Pol.* 1:2; Pol. *Phil.* 9:1.

The redundant address need not come at the beginning or middle of a clause. It is observed at the end as well, of both clauses and sections of discourse.[37] We observe this in their placement even with metacomments; they may come at the end of the metacomment, or between a frame of reference and the predicate if they are in the middle of a metacomment. Regardless of their location, the function is the same: accentuating a break in the discourse by making it more pronounced.

5.4.2 Attention-Getters as Forward-Pointing Devices

There are a handful of Greek idioms that fulfill a comparable function to attention-getting words and phrases that we use in English (e.g., "hey," "oh," "wow," "all of a sudden"). These idioms let a listener know that what follows is surprising or important. Very often attention-getters are imperative verbs that have become fixed expressions that function more like interjections than verbs. Here are the most frequently occurring NT idioms that are used to attract the reader's attention:

- ἰδού, "behold" or "look"
- ἀμήν, "amen/truly"[38]
- ἀληθῶς/ἀληθείας, "truly/certainly"
- οὐαί ὑμῖν, "woe to you"
- ὃς ἔχει ὦτα ἀκούειν ἀκουέτω, "let whoever has ears to hear, hear"

Attention-getters are an optional element that could have been omitted without significantly altering the propositional content, just like the other

---

37. Examples of redundant address at the end of a clause are Acts 2:37; 27:25; 28:17; Rom 7:1; 1 Cor 14:26; 15:31; 16:15; Gal 5:13; 6:18; Phil 3:17; 2 Thess 2:1, 13; Phm 1:7; Heb 3:12; 10:19; Jas 2:14; 3:1; 4:11; Rev 18:4. Examples of redundant address in the midst of metacomments are Rom 15:14; 1 Cor 1:10, 11; 15:31; 2 Thess 3:6. In each case, the vocative is followed by a buildup of the metacomment. It occurs between a topical frame and the metacomment in 1 Cor 12:1; 1 Thess 4:1.

38. Nolland comments, "The presence here of ἀμήν, 'amen,' the only Hebrew word retained by Luke, signals the presence of teaching considered to be of special importance by Luke" (John Nolland, *Luke 1:1–9:20* [WBC 35A; Dallas: Word, 1989], 200). Marshall observes, "H. Schlier, TDNT I, 335–338, and J. Jeremias, *Abba*, 145–152 (*The Prayers of Jesus*, London, 1967, 112–115) have argued that the use of the word to introduce an authoritative utterance (as distinct from the normal Jewish use, to confirm what has already been said) represents one of Jesus' characteristic and authentic forms of speech. This argument remains cogent despite the criticisms made by V. Hasler, *Amen*, Zürich, 1969, and K. Berger, *Die Amen-Worte Jesu*, Berlin, 1970 (Jeremias, *Theology*, I, 36 n. 2)" (*Gospel of Luke*, 187–88).

forward-pointing devices that we have seen. They have the effect of creating a break in the flow of the discourse that would not otherwise have been so noticeable, much like the use of metacomments. They often work in conjunction with metacomments, but they can occur by themselves as well. They may be placed either at the beginning of a clause or in the middle to create a break in the flow of the discourse. In the latter case, the attention-getter typically separates the topic from what is said about it. In either case, the delay has the effect of creating some measure of suspense.

In the following examples from Matthew, note how the attention-getter (identified by the ! symbol) immediately precedes the introduction of a new participant.

Example 77 :: Matthew 1:20

ταῦτα δὲ αὐτοῦ ἐνθυμηθέντος ⟨!ἰδοὺ!⟩ ἄγγελος κυρίου κατ᾽ ὄναρ ἐφάνη αὐτῷ λέγων· Ἰωσὴφ υἱὸς Δαυίδ, μὴ φοβηθῇς παραλαβεῖν Μαρίαν τὴν γυναῖκά σου· τὸ γὰρ ἐν αὐτῇ γεννηθὲν ἐκ πνεύματός ἐστιν ἁγίου.	But as he was considering these things, ⟨!behold,!⟩ an angel of the Lord appeared to him in a dream, saying, "Joseph, son of David, do not be afraid to take Mary as your wife, for what has been conceived in her is from the Holy Spirit."

This is the first appearance of the angel in the Gospel, and Hagner states, "ἰδού is Matthew's favorite device for calling attention to something extraordinary that is about to occur."[39] The words "about to" highlight a key observation by Hagner; they are forward-pointing. The instance in v. 20 is in the narrative, whereas the instance in v. 23 is within the angel's reported speech itself.

Example 78 :: Matthew 1:23

⟨!ἰδοὺ!⟩ ἡ παρθένος ἐν γαστρὶ ἕξει καὶ τέξεται υἱόν, καὶ καλέσουσιν τὸ ὄνομα αὐτοῦ Ἐμμανουήλ, ὅ ἐστιν μεθερμηνευόμενον μεθ᾽ ἡμῶν ὁ θεός.	⟨!"Behold,!⟩ the virgin will become pregnant and will give birth to a son, and they will call his name Emmanuel," which is translated, "God with us."

The next example also is taken from a reported speech, the accusation regarding Peter's association with Jesus while he waited outside Jesus' trial. The addition of the attention-getter has the effect of strengthening the accusation.

---

39. Hagner, *Matthew 1–13*, 18.

Example 79 :: Luke 22:59

καὶ διαστάσης ὡσεὶ ὥρας μιᾶς	And after about one hour had
ἄλλος τις διϊσχυρίζετο λέγων·	passed, someone else was insist-
⟨!ἐπ᾽ ἀληθείας!⟩ καὶ οὗτος μετ᾽	ing, saying, ⟨!"In truth!⟩ this man
αὐτοῦ ἦν, καὶ γὰρ Γαλιλαῖός ἐστιν.	also was with him, because he is
	also a Galilean!"

These examples illustrate the function of attention-getters when they occur alone. They serve the same purpose when co-occurring with a meta-comment, creating a more noticeable break in the discourse and attracting attention to the proposition that is introduced.

Summary

Metacomments play a key role in discourse by highlighting the introduction of important propositions. These propositions may occur at the beginning, middle, or conclusion of a paragraph. Other devices, such as redundant forms of address and attention-getters, can be combined with metacomments in order to signal a more significant break in the discourse. These have the effect of attracting more attention to what follows, whether it is a new pericope or an important proposition.

Suggested Reading

Levinsohn, Stephen H. *Self-Instruction Materials on Non-narrative Discourse Analysis*. chapter 7.

Mao, Luming R. "I Conclude Not: Toward a Pragmatic Account of Metadiscourse."

Mullins, Terence Y. "Disclosure: A Literary Form in the New Testament."

Runge, Steven E. "'I Want You to Know …': The Exegetical Significance of Meta-comments for Identifying Key Propositions."

Sanders, J. T. "The Transition from Opening Epistolary Thanksgiving to Body in the Letters of the Pauline Corpus."

White, John L. "Introductory Formulae in the Body of the Pauline Letter."

HISTORICAL PRESENT

Most of the time, present-tense verbs are used to refer to events or actions that are currently happening. Past-tense verbs are used to refer to past actions. This is how things normally work. There are certain contexts where these norms are regularly broken in order to accomplish certain pragmatic effects in Greek, in English, and many other languages. This usage of a present verb in a past context is referred to as a "historical present" (HP) in traditional grammars. In English, I could be telling a story (i.e., narrative genre) and very naturally change from past-tense verbs to present-tense verbs just before something surprising happens:

> I was camping this last weekend way out in the boonies. We had pitched camp and were sitting around the fire after dinner, when all of a sudden this bear *comes* out of the woods. I was scared to death. So I jumped up, and I *grab* some pans and *start beating* them together, but the bear just *keeps coming.*

Different languages use historical presents to accomplish different things. It is important to differentiate its function in English from its function in Koiné Greek.

6.1 Conventional Explanation

The phenomenon of using a present-tense verb to refer to a past action is well known by Greek grammarians; however, there are a number of opinions about what one should infer from its usage. Porter describes the three primary claims as:[1]

---

1. Stanley E. Porter, *Idioms of the Greek New Testament* (2nd ed.; Sheffield: Sheffield

A. dramatic use[2]
B. tense reduction[3]
C. change of setting or character[4]

Each of these proposals will be discussed in preparation for a discourse-based explanation.

The *dramatic use* explanation of the HP is the one most widely found in the commentary literature, and it seems to be based more upon modern vernacular usage in English than on premodern usage.[5] Most scholars claim that the effect of the HP is based upon the perceived semantic meaning of the present tense; since present tense is believed to grammaticalize present time, the HP usage is believed to essentially transport a past event into the reader's present experience. Wallace states, "The *reason* for the use of the historical present is normally to portray an event *vividly*, as though the reader were in the midst of the scene as it unfolds."[6] In other words, it is the semantics of the verb form that create the effect, not the nondefault usage of the present form in the "wrong" context. This explanation has muddied the meaning of the verb form itself, leading to the proposal that the HP has no tense—that is, tense reduction. Although the vividness proposal is attractive due to its compatibility with modern English usage, it cannot account for the variety of usages observed in the NT.

Academic, 1999), 30–31. The ongoing controversy over the nature of tense and aspect in Greek has significantly influenced the modern treatment of HP discussions. Porter rejects all but the third before introducing his explanation based on verbal aspect.

2. See MHT 3:61; BDF §321; Buist Fanning, *Verbal Aspect in New Testament Greek* (OThM; Oxford: Clarendon, 1990), 226; Daniel B. Wallace, *Greek Grammar beyond the Basics: An Exegetical Syntax of the New Testament* (Grand Rapids: Zondervan, 1999), 527.

3. See Paul Kiparsky, "Tense and Mood in Indo-European Syntax," *FL* 4 (1968): 30–57; John A. Battle, "The Present Indicative in New Testament Exegesis" (Th.D. diss., Grace Theological Seminary, 1975), 111–17; BDF §321; A. T. Robertson, *A Grammar of the Greek New Testament in the Light of Historical Research* (1919; repr., Bellingham, Wash.: Logos, 2006), 867; Fanning, *Verbal Aspect*, 227–31; Wallace, *Greek Grammar*, 527–28.

4. See Robertson, *Grammar*, 868; Randall Buth, "Mark's Use of the Historical Present," *Notes* 65 (1977): 7–13.

5. Brinton claims that the "vividness and excitement are a consequence of the text-organizing function of the historical present, not the primary function of the form" (Laurel J. Brinton, "Historical Discourse Analysis," in *The Handbook of Discourse Analysis* [ed. Deborah Schiffrin, Deborah Tannen, and Heidi Ehernberger Hamilton; Malden, Mass.: Blackwell, 2001], 143). Similarly, Kiparsky ("Tense and Mood," 30) also argues that the vivid and dramatic idea is a later development in Indo-European languages and hence is anachronistic to the Koiné Greek usage.

6. Wallace, *Greek Grammar*, 526.

The *tense reduction* view rejects understanding the present-tense verbs as true presents, viewing them instead as more of a sequential form like that found in Hebrew and other languages. Another factor lending credence to this view is that "their exegetical significance differs from other verbs which may appear as historical presents."[7] Battle seems to accept the idea that the historical present is indeed used for the sake of vividness, but he is more focused on the semantic issue of the tense's meaning than on its pragmatic effects in past-tense contexts.[8] He offers the following proposal to explain the usage:

> Matthew and Luke-Acts, especially the former, nearly always connect the historical present to the aorist. Very seldom is it tied to an imperfect. This fact can show either that the historical present is substituted for an aorist in what would normally be a chain of aorists, or that the historical present takes the place of the imperfect which would normally be used to break the monotony of continuous aorists. The first explanation seems simpler, and thus better.[9]

Battle's view appears to attribute the usage to stylistic variation, without a definable discourse function in the Gospels. He understands the HP as a substitute verb form, describing what is possible without providing a motivation for the departure from the norm.[10]

Wallace, while affirming the pragmatic effect of vividness, states,

> The *aspectual* value of the historical present is normally, if not always, reduced to zero. The verbs used, such as λέγει and ἔρχεται, normally introduce an action in the midst of aorists without the slightest hint that an internal or progressive aspect is intended. The historical present has suppressed its aspect but not its time. But the time element is rhetorical rather than real.[11]

In claiming this, Wallace is not taking a reductionist view so much as he is responding to the contextual factors. The context ostensibly expects an aorist form, with no semantic need for present tense or imperfective aspect. His claim about the usage being rhetorical rather than semantic evidences an understanding of markedness, even if unstated. His effort to minimize the aspect can reasonably be attributed to the HP's departure from expected norms.

---

7. Battle, "Present Indicative," 118.
8. Ibid., 125.
9. Ibid., 127–28.
10. Ibid., 128–30.
11. Wallace, *Greek Grammar*, 527.

The final proposal that one finds is that the HP is used to signal a *change of scene* or similar break in the discourse.[12] MHT cites the work of Thackeray in support of the HP usage to signal the open or close of a paragraph.[13] Porter finds this option the most attractive of the traditional explanations, yet "the instances where it does not mark significant change are too manifest to endorse this scheme as a sufficient explanation."[14] This explanation alone cannot explain the usage.

Aside from assigning a function, several observations have been made regarding the inequitable distribution of usage. First, the HP often is associated with vernacular speech and style as a way of accounting for Luke's infrequent use.[15] Also noteworthy is the tendency to view usage with verbs of speaking under a separate category: "With λέγει and other verbs introducing (in)direct discourse, the historical present is for the most part a stereotyped idiom that has lost its original rhetorical powers. λέγει/λέγουσιν is by far the most common verb used as a historical present, accounting for well over half of all the instances."[16] I will return to these claims below.

6.2   Discourse Explanation

Explaining the function and the distribution of usage of the HP requires reviewing some introductory principles and introducing some new ones. First, it is important to recognize that the use of the present form in a past-tense setting represents the choice to break with expected usage. The identification of a "historical present" is based on not following the expected rules. Randall Buth notes that HP usage breaks the rules not only in regard to tense, but also in regard to aspect.[17] In other words, not only is there a mismatch in the

---

12. Battle ("Present Indicative," 128) cites the following instances as support for this usage: Matt 2:13, 19; 3:1, 13; 9:14; 13:51; 15:1; 17:1; 26:31, 36; Mark 1:12, 21, 40; 3:13, 20, 31; 4:13, 35; 5:35; 6:30; 7:1; 8:1, 22; 9:2; 10:23, 35; 11:1, 15, 27; 12:13, 18; 13:1; 14:27, 32, 43, 66; 15:21; Luke 8:49; 11:37; John 1:29; 4:7, 16; 9:13; 11:38; 13:36; 18:28; 19:28; 20:1; 21:20; Acts 21:37; 26:24; Rev 17:15.

13. "Thackeray's thorough examination shows that in Mk as in 1 Kgd the historic present tends to come at or near the beginning of a paragraph. The exceptions are specially dramatic, as Mk 15$^{24.27}$ (pictorial). Verbs of (*a*) saying, (*b*) seeing, (*c*) coming and going, (*d*) bringing and sending, are conspicuous. The tense as a rule is dramatic in the sense that it serves to introduce new scenes in the drama" (MHT 2:456–57). See Robertson, *Grammar*, 868.

14. Porter, *Idioms*, 31. Cf. Buth, "Mark's Use," 7–13.

15. See Robertson, *Grammar*, 868; Wallace, *Greek Grammar*, 528; BDF §321.

16. Wallace, *Greek Grammar*, 527.

17. Buth (in personal correspondence). This idea is developed more fully in Steven E.

grammaticalized time with the discourse time, but also there is a mismatch in aspect. Most HP actions are perfective in nature, yet they are grammaticalized using an imperfective form.[18] This should not be understood to change the meaning of the verb; rather, it is simply another way in which the HP usage stands out in its context.

Recall that choice implies meaning, and that nondefault usage typically marks the presence of some feature that the default form would not have marked. In other words, the HP is not some special sense or abuse of the tense; it simply marks that some discourse feature is present. Why use an HP to accomplish this task? Why not use another verb form? Let's take a look at what options are available in Koiné Greek.

If I want to use a verb form as a prominence marker in a past-time context, there are few options available based on the discourse function of the other verb forms in Greek. The aorist conveys "perfective" aspect, portraying the action as "a complete and undifferentiated process."[19] It is the default form used for the mainline of the narrative; it is unmarked for any special features in narrative. The aorist form will be used here as the canon against which the other narrative verb forms are described and the discourse features that they signal.

Participles that precede the main verb have the effect of backgrounding the action with respect to the main verb of the clause, while most participles that follow the main verb elaborate the main verbal action.[20] Participles therefore are not an option for prominence marking, since they already mark something else. Using them in narrative would be understood to signal either backgrounding or elaboration.

Porter associates the perfect and pluperfect tenses with stative aspect, depicting "the action as reflecting a given (often complex) state of affairs."[21] This is something that cannot be explicitly signaled using the perfective aspect, hence the special function of stative verbs. Use of the perfect in an attempt to accomplish some prominence-marking function would likely not be differentiated from its expected stative function.

Both the imperfect and the present tenses grammaticalize imperfective aspect, depicting action that is ongoing or incomplete.[22] Imperfective aspect

Runge, "Reconsidering the Aspect of the Historical Present Indicative in Narrative" (paper presented at the annual meeting of the Society of Biblical Literature, New Orleans, La., 21–24 November 2009).

18. See Battle, "Present Indicative," 128.

19. Porter, *Idioms*, 21.

20. See chapter 12.

21. Porter, *Idioms*, 39.

22. Ibid., 21.

is generally associated across languages with offline, nonevent information in narrative.[23] In contrast, salient main events typically are communicated using the aorist or "perfective" aspect.

Since both present- and imperfect-tense forms grammaticalize imperfective aspect, theoretically either one could be used for offline information in narrative, but this is not the case. Since the imperfect-tense form is associated with past time and the present with present time,[24] there is a preference for using the form that best matches the temporal setting.[25] The imperfect is the default means of signaling the offline information in a past-time setting, freeing the present-tense form for use as a prominence marker.[26] Attempting to substitute a present for the imperfect would communicate some message other than offline information—that is, prominence marking. Based on the function of the verbal system that I am claiming here regarding past-time contexts, the imperfect marks the action as past-time and imperfective, whereas the function of HP is to highlight an event or speech that follows.

I contend that the present form is the most viable option for marking prominence in a past-time setting. Think about what it is that makes it stand out; the name associated with it says it all. It is a present verb, normally associated with present time, being used in a past-tense context.

---

23. See William A. Foley and Robert D. Van Valin Jr., *Functional Syntax and Universal Grammar* (CSL 38; Cambridge: Cambridge University Press, 1984), 371; Stephen H. Levinsohn, *Discourse Features of New Testament Greek: A Coursebook on the Information Structure of New Testament Greek* (2nd ed.; Dallas: SIL International), 172–75.

24. For those more advocating an "aspect only" understanding of the Greek verbal system, this differentiation is typically described as "remote" versus "nonremote" (see Rodney J. Decker, *Temporal Deixis of the Greek Verb in the Gospel of Mark in Light of Verbal Aspect* [SBG 10; New York: Peter Lang], 107) or "proximate" versus "nonproximate" (see Constantine Campbell, *Verbal Aspect, the Indicative Mood, and Narrative: Soundings in the Greek of the New Testament* [SBG 13; New York: Peter Lang], 48–57, 65).

25. Porter states that even in his nontemporal, aspect-oriented framework it is difficult not to find some temporal distinction between the present and the imperfect. "*The imperfect form* (along with the pluperfect …) *is the closest that the Greek language comes to a form actually related to time* (this does not mean that it is an absolute tense, however). Through a combination of features, including the added bulk of the augment and the secondary endings upon the present stem, Greek language users restricted its usage and meaning, often to past contexts" (*Idioms*, 33–34).

26. Battle has found that the HP is most heavily used in the Gospels; there is no substitution of the HP for the imperfect tense: "In Matthew and Luke-Acts, the historical present is not usually used in context with imperfects, suggesting that it is not substituted for the imperfect in these books" ("Present Indicative," 128). This corroborates the idea that it is the imperfect tense is associated with offline information in narrative, since the present is not substituted for it.

To reassert Buth's point, it is also an imperfective-aspect verb form used in an ostensibly perfective-aspect context, providing another reason that the usage stands out. Recall Battle's comments about the apparent "substitution" of the HP for only aorist forms, and Wallace's observation that the aspectual value is reduced to zero, i.e., no distinction from the perfective aorist.[27] Utilizing an imperfective aspect to describe a perfective action makes the HP stand out for two reasons. This is what creates the contrast, not some hidden semantic meaning of the verb form.

Most HPs are associated with mainline events, not background information. If an aorist tense/perfective aspect had been used, then there would be no break from the expected norm, and nothing would stand out. In order for something to mark prominence, it must stand out. This requires using something that is unexpected in the context. Otherwise, it would stand out about as much as Longacre's "black camels crossing black sands at night."[28]

Now that we know why the HP stands out, let's look at what it signals. Just like the forward-pointing devices that stand out because they are redundant, the HP's departure from the expected norm creates a break in the flow of the discourse. There is a very specific hierarchy of how these devices are interpreted by readers and hearers, based on how humans are wired to process discontinuity. I described this hierarchy in my dissertation as a way of unifying various claims that have been made about prominence-marking devices involving discontinuity or redundancy.[29]

There is a tendency to claim that a device can only do one thing or another, that it cannot accomplish more than one discourse task at a time. This tendency runs counter to the actual usage observed. Languages are more likely to multitask than to specialize. Rarely will one idiom ever accomplish only a single thing.

There is a rhyme and reason to how the tasks double up, described in the processing hierarchy of figure 3. Instead of creating an either/or opposition, the processing hierarchy posits that one function is entailed within the one above it.[30]

---

27. Ibid., 127–28; Wallace, *Greek Grammar*, 527.

28. See §1.4.2.

29. Steven E. Runge, "A Discourse-Functional Description of Participant Reference in Biblical Hebrew Narrative" (D.Litt. diss., University of Stellenbosch, 2007), 39.

30. Ibid.

Figure 3 :: Processing hierarchy

Discourse-pragmatic Function

which entails

Processing Function

which entails

Semantic Function[31]

Devices that play double-duty to signal different discourse functions always play a semantic role. They may not be semantically required, but they still communicate semantic content. This is the case with forward-pointing references, metacomments, redundant quotative frames (see chapter 7) and tail-head linkage (see chapter 8), and the thematic highlighting devices of part 4. The fact that the information that they provide is not semantically required moves the reader or hearer to the next level of the hierarchy for an explanation: the processing function. In other words, the element that is not semantically required is next expected to be serving a processing function, signaling a discontinuity in the discourse. It still serves a semantic function, but it serves a secondary function as well.

The processing task of the hierarchy refers to the segmentation of the discourse into smaller chunks for purpose of easier processing by the reader or hearer. We saw this in the case of forward-pointing references and metacomments, where they were used to signal the next major propositional topic of the discourse—that is, at a transition in the discourse. The discontinuity was already present. The discourse device has the effect of accentuating what was already there, helping the reader to successfully navigate the transition in the discourse.

In the case of the HP, I contend that the usage associated with discourse boundaries or paragraphing is best explained as the next step in the cognitive processing of discourse devices: segmentation for easier processing. The segmentation may be at discourse transitions—for example, the introduction of new participants into an existing scene. Alternatively, it may signal the transition to a new scene within the same narrative. In such cases, the HP functions

---

31. This explanation may sound like a stretch, but it has more to do with how we are wired to process language than it does with the specifics of HP usage in Greek. This framework was developed to describe phenomena in Hebrew but was based on empirical evidence drawn from English, Dutch, German, and several non-Western languages.

as a processing device, making the discontinuity that naturally existed stand out even more as a guide to the reader or hearer.

This processing explanation holds true also for the use of the HP in quotative frames, particularly where there are unexpected turns in the conversation.[32] The presence of the HP makes the discontinuity that was already present stand out all the more. This will be discussed further in the application section.

Now we move on to the claims regarding highlighting and prominence. The top level of the processing hierarchy describes the overuse of something, either where it is multiplied far more than is needed for segmentation or where there is little to no natural discontinuity present. In other words, if there is a clustering of devices that exceeds what is needed for semantic or processing reasons, the reader will process the usage as accomplishing some discourse-pragmatic function. In the case of forward-pointing devices, it is highlighting or prominence marking.[33]

To summarize, if a device is not needed for semantic reasons, it still plays a semantic role, but it also is doing something more. I claim that the first "something more" is to segment the discourse for easier processing, to accentuate a natural discontinuity that was already present. If the device is not needed or is excessive for processing, then it is deemed to accomplish something else, a discourse-pragmatic function. This describes the overuse of a device in a series of clauses, like building to a crescendo. It also accounts for the isolated use in a context where it is not needed either for semantic reasons or for processing a discontinuity in the discourse.

Just as metacomments and forward-pointing references can be used to highlight a discourse boundary or highlight an important proposition that follows, HPs can serve comparable functions. Instead of highlighting propositions, HPs highlight events or speeches that follow.[34] The HPs in the examples that follow are marked at each end by the ⊘ symbol.

---

32. The same will be claimed regarding the use of redundant quotative frames in the next chapter.

33. In the case of redundant thematic information, the information itself is highlighted. This typically has the effect of (re)characterizing the participant in a particular way in the particular context for some particular reason. See part 4 on thematic highlighting.

34. Levinsohn states, "What is highlighted by the HP is not so much the speech or act to which it refers but the event(s) that follow. In other words, like other devices employed for highlighting, the HP usually occurs *prior* to the event or group of events that are of particular significance" (*Discourse Features*, 200).

6.3   Application

6.3.1   Discourse-Processing and Segmentation

Recall my claim that things like contrast and discontinuity are not created by discourse features, though they may be highlighted or accentuated. Discontinuity is either present or not. If it is present, there are a number of means that can be used to attract more attention to it, as was seen in the usage of metacomments, redundant vocatives and nominatives of address, and attention-getters.[35] The same holds true for the use of HPs in contexts of discontinuity in a discourse. HPs do not create a discontinuity; they simply accentuate what discontinuity is already present. The break in the discourse would exist with or without a marker.

Writers use markers such as the HP to make sure that the reader does not miss changes or transitions in the discourse. They have the effect of slowing down the pace and attracting the reader's attention. Levinsohn notes, "In Matthew's gospel, nearly every non-speech HP occurs at a generally recognized paragraph boundary. Nevertheless, there is still no need to claim that the HP is *marking* the boundary. This is because other features that tend to occur at boundaries are also present."[36] This is another context where the distinction between semantic meaning and pragmatic effect is important. The HP does not create a boundary; it simply attracts extra attention to it, often because of the significance of the speech or event that follows. In Matthew's case, he regularly utilizes the HP at discourse boundaries to aid the reader in recognizing the transition, as in the following examples.

Example 80 :: Matthew 15:1

> [14:34] And after they had crossed over, they came to land at Gennesaret. [35] And when the men of that place recognized him, they sent word into that whole surrounding region, and they brought to him all those who were sick. [36] And they were imploring him that they might only touch the edge of his cloak, and all those who touched it were cured.

---

35. Part 3 describes the use of word order to structure information, providing another means of accentuating continuity or discontinuity in the discourse.

36. Levinsohn, *Discourse Features*, 202. Levinsohn lists the following in Matthew's gospel as examples of boundary markers: "τότε (e.g., in 26:36a …) or a temporal point of departure (3:1, 17:1, 25:11, 25:19), including a genitive absolute (2:13, 2:19). Matthew 26:40 (καὶ ἔρχεται 'and he comes') is an exception" (ibid.).

^{15:1} Τότε ⟨⦰προσέρχονται⦰⟩ τῷ   ^{15:1} Then Pharisees and scribes
Ἰησοῦ ἀπὸ Ἱεροσολύμων Φαρισαῖοι   ⟨⦰came⦰⟩ to Jesus from Jerusa-
καὶ γραμματεῖς λέγοντες·   lem, saying,

Most discourse boundaries are identified based on *thematic discontinui-ties*—for example, changes in time, place, participants or action.[37] Generally speaking, the more discontinuities that are present, the higher the level of the discourse boundary.[38] The transition from the scene at the end of Matt 14 to Matt 15:1 has few thematic discontinuities. There has been no change in time[39] or place; the primary change is the introduction of the Pharisees and scribes from Jerusalem. The reader does not know if the introduction of the new participants is the start of a new pericope or a continuation of the current one.

The use of the HP in combination with narrative τότε helps the reader identify the boundary in the discourse by attracting more attention to it than it would otherwise have received. The use of τότε provides little specific information about the amount temporal change; rather, it signals a new development by generically indicating that time has passed in the same way as "After that …" in English.[40] The HP plays a forward-pointing role by attracting attention to something important that follows. In this case, it is the introduction of the new participants whose question to Jesus forms the basis for the next pericope. The HP does not have the semantic meaning of "boundary marker"; it simply helps make the boundary easier to recognize and to process.

In the Synoptic parallel to Matt 15:1, one finds a different verb used to introduce the arrival of the Pharisees and scribes, yet the HP usage is maintained. [41]

---

37. See Robert A. Dooley and Stephen H. Levinsohn, *Analyzing Discourse: A Manual of Basic Concepts* (Dallas: SIL International, 2001), 37.

38. See Steven E. Runge, "Where Three or More Are Gathered, There Is Discontinuity" (paper presented at the international meeting of the Society of Biblical Literature, Edinburgh, 2–6 July 2006).

39. For a description of narrative τότε, see §2.4.

40. BDF states, "On the other hand, the use of τότε as a connective particle to introduce a subsequent event, but not one taking place at a definite time ('thereupon,' not 'at that time'), is unclassical; it is particularly characteristic of Mt, but is also found in Lk (especially Acts)" (§459[2]). Regardless of whether τότε is of Semitic origin or not (see MHT 3:341), it serves a describable role when functioning as a connective.

41. Porter observes that καί is often used in Mark at discourse boundaries along with the HP (see *Idioms*, 301–2). He cites Mark 1:9, 16, 21, 39, 40; 2:1, 13, 15, 18, 23; 3:1, 13, 20, 31; 4:13, 21, 24, 26, 30, 35; 5:1, 21, 24; 6:1, 14, 21, 30; 7:1, 14; 8:11, 14, 22, 27, 31, 34; 9:1, 9, 14, 33; 10:2, 13, 17, 23, 35, 41, 46; 11:11, 15, 20, 27; 12:1, 13, 18, 28, 35, 41; 13:1, 3; 14:3, 22, 26, 27, 32, 53, 65, 66; 15:21, 33; 16:1 as other examples of this usage. However, he attributes

Example 81 :: Mark 7:1

Καὶ ⟨Øσυνάγονται⟩ πρὸς αὐτὸν οἱ Φαρισαῖοι καί τινες τῶν γραμματέων ἐλθόντες ἀπὸ Ἱεροσολύμων.	And the Pharisees and some of the scribes who had come from Jerusalem ⟨Øgathered⟩ to him.

Levinsohn has noted the use of HPs in connection with the introduction of new participants,[42] and I have noted the use of verbs of motion as a form of "presentational" articulation that allows new participants to be introduced as subjects of a clause without violating Chafe's cognitive principle of only introducing one new thing at a time.[43] Note the pattern that is developing:

- HPs are often verbs of motion;
- new participants are often introduced by verbs of motion;
- introduction of new participants represents a natural discontinuity.

In examples 80 and 81, the verbs of motion introduce new participants, which also coincides with a transition in the discourse from Jesus healing to the dialogue with the religious leaders about eating with defiled hands. The HP here adds corroborating evidence for viewing these verses as transitions in the discourse, accentuating the discontinuity that was already present.

Example 82 introduces Jesus' speech to his disciples in the garden of Gethsemane, just after leaving the supper.

Example 82 :: Matthew 26:31

30 And after they had sung the hymn, they went out to the Mount of Olives.

31 Τότε ⟨Øλέγει⟩ αὐτοῖς ὁ Ἰησοῦς· πάντες ὑμεῖς σκανδαλισθήσεσθε ἐν ἐμοὶ ἐν τῇ νυκτὶ ταύτῃ, γέγραπται γάρ· πατάξω τὸν ποιμένα, καὶ διασκορπισθήσονται τὰ πρόβατα τῆς ποίμνης.	31 Then Jesus ⟨Øsaid⟩ to them, "You will all fall away because of me during this night, for it is written, 'I will strike the shepherd and the sheep of the flock will be scattered.'"

---

the marking of the boundary to the shift in tenses from aorist and imperfect to the present, not to the prominence associated with the marked use of the present form in a past context.

42. Levinsohn, *Discourse Features*, 210–13.
43. Runge, "Discourse-Functional Description," 103–5.

There is no change of time or participants, only a change of location and kind of action (i.e., a transition from narrative to reported speech). The HP attracts attention to the boundary where the thematic discontinuities are sparse. The use of τότε also confirms the presence of a boundary by indicating a generic change in time. The combination of markers helps the reader properly process the transition by serving as a signpost. It signals that the writer views this as a shift in the narrative despite the natural continuity of the content. One might also argue that the HP serves an additional function of attracting attention to Jesus' announcement that all of the disciples will fall away. In either case, the processing function would still be present based on the entailment of one function within another. There are twenty-four other instances in Matthew's gospel where the HP and τότε co-occur, all used in narrative proper.[44]

6.3.2   Discourse-Pragmatic Function/Prominence Marking

The other primary function of the HP in addition to processing is to highlight a significant speech or event that immediately follows. It is not the action of the HP verb itself that is prominent, but that which follows.[45] Callow notes that particularly in Mark and John, however, the HP

> does *not* draw attention to the event which the HP verb itself refers to, as those events, in themselves, are not particularly important—*to go, to say, to gather together, to see, etc.*… [I]t has a *cataphoric* function; that is, it points on beyond itself into the narrative, it draws attention to what is following.[46]

Grammarians have correctly associated the HP with prominence but have overlooked its forward-pointing nature. This explains why seemingly mundane actions are encoded by use of the HP. Attention should be directed to the speech or event that follows.

---

44. See Matt 3:13, 15; 4:5, 10, 11; 9:6, 14, 37; 12:13; 15:1, 12; 18:32; 22:8, 21; 26:31, 36 (HP 2x), 38, 45 (HP 2x), 52; 27:13, 38; 28:10.

45. Much of the criticism regarding the use of the HP as a prominence marker comes from the claim that the action grammaticalized by the HP itself is prominent. The frequent use of the HP with verbs of speaking and motion is the proof offered that the verb itself cannot be prominent. Instead, attention is drawn prospectively to the speech that the quotative frame introduces, not the action of speaking (e.g., John 1:15, 21, 29). Similarly, the verbs of motion often introduce significant participants or move the participants to the location of a significant event that is about to happen (e.g., the 23 instances in John 20). See Levinsohn, *Discourse Features*, 203–5.

46. John Callow, "The Historic Present in Mark" (seminar handout, 1996), 2, cited in Levinsohn, *Discourse Features*, 202.

The following example from John 14 illustrates how significant turns in a speech are signaled by use of the HP.

Example 83 :: John 14:5–6, 8–9

5 ⟨⦿Λέγει⦿⟩ αὐτῷ Θωμᾶς· κύριε, οὐκ οἴδαμεν ποῦ ὑπάγεις· πῶς δυνάμεθα τὴν ὁδὸν εἰδέναι;	5 Thomas ⟨⦿said⦿⟩ to him, "Lord, we do not know where you are going. How are we able to know the way?"
6 ⟨⦿λέγει⦿⟩ αὐτῷ [ὁ] Ἰησοῦς· ἐγώ εἰμι ἡ ὁδὸς καὶ ἡ ἀλήθεια καὶ ἡ ζωή· οὐδεὶς ἔρχεται πρὸς τὸν πατέρα εἰ μὴ δι' ἐμοῦ.	6 Jesus ⟨⦿said⦿⟩ to him, "I am the way, and the truth, and the life. No one comes to the Father except through me."

Thomas asks a question in v. 5 that Jesus redirects in v. 6. Instead of describing the way that Thomas asks about, Jesus claims that he *is* the way. These shifts in the direction of the conversation represent a thematic discontinuity or redirection. The use of the HP in such contexts is not required, but using it has the effect of accentuating the shift, effectively highlighting the speech that follows. The frequent use of HPs in the quotative frames of John's gospel can be attributed to the nature of their content.[47]

There is a similar usage just a few verses later that coincides with the introduction and redirection of a question from Philip.

8 ⟨⦿Λέγει⦿⟩ αὐτῷ Φίλιππος· κύριε, δεῖξον ἡμῖν τὸν πατέρα, καὶ ἀρκεῖ ἡμῖν.	8 Philip ⟨⦿said⦿⟩ to him, "Lord, show us the Father, and it is enough for us."
9 ⟨⦿λέγει⦿⟩ αὐτῷ ὁ Ἰησοῦς· τοσούτῳ χρόνῳ μεθ' ὑμῶν εἰμι καὶ οὐκ ἔγνωκάς με, ⟨☛Φίλιππε;☛⟩ ὁ ἑωρακὼς ἐμὲ ἑώρακεν τὸν πατέρα· πῶς σὺ λέγεις· δεῖξον ἡμῖν τὸν πατέρα;	9 Jesus ⟨⦿said⦿⟩ to him, "Am I with you so long a time and you have not known me, ⟨☛Philip?☛⟩ The one who has seen me has seen the Father! How can you say, 'Show us the Father'?"

Note that Jesus punctuates the end of his statement using a redundant vocative of address, which is not needed to identify the addressee. Jesus answers

---

47. Other devices may be used to accentuate such turns in a conversation—for example, overencoding of the participants, and the use of redundant quotative frames. See Levinsohn, *Discourse Features*, 133–65, 218–60.

Philip's question with a rhetorical one, conveying a rebuke to the nature of the question. The HP serves the processing function of marking transitions in the discourse (new speaker and redirection). It also serves to highlight the speech that follows. The HP is not required here; it represents the writer's choice.

The HP is used again in John 14:22 to introduce the next disciple's question. Jesus' response is introduced with a redundant quotative frame[48] instead of an HP. The use of the HP with quotative frames in John is often associated with a speaker moving the conversation in a new direction—for example, Jesus and Nicodemus in John 3.

Mark 14 records the final supper and the events in the garden of Gethsemane. Many of Jesus' actions are recorded by way of HPs, all of them forward-pointing. The first pair is found as Jesus instructs his disciples to arrange a room for the Passover meal (v. 14). The instructions foretell what they will find as they enter the city. The next occurrence is in v. 17, at the transition from the preparation to the arrival of the twelve disciples to eat the meal. There are two more HPs, one introducing the speech where Jesus predicts that all of them will fall away (v. 27), and the other where he predicts that Peter will deny him three times (v. 30).

Example 84 :: Mark 14:30

> [27] And Jesus said to them, "You will all fall away, because it is written, 'I will strike the shepherd and the sheep will be scattered.' [28] But after I am raised, I will go ahead of you into Galilee." [29] But Peter said to him, "Even if they all fall away, certainly I will not!"

[30] καὶ ⟨ⓄλέγειⓄ⟩ αὐτῷ ὁ Ἰησοῦς· ⟨!ἀμὴν!⟩ ⟨⎃λέγω σοι⎃⟩ ὅτι σὺ σήμερον ταύτῃ τῇ νυκτὶ πρὶν ἢ δὶς ἀλέκτορα φωνῆσαι τρίς με ἀπαρνήσῃ.	[30] And Jesus ⟨ⓄsaidⓄ⟩ to him, ⟨!"Truly,!⟩ ⟨⎃I say to you⎃⟩ that today—this night—before the rooster crows twice, you will deny me three times!"

The speech of v. 30 represents the climax of the conversation. Peter has just emphatically denied that he would ever desert Jesus (v. 29). Jesus' speech itself is also highlighted using an attention-getter and a metacomment.[49]

The transition from the upper room to the garden is also highlighted through the repeated use of the HP. The clustering serves to build the sus-

---

48. See chapter 7.
49. For similar usage of these devices before a significant pronouncement, see Mark 14:9, 18b, 25.

pense that something significant is about to happen, since it is more than what is needed to process the transition from the upper room to the garden.[50]

Example 85 :: Mark 14:32–33

[32] Καὶ ‹ØἔρχονταιؘØ› εἰς χωρίον οὗ τὸ ὄνομα Γεθσημανὶ καὶ ‹ØλέγειؘØ› τοῖς μαθηταῖς αὐτοῦ· καθίσατε ὧδε ἕως προσεύξωμαι.	[32] And they ‹Øthey cameؘØ› to a place named Gethsemane, and ‹Øhe saidؘØ› to his disciples, "Sit here while I pray."
[33] καὶ ‹ØπαραλαμβάνειؘØ› τὸν Πέτρον καὶ [τὸν] Ἰάκωβον καὶ [τὸν] Ἰωάννην μετ᾽ αὐτοῦ καὶ ἤρξατο ἐκθαμβεῖσθαι καὶ ἀδημονεῖν	[33] And ‹Øhe tookؘØ› along Peter and James and John with him, and he began to be distressed and troubled.

There are a total of seventeen HPs in Mark 14, the most in any single chapter of Mark.[51]

One finds another such clustering in John 20, just before the women discover that Jesus has risen from the dead.

Example 86 :: John 20:1–2

[1] Τῇ δὲ μιᾷ τῶν σαββάτων Μαρία ἡ Μαγδαληνὴ ‹ØἔρχεταιؘØ› πρωῒ σκοτίας ἔτι οὔσης εἰς τὸ μνημεῖον καὶ ‹ØβλέπειؘØ› τὸν λίθον ἠρμένον ἐκ τοῦ μνημείου.	[1] Now on the first day of the week, Mary Magdalene ‹ØcameؘØ› to the tomb early, while it was still dark, and ‹ØsawؘØ› the stone had been taken away from the tomb.
[2] ‹ØτρέχειؘØ› οὖν καὶ ‹ØἔρχεταιؘØ› πρὸς Σίμωνα Πέτρον καὶ πρὸς τὸν ἄλλον μαθητὴν ὃν ἐφίλει ὁ Ἰησοῦς καὶ ‹ØλέγειؘØ› αὐτοῖς· ἦραν τὸν κύριον ἐκ τοῦ μνημείου καὶ οὐκ οἴδαμεν ποῦ ἔθηκαν αὐτόν.	[2] So ‹Øshe ranؘØ› and ‹ØwentؘØ› to Simon Peter and to the other disciple whom Jesus loved and ‹ØsaidؘØ› to them, "They have taken away the Lord from the tomb and we do not know where they have put him!"

---

50. See Robert E. Longacre, "Discourse Peak as Zone of Turbulence," in *Beyond the Sentence: Discourse and Sentential Form* (ed. Jessica R. Wirth; Ann Arbor, Mich.: Karoma, 1985), 81–98. Longacre claims that the "peak" (i.e., the climax of a narrative) often is marked by an unusual clustering of prominence markers in one place. He likens it to a "zone of turbulence" where marked usage replaces the expected default.

51. For a discussion of the clustering of HPs in Mark 15, see Campbell, *Verbal Aspect*, 69–71.

The repeated use of the HP here has the effect of building to a dramatic peak, yet this should not be construed as the semantic meaning of the HP. Each HP portrays the action as though it were a transition to some new stage of the discourse. The net effect is to slow the discourse flow and build anticipation. Each one also highlights the next event, only to have the resolution deferred by the presence of another HP. This seems to be the effect of the clustering of HPs into series in John's gospel. In this same chapter there is another series of three HPs in vv. 5–6 as the disciples investigate the empty tomb, and another one as Jesus appears to Mary in vv. 14–18.

Matthew, Mark, and John are best known for using the HP, while in Luke-Acts HPs are only sparsely found. Of the uses in Luke, all but one occur with verbs of speaking, in each case at the beginning or at a significant transition in the dialogue, highlighting the speech that follows. The one exception encodes Peter seeing that the tomb is empty.

Example 87 :: Luke 24:12

Ὁ δὲ Πέτρος ἀναστὰς ἔδραμεν ἐπὶ τὸ μνημεῖον καὶ παρακύψας ⟨ⓄβλέπειⓄ⟩ τὰ ὀθόνια μόνα, καὶ ἀπῆλθεν πρὸς ἑαυτὸν θαυμάζων τὸ γεγονός.

But Peter got up and ran to the tomb, and bending over to look, ⟨Ⓞhe sawⓄ⟩ only the strips of linen cloth, and he went away to his home wondering what had happened.

Usage in a context where there is thematic continuity has the effect of highlighting the event that follows.

Similarly in Acts, all but two of the HPs found are verbs of speaking. The nonspeech uses are associated with Peter's ministry to Cornelius's family. The HPs draw attention to the significance of these events. Cornelius and his family are the first people (Gentile or otherwise) to receive the Holy Spirit without the laying on of hands since the initial outpouring on the apostles at Pentecost in Acts 2. Verse 11 highlights the vision that teaches Peter that nothing God has made is unclean.

Example 88 :: Acts 10:11

καὶ ⟨ⓄθεωρεῖⓄ⟩ τὸν οὐρανὸν ἀνεῳγμένον καὶ καταβαῖνον σκεῦός τι ὡς ὀθόνην μεγάλην τέσσαρσιν ἀρχαῖς καθιέμενον ἐπὶ τῆς γῆς....

And ⟨Ⓞhe sawⓄ⟩ heaven opened and an object something like a large sheet coming down, being let down to the earth by its four corners....

The very next HP is just before Peter applies this lesson in proclaiming the gospel to Cornelius. It is the only other HP in Acts that does not use a verb of speaking.

Example 89 :: Acts 10:27–28

²⁷ καὶ συνομιλῶν αὐτῷ εἰσῆλθεν καὶ ‹ⓄεὑρίσκειⓄ› συνεληλυθότας πολλούς,	²⁷ And as he conversed with him, he went in and ‹ⓄfoundⓄ› many people gathered.
²⁸ ἔφη τε πρὸς αὐτούς· ὑμεῖς ἐπίστασθε ὡς ἀθέμιτόν ἐστιν ἀνδρὶ Ἰουδαίῳ κολλᾶσθαι ἢ προσέρχεσθαι ἀλλοφύλῳ· κἀμοὶ ὁ θεὸς ἔδειξεν μηδένα κοινὸν ἢ ἀκάθαρτον λέγειν ἄνθρωπον·	²⁸ And he said to them, "You know that it is forbidden for a Jewish man to associate with or to approach a foreigner. And to me God has shown that I should call no man common or unclean."

Whether this usage was intended to connect these two events or not is unclear. There are no textual variants listed in NA²⁷ to call either of these instances into question.

As with the other prominence markers, HPs tend to highlight some kind of discontinuity in the discourse. Usage of the HP at a boundary attracts extra attention to it, helping the reader process the transition to a new topic or pericope. Usage before a significant event or speech accomplishes the same processing task.

Usage that is unneeded for processing serves the pragmatic function of highlighting the speech or event that follows. It directs the reader to pay closer attention to something important. The HP achieves this effect by standing out in its context, on the basis of both temporal reference and aspect. If it did not stand out, it would not achieve these effects. One must differentiate the semantic meaning of the tense form from the effect of using it to describe past-time, perfective action. The HP should be regarded as a marked usage to accomplish a specific pragmatic effect, not a special submeaning of the tense.

Suggested Reading

Battle, John A. "The Present Indicative in New Testament Exegesis."
Blass, F., A. Debrunner, and R. W. Funk. *A Greek Grammar of the New Testament and Other Early Christian Literature.* §321.
Beekman, John, and John Callow. *Translating the Word of God.* Chapter 14.
Black, Stephanie L. "The Historic Present in Matthew: Beyond Speech Margins."

Brinton, Laurel J. "Historical Discourse Analysis."

Buth, Randall. "Mark's Use of the Historical Present."

Campbell, Constantine. *Verbal Aspect, the Indicative Mood, and Narrative: Soundings in the Greek of the New Testament.* 57–76.

Comrie, Bernard. *Tense.* 36–55.

Fludernik, Monika. "The Historical Present Tense in English Literature: An Oral Pattern and Its Literary Adaptation."

Kiparsky, Paul. "Tense and Mood in Indo-European Syntax."

Leong, Siang-Nuan. "Macro-Structure of Mark in Light of the Historic Present and Other Structural Indicators."

Levinsohn, Stephen H. *Discourse Features of New Testament Greek: A Coursebook on the Information Structure of New Testament Greek.* 200–212.

Reynolds, Stephen M. "The Zero Tense in Greek."

Runge, Steven E. "Reconsidering the Aspect of the Historical Present Indicative in Narrative."

———. "The Verbal Aspect of the Historical Present Indicative in Narrative."

Wallace, Daniel B. *Greek Grammar beyond the Basics: An Exegetical Syntax of the New Testament.* 526–32.

REDUNDANT QUOTATIVE FRAMES

Most speeches are introduced using what are called "quotative frames" (e.g., "They said ..."). Quotative frames signal a transition from narrative proper to a speech or dialogue embedded within the narrative. Once the speech has been introduced, there is no need for another quotative frame unless there is a change in speakers (e.g., "He said..., then she said ...").

This chapter describes the discourse function of redundant quotative frames, those that are not needed to determine who is speaking to whom. Here is the definition used in the *LDGNT* glossary to describe the phenomenon:

> **Redundant Quotative Frame**—The use of extra verbs of speaking to "frame" or introduce a speech, which is meant to draw attention to a surprising or important speech that follows.

There are two different uses of redundant quotative frames. The first concerns using more than one verb of speaking to introduce a speech (e.g., "He answered and said to him ..."); the second concerns reintroducing the same speaker within a single speech—that is, where there has been no change of speakers (e.g., "The angel said ... The angel continued, saying ..."). Both of these uses have the pragmatic effect of highlighting a discontinuity in the text, specifically within the context of the speech. Both have the effect of attracting more attention to the speech or segment of speech that follows.

7.1 Conventional Explanation

The use of multiple verbs of speaking to frame a quotation is widely acknowledged, but NT scholars have focused more interest on explaining its origins or proper translation than on explaining its exegetical contribution to the discourse. The use of a participial form of ἀποκρίνομαι with a finite form of λέγω represents what Wallace refers to as a pleonasm: "A verb of saying (or sometimes thinking) can be used with a participle with basically the same meaning (as in ἀποκριθεὶς εἶπεν)."[1] This collocation is viewed as redundant because the finite verb communicates essentially the same semantic information as the participle. Wallace attributes the usage in the Synoptic Gospels to a Semitic idiom but does not assign special significance to it. In John's gospel, one also finds ἀποκρίνομαι occurring with λέγω where both verbs are finite. This usage is also attributed to a Semitic idiom, deriving from either Hebrew (וַיַּעַן וַיֹּאמֶר, "And he answered and said …") or Aramaic (עָנֵה וְאָמַר, "Answering, he said …").

MHT states, "This Hebrew construction [וַיַּעַן וַיֹּאמֶר] is copied by the LXX and the Targums and in Biblical Aramaic עָנֵה וְאָמַר is often found,"[2] but it is not found in later Aramaic. However, they do cite Dalman's observation that the redundant use of a different Aramaic pleonasm for speaking "appears to be as yet a learned term for making good an objection" in Targum Onkelos.[3]

Dalman is not the only scholar who connects the use of redundant quotative frames to framing speeches that contain an objection or similar change in the course of a conversation. Similar observations are occasionally made by commentators, particularly in contexts where ἀποκρίνομαι ("I answer") is used where there is no question or command in the preceding context that is being answered.

France notes in his comments on Mark 9:5–6 that the redundant quotative frame does more than just introduce a reply, since it follows not a reported speech but rather the transfiguration of Jesus. "Peter's words are a response not to any words already spoken, but to the whole bewildering situation in which the disciples find themselves."[4] Regarding Mark 7:28, he characterizes the Syrophoenecian woman's response to Jesus as "refutation" that is "defiant."[5] Finally, regarding Jesus' address to the fig tree in Mark 11:14,

---

1. Daniel B. Wallace, Greek *Grammar beyond the Basics: An Exegetical Syntax of the New Testament* (Grand Rapids: Zondervan, 1999), 650; See A. T. Robertson, *A Grammar of the Greek New Testament in the Light of Historical Research* (1919; repr., Bellingham, Wash.: Logos, 2006), 1126.

2. MHT 2, §174. Hendriksen also characterizes the use of "characteristic expressions (like 'answered and said')" as evidence of Aramaic influence (*Exposition of the Gospel According to John* [NTC; Grand Rapids: Baker, 1953], 64).

3. Gustaf Dalman, *The Words of Jesus: Considered in the Light of Post-Biblical Jewish Writings and the Aramaic Language* (trans. D. M. Kay; Edinburgh: T & T Clark, 1902), 25, cited in MHT 2, §174.

4. R. T. France, *The Gospel of Mark: A Commentary on the Greek Text* (NIGTC; Grand Rapids: Eerdmans, 2002), 353.

5. Ibid., 298

he states, "Here is a classic case of ἀποκριθείς used, as often in Mark, to mean not a reply to anything said but a response to a situation. Jesus is 'replying' to the tree's failure to provide what he wanted."[6]

This usage of ἀποκρίνομαι in a less specific sense than literally "answering" a question or command is so pervasive that BDAG provides an alternate definition of "the continuation of discourse like עָנָה" to try to describe it.[7]

At the same time, the usage can be a source of befuddlement for commentators. Some want to find an implicit question that is being answered from the preceding context. Kistemaker observes regarding the usage in Act 5:8 that "usually the idiom is fully written out: 'he answered and said.' But occasionally the verb *said* is omitted. The construction means 'to address.' Nevertheless, the possibility that Sapphira asked Peter about her husband is not remote."[8] In his volume on John's gospel, Hendriksen comments regarding 3:13, "Nicodemus has not asked any question. Nevertheless, Jesus *answers* him, for he read the question which was buried deeply in the heart of this Pharisee."[9]

There is second kind of redundant quotative frame found in the NT in which a verb of speaking is used to reintroduce the same speaker in the midst of a single speech. In other words, there has been no switch of speakers, yet there is an extra quotative frame. This other redundant usage has been acknowledged by interpreters as an odd phenomenon. However, the proposed explanations offer little help in understanding its discourse function.

For instance, Nolland states regarding the redundant use of εἶπεν in the midst of a speech in Luke 4:24, "Jesus is reintroduced as though there were a change of speaker, since he has in v. 23 been voicing the people's sentiment. [Verse] 24 is thus a response to v. 23."[10] Plummer associates a similar usage with a temporal gap in the speech in Luke 4:24: "When these words occur between two utterances of Christ, they seem to indicate that there is an interval between what precedes and what follows."[11]

To summarize, the traditional approach to redundant quotative frames in NT studies has been to explain the origins of the phenomenon without answering the exegetical question of why the device is used in some cases and not in others. These redundant frames may indeed represent a borrowing from Semitic sources, as some have claimed. However, the usage represents

---

6. Ibid., 443.

7. BDAG, 114.

8. Kistemaker, *Exposition of the Acts of the Apostles* (NTC; Grand Rapids: Baker, 1990), 189.

9. Hendriksen, *Gospel According to John,* 132.

10. John Nolland, *Luke 1:1–9:20* (WBC 35A; Dallas: Word, 1989), 200.

11. Alfred Plummer, *A Critical and Exegetical Commentary on the Gospel According to S. Luke* (ICC; Edinburgh: T & T Clark, 1896), 127.

more than a stylistic borrowing, since they are used to accomplish the same kinds of discourse tasks in Greek as in Biblical Hebrew.

Furthermore, any claim of Semitic influence must account for the attestation of redundant quotative frames in Greek that is not viewed as Semitically influenced. BDAG cites Homer's use of ἀμειβόμενος προσέειπε as accomplishing a comparable effect to NT usage,[12] while BDF correlates the NT usage of redundant quotative frames to the use of ἔφη λέγων, εἰρώτα λέγων, ἔλεγε φάς and the like in Herodotus, and ἀποκρινόμενος εἶπεν in Plato, *Protagoras*.[13] One also finds redundant quotative frames heavily used in *The Shepherd of Hermas* in discourse contexts comparable to the NT. Further study is needed to determine whether it is a case of borrowing. It is more likely that both languages use the same grammatical device to accomplish similar discourse tasks, meaning that redundant quotative frames are a cross-linguistic discourse convention.

I stated in chapter 1 that if there is more than one way of accomplishing a discourse task, there is most likely a meaning associated with each choice. In this case, the default manner of introducing a reported speech would be to use a single verb of speaking. The redundant use of quotative frames is intended by the writer to accomplish a discourse task that default encoding would not have accomplished.

7.2   Discourse Explanation

The functions associated with redundant quotative frames by some NT commentators and grammarians are not far from those proposed by linguists studying biblical languages. This should not be a surprise, since these NT scholars, in most cases, have internalized the grammar; they simply lacked a proper framework for clearly describing the phenomenon they observed.

If we accept MHT's claim that ἀποκριθεὶς εἶπεν is truly a borrowing of וַיַּעַן וַיֹּאמֶר from the Hebrew Bible, the question still remains as to what this usage signals. Miller notes that וַיַּעַן וַיֹּאמֶר "often introduces a second pair-part [of a dialogue] that gives an appropriate response to a first-pair-part," especially in commands, protests, accusations and inquiries.[14] What Miller describes represents the expected usage, where a verb of answering introduces a response to some precipitating utterance.

---

12. BDAG, 114.

13. BDF §420.

14. Cynthia L. Miller, *The Representation of Speech in Biblical Hebrew Narrative: A Linguistic Analysis* (corrected ed.; HSM 55; Winona Lake, Ind.: Eisenbrauns), 320.

Miller further notes that since most conversations are introduced using a single verb of speaking, the multiple-verb frames are found only once or twice at most in a conversation. This leads her to claim that "the use of עֲנָה in a multiple-verb frame thus seems to signal the most salient or important response in the conversation."[15] Miller is not the only scholar who correlates multiple-verb frames to a prominent speech that follows. Wenham observes that the collocation "answered and said" often precedes a "significant remark," citing Gen 18:27; 23:5, 10, 14; 24:50; 27:37, 39; 40:18 as examples.[16]

If we accept that the use of a multiple-verb quotative frame using ἀποκρίνομαι is motivated by the usage of its Hebrew counterpart, it would be reasonable to expect it to be used in comparable contexts. This is indeed the case, as demonstrated by similar claims cited earlier regarding the usage in NT Greek. The use of multiple-verb frames is also attested in literature unlikely to have experienced Semitic influences.[17]

On the basis of the diversity of distribution and the similarity in function, it is more reasonable to understand the use of redundant quotative frames for accentuating discontinuity in the discourse as a broader cross-linguistic convention than as a Hebrew convention simply borrowed by NT writers. Regardless of whether the convention is borrowed or not, the attested usage plays a strikingly similar function within the respective discourses. I now move to the NT evidence, beginning with quotative frames that introduce a change in speakers, followed by those that reintroduce the same speaker.

7.2.1   At Changes in Speaker and Hearer

From a cross-linguistic standpoint, when a conversation follows an expected path, the expected conventions tend to be observed. On the contrary, it is reasonable to suppose that departures from the expected flow of a conversation could somehow be marked to make sure that the reader properly tracks the flow. Dooley and Levinsohn describe such departures in this way:

> Sometimes, instead of taking up the same topic as that of the previous speech and developing the conversation from the point at which the last speaker left off, the new speaker may change the direction of the conversation with a

---

15. Ibid., 321.

16. Gordon J. Wenham, *Genesis 16–50* (WBC 2; Dallas: Word, 1994), 272. Regarding the use Gen 40:18, he comments, "To 'answer and say' may suggest a brusque impatience on Joseph's part and the momentous nature of his comment" (ibid., 384).

17. Consider the forty uses of the collocation ἀπαμειβόμενος προσέφη ("answered and said") in comparable contexts of shifts in the conversation in Homer's *Iliad* (e.g., 1.84, 130; 2.369; 5.764).

countering move.... Such counters generally are marked in some way. In Koiné Greek, for instance, the verb *apokrínomai*, which is usually glossed "answer," typically signals a change of direction in a reported conversation.[18]

So if there is an unexpected or significant turn in a speech, the writer may choose to mark it in some way. This marking is not a requirement; it is a pragmatic choice made to ensure that the reader does not overlook the change. Based on the similarity in usage and context with Hebrew, it is reasonable to view redundant quotative frames as serving the same discourse function in Greek as in biblical Hebrew. In other words, the redundant frame serves to highlight a shift in the conversation in ways comparable to the other forward-pointing devices discussed so far.[19]

The most commonly occurring multiple-verb frame consists of a form of ἀποκρίνομαι with a finite form of λέγω. The pragmatic effect is to accentuate a discontinuity or transition in the dialogue, thereby directing attention to the speech that follows. This usage is most typically found in contexts where there is a change in the direction of the conversation initiated by the new speaker, or where the new speaker is about to make what Levinsohn describes as "an authoritative pronouncement."[20] Redundant quotative frames in Mathew, Mark, and Luke typically consist of a participial form of ἀποκρίνομαι with a finite verb of speaking. [21] In John's gospel, both verbs take a finite form.[22]

---

18. Robert A. Dooley and Stephen H. Levinsohn, *Analyzing Discourse: A Manual of Basic Concepts* (Dallas: SIL International, 2001), 51–52. Carl Conrad (in personal correspondence) notes that "in older Greek (6th–5th c. Attic) ὑποκρίνομαι is the major word for 'answer' until it is replaced by ἀποκρίνομαι; at the point when a second and third actor was added in the early tragic performances, they were called ὑπόκριται, 'respondents.'"

19. Redundant quotative frames are not the only means for highlighting significant speeches. Recall the frequent use of the historical present (HP) with verbs of speaking described in chapter 6. The two devices co-occur in Mark 3:33; 7:28; 8:29; 9:5; 10:24; 11:22, 33; 15:2; Luke 11:45; 13:8; 17:37. The HP is also used with a single redundant verb of speaking that interrupts the same speaker's speech in Mark 4:13; John 1:51; 11:11; 21:16, 17; Rev 17:15; 19:19.

20. Stephen H. Levinsohn, *Discourse Features of New Testament Greek: A Coursebook on the Information Structure of New Testament Greek* (2nd ed.; Dallas: SIL International), 231.

21. Levinsohn considers Acts to follow a slightly different pattern of usage: "In *Acts*, the combination of the participle plus εἶπεν is used sparingly. Typically, it is accompanied by a full noun phrase reference to the subject. With one exception..., it is used when the counter or new initiative concerned would not have been expected. Furthermore, this counter or new initiative is decisive in determining the outcome of the exchange (contrast Acts 9:13–14 ...). It seems reasonable, therefore, to assume that the longer form of the speech orienter has been chosen to highlight the speech" (ibid., 232).

22. Levinsohn states, "In sec. 14.1 we saw that forms of ἀποκρίνομαι are used in the Synoptic Gospels and Acts to break the tight-knit nature of a closed conversation. This

As in English, the different Greek verbs of speaking signal differing degrees of continuity, based on their semantic value. Stating that "he said …" conveys much more continuity (and less emotion and friction) than "he retorted.…" It appears that both ἀποκρίνομαι and the Hebrew יען convey a stronger semantic encoding than the typical quotative verbs λέγω and אמר. Using these semantically stronger verbs in contexts where they are not semantically "appropriate" effectively accentuates some discontinuity that the writer wants to represent. Therefore, I do not claim that every occurrence of ἀποκρίνομαι is marked, but only those where it is redundant in a compound collocation with another verb of speaking. Although ἀποκρίνομαι does convey a semantically sharper change in the conversation, I limit my claim of a prominence-marking effect to its use with another verb of speaking.

7.2.2   Within the Same Speaker's Speech

So far, I have considered the redundant use of quotative frames only in contexts where there is a change of speakers. There are a number of instances in both the Greek NT and the Hebrew Bible where quotative frames are observed in the middle of speeches, where there has been no change of speakers. Since the same person is speaking, there is no semantic need for reintroduction. Levinsohn states,

> If an orienter is repeated in the middle of a speech, you should assume that its presence is motivated. Typically, orienters are repeated:
> - to mark the introduction of a new point within the same reported speech
> - to slow down the discourse immediately preceding a key assertion.[23]

They are typically found within a single speech at shifts from one topic to another. They function to segment the speech into logical parts, based on content. They also can be used to create something of a dramatic pause just before a (or the) significant point of the speech. In this way, the redundant frame

---

effect is achieved in John by what I shall call the *long* orienter of ἀπεκρίθη καὶ εἶπεν" (ibid., 247). He later elaborates: "When a form of ἀποκρίνομαι occurs in a speech orienter in John's Gospel, it is always a finite verb. Whereas the short orienter ἀπεκρίθη is the default way of introducing a response to a previous speech or non-verbal stimulus…, the long orienter ἀπεκρίθη καὶ εἶπεν *highlights* the response. The response is most often highlighted because it represents a significant counter.… Sometimes, it represents a significant new initiative, usually by other than the addressee of the previous speech. Occasionally, a direct answer to a question is highlighted because of its importance" (ibid., 255–56).

23. Ibid., 53.

serves to separate what is less important from a more important portion that follows. Creating the break in the flow also serves the same delay tactic seen with other forward-pointing devices, building suspense through the delay.

7.3   Application

I will now present examples of redundant quotative frames used in the two different contexts described above. The redundant frames used at changes of speaker and hearer can serve either to signal a change in the direction of the speech or to highlight the salient speech of the discourse. The quotation symbol "" will be used to identify the redundant frames.

7.3.1   At Changes in Speaker and Hearer

Both Matthew and Mark use redundant quotative frames to highlight Jesus' proclamation that the one having faith can move mountains. However, the statements that are highlighted differ from one another both in wording and in how they are introduced. In Mark 11:22, the finite verb in the quotative frame is a historical present (HP). The use of ἀποκριθείς is not preceded by a question in v. 21, but by a statement that is also introduced using an HP.

Example 90 :: Mark 11:22–23 and Matthew 21:21

^{22} καὶ ⟨"ἀποκριθεὶς"⟩ ὁ Ἰησοῦς ^{22} And Jesus ⟨"answered"⟩ and
λέγει αὐτοῖς· ἔχετε πίστιν θεοῦ.   said to them, "Have faith in God!"

^{23} "⟨!Truly!⟩ ⟨I say to you⟩ that whoever says to this mountain ..."

Peter's precipitating statement and Jesus' pronouncement are highlighted by a combination of discourse devices. In v. 21, the writer uses an HP (λέγει), and Peter's statement uses two delaying devices: redundant thematic address and an attention-getter. Jesus' response uses a redundant quotative frame, ἀποκριθείς, followed by an HP form of the finite verb. His speech begins with both an attention-getter and a metacomment. This clustering of devices provides corroborating evidence regarding the significance of this exchange. Peter seems shocked at what he sees. Jesus redirects the direction of the conversation by essentially rejecting Peter's premise. More colloquially in English, we might paraphrase Jesus as saying, "You ain't seen nothing yet." All the forward-pointing devices serve to accentuate the redirection by Jesus.

In contrast, Matthew's account in 21:21 uses an aorist form for the finite verb instead of an HP. The disciples' statement that precipitates Jesus' response is introduced with an HP. In Mark's version, the redundant frame follows a declaration, whereas in Matthew's account it is punctuated as a question. In

Matthew's version, as in Mark's, Jesus' statement is introduced with an attention-getter combined with a metacomment.

Example 91 :: Matthew 21:21

²¹ ⟨ᵫ⁣"ἀποκριθεὶςᵫ⁣"⟩ δὲ ὁ Ἰησοῦς εἶπεν αὐτοῖς· ⟨!ἀμὴν!⟩ ⟨⊡λέγω ὑμῖν,⊡⟩ ἐὰν ἔχητε πίστιν καὶ μὴ διακριθῆτε, οὐ μόνον τὸ τῆς συκῆς ποιήσετε, ἀλλὰ κἂν τῷ ὄρει τούτῳ εἴπητε· ἄρθητι καὶ βλήθητι εἰς τὴν θάλασσαν, γενήσεται·

²¹ And Jesus ⟨ᵫ⁣"answeredᵫ⁣"⟩ and said to them, ⟨!"Truly!⟩ ⟨⊡I say to you,⊡⟩ if you have faith and do not doubt, you will do not only what was done to the fig tree, but even if you say to this mountain, 'Be lifted up and thrown into the sea,' it will happen!"

 In both Gospels, the speeches could have been introduced by a single, simple aorist quotative frame, εἶπεν. Based on the significance of the speech that is introduced to the discourse context, as well as the co-occurrence of other forward-pointing devices both in the frame and in the speech itself, the use of the redundant quotative frame is reasonably understood as further contributing to the highlighting associated with the other devices.

 Matthew 21:23–27 records Jesus' interaction with the Jewish leaders regarding the source of his authority. The conversation takes some dramatic turns as it progresses, a few of which are marked with redundant quotative frames. Jesus is asked the initial question about the source of his authority in Matt 21:23. The replies recorded in Matt 21:24 and Luke 20:3 use redundant quotative frames, though Luke's version differs slightly.

Example 92 :: Matthew 21:24 and Luke 20:3

Here is the reading in Matt 21:24:

⟨ᵫ⁣"ἀποκριθεὶςᵫ⁣"⟩ δὲ ὁ Ἰησοῦς εἶπεν αὐτοῖς· ἐρωτήσω ὑμᾶς κἀγὼ λόγον ἕνα, ὃν ἐὰν εἴπητέ μοι κἀγὼ ὑμῖν ἐρῶ ἐν ποίᾳ ἐξουσίᾳ ταῦτα ποιῶ·

And Jesus ⟨ᵫ⁣"answeredᵫ⁣"⟩ and said to them, "I also will ask you one question. If you tell the answer to me, I also will tell you by what authority I am doing these things."

Following is the reading in Luke 20:3:

⟨ᵫ⁣"ἀποκριθεὶςᵫ⁣"⟩ δὲ εἶπεν πρὸς αὐτούς· ἐρωτήσω ὑμᾶς κἀγὼ λόγον, καὶ εἴπατέ μοι·

And ⟨ᵫ⁣"he answeredᵫ⁣"⟩ and said to them, "I also will ask you a question, and you tell me:"

The effect in both readings is to attract more attention to the "turning of the tables" as Jesus refuses to answer their question, although Luke's version uses neither thematic addition (see chapter 16) nor a conditional frame of reference (see §11.1).

Jesus' reply in the parallel account of Mark 11:29 is encoded with a default quotative frame, ὁ δὲ Ἰησοῦς εἶπεν αὐτοῖς.[24] The leaders' answer to Jesus' question is introduced in Matt 21:27 and Mark 11:33 using redundant quotative frames,[25] while Luke 20:7 uses the aorist indicative ἀπεκρίθησαν. The use of the redundant quotative frames has the effect of accentuating a discontinuity in order to attract attention to the speech that follows. In this instance, it highlights the changes in direction of the speeches that follow. Jesus refused to answer the leaders' question, and they in turn refused to answer his.

There are plenty of instances where answers to questions are framed using only a form of λέγω, or using only a form of ἀποκρίνομαι, as in Luke 20:7. The choice to use a second verb has the effect of slowing the discourse like a speed bump, attracting attention to what follows.

Mark 12:34 relates how, as a result of how well Jesus had refuted attempts to trap him, no one dared ask him any more questions. Despite the fact that people had ceased to ask Jesus questions, Mark begins the pericope about the Christ being David's son with a redundant quotative frame using ἀποκριθείς.

Example 93 :: Mark 12:35

Καὶ ‹«"ἀποκριθεὶς«"›› ὁ Ἰησοῦς ἔλεγεν διδάσκων ἐν τῷ ἱερῷ· πῶς λέγουσιν οἱ γραμματεῖς ὅτι ὁ χριστὸς υἱὸς Δαυίδ ἐστιν;	And ‹«"continuing,«"›› Jesus said while teaching in the temple courts, "How can the scribes say that the Christ is David's son?"

---

24. The reply is default with respect to the quotative frame used. Note that a full noun phrase, ὁ Ἰησοῦς, is used, as opposed to the standard articular pronoun + development marker ὁ δέ. The overencoding of noun phrases is another means of attracting prominence in both Greek (see Levinsohn, *Discourse Features*, 135–42) and Hebrew (see Steven E. Runge, "A Discourse-Functional Description of Participant Reference in Biblical Hebrew Narrative" [D.Litt. diss., University of Stellenbosch, 2007], 209–16). Note that Luke does not overencode the noun phrase, while Matthew does. Thus Matthew, Mark, and Luke each use a different combination of forward-pointing devices to accomplish the same discourse task of highlighting the speech that follows by accentuating a discontinuity. This represents stylistic variation within Synoptic consistency, from the standpoint of text linguistics and discourse grammar.

25. Mark's version uses an HP for the finite verb form, as is commonly found elsewhere in his gospel.

Note that the LEB's translation is "continuing," the same sense that BDAG attributes to ἀποκρίνομαι when it is not used to answer a question.[26]

Are the uses of ἀποκρίνομαι in redundant quotative frames what lead to this second sense of "continuing"? It is better explained as an effect of its redundant use to mark either a shift or a significant speech that follows, rather than as some special semantic meaning of the word. In the Synoptic parallels to Mark 12:35, Matt 22:39 frames Jesus' question using ἐπηρώτησεν; Luke 20:41 uses the default εἶπεν. This difference in usage illustrates the different interests of the writers based on the choices made. Mark's version frames the speech in such a way as to build anticipation, using "answer" after just stating that no one was asking Jesus questions anymore. Luke simply reports the conversation.

The next example illustrates the use of redundant quotative frames just before an authoritative announcement. Peter and the apostles have been arrested for teaching about Jesus and have been commanded by the Sanhedrin to stop (see Acts 5:26–28). In response to this prohibition, Peter refuses to obey the order by appealing to a higher authority.

Example 94 :: Acts 5:29

⟨ᴌ"ἀποκριθεὶςᴌ"⟩ δὲ Πέτρος καὶ οἱ ἀπόστολοι εἶπαν· πειθαρχεῖν δεῖ θεῷ μᾶλλον ἢ ἀνθρώποις.	But Peter and the apostles ⟨ᴌ"answeredᴌ"⟩ and said, "It is necessary to obey God rather than men!

The use of the redundant frame here could be attributed either to Peter's rejection or to the significance of his speech to the pericope. Using the redundant frame here accentuates Peter's rejection and redirection by using a semantically charged verb of speaking in a context where it is not necessary. Both factors appear to motivate the redundant usage here.[27]

When Jesus interacts with the Syrophoenecian woman in Mark 7:28, he makes a rather blunt statement that seems to preclude her request being ful-

---

26. BDAG, 115.

27. Levinsohn provides a more specific analysis stating, "After the high priest's assertion of Acts 5:28, the apostles would have been expected either to stay silent or to offer some excuse for their conduct. Instead, they counter with a decisive appeal to higher authority for what they are doing (vv. 29ff.). This largely determines the outcome of the trial (see Gamaliel's warning in v. 39 that the authorities might be found to be fighting against God if they put the apostles to death)" (*Discourse Features*, 232). Note also that the level of encoding used for "Peter and the apostles" is more than is needed, providing another indicator that what follows is highlighted (see ibid., 135–42).

filled because she is not a Jew. Her answer in v. 28 represents a significant counter to this assertion, and it is framed accordingly.

Example 95 :: Mark 7:28

ἡ δὲ ⟨«"ἀπεκρίθη«"⟩ καὶ ⟨ⓄλέγειⓄ⟩ αὐτῷ· κύριε· καὶ τὰ κυνάρια ὑποκάτω τῆς τραπέζης ἐσθίουσιν ἀπὸ τῶν ψιχίων τῶν παιδίων.	But she ⟨«"answered«"⟩ and ⟨ⓄsaidⓄ⟩ to him, "Lord, even the dogs under the table eat the children's crumbs."

The woman's response concedes Jesus' premise that the Jews have priority over the Gentiles, but it asserts that she still qualifies for the leftovers. Notice that Mark uses an HP for the finite verb form. Matthew's version in 15:27 uses a default frame: ἡ δὲ εἶπεν.[28] Here again we see evidence of authorial choice in how the scenes are represented.

The confession of John the Baptist that he was not the Christ uses literal redundancy to build the anticipation of his actual claim, repeating the same verb along with a second verb of speaking in a three-part quotative frame.

Example 96 :: John 1:20

καὶ ὡμολόγησεν καὶ ⟨«"οὐκ ἠρνήσατο,«"⟩ καὶ ⟨«"ὡμολόγησεν«"⟩ ὅτι ἐγὼ οὐκ εἰμὶ ὁ χριστός.	And he confessed—and ⟨«"he did not deny,«"⟩ and ⟨«"confessed«"⟩— "I am not the Christ!"

Note that the writer uses αὕτη as a forward-pointing reference in v. 19 as another means of adding to the anticipation of how John will respond to the questions put to him by the Jews.[29] Using ὡμολόγησεν by itself would have been sufficient to introduce the speech, or even εἶπεν for that matter. The redundant verbs in the quotative frame have the effect of interrupting the flow of the discourse as a means of building suspense, postponing the disclosure of the Baptist's answer.

---

28. Note that in Matthew's version the information structure of the woman's speech bears a small change, rendering "even the dogs" as emphasized rather than functioning as a topical frame of reference, based on the fronting of only the most salient elements of the noun phrase. See chapters 10–13.

29. See chapter 3.

7.3.2   Within the Same Speaker's Speech

I now move on to illustrate the effect of using a quotative frame in the midst
of a single speech, where there has been no switch of speakers. There are two
effects associated with this use. First, the midspeech quotative frame serves
to segment a larger speech into smaller units, typically based on content or
theme. Second, they can serve to slow the pace of the discourse just before
a significant pronouncement. This has the effect of separating what is less
important from what is more important, with the latter typically following the
midspeech frame.

It is important to note that these frames have been inserted by the writer,
not the speaker. Their use represents the writer's choice to interrupt the speech
by inserting the redundant frame.

Midway through Jesus' teaching about the purpose of the Sabbath, there
is a redundant midspeech quotative frame that creates a break in the speech
between the illustration of David taking the bread of the presence and the
principle that Jesus draws from this illustration.

Example 97 :: Luke 6:5

> [2] But some of the Pharisees said, "Why are you doing what is not per-
> mitted on the Sabbath? [3] And Jesus answered and said to them, "Have
> you not read this, what David did when he and those who were with
> him were hungry— [4] how he entered into the house of God and took
> the bread of the presentation, which it is not permitted to eat (except
> the priests alone), and ate it and gave it to those with him?"

⟨«"καὶ ἔλεγεν αὐτοῖς·«"⟩ κύριός ἐστιν τοῦ σαββάτου ὁ υἱὸς τοῦ ἀνθρώπου.	⟨«"And he said to them,«"⟩ "The Son of Man is Lord of the Sabbath."

Mark's version also uses a redundant quotative frame, although the saying
that follows is somewhat different.

Example 98 :: Mark 2:27

⟨«"καὶ ἔλεγεν αὐτοῖς·«"⟩ τὸ σάββατον διὰ τὸν ἄνθρωπον ἐγένετο καὶ οὐχ ὁ ἄνθρωπος διὰ τὸ σάββατον·	⟨«"And he said to them,«"⟩ "The Sabbath was established for people, and not people for the Sabbath.

It is noteworthy that even though Luke and Mark differ in the wording of

Jesus' pronouncement about the Sabbath, they both use the same device to set
it off from the illustration of David. The effect is to attract more attention to
it than it otherwise would have received. Both writers could have more easily
omitted the redundant frame, as is in Matt 12:8. Highlighting a discontinuity
using the redundant frame slows the flow of the discourse and creates anticipation for what follows.

Mark 4 contains a series of teachings that are not interrupted by speeches
from others except in vv. 10–11. However, it is segmented into smaller units
by redundant quotative frames that reintroduce Jesus as the speaker. Although
they are semantically redundant, they perform an important pragmatic function.[30] We find the first redundant frame of the chapter in v. 9, just as Jesus
finishes telling a parable. It separates the concluding warning from the parable
itself.

Example 99 :: Mark 4:9, 13, 21, 24, 26, 30

[9] ⟨ꞈ"καὶ ἔλεγεν·ꞈ"⟩ ὃς ἔχει ὦτα ἀκούειν ἀκουέτω.	[9] ⟨ꞈ"And he said,ꞈ"⟩ "Whoever has ears to hear, let him hear!"
[13] ⟨ꞈ"Καὶ λέγει αὐτοῖς·ꞈ"⟩ οὐκ οἴδατε τὴν παραβολὴν ταύτην, καὶ πῶς πάσας τὰς παραβολὰς γνώσεσθε;	[13] ⟨ꞈ"And he said to themꞈ"⟩, "Do you not understand this parable? And how will you understand all the parables?"
[21] ⟨ꞈ"Καὶ ἔλεγεν αὐτοῖς·ꞈ"⟩ μήτι ἔρχεται ὁ λύχνος ἵνα ὑπὸ τὸν μόδιον τεθῇ ἢ ὑπὸ τὴν κλίνην; οὐχ ἵνα ἐπὶ τὴν λυχνίαν τεθῇ;	[21] ⟨ꞈ"And he said to them,ꞈ"⟩ "Surely a lamp is not brought so that it may be put under a bushel basket or under a bed, is it? Is it not so that it may be put on a lampstand?"
[24] ⟨ꞈ"Καὶ ἔλεγεν αὐτοῖς·ꞈ"⟩ βλέπετε τί ἀκούετε. ἐν ᾧ μέτρῳ μετρεῖτε μετρηθήσεται ὑμῖν καὶ προστεθήσεται ὑμῖν.	[24] ⟨ꞈ"And he said to them,ꞈ"⟩ "Take care what you hear! With the measure by which you mea-sure out, it will be measured out to you, and will be added to you."

---

30. Some might argue that these quotative frames are evidence of redaction or of
an underlying oral form of the sayings. Regardless of the origins of the current text, the
writer/editor could have removed the quotative frames instead of leaving them in, if this is
even what happened. Removing them would have unified the sayings into a single speech
instead of a series of speeches. Their presence, regardless of origins, has the effect of segmenting what could have been a long speech into smaller chunks.

26 ⟨«"Καὶ ἔλεγεν·«"⟩ οὕτως ἐστὶν ἡ βασιλεία τοῦ θεοῦ ὡς ἄνθρωπος βάλῃ τὸν σπόρον ἐπὶ τῆς γῆς

26 ⟨«"And he said,«"⟩ "The kingdom of God is like this: like a man scatters seed on the ground."

30 ⟨«"Καὶ ἔλεγεν·«"⟩ πῶς ὁμοιώσωμεν τὴν βασιλείαν τοῦ θεοῦ ἢ ἐν τίνι αὐτὴν παραβολῇ θῶμεν;

30 ⟨«"And he said,«"⟩ "With what can we compare the kingdom of God, or by what parable can we present it?"

Note that aside from the historical present in v. 13, the verb form used in each redundant frame is imperfect (ἔλεγεν), not aorist. Wallace refers to this usage as the "instantaneous imperfect," where the imperfect is used "just like the aorist indicative, to indicate simple past."[31] He notes that the usage "is virtually restricted to ἔλεγεν in narrative literature."[32] In contrast, Levinsohn remarks that the imperfect is used "to portray events as incomplete."[33] Note that the primary reason for placing the frame here is to segment an ongoing speech, not to indicate that the speech is completed.

Imperfect forms of λέγω characteristically are used either to introduce an initial speech that is more of a monologue than a dialogue[34] or to record the responses of multiple groups to one thing.[35] They can also be used in the expected imperfective sense of ongoing or repeated events.[36]

Note that when one comes across an aorist verb of speaking without a full noun phrase (e.g., εἶπεν or ὁ εἶπεν), the default expectation is that there has been a change of speaker and hearer. Since underspecified aorist quotative frames are most often associated with changes in speakers, using such a frame might create the impression that there was a switch of speakers.[37] Alternatively, the use of a present-tense quotative frame would have created an HP, adding extra prominence in addition to the redundant frame itself.[38]

---

31. Wallace, *Greek Grammar*, 542.

32. Ibid.

33. Levinsohn, *Discourse Features*, 175.

34. Robertson (*Grammar*, 885) refers to this usage as an "inchoative imperfect" (e.g., Matt 9:11, 21, 23, 34; 26:5; Mark 2:16; 24; 3:23; 5:30).

35. For example, Matt 12:23; 21:11; 27:41, 47, 49; Mark 3:21, 22; 4:41.

36. Such clauses often begin with γὰρ and provide background to the situation describing ongoing actions (e.g., Matt 14:4; Mark 3:30; 4:2; 5:8, 28).

37. See the discussion by Levinsohn (*Discourse Features*, 135–47) of the encoding of participants in narrative contexts.

38. There are only a handful of instances where an HP verb of speaking is used mid-speech: Mark 4:13; John 1:51; 21:16, 17. In each case, significant pronouncements follow.

If a writer is going to insert an underspecified redundant frame with the goal of continuing the speech, the imperfect is the most natural choice. Although it segments the speech, it does not signal closure or switch. The aspect of the imperfect itself is used for ongoing or incomplete action. This discourse-based explanation of the instantaneous imperfect provides a reasonable account of the data without needing to postulate another sense. The fact that Wallace's data is "virtually restricted to ἔλεγεν in narrative literature" makes this explanation even more compelling.[39]

The imperfect quotative frame ἔλεγεν is used redundantly four more times in Mark 4. The frame in v. 21 separates the explanation of the parable of the sower from the parable of the light under a bushel. The frame in v. 26 segments the light under the bushel from the parable of the growing seed. The frame in v. 30 segments the text again just before the parable of the mustard seed.

There is a comparable chaining together of parables in Matt 13. Rather than using an imperfect verb of speaking to segment the text, Matthew inserts a redundant narrative comment to accomplish the very same effect.

Example 100 :: Matthew 13:24, 31, 33

[24] ⟨ᵤᵢ."Ἄλλην παραβολὴν παρέθηκεν αὐτοῖς λέγων·ᵤ."⟩ ὡμοιώθη ἡ βασιλεία τῶν οὐρανῶν ἀνθρώπῳ σπείραντι καλὸν σπέρμα ἐν τῷ ἀγρῷ αὐτοῦ.

[24] ⟨ᵤᵢ."He put before them another parable, saying,ᵤ."⟩ "The kingdom of heaven may be compared to a man who sowed good seed in his field."

Matthew's strategy accomplishes the same purpose of segmenting the text by redundantly introducing what follows as another parable, even though he uses different words. The technique is repeated in vv. 31 and 33.

[31] ⟨ᵤᵢ."Ἄλλην παραβολὴν παρέθηκεν αὐτοῖς λέγων·ᵤ."⟩ ὁμοία ἐστὶν ἡ βασιλεία τῶν οὐρανῶν κόκκῳ σινάπεως, ὃν λαβὼν ἄνθρωπος ἔσπειρεν ἐν τῷ ἀγρῷ αὐτοῦ·

[31] ⟨ᵤᵢ."He put before them another parable, saying,ᵤ."⟩ "The kingdom of heaven is like a mustard seed that a man took and sowed in his field."

[33] ⟨ᵤᵢ."Ἄλλην παραβολὴν ἐλάλησεν αὐτοῖς·ᵤ."⟩ ὁμοία ἐστὶν ἡ βασιλεία

[33] ⟨ᵤᵢ."He told them another parable:ᵤ."⟩ "The kingdom of

---

39. Wallace, *Greek Grammar*, 542.

τῶν οὐρανῶν ζύμῃ, ἣν λαβοῦσα γυνὴ ἐνέκρυψεν εἰς ἀλεύρου σάτα τρία ἕως οὗ ἐζυμώθη ὅλον.

heaven is like yeast that a woman took and put into three measures of wheat flour until the whole batch was leavened."

It is very important for readers to know how and where to break a text down into smaller chunks for easier processing. Use of redundant quotative frames in the middle of a speech is a common way for the writer to provide the reader with instructions about where to segment the text.[40]

Midspeech quotative frames are also used to segment a speech at thematic boundaries, which also slows the pace of the discourse. As Jesus asks Peter to reaffirm his love for him, redundant frames segment each of the exchanges.

Example 101 :: John 21:16–17

16 ⟨„" ⟨⊘λέγει⊙⟩ αὐτῷ πάλιν δεύτερον·„"⟩ Σίμων Ἰωάννου, ἀγαπᾷς με; λέγει αὐτῷ. ναὶ κύριε, σὺ οἶδας ὅτι φιλῶ σε. λέγει αὐτῷ· ποίμαινε τὰ πρόβατά μου.

17 ⟨„" ⟨⊘λέγει⊙⟩ αὐτῷ τὸ τρίτον·„"⟩ Σίμων Ἰωάννου, φιλεῖς με; ἐλυπήθη ὁ Πέτρος ὅτι εἶπεν αὐτῷ τὸ τρίτον· φιλεῖς με; καὶ λέγει αὐτῷ· κύριε, πάντα σὺ οἶδας, σὺ γινώσκεις ὅτι φιλῶ σε. λέγει αὐτῷ [ὁ Ἰησοῦς]· βόσκε τὰ πρόβατά μου.

16 ⟨„" ⟨⊘He said⊙⟩ to him again a second time,„"⟩ "Simon son of John, do you love me?" He said to him, "Yes, Lord, you know that I love you." He said to him, "Shepherd my sheep!"

17 ⟨„" ⟨⊘He said⊙⟩ to him a third time,„"⟩ "Simon son of John, do you love me?" Peter was distressed because he said to him a third time, "Do you love me?" and he said to him, "Lord, you know everything! You know that I love you!" Jesus said to him, "Feed my sheep!"

The writer takes steps to make sure that the reader does not miss the repetition of the question. The use of the adverbs "second" and "third" accomplishes this, as do the redundant frames in vv. 16a and 17a. Each of them is framed using an HP, calling further attention to them.

---

40. See §6.2 and the discussion of the cross-linguistic processing hierarchy. Based on this theoretical framework, the redundant quotative frames are understood first to be accomplishing a processing function, guiding the reader's judgments about where to segment the text into smaller pieces for easier processing.

The use of quotative frames in the midst of a speech is unnecessary, which has the effect of making it stand out. The use also represents the writer's choice to highlight a break in the flow of the text that would not otherwise have stood out nearly so much. Each frame falls in an appropriate place based on the content of the speeches. Minimally, the breaks in the speech signal to the reader where to segment the text into smaller chunks. Because the segments are so clear, the frames also accomplish a pragmatic function. Such discontinuities are often created just before a significant statement or portion of the speech.

When redundant frames are used in contexts where there is a change of speakers, the effect is to attract more attention to the change. One common motivating factor is the writer's desire to signal redirection of the speech: the new speaker will take the conversation somewhere other than where the previous speaker was directing it. Another common motivation is the writer's wish to draw attention to a significant statement or pronouncement that follows.

Suggested Reading

Blass, F., A. Debrunner, and R. W. Funk. *A Greek Grammar of the New Testament and Other Early Christian Literature.* §420.

Dooley, Robert A., and Stephen H. Levinsohn. *Analyzing Discourse: A Manual of Basic Concepts.* 50–52.

Levinsohn, Stephen H. *Discourse Features of New Testament Greek: A Coursebook on the Information Structure of New Testament Greek.* 231–70.

———. *Self-Instruction Materials on Narrative Discourse Analysis.* 45–54.

Miller, Cynthia L. "Introducing Direct Discourse in Biblical Hebrew Narrative."

Revell, E. J. "The Repetition of Introductions to Speech as a Feature of Biblical Hebrew."

Runge, Steven E. "The Effect of Redundancy on Perceptions of Emphasis and Discontinuity."

Wallace, Daniel B. *Greek Grammar beyond the Basics: An Exegetical Syntax of the New Testament.* 649–50.

TAIL-HEAD LINKAGE

This chapter describes the function of a certain kind of repetition called "tail-head linkage." This device involves the repetition of some action from one clause at the beginning of the next clause, often as a circumstantial participial clause. In other words, the "tail" of one clause becomes the "head" of the next. Here is the definition from the *LDGNT* glossary:

> **Tail-Head Linkage**—The process of restating an action from the previous clause (the tail) at the beginning of the following clause (the head) in order to more closely link it to the preceding clause. It has the effect of slowing down the flow of the discourse before something surprising or important.

Instances of tail-head linkage are graphically represented by the ↻ symbol at the beginning and the end.

We often use tail-head linkage in English to build suspense by slowing down the flow of the story with redundant information. Even though the information is not semantically necessary for understanding the story, it plays an important role in the discourse. Imagine that I wanted to tell you about something surprising that happened to me in the basement of my house.

> While eating dinner, I heard a crash in the basement, so I decided to go downstairs and see what had happened. *As I was going downstairs …*

You can picture what might follow. Levinsohn states regarding tail-head linkage, "Its rhetorical effect is to slow down the story and thus highlight a significant event that follows."[1]

---

1. Stephen H. Levinsohn, *Discourse Features of New Testament Greek: A Coursebook on the Information Structure of New Testament Greek* (2nd ed.; Dallas: SIL International), 290.

8.1   Conventional Explanation

The kind of repetition found in tail-head linkage is typically attributed to a redactor or editor who has inserted the extra information in order to smooth a transition from older material to new material that has been added to a discourse. This is especially true in the Synoptic Gospels where there are similar versions of a discourse. The reasoning goes that the only explanation for the presence of such repetition is the work of an editor at some point in the compositional process.

For instance, in Matt 9, Jesus has been teaching about putting new wine into old wineskins. In v. 18 there is a reiteration of the fact that he has been speaking, provided in the form of a circumstantial frame at the beginning of the verse:

Example 102 :: Matthew 9:18

‹☌Ταῦτα αὐτοῦ λαλοῦντος αὐτοῖς,☌› ‹!ἰδοὺ!› ἄρχων εἷς ἐλθὼν προσεκύνει αὐτῷ λέγων ὅτι ἡ θυγάτηρ μου ἄρτι ἐτελεύτησεν· ἀλλὰ ἐλθὼν ἐπίθες τὴν χεῖρά σου ἐπ᾽ αὐτήν, καὶ ζήσεται.	‹☌As he was saying these things to them,☌› ‹!behold,!› one of the rulers came and knelt down before him, saying, "My daughter has just now died, but come, place your hand on her and she will live!"

Davies and Allison construe the repetition at the beginning of the verse to be "a redactional introduction which replaces Mk 5:21, a verse which would be inappropriate for the new, Matthean context."[2] They view it as providing an appropriate introduction to its new context in Matthew compared to its placement in the Gospel of Mark.[3] In Hendriksen's view, repeating the action highlights the simultaneity of the events: "while Jesus was still answering the question regarding fasting."[4]

---

2. W. D. Davies and Dale C. Allison, *A Critical and Exegetical Commentary on the Gospel According to Saint Matthew*, vol. 2 (ICC; Edinburgh: T & T Clark, 2004), 125.

3. Allen comes to a similar conclusion about the repetition: "The editor now, as before (see on 8:18), postpones Mk 2:23–4:34. He has already inserted 4:35–5:20. This brings him therefore to Mk 5:21–43, which contains two miracles, one set within the other. The editor probably counted this as one incident rather than as two miracles" (Willoughby C. Allen, *A Critical and Exegetical Commentary on the Gospel According to S. Matthew* [ICC; Edinburgh: T & T Clark, 1907], 94).

4. William Hendriksen, *Exposition of the Gospel According to Matthew* (NTC; Grand Rapids: Baker, 1973), 430.

There are similar views postulated regarding the repetition observed in Matt 12:46.

Example 103 :: Matthew 12:46

⟨↻Ἔτι αὐτοῦ λαλοῦντος τοῖς ὄχλοις↻⟩ ⟨!ἰδοὺ!⟩ ἡ μήτηρ καὶ οἱ ἀδελφοὶ αὐτοῦ εἱστήκεισαν ἔξω ζητοῦντες αὐτῷ λαλῆσαι.	⟨↻While he was still speaking to the crowds,↻⟩ ⟨!behold,!⟩ his mother and brothers were standing there outside, desiring to speak to him.

Commentators have recognized the repetition and construed it as evidence of redaction by some editor in the Gospel's development. Yet claiming that it is a sign of redaction simply sidesteps the exegetical issue. It provides no insight into why the redactor included it or into what the device contributes to the discourse. Regardless of who placed it there or what it might be evidence of, it accomplishes a very specific discourse function.

The redactor often is pictured as incompetent or inept, unable to remove "extra" words, as in these passages from Matthew. Berlin makes some helpful comments regarding form and source criticism:

> [In form criticism], as in source criticism, the burden of reading and interpreting is shifted from the reader to the author, and qualities which in modern literature would be valued—e.g., complexity, multiple meanings, allusions to earlier ideas—are discredited for their literary worth and understood as evidence of "layers."[5]

This is not to claim that the ancients have the same literary sensibilities as moderns. However, moderns are often quick to discount literary sophistication, particularly where there is a mismatch between modern and ancient literary devices. Nearly every prominence-marking device described so far has used a redundant element of some kind, and tail-head linkage is no exception. Regardless of origins, it accomplishes a describable task in the discourse, one quite comparable to our modern usage.

Similar appeals to "signs of redaction" have been made in regard to repetition in the Hebrew Bible, especially regarding what Berlin describes as "resumptive repetition." After presenting examples from 1 Kings, she comments,

---

5. Adele Berlin, *Poetics and Interpretation of Biblical Narrative* (BLS 9; Sheffield: Almond, 1983), 123.

These examples are convincing because in both cases the intervening material seems, on the basis of its content or by comparison with a parallel account, to have been a later edition. But, as Talmon has demonstrated, this technique of resumptive repetition occurs elsewhere, in some cases where there is no question of later additions, and is to be explained as a technique whereby the narrative can convey simultaneous events.[6]

In other words, if tail-head linkage is indeed a device for tightening connections between events in order to create a sense of simultaneity and suspense, then someone has made the choice to insert it to accomplish this task in the discourse.

The point to be gleaned here is the mandate to exegete all of the text, regardless of its hypothesized origins. Form and redaction criticisms were developed to explain anomalies in the text that could not adequately be accounted for using traditional methods. Critical scholars hypothesized that a complex compositional history involving multiple editors or redactors provided the best explanation for such discordant or redundant information. Signs of redaction like tail-head linkage may be better explained as indications of literary skill rather than editorial bungling, based on their broader usage in the world's languages, both ancient and modern.

This point raises important methodological questions for form and redaction criticisms: on what basis can one claim a complex redactional history if significant bellwethers of its existence are removed? How might commonly-held compositional assumptions need to be changed? Regardless of where one stands on such matters, all of the text requires our attention. Instead of merely claiming redactional activity, we must consider the exegetical implications associated with it.

8.2   Discourse Explanation

Levinsohn defines tail-head linkage in the NT[7] as "the repetition, in an adverbial or participial clause at the beginning (the head) of the new sentence, of

---

6. Ibid., 126. Berlin raises an important methodological question regarding the insights from poetics (and discourse studies), and the impact that they should have on reassessing critical methodologies. "So it remains a methodological question whether, having explained a piece of evidence synchronically, we can then use the same piece of evidence for a diachronic reconstruction. That is, if a phrase like ויהי is part of the present discourse, serving a poetic function in the present text, can it also be taken as proof that the story which it opens once existed outside of the context in which it is now located?" (ibid., 126–27).

7. Tail-head linkage is found in many other languages besides Koiné Greek. Dooley

the main verb and other information that occurred in the previous sentence (the tail)."[8] As Berlin indicates, repeating a previous action can accomplish a number of things. In English, the idiom "meanwhile, back at the ranch" generically signals a switch from the current story line to some other story line that is simultaneously occurring. Tail-head linkage is similar, in that repeating some preceding event as the circumstantial context for whatever action follows creates a much closer connection between the two than foregoing the repetition.

Tail-head linkage also has the effect of slowing the pace of the narrative, since the information is redundant.[9] As I have shown, doing something that slows the pace is an oft-used highlighting device to point forward to something important. Levinsohn states, "This repetition may be thought of as a rhetorical device that slows the story down prior to the significant event or speech."[10]

Think about the role that this device plays in English storytelling. If I were to say, "So I walked upstairs. And as I was walking up the stairs…," and nothing significant happened in the main clause that follows, you probably would be disappointed or perhaps frustrated. This device is used in various languages of the world to accomplish the same basic task: slowing down the narrative just before something surprising or important. In light of the pervasive use of this device in a variety of languages, it is fanciful to believe that the only role it plays is that of a telltale sign of an inept redactor.

8.3   Application

The first example is taken from John's account of the healing of the official's son. The story involves two different locations: where the official and Jesus talk, and where his son lies sick in bed. At the point that John switches from the one to the other, tail-head linkage is used to indicate that these potentially

---

and Levinsohn provide the following description: "A distinctive form of repetition frequently found in oral material is **TAIL-HEAD LINKAGE** (Thompson and Longacre, 'Adverbial Clauses,' 209–13). This consists of the repetition in a subordinate clause, at the beginning (the 'head') of a new sentence, of at least the main verb of the previous sentence (the 'tail'), as in … **he arrived at the house**. **When he arrived at the house**, *he saw a snake.* Johnston (1976:66) found that tail-head linkage, considered the 'life blood of narrative discourse in most Papua New Guinea languages', was edited out of written texts by native speakers" (*Analyzing Discourse*, 16).

8. Levinsohn, *Discourse Features*, 197.

9. According to Callow, "Whatever form of repetition is used, the effect is always the same. The second mention of the event provides virtually no new information in itself, hence it slows down the information rate considerably" (Kathleen Callow, *Discourse Considerations in Translating the Word of God* [Grand Rapids: Zondervan, 1974], 74).

10. Levinsohn, *Discourse Features*, 197.

unrelated events are indeed closely connected, fostering a sense of simultaneity. John's usage makes clear the connection between Jesus' announcement of healing and the timing reported by the servants.

Example 104 :: John 4:51

⟨☉ἤδη δὲ αὐτοῦ   ⟨☉Now as he was going down,☉⟩
καταβαίνοντος☉⟩ οἱ δοῦλοι αὐτοῦ his slaves met him, saying that his
ὑπήντησαν αὐτῷ λέγοντες ὅτι ὁ   child was alive.
παῖς αὐτοῦ ζῇ.

John further reinforces the simultaneity by including in v. 52 the dialogue between the official and his servants regarding the specific time.[11] The same information could have been communicated without the repetition: "He departed. His slaves met him, saying...." Although this communicates the same content, it does not make the temporal correlation as explicit as using the tail-head linkage.

Acts 4 recounts the story of Peter and the apostles' imprisonment and release. Verse 21a states that they were released, and vv. 21b–22 elaborate on exactly why the officials released them. In other words, the apostles have left the Sanhedrin, and the story remains focused on this location based on the elaboration. The reader needs to be aware of the switch to the new scene of the apostles returning to report what has happened to them.

Example 105 :: Acts 4:23, 24

21 So after threatening them further, they released them, finding no way to punish them on account of the people, because they were all praising God for what had happened. 22 For the man on whom this sign of healing had been performed was more than forty years old.

23 ⟨☉Ἀπολυθέντες☉⟩ δὲ ἦλθον   23 And ⟨☉when they were
πρὸς τοὺς ἰδίους καὶ ἀπήγγειλαν released,☉⟩ they went to their
ὅσα πρὸς αὐτοὺς οἱ ἀρχιερεῖς καὶ own people and reported all that
οἱ πρεσβύτεροι εἶπαν.   the chief priests and the elders had
                               said to them.

---

11. Neither Matthew nor Luke uses tail-head linkage in their account, nor do they include the clarification of John 4:53. This suggests that the writers had different objectives in what each wanted to highlight, based on the overall objectives for their Gospels. We should not be surprised at differences like these, in that they point to differing purposes among the Gospel writers in reporting the events.

The tail-head linkage explicitly signals to the reader that there has been a switch and portrays it as "meanwhile, back at the ranch" from the standpoint of time. While the members of the Sanhedrin are scratching their heads about the matter, the apostles go and report to the disciples. The tail-head linkage in v. 23 stands out somewhat in that it is not needed to signal a switch from the Sanhedrin to the apostles. The effect of using it in this context is twofold. There is still the close connection made between the events, but the slowing of the narrative has the prototypical effect of attracting extra attention to the event or speech that follows. In this case, it is the response of the disciples to the apostles' report from v. 24, which likewise is introduced through tail-head linkage.

οἱ δὲ ⟨↺ἀκούσαντες↻⟩ ὁμοθυμαδὸν ἦραν φωνὴν πρὸς τὸν θεὸν καὶ εἶπαν· δέσποτα, σὺ ὁ ποιήσας τὸν οὐρανὸν καὶ τὴν γῆν καὶ τὴν θάλασσαν καὶ πάντα τὰ ἐν αὐτοῖς,	And ⟨↺when they heard it,↻⟩ they lifted their voices with one mind to God and said, "Master, you are the one who made the heaven and the earth and the sea and all the things in them,"

The response could have been reported more easily and efficiently without the repetition, but it would not have had the same highlighting effect. The use of tail-head linkage helps the reader to better understand how the writer viewed the contribution of these events to the overall discourse.

The next example recounts the beheading of John the Baptist by Herod. There is a switch from the story of the beheading to Jesus feeding the five thousand beginning in v. 13. The tail-head linkage has the effect strengthening the link between these events, as though Jesus' departure was a direct response to Herod's actions.

Example 106 :: Matthew 14:13

⟨↺Ἀκούσας δὲ ὁ Ἰησοῦς↻⟩ ἀνεχώρησεν ἐκεῖθεν ἐν πλοίῳ εἰς ἔρημον τόπον κατ' ἰδίαν· καὶ ἀκούσαντες οἱ ὄχλοι ἠκολούθησαν αὐτῷ πεζῇ ἀπὸ τῶν πόλεων.	⟨↺Now when Jesus heard it,↻⟩ he withdrew from there in a boat to an isolated place by himself. And when the crowds heard it, they followed him by land from the towns.

Although there is a switch from the scene of Herod's birthday and John's beheading to Jesus' teaching, the repetition of "hearing" (as opposed to some other action) implies that Jesus' decision to depart was tied to hearing the report about John. The transitions in the Synoptic parallels in Mark 6:29–30 and Luke 9:9–10 represent the default choice to simply place the events in order without specifying any particular relation between John's beheading and the feeding of the five thousand. This again suggests differing objectives in relating the stories as evidenced by the choices made by each writer in relating the story.

Matthew 17 describes Jesus' transfiguration and the annunciation from heaven. Before the annunciation, Peter suggests in v. 4 that tabernacles be built for Jesus and the two men who appear with him. Tail-head linkage is used in v. 5 to explicitly portray what follows as being closely linked with Peter's speech. Again, since there is no switch of location, the tail-head linkage has a slowing effect, closely connecting potentially unrelated events and attracting extra attention to the proclamation from the cloud.

Example 107 :: Matthew 17:5

⟨🗲ἔτι αὐτοῦ λαλοῦντος🗲⟩ ⟨!ἰδοὺ!⟩ νεφέλη φωτεινὴ ἐπεσκίασεν αὐτούς, καὶ ⟨!ἰδοὺ!⟩ φωνὴ ἐκ τῆς νεφέλης λέγουσα· οὗτός ἐστιν ὁ υἱός μου ὁ ἀγαπητός, ἐν ᾧ εὐδόκησα· ἀκούετε αὐτοῦ.	⟨🗲While he was still speaking,🗲⟩ ⟨!behold,!⟩ a bright cloud overshadowed them, and ⟨!behold,!⟩ a voice from the cloud said, "This is my beloved Son, with whom I am well pleased. Listen to him!"

Note the use attention-getter "behold" before the introductions of both the cloud and the voice, attracting even more attention to the proclamation that follows. The same information could have been related without the tail-head linkage, as in Mark 9:6–7, but without achieving the same effect. Luke 9:34 uses tail-head linkage, suggesting a similar interest in highlighting the speech that it introduces.

Example 108 :: Luke 9:34

⟨🗲ταῦτα δὲ αὐτοῦ λέγοντος🗲⟩ ἐγένετο νεφέλη καὶ ἐπεσκίαζεν αὐτούς· ἐφοβήθησαν δὲ ἐν τῷ εἰσελθεῖν αὐτοὺς εἰς τὴν νεφέλην.	⟨🗲And while he was saying these things,🗲⟩ a cloud came and overshadowed them, and they were afraid as they entered into the cloud.

We again find evidence of differences in the writer's priorities or intentions based on the kinds of discourse devices used to represent the propositional content.

I have only observed one instance of tail-head linkage in Mark: at Jesus' arrest in the garden of Gethsemane. The device is also found in the Synoptic parallels.[12]

Example 109 :: Mark 14:43

Καὶ εὐθὺς ‹↻ἔτι αὐτοῦ λαλοῦντος↻› παραγίνεται Ἰούδας εἷς τῶν δώδεκα καὶ μετ' αὐτοῦ ὄχλος μετὰ μαχαιρῶν καὶ ξύλων παρὰ τῶν ἀρχιερέων καὶ τῶν γραμματέων καὶ τῶν πρεσβυτέρων.	And immediately, ‹↻while he was still speaking,↻› Judas—one of the twelve—arrived, and with him a crowd with swords and clubs, from the chief priests and the scribes and the elders.

The two events could simply have been placed together without any repetition. Note also that the tail-head linkage co-occurs with the use of the historical present, another forward-pointing device that highlights what follows.[13] The effect of the repetition is to create the sense that Judas arrives just as Jesus finishes speaking to the disciples. This is important to the writer, since in v. 42 Jesus says, "Get up, let us go! Behold, the one who is betraying me is approaching!" The effect of using the tail-head linkage in v. 43 is to attract more attention to an important event that follows, Jesus' dialogue with Judas, who Mark reminds us is "one of the twelve," using an overspecified noun phrase to thematically highlight this information.[14]

The account in Luke 18:18–30 consists of a dialogue between Jesus and a rich ruler who wants to make sure that he will inherit eternal life. Tail-head linkage is used in a series of three verses to slow the pace of the dialogue, effectively highlighting each speech that follows. Note that this linkage represents the writer's choice about how to represent the material.

Example 110 :: Luke 18:22–24

22 ‹↻ἀκούσας δὲ ὁ Ἰησοῦς↻› εἶπεν αὐτῷ· ἔτι ‹→ἕν→› σοι λείπει· ‹⊙πάντα ὅσα ἔχεις πώλησον	22 And ‹↻when he heard this,↻› Jesus said to him, "You still lack ‹→one thing:→› ‹⊙›Sell all that

---

12. Note that John's gospel uses tail-head linkage in this pericope, but not to highlight Judas's arrival. Instead, it is used in 18:1 to highlight the transition from the discourse in the upper room to the scene in the garden.

13. See chapter 6.

14. See §15.2.1.

καὶ διάδος πτωχοῖς, καὶ ἕξεις
θησαυρὸν ἐν [τοῖς] οὐρανοῖς, καὶ
δεῦρο ἀκολούθει μοι.☉⟩

you have, and distribute the proceeds to the poor—and you will
have treasure in heaven—and
come, follow me."☉⟩

23 ὁ δὲ ⟨☉ἀκούσας ταῦτα☉⟩
περίλυπος ἐγενήθη· ἦν γὰρ
πλούσιος σφόδρα.

23 But ⟨☉when he heard these
things☉⟩ he became very sad,
because he was extremely wealthy.

24 ⟨☉Ἰδὼν δὲ αὐτὸν ὁ Ἰησοῦς
[περίλυπον γενόμενον]☉⟩ εἶπεν·
πῶς δυσκόλως οἱ τὰ χρήματα
ἔχοντες εἰς τὴν βασιλείαν τοῦ
θεοῦ εἰσπορεύονται·

24 And ⟨☉when Jesus saw him
becoming very sad,☉⟩ he said,
"How difficult it is for those who
possess wealth to enter into the
kingdom of God!"

The answer that the rich ruler provides to Jesus in v. 21 sets the stage for Jesus to redirect him to something more costly than keeping the commandments: selling all that he has and giving it away in preparation for following Jesus. This change in direction also could have been communicated by way of a redundant quotative frame. However, doing so may have made the exchange look more like an argument than a push to make the rich man to look deeper. A quotative frame is not an option in v. 23, since it is a narrative comment and not the introduction of a speech.

Another effect of the tail-head linkage in this context is to closely relate the events to one another. Far from being a sign of redaction, the use of tail-head linkage here suggests an intimacy in this dialogue. Each response is explicitly tied back to the other speaker's action. In other words, the idea of selling everything is portrayed not as some idea that Jesus pulls out of thin air, but as a direct response to the rich man's answer. The rich man's sadness is directly linked to Jesus' request that he sell everything. Jesus' statement in vv. 24–25 is portrayed as a direct response to the rich man's response to Jesus' command to sell, distribute, and follow.

The Synoptic parallels in Mark 10 and Matthew 19 do not use tail-head linkage. The events are simply related to one another implicitly by virtue of their linear placement in the text. Luke's usage suggests a much greater inter-est in highlighting the relationships between the events. It also has the effect of slowing the pace, attracting more attention to what follows.[15]

---

15. The question posed by the rich man in Matt 19:20, "What do I still lack?" has a comparable effect of slowing the flow, compared to Jesus telling him that he yet lacks

The next example is from Matthew's description of Jesus' prediction of his death as he makes his way to Jerusalem. In this case, the repetition is in the dialogue itself rather than in narrative proper. There is no need for both statements. The inclusion of the circumstantial clause in the narrative of v. 17 sets the stage for processing Jesus' first comment as tail-head linkage in v. 18.

Example 111 :: Matthew 20:18

[17] And as Jesus was going up to Jerusalem, he took the twelve disciples by themselves and said to them on the way,

[18] ‹!ἰδού!› ‹↻ἀναβαίνομεν εἰς Ἰεροσόλυμα,↻› καὶ ὁ υἱὸς τοῦ ἀνθρώπου παραδοθήσεται τοῖς ἀρχιερεῦσιν καὶ γραμματεῦσιν, καὶ κατακρινοῦσιν αὐτὸν θανάτῳ….	[18] ‹!"Behold,!› ‹↻we are going up to Jerusalem,↻› and the Son of Man will be handed over to the chief priests and scribes, and they will condemn him to death…."

In v. 17 we learn that Jesus and his disciples are heading up to Jerusalem. The disciples likely knew where they were going, so there would have been no need for repeating this information from the narrative in the speech of v. 18.[16] The effect of having these statements repeated is to slow the pace of the narrative for the reader. Matthew could have simply allowed Jesus' words to report that they were going to Jerusalem, instead of stating it in the narrative before the speech. Choosing to repeat the information slows the pace of the discourse just before Jesus' announcement about the Son of Man. This prediction that Jesus is to be handed over to the chief priests and scribes comes just before the triumphal entry. The statements regarding Jesus' betrayal and death become increasingly more specific as the passion story unfolds.[17] Jesus' statements play a crucial role in processing the events that follow. He fully understood what lay ahead, and the writer understandably draws attention to the important pronouncement here using tail-head linkage.

Another example of tail-head linkage is found in the scene where Mary goes to visit Elizabeth after hearing from the angel that both she and Elizabeth are to give birth to sons, and that Elizabeth is already in her third month of the pregnancy.

---

something, as in Luke's account. This question draws extra attention to the answer that is to follow, just as Luke's use of a forward-pointing reference and target.

16. The same kind of repetition occurs in Josh 13:1: "Now Joshua was old and advanced in years when the Lord said to him, 'You are old and advanced in years, and very much of the land remains to be possessed'" (NASB).

17. See Matt 12:40; 17:9–12, 22.

Example 112 :: Luke 1:41

καὶ ἐγένετο ‹✿ὡς ἤκουσεν τὸν ἀσπασμὸν τῆς Μαρίας ἡ Ἐλισάβετ,✿› ἐσκίρτησεν τὸ βρέφος ἐν τῇ κοιλίᾳ αὐτῆς, καὶ ἐπλήσθη πνεύματος ἁγίου ἡ Ἐλισάβετ….	And it happened that ‹✿when Elizabeth heard the greeting of Mary,✿› the baby in her womb leaped and Elizabeth was filled with the Holy Spirit….

Elizabeth's baby is John the Baptist, who will prepare the way for Jesus' ministry. His leaping in the womb is portrayed as a direct response to hearing Mary's greeting, based on the use of the tail-head repetition. It is also something of a foretaste of what is to come. His response to Mary's greeting precipitates a series of significant speeches that are related to one another. In v. 42, Elizabeth asks Mary why she has come to visit in light of how blessed she is by God to be the mother of the Lord. Participles are used to background the circumstances,[18] as if to say, "In light of the fact that you are blessed among women, and that the fruit of your womb is blessed, why in the world would you visit me?" Mary responds in vv. 46–55 with what has come to be known as the Magnificat, a prayer of thanksgiving and praise to the Lord for all that he has done and is doing in her life.

To summarize, the repetition of "heard the greeting" does several things. It creates an explicit connection between John's leaping in the womb and Elizabeth's hearing of Mary's greeting. Omitting the repetition would have left this relationship implicit by virtue of the ordering of the events. The repetition also has the effect of slowing the narrative just before the significant event of John's leaping that precipitates the series of speeches that follow.

The last part of Luke 9 contains a series of brief interactions between would-be followers and Jesus as he travels to a new village.

Example 113 :: Luke 9:57

Καὶ ‹✿πορευομένων αὐτῶν ἐν τῇ ὁδῷ✿› εἶπέν τις πρὸς αὐτόν· ἀκολουθήσω σοι ὅπου ἐὰν ἀπέρχῃ.	And ‹✿as they were traveling on the road,✿› someone said to him, "I will follow you wherever you go!"

The use of the tail-head linkage accomplishes several things. First, the repetition has the effect of slowing the pace of the narrative, creating anticipation. Second, it suggests a simultaneous relationship between the events, as though

---

18. See chapter 12.

the people are making these pronouncements to Jesus as he is walking along. It portrays Jesus as focused on the journey and possibly not stopping for the conversations. Finally, the slowing down through repetition draws attention to the significant speeches that follow. These include the Son of Man having nowhere to lay his head (vv. 57–58), letting the dead bury the dead (vv. 59–60), and not looking back once one has put a hand to the plow (vv. 61–62).

Each one of the would-be followers has the same problem: placing a higher priority on something other than following Jesus. There is no indication from Luke that any of these potential disciples responded by following Jesus. Luke's use of tail-head linkage creates the impression that these interactions occur while Jesus is mission-focused, moving from one ministry place to the next. In each interaction, Jesus challenges the person to count the cost of following him. This results in Jesus speaking about mission while he is actively carrying it out, moving from place to place. Matthew's account beginning in 8:18 implies travel but does not make it explicit. Luke's use of tail-head linkage represents the choice to place these interactions about "following" in a particular narrative context, based on his communicative objectives.

The story of raising Lazarus from the dead in John 11 exhibits heavy use of tail-head linkage to slow the narrative flow in order to draw attention to significant speeches or events that follow. In v. 3, Jesus is told that "the one whom he loves" is sick. The implication is that they are informing him in order to have Jesus heal Lazarus, to prevent him from dying. Verse 4 records Jesus' response to this situation.

Example 114 :: John 11:4

⟨↻ἀκούσας↻⟩ δὲ ὁ Ἰησοῦς εἶπεν· αὕτη ἡ ἀσθένεια οὐκ ἔστιν πρὸς θάνατον ἀλλ᾽ ὑπὲρ τῆς δόξης τοῦ θεοῦ, ἵνα δοξασθῇ ὁ υἱὸς τοῦ θεοῦ δι᾽ αὐτῆς.	And ⟨↻when he heard it,↻⟩ Jesus said, "This sickness is not to death, but for the glory of God, in order that the Son of God may be glorified through it."

Jesus' statement makes it appear as though he is not worried about Lazarus's sickness. However, Lazarus does die, and questions remain about why Jesus allowed this to happen and whether or not Lazarus will be raised. The writer uses a number of devices to slow the flow and build up the suspense by delaying the conclusion.

In the intervening verses leading up to v. 28, Lazarus has died and Martha has conveyed to Jesus that had he been there Lazarus would not have died. After this interaction with Jesus, Martha returns to the house and informs Mary that Jesus has arrived.

Example 115 :: John 11:28–29

²⁸ Καὶ ‹⊕τοῦτο εἰποῦσα⊕› ἀπῆλθεν καὶ ἐφώνησεν Μαριὰμ τὴν ἀδελφὴν αὐτῆς λάθρᾳ εἰποῦσα· ὁ διδάσκαλος πάρεστιν καὶ φωνεῖ σε.	²⁸ And ‹⊕when she had said this,⊕› she went and called her sister Mary privately, saying, "The Teacher is here and is calling for you."
²⁹ ἐκείνη δὲ ‹⊕ὡς ἤκουσεν⊕› ἠγέρθη ταχὺ καὶ ἤρχετο πρὸς αὐτόν.	²⁹ So that one, ‹⊕when she heard it,⊕› got up quickly and went to him.

This twofold use of tail-head linkage is followed by more background information in vv. 30–31 that Jesus had not yet entered the village, and that the Jews followed Mary out of town, assuming that she was going to mourn at the tomb. The net result of all of this repetition and background information is to delay the expected dialogue between Mary and Jesus, one of the climaxes of the story. We are not told what Mary was thinking or feeling, so readers are left to place themselves in her shoes, so to speak. The speeches between Mary and Jesus are sprinkled with highlighting devices, especially the historical present. They have the effect of drawing attention to the speech that follows.

As Jesus finally reaches the tomb and prepares to raise Lazarus, his prayer in vv. 41–42 has the effect of delaying the expected event. Jesus' call for Lazarus to come out in v. 43 is framed using tail-head linkage, repeating the action of saying the prayer in a backgrounded participial clause.

Example 116 :: John 11:43

⁴¹ So they took away the stone. And Jesus lifted up his eyes above and said, "Father, I give thanks to you that you hear me. ⁴² And I know that you always hear me, but for the sake of the crowd standing around I said it, so that they may believe that you sent me."

⁴³ καὶ ‹⊕ταῦτα εἰπὼν⊕› φωνῇ μεγάλῃ ἐκραύγασεν· Λάζαρε, δεῦρο ἔξω.	⁴³ And ‹⊕when he had said these things,⊕› he cried out with a loud voice, "Lazarus, come out!"

This story illustrates well the use of delay tactics such as repetition and background information to slow the pace of the story, drawing it out in order to build suspense. The same kind of delay strategies could be put to use in teaching or preaching the text.

The use of tail-head linkage in this chapter fits well with the use of other forward-pointing devices we have observed in the Synoptic gospels and Acts.

Understanding devices such as tail-head linkage will pay dividends not only in exegesis, but also in exposition. The same kinds of strategies that we see the biblical writers use to convey their message can also be used when preaching or presenting the content to English speakers. Understanding the function of the device will also aid in the proper representation of the story in exposition.

Suggested Reading

Berlin, Adele. *Poetics and Interpretation of Biblical Narrative.* 122–28.

Callow, Kathleen. *Discourse Considerations in Translating the Word of God.* 74–81.

Dooley, Robert A., and Stephen H. Levinsohn. *Analyzing Discourse: A Manual of Basic Concepts.* 15–18.

Levinsohn, Stephen H. *Self-Instruction Materials on Narrative Discourse Analysis.* 197–200.

.

PART 3   INFORMATION STRUCTURING DEVICES

Greek is a highly inflected language, making extensive use of case-marking to represent syntactic relationships. In contrast, English heavily relies upon the ordering of clause components to convey syntactic roles. This mismatch in syntactic encoding has led to significant misunderstandings about the nature of word order in Greek.

Part 3 describes how variation in the ordering of propositions is used to pragmatically structure the flow of the discourse.

INFORMATION STRUCTURE

This chapter provides an introduction to "information structure," which is most often referred to in NT studies as "word order" analysis.[1] Discussions of word order in Greek have been fundamentally interested in determining the preferred or "normal" ordering of clause components. Some of this interest is typologically motivated, seeking to properly classify Greek with similar languages. Such study ends up telling us what orders are possible and perhaps preferred. But it offers little explanatory help for understanding the meaningful difference in using one order compared to another. Is there a better explanation than claiming "stylistic variation" or "emphasis"?

Most languages have some means by which writers can structure discourse, prioritizing and organizing it based on their communication goals. As we will see, English relies heavily upon intonation to accomplish this task, whereas Koiné Greek relies upon its flexible word order to structure the information. The goal of this chapter is to introduce the principles used for structuring information across languages, principles that apply equally well to English and Greek, even though the languages use different means of conveying the same discourse function. These principles provide insight into the writers' intention and motivation for changing the order of the clause components from the patterns expected in the Greek NT.

---

1. Portions of the chapter are excerpted from Steven E. Runge, "What Difference Does It Make If NT Greek Has a Default Word Order or Not?" (paper presented at the annual meeting of the Evangelical Theological Society, Washington, D.C., 15–17 November 2006).

9.1   Conventional Explanation

Greek grammarians seem to have a love-hate relationship with the issue of word order. Most seem to believe that there is some significance to the variation observed, yet it has proven difficult to delineate principles that accurately describe the variation. Porter states, "Many of the standard reference grammars of the Greek of the NT are convinced that standard NT Greek 'word order' is verb-subject-object."[2] These grammarians are Winer,[3] Robertson, BDF, MHT, Moule,[4] and Schwyzer.[5] Although each recognized a tendency toward VSO (verb-subject-object), most were reluctant to say much more.

It seems that these grammarians had a rather strict conception of word order. Unless the language nearly always followed a certain pattern, little could legitimately be claimed about word order. This view seems to be based upon using English as the standard: since it exhibits a very rigid word order, it is therefore easily describable. Greek and Hebrew exhibit what has been called "free word order." The great disparity in ordering principles between English and the biblical languages has led some to despair that anything can be conclusively claimed regarding ordering principles. It is critical to note that the preoccupation with describing the typology of the language has provided little understanding of how and why the language structures clauses as it does. Little attention has been given to insights from the field of information structure.

The accepted view seems to be that the most emphatic or prominent part of the sentence is placed at the beginning, although most have recognized that this was not a rule.[6] Robertson's comment on the matter illustrates well this tension regarding word order: "The predicate very commonly comes first … simply because the predicate is most frequently the main point in the clause."[7] He then goes on to criticize Blass for making too strong a claim on the matter of VSO ordering, concluding that there is no "unalterable rule in the Greek

---

2. Stanley E. Porter, *Idioms of the Greek New Testament* (2nd ed.; Sheffield: Sheffield Academic, 1999), 293.

3. G. B. Winer, *A Treatise on the Grammar of New Testament Greek* (trans. and rev. W. F. Moulton; 3rd ed.; Edinburgh: T & T Clark, 1882).

4. C. F. D. Moule, *An Idiom Book of New Testament Greek* (Cambridge: Cambridge University Press, 1959).

5. Eduard Schwyzer, *Griechische Grammatik: Auf der Grundlage von Karl Brugmanns Griechischer Grammatik* (2 vols.; Munich: Beck, 1939–1950), 2:693.

6. See A. T. Robertson, *A Grammar of the Greek New Testament in the Light of Historical Research* (1919; repr., Bellingham, Wash.: Logos, 2006), 417.

7. Ibid. Porter arrives at the same conclusion: "The importance of the verb for Greek is confirmed by the central place occupied by the predicate in clause structure" (*Idioms*, 296).

sentence save that of spontaneity."[8] Even though Robertson ostensibly rejects the idea of a standard order in Koiné Greek, only three sentences later he states that emphasis is indicated by "removing a word from its *usual* position to an *unusual* one."[9] Such a claim presupposes that an underlying usual order exists, even though Robertson himself may not have been able to adequately describe it.[10] When this "usual" pattern is broken, it stands out as "unusual."

In many cases, statistical analysis of the various orders is used to justify a certain order as preferred. However, the complexity of the Greek data creates something of a conundrum, illustrating the limited utility of statistics. Porter states that there are two major problems with statistical analyses: unlike English, "the majority of Greek clauses do not express all of the elements used in the formulation" (i.e., predicate, subject, and object), and "to base one's formulation of standard order on instances where all three elements are present misrepresents the evidence and the results."[11] The net result of this is guarded reference to word order in most grammars, other than to say that the order is fairly free and seems to be motivated by emphasis and/or contrast.[12]

In spite of Porter's reservations regarding the statistical data, he does make some insightful observations about the positioning of the subject when it is present.[13] When it occurs at the beginning of a clause, it "gives new or

---

8. Robertson, *Grammar*, 417.

9. Ibid. (italics added).

10. I contend that Robertson and others had spent enough years living in the language that they had internalized the syntax sufficiently to be able to intuitively analyze it. In other words, their gut instinct was their guide. What they lacked was not an understanding of the language, but rather a framework for describing it. I will bolster this claim by showing how the contradictory claims that they made are valid in certain contexts. They got it, but they had difficulty communicating what they got.

11. Porter, *Idioms*, 293.

12. Wallace is representative of this, in that he does not systematically discuss the issue of word order in the clause, focusing instead on the classification of clauses. He does discuss the impact of word order on certain constructions. For instance, he notes that word order is not a reliable guide in distinguishing between the subject and object of infinitival constructions, where both are accusatives: "Just as with S[ubject]-P[redicate]N[ominative], if one of the two substantives is a pronoun and the other is articular (or a proper name), the pronoun is the subject term (again, regardless of word order)" (Daniel B. Wallace, *Greek Grammar beyond the Basics: An Exegetical Syntax of the New Testament* [Grand Rapids: Zondervan, 1999], 196). Word order is also discussed in conjunction with Colwell's Rule (ibid., 256–70), and in distinguishing different kinds of participles (e.g., participles describing attendant circumstance will precede the main verb [ibid., 641–42]), while "the result participle will be a *present* tense participle and will *follow* (in word order) the main verb" (ibid., 638).

13. Porter's interest in statistical data is motivated by the presuppositions of his

emphatic information and the predicate elucidates it."[14] He notes a correlating effect associated with placement in a noninitial position: "When the subject is placed in the second or third position in the clause (i.e., after the predicate and/or complement), its markedness or emphasis apparently decreases.... Moving the subject to a subsidiary position, however, does not necessarily elevate another element in the clause to a position of prominence."[15] Such comments are representative of the conundrum with respect to word order in Koiné Greek: placing some elements at the beginning of the clause in some contexts can result in emphasis, but not always. Although the grammarians provide only very general principles describing word order, there is consensus that something related to emphasis or contrast motivated the NT writers to change the order of certain words, and context is the determining factor.

To summarize, there seems to have been an underlying sense about what "standard" order was, yet the complexity and frequency of the variation precluded anything more than general statements from being made on the issue. Judgments regarding the exegetical significance of variation in word order seem based more on intuition about the language than on a clearly defined understanding of information structure. As we will see, this intuition is often correct, suggesting that the classic grammarians internalized principles of information structure. They could intuitively describe the meaning associated with the patterns, even if they could not clearly express the principles in a unified framework.

The claims and principles described in this section form the backdrop for the linguistic description that follows. Most of them will be shown to hold true in certain instances. What has been lacking is a descriptive framework that is sufficiently flexible and robust to account for the variety of data attested in a form that is accessible to nonlinguists.

---

methodology—a modified version of Systemic Functional Linguistics (SFL)—which utilizes statistical analyses to create a hierarchy or "cline" of clause types. SFL provides an adequate description of information structure in English but was not originally formulated to describe nonconfigurational (i.e., flexible word order) languages such as Koiné Greek. Porter's presuppositions also differ from other functional theories in significant ways, though these differences are rarely discussed in the NT literature. For an overview of the SFL approach to word order in Koiné Greek, see Ivan Shing Chung Kwong, *The Word Order of the Gospel of Luke: Its Foregrounded Messages* (LNTS 298; SNTG 12; London: T & T Clark, 2005); Steven E. Runge, review of Ivan Shing Chung Kwong, *The Word Order of the Gospel of Luke: Its Foregrounded Messages*, *RBL* (26 April 2008).

14. Porter, *Idioms*, 296.

15. Ibid.

9.2   Discourse Explanation

9.2.1   Introduction

In §1.3, I introduced the idea of *markedness* as a strategy for organizing the choices available to a writer into a coherent and unified framework. This qualitative approach to markedness presupposed that in each set of choices there will be one that is the most basic, called the *default*. This is the option used when the writer chooses not to signal the presence of some qualitative feature. The feature may or may not be present in the default; it is *unmarked* for the feature. Based on the unmarked option, all the other options are described based upon what they signal, or *mark*, as being present. Generally speaking, the unmarked option is the one most frequently used, though not always.[16] When there are more than two or three options available, statistics can be misleading, particularly if there are other meaningful variables that need to be factored into the identification of a default (e.g., genre or content).[17]

Most inquiries into Greek word order have focused upon establishing the most frequently occurring pattern rather than the most basic, unmarked pattern.[18] Although I will occasionally refer to statistics, establishing the most basic form is far more important than finding the most frequently occurring one. They are not necessarily the same.

Because of the importance of understanding the concepts that follow, I will start by describing the use of information structuring principles in English. This explanation will allow us then to return in the next five chapters to how these same principles operate in Koiné Greek.

9.2.2   Information Structure

Studies of information structure focus on the ordering of clause components, not just single words. These clause components include the subject, verb/predicate, direct and indirect objects. Clauses may also contain embedded clauses, such as subordinate or relative clauses. There are certain ordering principles followed in each language,[19] but even in rigidly ordered languages

---

16. Regarding the perils of using statistics alone to isolate a default, see Edna Andrews, *Markedness Theory: The Union of Asymmetry and Semiosis in Language* (Durham, N.C.: Duke University Press, 1990), 137–39.

17. See the discussion of certain adverbial clauses in chapter 11.

18. See Kwong, *Word Order*; James D. Dvorak, "Thematization, Topic, and Information Flow," *JLIABG* 1 (2008): 17–37.

19. For some examples from Greek, see Porter, *Idioms*, 291–93.

such as English there is quite a bit of flexibility. The information of the overall discourse is structured in such a way as to best communicate the speaker's or writer's intended message, based upon the constraints and conventions of the particular language.

Craige Roberts notes that English uses intonation, or *prosody*, in ways that are language-specific and that should not be expected to universally apply. "We might expect that other languages would use very different means to achieve some of the same ends, or would use similar means to encode other kinds of information."[20] She is correct: Greek uses changes in word order to accomplish the same discourse tasks that are predominantly accomplished in English using prosody. All languages must accomplish the same basic set of tasks. We should not be surprised that they use different grammatical devices to accomplish them, based upon the constraints of each language. In both Greek and English, the devices are employed to accomplish specific communicative tasks. The attested variations can be correlated to the content and objectives present in the discourse context.

9.2.3   Mental Representations

As people hear or read a discourse, they do not simply store all of the words in their head. Instead, they take the ideas and concepts and essentially file them away in what Lambrecht calls a *mental representation* of the discourse.[21] This mental representation has been likened to a filing cabinet, where the basic topics of the discourse are the file folders. As new information is added to the mental representation, it is placed into the appropriate file based on its content and relationship to the discourse. The topical files could also be conceived as being filed in drawers of a file cabinet, based on how each relates to the overall discourse.[22]

The writer's goal is to make sure that readers build their mental representation of the discourse in a way that accords with the writer's intended message. Dooley and Levinsohn state,

---

20. Craige Roberts, "Information Structure: Towards an Integrated Formal Theory of Pragmatics," in *Papers in Semantics* (ed. Jae-Hak Yoon and Andreas Kathol; WPL 49; Ohio State University Department of Linguistics, 1999), 2.

21. Knud Lambrecht, *Information Structure and Sentence Form: Topic, Focus, and the Mental Representations of Discourse Referents* (CSL 71; Cambridge: Cambridge University Press, 1996), 74.

22. This analogy is based on Talmy Givón, "The Grammar of Referential Coherence as Mental Processing Instructions," *Linguistics* 30 (1992): 5–55; cf. Lambrecht, *Information Structure*, 74–113.

The organization that hearers associate with a discourse is not simply a matter of the linguistic structure that appears. Rather, on a more fundamental level, it is a reflection of how the content comes together and is stored in the mind. The forms of language that the speaker uses certainly play a part in this, but psychological research shows that the way hearers understand, store, and remember a discourse corresponds only partially with what was actually said.[23]

9.2.4 Natural Information Flow

There is a tendency in discourse to move from what is most known to what is least known, as much as the constraints of the language allow.[24] Speakers tend to start with what is already established or knowable in the context and then add new or "nonestablished" information to it. This principle is easily observed at the beginning of a story. In a context where there is no ongoing situation (i.e., starting from scratch), the story begins by predicating the existence of something before saying anything about it. The use of "dummy" subjects such as *there* (e.g., "There was an X") allows a new person or concept to be introduced as the object of the clause instead of as the subject. Dummy subjects allow us to introduce something while not violating natural information flow.

For example, if you knew that I had a friend named Mike, and he was the only "Mike" we ever discussed, I could say something like "Mike and I had lunch today" without causing confusion. If you did not know this particular Mike or if there are several "Mikes" to choose from, I would need to introduce him before talking about him: "There is a friend of mine named Mike. He ..." There are also streamlined introductions, such as "This friend of mine named Mike, he..."[25] Both of these conventions introduce what is going to be talked about before talking about it. Using the dummy subject allows me to introduce "Mike" as the object of the clause instead of as the subject. Alternatively, I could simply introduce "Mike" as the object in a clause using some other subject knowable from an established context: "I had lunch today with a friend of mine named Mike."

---

23. Robert A. Dooley and Stephen H. Levinsohn, *Analyzing Discourse: A Manual of Basic Concepts* (Dallas: SIL International, 2001), 10.

24. See Bernard Comrie, *Language Universals and Linguistic Typology: Syntax and Morphology* (Chicago: University of Chicago Press, 1989), 127–28.

25. This second option uses what is called a left-dislocation or *pendens* construction, which is widely used in the NT for the same kind of task as illustrated here in English. This device is discussed in more detail in chapter 14.

These examples illustrate "natural information flow" within a clause. This principle also operates at higher levels of the discourse. Think about how the typical story develops. Generally speaking, most clauses have a topic followed by some kind of comment about it. Oftentimes, information from the comment of one clause becomes the topic of the next one. For example:

> Once upon a time *there* was a **prince**.
> The *prince* lived in a **castle**.
> The *castle* had a huge **moat** around it.

This may sound very simplistic, but it is key to understanding information structure. Consider the following NT example:

Example 117 :: Natural information flow Mark 8:1

(a) Ἐν ἐκείναις ταῖς ἡμέραις πάλιν πολλοῦ ὄχλου ὄντος	(a) In those days there was again a large crowd,
(b) καὶ μὴ ἐχόντων τί φάγωσιν,	(b) and they did not have anything they could eat.
(c) προσκαλεσάμενος τοὺς μαθητὰς λέγει αὐτοῖς.…	(c) Summoning the disciples, he said to them.…

Notice that the verb in clause (a) uses a dummy subject, "there was," to predicate the existence of the crowd. Once the crowd is established in the discourse, it then becomes the topic of the following clause, grounding clause (b) to what precedes. This quick introduction in Mark 8:1 provides the background for the story of feeding the four thousand.

Most every clause in a discourse is a combination of *established* information and *nonestablished* information. The established information may derive from the preceding discourse content, or from generally accessible knowledge about the world around us. A discourse that asserts nothing new would be pointless; a discourse composed of only new information, ungrounded in what was already known, would be difficult (or impossible) to understand. The established information provides the grounding and framework within which we process and store the newly asserted information. Communicating new information is the ultimate goal of a discourse. The established information in the mental representation provides the basis and framework for understanding the new. The two work together.

Understanding the distinction between established and nonestablished information is critical to understanding information structure. Nonestablished information refers to newly asserted ideas or concepts, not just to the new words themselves. The newly asserted information is called the *focus* of the clause because it is what the writer or speaker wants you to know as a result of the utterance. Communicating the focal information is the *raison d'être* for the utterance.

Since each clause contains a mix of presupposed and newly asserted information, the focus of the clause may be more specifically defined as the difference between what is presupposed in a context and what is asserted in a given proposition.[26] This means that what is focal in any given context will change as the discourse develops. The newly asserted information of one clause will become part of the presupposed information of the next clause. This constant change in information status is what complicates an understanding of information structure.

The key thing to remember is that each clause will contain a mix of established and newly asserted information. The goal of the communication is to convey the newly asserted information; it is the focus of the utterance. The presupposed information provides the framework for processing and understanding the focal information. As new information is asserted, the body of presupposed information will grow. Thus, differentiating what is presupposed from what is focal is entirely context-dependent. As the context changes, so will the determinations about the status of information.

What I have described so far represents the default strategy for structuring a discourse and the flow of information. This does not mean that it is always followed. The default strategy typically is used when there is nothing special that the writer wants to signal. As I have pointed out in earlier chapters, breaking default expectations has the effect of making something stand out in ways that the default form would not have accomplished. The resulting prominence accomplishes various pragmatic effects (recall the distinction between semantic meaning and pragmatic effect in §1.2). These effects are not an inherent meaning of the syntactic form; rather, they are an effect of using a form or structure in some marked way that breaks with the expected norm for that context.

9.2.5   Violating Natural Information Flow and Prominence

Simon Dik has proposed that there are two different preverbal positions that may or may not be filled in any given clause, which he calls Position 1

---

26. Lambrecht refers to newly asserted information as the *focus* of the clause, defining it as "the semantic component of a pragmatically structured proposition whereby the assertion differs from the presupposition" (*Information Structure*, 213).

(P1) and Position 2 (P2).[27] Placing a clause component in one of these positions upsets the principle of natural information flow and has the effect of assigning prominence to the component that it would not otherwise have received in its standard position. Dik's model has successfully been applied to diverse languages, but most importantly to English, Greek, and Hebrew.[28] The meaningful distinction between P1 and P2 is based solely upon whether the information is presupposed or newly asserted, respectively.

One or more established (i.e., topical) elements of the clause may be placed in position P1. These P1 elements establish a new *frame of reference*,[29] creating an explicit mental grounding point for the clause that follows. Position P2, on the other hand, is where newly asserted or focal information is placed. The prominence added to the P2 element marks it as "what is relatively the most important … information in the setting."[30]

The default expectation of natural information flow is that focal information will be placed as close to the end of the clause as the typology of the language allows. Placing focal information in the P2 position represents the choice to take what was already the most important part of the clause (i.e., newly asserted, focal information) and to attract even more attention to it by moving it from its default position to a marked one. Linguists refer to this as *marked focus*.

---

27. Simon Dik, *The Theory of Functional Grammar: Part I: The Structure of the Clause* (FGS 9; Dordrecht; Providence, R.I.: Foris, 1989), 363.

28. Its application to Koiné Greek and biblical Hebrew is particularly relevant because the verb quite often occurs clause-initially (see Stephen H. Levinsohn, *Self-instruction Materials on Narrative Discourse Analysis* [Dallas: SIL International, 2007], §§4A.2.2, 4B.2.2]; Porter, *Idioms*, 293). From its inception, Dik's "functional grammar" model focused on providing typologically based descriptions of language rather than restricting itself to English and European languages.

29. What I refer to here as a "frame of reference" traditionally has been called "topicalization" (Lambrecht, *Information Structure*, 6), a "point of departure" (PoD) (Stephen H. Levinsohn, *Discourse Features of New Testament Greek: A Coursebook on the Information Structure of New Testament Greek* [2nd ed.; Dallas: SIL International], 8), or a "contextualizing constituent" (Randall Buth, "Word Order in the Verbless Clause: A Generative-Functional Approach," in *The Verbless Clause in Biblical Hebrew: Linguistic Approaches* [ed. Cynthia L. Miller; Winona Lake, Ind.: Eisenbrauns, 1999], 107). According to Levinsohn (*Discourse Features*, 8), a PoD accomplishes two functions: (1) it provides a starting point for the communication; (2) it cohesively anchors the subsequent clause(s) to something that is already in the context (i.e., something accessible in the hearer's mental representation).

30. Dik, *Functional Grammar*, 19. Most linguists use the term *focus* to refer to the new information added in each clause. Lambrecht (*Information Structure*, 206) offers a more precise definition, describing it as the difference between that which is presupposed at the time of the utterance and that which is asserted in the utterance.

Greek grammarians traditionally have referred to marked focus as a subcategory of *emphasis*. I will use the term *emphasis* in a technical sense throughout this volume. It will *only* refer to focal information (that which is already the most important in the clause) that has been placed in a marked position or construction in order to attract more prominence to it.[31]

Dik's template is summarized below:

Figure 4 :: Simon Dik's preverbal template

(P1) (P2) VERB X, where

::Position P1: may contain one or more established clause component;

::Position P2: may contain a nonestablished clause component;

::X represents the other nonverbal components of the clause.[32]

The parentheses signify that neither of the P elements is required; however, when both are present, they will be placed in the order indicated. Position P1 will be indicated graphically in the examples by ⌈superscripted brackets⌉ and hereafter be referred to as a *frame of reference*. Position P2 will be indicated by **boldface type** and hereafter referred to as *emphasis*.

The framework that I am advocating here likely sounds novel to those with a background in NT studies because of the predominance of statistics-based studies of word order. This could create the impression that the work of Dik, Lambrecht, and Levinsohn represents a nonstandard model used by only a few linguists, with statistics-based methods being the overwhelming norm. In reality, the opposite is far closer to the truth in the field of linguistics. Most functional linguistic frameworks utilize a "Dikian" or "Lambrechtian" scheme as their foundation, differing primarily on the specific question that they are seeking to answer. In other words, the statistically based approaches—like those used in Porter's application Systemic Functional Linguistics—will not be found among linguists working in nonconfigurational or "flexible word-

---

31. The term "emphasis" has been much abused, being used to justify virtually anything that a commentator thinks is special or important. Claims of emphasis often indicate that they knew *something* was going on, even if they could say exactly what. Levinsohn claims "Greek grammarians tend to employ the term 'emphasis' to denote any kind of *prominence*" (*Discourse Features*, 7). In light of its checkered past, I reluctantly chose to assign this term a more technical meaning. Despite its past, it is the most elegant term to describe the effect of placing focal information in position P2.

32. Dik, *Functional Grammar*, 363.

order" languages. Such approaches are unable to adequately describe the data attested in the world's languages. This latter approach was developed almost exclusively with respect to English, and Porter's statistically based methodology appears to be his own reformulation of the Systemic Functional approach. In either form, the methodology has proven largely ineffective as a framework for describing nonconfigurational languages like Greek and Hebrew.[33]

9.2.6   Position P2: Emphasis

A helpful way of understanding emphasis is to look at question and answer pairs. Most questions are asking for some piece of information to be filled in by the answer. The question encapsulates what is known or presupposed, and the blank that is to be filled is represented by the question word (e.g., *who*, *what*, *when*). In English, new/focal information receives primary accent in the sentence. In prototypical contexts, the question words will be what is most important. As stated above, context is the determining factor, based on what is presupposed and what is being asserted.

Here are some examples of question/answer pairs. I provide the question, stating what is presupposed from the previous context in parentheses; then two possible ways of answering the question are provided. The **bolded** words mark what would most naturally receive stress if the sentences were aloud based on the presupposition provided.

Example 118 :: Questions, presuppositions, and answers

(a) **To whom** did you give the book? (Presupposition: You gave the book **to someone**.)

Default answer: I gave the book **to James**, or **To James**.
Marked answer: (It was) **to James** I gave the book (and not to someone else).

(b) **Where** did you put my book? (Presupposition: You put my book **somewhere**.)

Default answer: I put your book **on the table**, or **On the table**.
Marked answer: (It was) **on the table** I put your book (and not somewhere else).

---

33. For a more detailed discussion of these issues, see §9.4.

(c) **When** did you arrive? (Presupposition: You arrived **sometime**.)

Default: I arrived **yesterday**, or **Yesterday**.
Marked: (It was) **yesterday** I arrived (and not at some other time).

In each case, the bolded word(s) fill in the blank created by the question words. This information is the most important, regardless of its location in the clause. Placing it at the beginning of the clause has the effect of attracting more attention to it than in the default answers. The effect of this added attention is to emphasize the focal information. In colloquial English, one might even omit the "it was" part of the construction and keep the new information in the initial position—e.g., "**Yesterday** I arrived."

Even though English rigidly orders its clauses, there is still some degree of flexibility using "It is …" cleft constructions. Theoretically, every clause asserts new (i.e., focal) information. The choice to take what is already important and to assign it more prominence has the effect of emphasizing it.

Recall that the new or focal information is defined as the difference between what is presupposed and what is being asserted in the context—that is, what "fills in the blank." This means that the presupposed information changes with each new clause, based upon what it contributes to your mental representation of the discourse. As the presupposed information changes, so will the analysis of what is focal. In other words, the information that answers the question is most important only because the question has been asked. "James" and "on the table" are not inherently important words; it is context that determines this. This means that if the context changes, the importance of this information relative to the other parts of the clause might change as well.

9.2.7   Position P1: Frames of Reference

I will now take the answers to the questions above and place them in a different context to illustrate its impact on the status of information.

Example 119 :: Presuppositions and frames of reference

What did you give to James and Elizabeth?
(a) [To James] I gave **the book**, [to Elizabeth] I gave **the backpack**.

What did you do this week?
(b) [Yesterday] I **arrived**, [today] I will **go sightseeing**.

Notice the changes in the status of the information based on the changes in context. I am using the same marked answers without the "it was …" cleft construction, but it does not have the same pragmatic effect of emphasis. This information is no longer the most important part of the clause; it is now presupposed information. The *what* question in example 119(a) means that the object given is the most important part of the clause, not the subject or the time. In example 119(b), the action is the most important information of the clause. However, if these words were read with stress, they would still stand out and still have some pragmatic effect. This is where the P1 slot comes into play. Placing presupposed information in a place of prominence has the effect of establishing an explicit frame of reference, providing the reader with the primary basis for connecting what follows with what precedes.

In the case of example 119(a), the added attention drawn to "James" sets the stage for the switch to the new topic, "Elizabeth," in the next clause.[34] "James" is not the most important information in the context; what was given to him is. Thus, primary stress would still be placed on the bolded words, since primary sentence stress is used to mark the new or focal information in English. Adding secondary stress to "Elizabeth" signals that it is a frame of reference, providing the primary basis for relating the following clause to the one that precedes.

Similarly, in example 119(b), adding secondary stress to "yesterday" establishes a specific temporal frame of reference for what follows, indicating that you are talking about yesterday as opposed to some other day. Based on the question, the action of arriving is what is most important, not when. Placing the time in P1 sets the stage for a switch to a different temporal frame in the next clause (i.e., "today").

A very important distinction must be drawn between P1 and P2, between frames of reference and marked focus/emphasis. Both use a marked position to attract extra attention to information. Since there is a difference in the status of the information, there is a corresponding difference in the pragmatic effect achieved by each. By definition, P1 refers to placing known or knowable information in a marked position, resulting in an explicit frame of reference for relating what follows to what precedes. P2 refers to placing newly asserted information in a marked position and has the effect of emphasizing it. Placing exactly the same sentence in different contexts can completely change the pragmatic effect achieved.[35] Consider this statement: "**Today** I got here." In

---

34. In terms of traditional Greek grammar, "James" and "Elizabeth" would be called "contrastive topics."

35. An anonymous reviewer made this point well: "In question (a) in example 118, if I wanted to know to whom you gave the book, not some other object, I would emphasize thus: "To whom did you give **the book**?" (Presupposition: I'm interested in what you did with the book, not something else). Likewise in (b), "Where did you put **my book**?" (as

answer to the question "**When** did you get here?" "today" is construed as in marked focus. In answer to the question "**What** did you do today?" "today"is construed as a temporal frame of reference. Placing the same word in the same initial slot of the clause can have different pragmatic effects, depending on the context. It is the status of the information that determines the role, not the special syntactic position. This holds true for English, Greek, and many other languages.

Frames of reference play a very important role in helping readers successfully break down and organize their mental representation of a discourse. The reader needs to know who is doing what to whom, to be able to track changes in time, place, and circumstance, and to know where one part of the story ends and another begins. Frames of reference are commonly used to attract extra attention to such changes.

You have likely experienced the confusion associated with losing track of where a speaker was going with a story, asking the speaker to stop and help you "catch up." One of the ways of making sure that changes and transitions are not missed is to make them stand out more. This is not a requirement but a choice. If there is going to be a change of some sort, I could use the default way of communicating it or I could make it stand out more by using a frame of reference. Using the default method risks the reader missing the transition. Frames of reference play a significant role in marking these kinds of changes, making the framing information stand out more. Generally speaking, the bigger the change or transition, the more marking it will receive.[36]

9.3   Application to English

Since context is critical for determining whether or not an element is established, I will use longer examples that include context. I will analyze the English translations of some NT passages for my examples. The analysis is of the English, not the Greek that underlies it.

---

opposed to, say, "Where did you put **my apple**?"). And in (c), "When did you **arrive**?" (as opposed to, say, "When did you **leave**?")." The reviewer's reformulation of the context illustrates the impact that contextual changes can have on judgments about the status of information.

36. See Steven E. Runge, "Where Three or More Are Gathered, There Is Discontinuity" (paper presented at the international meeting of the Society of Biblical Literature, Edinburgh, 2–6 July 2006).

Example 120 :: Matthew 10:17–20

> [17] But beware of people, because they will hand you over to councils, and they will flog you in their synagogues. [18] And you will be brought before both governors and kings because of me, for a witness to them and to the Gentiles.
>
> [19] But [whenever they hand you over,] do not be anxious **how** to speak or **what** you should say, for what you should say will be given to you at that hour.
>
> [20] For ⟨✗[it is not] **you** who are speaking,✗⟩ but ⟨✓**the Spirit of your Father** who is speaking through you.✓⟩ [LEB, modified]

This excerpt comes from Jesus' instructions to the disciples about what lies ahead for them. We read in v. 17 that they will be delivered over to the courts, which then becomes established information to ground what follows. In v. 19, Jesus gives them specific instructions about how they are to respond when this handing over happens. The verse begins with a subordinate clause that restates some established information. The effect is to create a specific temporal frame of reference for what follows. Temporal information can be placed at either the beginning or the end of the clause in Greek and English. The admonition not to be anxious is applied to a specific context established using the frame of reference—that is, "When this happens, at that time …" The same information could have been communicated using unmarked or default clause order, placing the subordinate clause after the main clause rather than before it:[37]

> Do not be anxious when they deliver you over, **how** you are to speak or **what** you are to say.

Thompson states that the default expectation is that narratives will develop one event after another, based on the ordering of events. In this case, the expectation of chronological ordering is not met, so a marker is used to help the reader process the transition.[38] Placing the temporal information in

---

37. For discussions of the default position in English for adverbial expressions, see Stephen H. Levinsohn, "Preposed and Postposed Adverbials in English," *Work Papers of the Summer Institute of Linguistics, University of North Dakota Session* 36 (1992): 19–31; Sandra A. Thompson and Robert E. Longacre, "Adverbial Clauses," in *Complex Constructions* (vol. 2 of *Language Typology and Syntactic Description*; ed. Timothy Shopen; Cambridge: Cambridge University Press, 1985), 212–25.

38. Sandra A. Thompson, "Subordination and Narrative Event Structure," in *Coher-*

a frame of reference explicitly signals that the comment that follows applies to a specific context, the context described in the temporal frame of reference. Jesus essentially backtracks a bit and comments on how the disciples should respond when these things happen.

Later in v. 19, notice how the bolded question words open specific blanks about what is not to make them anxious. Verse 20 provides support for why they should not be anxious in the form of a point/counterpoint set.

> For ‹✗[it is not] **you** who are speaking,✗› but ‹✓**the Spirit of your Father** who is speaking through you.✓›

The counterpoint uses an *it*-cleft construction to unambiguously mark that "you" is being emphasized. The point that replaces the counterpoint could also be stated with an *it*-cleft, but it has been dropped because there is little ambiguity that "the Spirit of your Father" is intended to replace "not you." If the *it*-cleft construction had not been used, "you" would have looked like a simple subject, and its significance might have been overlooked by the reader:

> You are not the one speaking. The Spirit of your Father is the one speaking.

Stated in this way, it is unclear whether "you" and "The Spirit of your Father" are frames of reference or receiving emphasis. Using the *it*-cleft makes clear that emphasis is intended.

Example 121 :: Philippians 2:12–13

> ¹² Therefore my dear friends, [just as you have always obeyed,] not as in my presence only but now much more in my absence, *work out your own salvation with fear and trembling*. ¹³ For it is **God** who is at work in you, both to will and to work for his good pleasure. [LEB, modified]

The comparison "as you have obeyed" is placed in position P1 to create an explicit frame of reference for what follows. This information is known to the Philippians, even though it may not have been specifically mentioned in the

---

ence and Grounding in Discourse (ed. Russell S. Tomlin; Amsterdam: John Benjamins, 1987), 435–54, esp. 448. In this case, the fronted adverbial explicitly signals that the narrative timeline is backtracking somewhat to look at what the disciples should be doing at the same time that their adversaries are handing them over.

discourse. This information draws a specific comparison between the manner in which they have obeyed and the comment that follows in the main clause. The comparative frame is elaborated through the use of a point/counter-point set, specifying that it is not just how they obeyed when Paul was there watching them, but also how they obeyed in his absence. Putting all of this information at the beginning of the clause provides something of a buildup. It delays the disclosure of what they are actually supposed to do in the same way that they have obeyed (the main clause in v. 12 above is indicated by italics).

Verse 13 contains an *it*-cleft construction to explicitly emphasize that God is the one working in them, as opposed to someone else. It is not their own ability that will enable them to work out their salvation, but God working in them. Stating that "God works in you both to will and to work for his good pleasure" does not specify whether "God" is a topical frame or receiving emphasis. It is the subject of the clause in either case, and subjects in English normally function as topical frames. Use of the *it*-cleft construction disambiguates the role that "God" is playing, indicating that it is being emphasized and is not a frame of reference.

The next example also uses a cleft construction to explicitly mark that something is being emphasized. This verse is taken from the story of Jesus walking on the water, at the point where the disciples are afraid that Jesus is in fact a ghost.

Example 122 :: Mark 6:50

for they all saw him and were terrified. But immediately he spoke to them and said, "Take heart; it is I. Do not be afraid." (ESV)

To allay their fears, Jesus tells them that it is he, not a ghost or something else. In languages such as Greek, independent pronouns often can be dropped because the verb encodes most of the same information (e.g., the verb form εἰμι on its own indicates that the subject is first-person singular, "I"). English requires the use of pronouns, and in most cases they cannot be dropped. If in v. 50 the translation had been "I am," it most likely would be understood as an existential claim of "being." The cleft construction disambiguates the role that "I" plays: it receives emphasis instead of functioning as a topical frame of reference.

Example 123 :: Romans 2:12–13

12 For ⌊as many as have sinned without law⌋ will also perish without law, and ⌊as many as have sinned under the law⌋ will be judged by the law.

¹³ For it is not **the hearers of the law** who are righteous in the sight of God, but **the doers of the law** will be declared righteous.

There are two frames of reference used in v. 12 that present new topics about which the rest of the clause comments. Look at how closely they match in content, the only difference being *without* the law compared to *under* the law. The effect of having such similar topics and yet completely opposite is to create a sharp contrast. The contrast comes not from the syntax, but from the opposite nature of the content. Syntax can sharpen the contrast that is present in the context by attracting more attention to it, but it cannot create what is not already there. I will illustrate this much more in chapters 10 and 11.

Verse 13 uses an *it*-cleft construction to explicitly indicate that the subject is not functioning as a frame, as in v. 12. It is filling the P2 slot, something that would have been ambiguous without the cleft. The context presupposes that someone is righteous before God and will be justified, but the question is who that someone is. The subjects of the two clauses in v. 13 fill in the blank. The contrast that was already present in this verse is sharpened through the use of a point/counterpoint set. Both subjects concern someone doing something with the law; there is only one word that is different: "hearer" versus "doer." Contrast would have been present with or without the use of the point/counterpoint set. The same point could have been clearly communicated without using the negative counterpoint. Its use simply draws more attention to the contrast that was already present in the context.

Example 124 comes from Paul's exposition on the spiritual plight of Israel.

Example 124 :: Romans 11:5–6

⁵ So in this way also ⌊at the present time,⌋ there is a remnant **selected by grace**.

⁶ But ⌊if by grace,⌋ it is no longer by works, for otherwise ⌊grace⌋ would **no longer** be grace.

Verse 5 begins with a temporal frame of reference to ground the statement that a remnant exists at the present time. The verse establishes that the remnant will be chosen on the basis of grace, as opposed to some other basis such as their own merit. This established information becomes the basis for a conditional frame of reference at the beginning of v. 6. Conditional frames most often are used in the NT to create an explicit context for a statement that follows, one that might not hold true unless the condition is met. In this case, Paul wants to drive home the point that Israel's election is not based on their works. He could have stated, "It is no longer on the basis of works if it is by grace." Adverbial clauses can play different roles depending upon their placement before or after the main clause. Placing the condition at the end of the clause makes it function as a caveat rather than as a frame of reference.[39] The condition is not the most important information in the clause; "no longer by works" is. If the condition plays a crucial role in processing the main clause, it typically will be placed in position P1 to create an explicit frame of reference.

These examples illustrate the important distinction to be made between frames of reference and emphasis. Placing either established or newly asserted information in a marked position in the clause adds prominence to the clause component. However the difference in the information status dramatically impacts the effect that each achieves. Since the P1 information is either known or knowable by definition, it creates an explicit frame of reference for the clause that follows. In English, the subject most often fills this slot, but comparative, temporal, and conditional clauses also can fill this P1 slot.

On the other hand, placing newly asserted information in position P2 has the effect of adding emphasis to the fronted component. By definition, the new information is the most important component of the clause, regardless of its placement. Placing it in a marked position has the effect of emphasizing what was already most important.

9.4   Information Structure Methodologies and the Broader Field of Linguistics

As I mentioned at the end of §9.2.5, the preponderance of statistically based approaches to the study of NT Greek information structure might lead you to believe that this kind of approach is used by most linguists working outside of Koiné Greek, that NT studies are a representative microcosm of the broader field of linguistics. This is very far from the case. Too often the NT studies are conducted by nonspecialists who have ventured only part way into the linguistic realm. Alternatively, there are linguists applying methodologies that are largely designed for English-like languages, which are not robust enough to account for the complexity of Greek syntactic data. For the sake of clarification, the following material is meant to provide perspective on the current state of affairs regarding information structure in the broader field of linguistics.

In linguistics proper, most functional grammatical theories of information structure begin with the distinction, originating from the Prague school,

---

39. For a more thorough discussion of adverbial subordinate clauses within information structure, see chapter 10.

of *theme* and *rheme*. The theme corresponds to the "established" material of the clause, while the rheme corresponds to the newly asserted or focal information. These concepts correspond very closely with Simon Dik's Functional Grammar (FG) categories of P1 and P2, as long as one distinguishes between default and marked focus. Theme and rheme need not be placed at the beginning of the clause. P1 and P2 describe the effects of placing them in a marked position at the beginning of the clause. The Prague school claimed that clause-initial thematic information "cohesively anchors that subsequent clause(s) to something which is already in the context (i.e., to something accessible in the hearer's mental representation)," and it was referred to as a "point of departure."[40]

Lambrecht, using a *cognitive-functional* approach to describe the pragmatics of information structure, employs the traditional term *topicalization* to refer to P1, and the term *marked focus structure* to refer to P2.[41] Van Valin and LaPolla's Role and Reference Grammar (RRG) also uses Lambrecht's model, hence their notions of topicalization and marked focus also correspond to Dik's P1/P2.[42]

Sperber and Wilson's description of information structure according to Relevance Theory (RT) is similarly consistent with Dik's P1/P2 framework. Practitioners of RT are interested in describing the cognitive processing of new, foregrounded information, and thus they build upon the foundational elements established within the other functional approaches to information structure, without making revisions to it.[43]

Head-driven Phrase Structure Grammar (HPSG), an offshoot of Chomsky's generative approach, makes claims regarding "information packaging" that also correspond closely with Lambrecht and Dik, using the terms "focus" and "ground."[44]

---

40. Dooley and Levinsohn, *Analyzing Discourse*, 68. Hence Levinsohn uses the term "point of departure" to refer to P1 material.

41. Lambrecht, *Information Structure*, 201–17.

42. See Butler, "Focusing on Focus," 590.

43. See Dan Sperber and Deirdre Wilson, *Relevance: Communication and Cognition* (Oxford: Blackwell, 2001), 202–16.

44. See Sebastiaan J. Floor, "From Information Structure, Topic and Focus, to Theme in Biblical Hebrew Narrative" (D.Litt. diss., University of Stellenbosch, 2004), 42–45, 125–29. The generativists differ in their objectives compared to the functional approaches listed above. Floor states, "Generative linguists limit the study of information structure to the clause-level. For them the focus is not on functional issues, but mainly on explaining syntactic movement at the clause or sentence level"—that is, describing the "deep structure" that underlies the changes (ibid., 42).

The primary differences among these four approaches lie in how they came to the problem, and why they are seeking to solve it. Each methodology has a slightly different motivation for conducting the study, yet each has reached largely compatible conclusions regarding the means and motivations for pragmatically structuring information in discourse. The four approaches mentioned make at least a twofold distinction between what is presupposed and what is asserted. Furthermore, all four recognize a similar effect of pragmatically moving elements from their default position to a position of prominence, consistent with Dik's P1/P2 model. The further one moves beyond these foundational understandings, the more the views begin to diverge based upon their differing objectives. There is one main point that I want to make from this survey: there is far greater consensus on the matters of information structure within the field of linguistics than one would be led to believe based on recent studies of NT information structure.[45]

The predominant linguistic approach in NT studies today is Systemic Functional Linguistics (SFL), originated by M. A. K. Halliday.[46] Halliday's account of information structure derives also from the Prague school, yet with some significant differences. Halliday's SFL subdivides the Prague school's notion of given-new/theme-rheme into new subcategories rather than using them as synonymous terms. The given-new distinction he assigns to the "tone group," which does not correlate to any specific grammatical unit such as a clause or sentence. In other words, given-new corresponds to the primary device that English uses for information structuring: intonation or prosody. Theme and rheme are viewed as corresponding to constituents of the clause— that is, to syntax instead of prosody.[47] This differentiation into tone units versus clause units leads to significant differences in analysis in SFL compared to FG, RRG, or the other functional approaches discussed above.

Most all of Halliday's theoretical work to develop his framework was conducted on rigidly ordered languages, particularly English. Halliday's defi-

---

45. There is a similar consensus in the field of biblical Hebrew information structure, where Lambrecht and HPSG are the two primary methods that have been adopted. For monographs utilizing primarily Lambrecht and Dik, see Floor, "Information Structure"; Jean-Marc Heimerdinger, *Topic, Focus and Foreground in Ancient Hebrew Narratives* (JSOTSup 295; Sheffield: Sheffield Academic, 1999). For studies applying a generative perspective, see Robert D. Holmstedt, "Word Order and Information Structure in Ruth and Jonah: A Generative-Typological Analysis," *JSS* 54 (2009): 111–39; "The Relative Clause in Biblical Hebrew" (Ph.D. diss., University of Wisconsin - Madison, 2002).

46. See M. A. K. Halliday, "Notes on Transitivity and Theme in English, Part 2," *JL* 3 (1967): 199–244; also his revised introduction to M. A. K. Halliday and Christian M. I. M. Matthiessen, *An Introduction to Functional Grammar* (London: Arnold, 2001).

47. See Butler, "Focusing on Focus," 592.

nition of "focus" is inextricably tied to stress and intonation, just as in English. His theory is well suited for English because prosody is the primary means of marking focus in rigidly ordered languages.[48] However, SFL has received criticism from outside the SFL school, as well as from within, regarding its documented deficiencies in the area of syntax. Robin Fawcett's *Theory of Syntax for Systemic Functional Linguistics* has been praised for addressing the rather flagrant flaws in Halliday's conceptions of syntax.[49] It has also resulted in something of a split between the "Cardiff school" of SFL, led by Fawcett, and Halliday's "Sydney school," resulting from Halliday's unwillingness to address the criticisms leveled against his theory.

SFL postulates that the initial element in a clause, be it a conjunction, subject, or fronted focal constituent, is always the "theme." This idea works fairly well in a rigidly configurational language, but it proves inadequate for non-configurational languages. This pitfall is a natural consequence of formulating the theory without a sound cross-linguistic framework like that of Dik. The choice to link theme-rheme only to intonation has significant consequences when applied more broadly to flexibly ordered languages.

Floor states regarding the work of Gómez-González's application of SFL to English, "English as a fixed word-order language lends itself rather nicely to the SFL thematic analysis, as her study in the wide corpus shows. But in basic VSO languages like biblical Hebrew, such analyses are not as straightforward."[50] Thus, when SFL studies speak of marked focus, theme, and rheme, the meaning is quite different from most every other approach using these terms. In some cases, they are completely opposite.[51] This difference in meaning for the same terms has led to confusion within NT studies about the use and meaning of terminology.

In its present form, SFL is ill suited to tackle flexibly ordered languages such as Greek and Hebrew.[52] Furthermore, since the ancient forms of both

---

48. See ibid., 602–4.

49. Robin Fawcett, *A Theory of Syntax for Systemic Functional Linguistics* (Amsterdam: John Benjamins, 2000).

50. Floor, "Information Structure," 30. See María Ángeles Gómez-González, *The Theme-Topic Interface: Evidence from English* (Amsterdam: John Benjamins, 2001).

51. See Butler, "Focusing on Focus," 600.

52. Butler (ibid., 613–14) summarizes the situation, saying, "The crucial stages in the development of SFL, on the other hand, were based largely on the study of English, though there has been much more interest in other languages in recent years, and this trend looks set to continue (see, e.g., Caffarel et al., 2004). It is nevertheless still the case that the major accounts of systemic theory and description, such as Halliday (2004), Halliday and Matthiessen are devoted almost entirely to English, though with occasional mention of other languages (about 5 percent of the Halliday and Matthiessen book is devoted to Chinese).

languages are no longer spoken, any discussion of prosody would of necessity represent a theoretical reconstruction. The SFL framework would need to be reformulated before it could appropriately be applied to an ancient, unspoken language. Unfortunately, most recent NT studies of word order have followed Halliday's Sydney school of SFL, without addressing the fundamental problems raised within the linguistic community. SFL's approach to syntax may hold promise, but only as its documented weaknesses are remedied.

No single linguistic theory is robust enough on its own to adequately account for every aspect of language. It is too diverse and complex to make this a realistic expectation. Each different linguistic framework was developed to tackle different problems, typically ones left unaddressed by other existing frameworks. Viewed in this way, Dik's FG, Lambrecht's cognitive-functional approach, and RT are in fact complementary, based on the unity of their presuppositions. In light of this complexity, a complete theoretical framework will also of necessity be somewhat eclectic.

The approach taken in this discourse grammar begins with the Prague school's notions of theme and rheme as the basic understanding of the kinds of information found in any given clause. This basic understanding is enriched using Dik's FG notions of P1/P2 to refer to pragmatic movement of clause elements from a cross-linguistic perspective, with P1 corresponding to thematic elements used to create explicit frames of reference for the clause that follows, and P2 corresponding to emphasis, taking what was already the most important element of the clause (i.e., the focus) and pragmatically placing it in a marked position for added prominence (i.e., marked focus). Finally, the given-new distinction based on the words or concepts previously mentioned in discourse is too simplistic to account for the usage observed. A cognitive component is needed in order to accurately describe and account for this distinction. Thus, I utilize Lambrecht's cognitive-functional model of mental representation and activation states to complete my information structure theoretical framework.

In principle, one might think that the separation between grammatical and phonological systems in the SFL account of information distribution could be an advantage, in that it would allow an assessment of the respective roles of the two systems in various languages. Nevertheless, because of the low priority assigned to typological adequacy in SFL, and the emphasis on describing single languages in some detail, rather than looking at particular phenomena across a range of languages, it is unlikely that SFL grammarians would be interested in, for example, the syntactic restrictions on focus placement which have been studied in RRG." This issue of "typological adequacy" is significant, in that it limits the ability of SFL to accurately and adequately describe languages that differ significantly in typology from English.

Suggested Reading

Andrews, Avery. "The Major Functions of the Noun Phrase."

Butler, Christopher C. "Focusing on Focus: A Comparison of Functional Grammar, Role and Reference Grammar and Systemic Functional Grammar."

Delin, J. *The Focus Structure of It-Clefts.*

Diessel, Holger. "Competing Motivations for the Ordering of Main and Adverbial Clauses."

———. "The Ordering Distribution of Main and Adverbial Clauses: A Typological Study."

Funk, Robert W. *A Beginning-Intermediate Grammar of Hellenistic Greek.* 1:3–14.

Givón, Talmy. "The Grammar of Referential Coherence as Mental Processing Instructions."

Levinsohn, Stephen H. "*Also, Too* and *Moreover* in a Novel by Dorothy L. Sayers."

Pavey, Emma. "An Analysis of *It*-Clefts within a Role and Reference Grammar Framework."[53]

Runge, Steven E. "Relative Saliency and Information Structure in Mark's Parable of the Sower."

---

53. See Pavey's dissertation on the same topic, "The English It-Cleft Construction: A Role and Reference Grammar Analysis" (Ph.D. diss., University of Sussex, 2004).

FRAMING DEVICES (1)

This chapter introduces the first half of the various kinds of frames found in the NT. The kinds of frames are differentiated by their content, specifically by the subordinating conjunction or verb form of the subordinate clause. Although they differ in content, all of them serve the same basic function of establishing an explicit frame of reference for the clause that follows. A basic overview of each kind of frame will be provided, followed by five examples taken from the NT. Most of the frames are retained in English translations, making it easier to discuss them in teaching or preaching.

Most frames are indicated by the use of superscripted brackets. The type of frame is specified using the following symbols:

[TPWord^TP]	Topical frames
[TMWord^TM]	Temporal frames
[CEWord^CE]	Conditional/Exceptive frames
[SPWord^SP]	Spatial frames
[CPWord^CP]	Comparative frames
[RRWord^RR]	Reason/Result frames
[LDWord^LD]	Left-dislocations
[TWord^T]	Topic of nonfinite clause

Koiné Greek is a verb-prominent language, where the least-marked and most basic order of clause components is for the verb to be placed in the initial position. When other elements are placed in the initial position, such placement is motivated by some pragmatic reason. This claim is based not on statistics, but on the varying effects that are achieved by "fronting" of clause elements. I have already cited Porter's observations regarding subject placement that support this view (see §9.1). The case of adverbial clause elements requires further explanation.

The placement of adverbial clauses (e.g., temporal, spatial, conditional, reason/result, and causal) manifests the same kind of meaningful distinction as subjects. In the case of adverbials, there are other determining factors that compete with information-structuring principles. Understanding these factors requires some background.

Diessel distinguishes six different distributional classes of languages, based upon the location of adverbial clauses. They range from rigidly ADV-S/VP, where the adverbial clause always precedes the main clause (i.e. the subject and verb phrase), to rigidly S/VP-ADV languages, where the adverbial clause always follows the main clause.[1] Koiné Greek and English both fall into the mixed/flexible portion of the continuum.

Diessel then moves on to consider the distribution of specific classes of adverbial clauses. He finds a tendency for certain classes of adverbials to occur in similar places, regardless of the overall preference of the language regarding adverbs, summarized in the following chart:

Figure 5 :: Location of subordinate adverbial clauses within main clause

Conditional   Temporal   Causal   Result/purpose
Clause-initial <--> Clause-final[2]

Note the overwhelming preference for conditional adverbials to occur clause-initially, whereas result/purpose and causal adverbials are predominately clause-final, with temporal adverbials showing much more varied distribution. Diessel notes that English demonstrates the same kinds of distributional preferences as those found in the other mixed/flexible languages.[3]

In a follow-up study, Diessel describes the factors influencing these distributional patterns. He claims that, rather than being driven by purely typological factors, other competing factors influence the placement of adverbial clauses based on the kind of adverbial. He claims that adverbial clauses serve different pragmatic functions, depending upon their initial or final position in the clause. The clause-initial adverbials "provide a thematic ground or orientation for subsequent clauses,"[4] or what I refer to as a "frame of reference."

In addition to the pragmatic factors influencing adverbials, there are semantic ones that have a high degree of influence. Regarding the distribution

---

1. Holger Diessel, "The Ordering Distribution of Main and Adverbial Clauses: A Typological Study," *Language* 77, no. 2 (2001): 440–41.

2. Ibid., 446.

3. Ibid.

4. Holger Diessel, "Competing Motivations for the Ordering of Main and Adverbial Clauses," *Linguistics* 43, no. 3 (2005): 459.

of conditional adverbials, Diessel notes that they do more than simply provide a thematic frame of reference for what follows. Instead,

> They describe a contrastive situation that establishes a specific framework—a specific semantic constellation—for the discourse that follows. In other words, conditional clauses predominantly precede the main clause, providing an orientation for interpreting subsequent clauses, because of their meaning.… In fact, the meaning of conditional clauses favors initial occurrence so strongly that the occurrence of final conditional clauses requires a particular explanation.[5]

In other words, conditional clauses play such an important role in the processing of main clauses—establishing the condition that must be met for the main clause to hold true—that placing them in the final position is almost not an option without some other mechanism to let the reader know that the condition is coming.[6] Placing the conditional in the final position may in fact cause confusion, since the reader might interpret the main clause as factual instead of being contingent upon a condition being met.[7]

The distribution of temporal and causal adverbials can also be attributed to factors other than typological preference:

> In contrast to conditional clauses, temporal and causal clauses do not affect the factivity of the associated main clause. In sentence-final position they either add new information to the preceding main clause or function as afterthoughts. Preposing of temporal and causal clauses is primarily motivated by general discourse pragmatic considerations; that is, temporal and causal clauses precede the main clause if they function to provide a thematic ground for the subsequent discourse.[8]

The model of information structure that I utilize is largely based on the distinction between what is presupposed and what is asserted. Adverbials can serve different discourse functions, based on their informational status in the context. In most cases, adverbial subordinate clauses that are placed before the main clause serve the pragmatic purpose of establishing an explicit frame

---

5. Ibid., 461–62.

6. "There are various linguistic means that may indicate the occurrence of a final conditional clause preventing the hearer from interpreting the main clause as a factual statement. In spoken discourse, the occurrence of a final adverbial clause can be indicated by intonation.… If the occurrence of a final conditional clause is not announced in the main clause, the conditional clause usually functions as an afterthought" (ibid., 462–63).

7. Ibid., 462.

8. Ibid., 463.

of reference for the clause that follows. This is especially true of conditional adverbials, not on the basis of frequency, but on the basis of the special semantic role that they play in establishing an interpretive framework for the clause that follows.

Keep in mind that the writer's choice to create a frame has meaning associated with it. The same information could have been communicated by placing the component somewhere after the verb. In many cases, the subordinate clauses could have been main clauses in their own right. The choice to use a frame of reference represents the choice not to take one of these other options.

10.1   Topical Frames

Topical frames are commonly found both in narrative proper and in non-narrative such as the NT Epistles and reported speeches of the Gospels and Acts. The two primary uses of topical frames are:

* to highlight the introduction of a new participant or topic, or
* to draw attention to a change in topics.

One frequently finds chains of topical frames used to help structure the discourse by clearly delineating transitions from one topic to another. Recall that the unmarked position for the subject in Greek is following the main verb, not preceding it.[9] The choice to place it in a frame of reference indicates the writer's choice to draw attention to it, but not because it is the most important information in the clause. In most cases, the comment about the topic is what is newly asserted and hence most important.

Consider the use of frames to mark the topic changes in John 1.

Example 125 :: John 1:1–5

1 [TM'Εν ἀρχῇTM] ἦν ὁ λόγος, καὶ [TPὁ λόγοςTP] ἦν πρὸς τὸν θεόν, καὶ **θεὸς** ἦν ὁ λόγος.

2 [TPοὗτοςTP] ἦν ἐν ἀρχῇ πρὸς τὸν θεόν.

1 [TMIn the beginningTM] was the Word, and [TPthe WordTP] was with God, and the Word was **God**.

2 [TPThis oneTP] was in the beginning with God.

---

9. See Stanley E. Porter, *Idioms of the Greek New Testament* (2nd ed.; Sheffield: Sheffield Academic, 1999), 296; Stephen H. Levinsohn, *Discourse Features of New Testament Greek: A Coursebook on the Information Structure of New Testament Greek* (2nd ed.; Dallas: SIL International), 29–30.

³ [TPπάντα^TP] **δι' αὐτοῦ** ἐγένετο, καὶ [TPχωρὶς αὐτοῦ^TP] ἐγένετο **οὐδὲ ἕν** ὃ γέγονεν

³ [TPAll things^TP] came into being **through him,** and [TPapart from him^TP] **not one thing** came into being that has come into being.

⁴ [TPἐν αὐτῷ^TP] **ζωὴ** ἦν, καὶ [TPἡ ζωὴ^TP] ἦν τὸ φῶς τῶν ἀνθρώπων·

⁴ [TPIn him^TP] was **life,** and [TPthe life^TP] was the light of humanity.

⁵ καὶ [TPτὸ φῶς^TP] ἐν τῇ σκοτίᾳ **φαίνει,** καὶ [TPἡ σκοτία^TP] αὐτὸ οὐ **κατέλαβεν.**

⁵ And [TPthe light^TP] **shines** in the darkness, and [TPthe darkness^TP] **did** not **overcome** it.

This Gospel begins with a temporal frame that establishes a context "in the beginning," and then "the word" is introduced at the end of the clause, just as expected by the principle of natural information flow.[10] In v. 1b, ὁ λόγος is placed in a frame of reference, elevating its status in the context as the main topic.

The next clause places θεός in position P2 for the sake of emphasis. The omission of the article serves to disambiguate whether θεός is the subject or direct object. Since both λόγος and θεός are established and known, the article is omitted to identify it as the predicate nominative and not the subject, since it is fronted. Including the article would have created ambiguity as to whether ὁ θεός was in a topical frame or being emphasized.[11] Since λόγος is the topic of v. 1c, the switch in v. 2 to a pronoun (the near demonstrative) is possible. The anarthrous reference to θεός indicates that it is part of the predicate, not a topic of this pericope.

Verses 3–5 contain a rapid series of topic switches. John characteristically uses topical frames to help the reader track such changes. Verse 3 makes a comment about "all things," emphasizing that they came about "through him" as opposed to through some other means. The second clause of the verse makes a similar point by excluding the Word through the use of a topical frame[12]

---

10. See §9.2.4.

11. Mistaking a definite ὁ θεός as the subject would have been very likely, since the object of one clause often becomes the subject of the following clause—for example, vv. 4–5 switch from life > light > darkness in succession. Furthermore, since both θεός and λόγος are established, the omission of the definite article serves to portray θεός as though it were new information. The choice to emphasize θεός virtually precludes the possibility of including a definite article with this noun. To do so would introduce all kinds of problems from a discourse point of view as to the identification of the topic.

12. One might argue that this frame should be construed as a spatial or exceptive frame because of the preposition. My approach is more functional than formal, though I

and emphasizes that "not one thing" came about apart from him. Verse 4 uses another prepositional phrase as a topical frame, setting the stage for another comment about what was in the Word. Verses 4b–5 illustrate the use of topical frames to create a tightly connected chain of clauses, with the object of one clause becoming the topic of the next. This strategy is not required; it represents the writer's choice to increase the cohesion of these clauses.

In Gal 5, Paul talks about the Galatians, himself, and those who are advocating circumcision as part of the gospel. The topic of v. 12 is the advocates of circumcision (i.e., "who are disturbing you"), but then it switches back to the Galatian believers in v. 13.

Example 126 :: Galatians 5:13–14

¹² I wish that the ones who are disturbing you would also castrate themselves!

¹³ [TP·Ὑμεῖς^{TP}] γὰρ ἐπ' ἐλευθερίᾳ ἐκλήθητε, ἀδελφοί· μόνον μὴ [^Tτὴν ἐλευθερίαν^T] εἰς ἀφορμὴν τῇ σαρκί, ἀλλὰ διὰ **τῆς ἀγάπης** δουλεύετε ἀλλήλοις.

¹⁴ [TP·ὁ γὰρ πᾶς νόμος^{TP}] **ἐν ἑνὶ λόγῳ** πεπλήρωται, ἐν τῷ· ἀγαπήσεις τὸν πλησίον σου ὡς σεαυτόν.

¹³ For [TPyou^{TP}] were called **to freedom**, brothers. Only do not let [^T your freedom^T] become an opportunity for the flesh, but **through love** serve one another.

¹⁴ For [TPthe whole law^{TP}] is fulfilled **in one statement**, namely, "You shall love your neighbor as yourself."

Most Bibles have some sort of a break between v. 12 and v. 13, indicating that a new paragraph or section has begun. The topical frame makes this change really stand out. The pronoun Ὑμεῖς is not semantically required, since the morphological information about the subject is contained in the verb ἐκλήθητε. The pronoun is not emphatic but required to signal the presence of a topical frame.

This usage of an independent pronoun in such contexts has led grammarians to call this a "contrastive" pronoun. The pronoun is the same as any other one; the contrast brought about by the change in topics would have been present with or without the use of a topical frame. The effect of using the semantically redundant pronoun in this context is to make the switch of

strive to maintain as much consistency as possible. Since the prepositional phrase conveys topical information in the context, I construe it as a topical frame of reference.

topics stand out more. An added effect of the topical frame is to help signal a higher-level break in the discourse—that is, a new section of the epistle.

Note that another topical frame is found in v. 14, one that was not considered to signal a new paragraph. This frame takes a topic that is accessible from the context and attracts attention to it in order to make the comment about it all the more poignant. The topic is not the most important part of the clause; ἐν ἑνὶ λόγῳ is. The clause could have alternatively read ἐν ἑνὶ λόγῳ γὰρ πεπλήρωται ὁ πᾶς νόμος, but this might have caused confusion about the information status of ἐν ἑνὶ λόγῳ, whether it is a spatial frame of reference or whether it is emphasized. Using a topical frame removes the ambiguity and clearly marks the switch.

Another chain of topical frames is found in James 1 to help the reader track the succession of topics.

Example 127 :: James 1:3–4

² Consider it all joy, my brothers, whenever you encounter various trials,

³ γινώσκοντες ὅτι [TPτὸ δοκίμιον ὑμῶν τῆς πίστεως TP] κατεργάζεται ὑπομονήν.	³ because you know that [TPthe testing of your faith TP] produces endurance.
⁴ [TPἡ δὲ ὑπομονὴ TP] **ἔργον τέλειον** ἐχέτω, ἵνα ἦτε τέλειοι καὶ ὁλόκληροι ἐν μηδενὶ λειπόμενοι.	⁴ And let [TPendurance TP] have **its perfect effect**, so that you may be mature and complete, lacking in nothing.

There is a switch of topics from "you" in v. 2 to the more complex "the testing of your faith" in v. 3. The effect is to recast "various trials" as something more than just trials: they are "the testing of your faith." The topical frame draws attention to this change, since the default expectation is to use the same terminology when promoting the object of one clause to the topic of the next. James challenges the reader to consider trials joy for good reason. Trials are portrayed as a means of testing one's faith, which he claims will produce endurance. The use of the topical frame attracts attention to the topic, helping the reader understand that he is talking about one and the same thing, not a brand new topic.

He then switches in v. 4 from "testing" to comment about "endurance," emphasizing that it must have its "perfect effect." The topical frames aid the reader in tracking the changes, as well as draw attention to the topics that are commented on.

Example 128 :: Matthew 12:1–2

¹ [TMἘν ἐκείνῳ τῷ καιρῷTM] ἐπορεύθη ὁ Ἰησοῦς τοῖς σάββασιν διὰ τῶν σπορίμων· [TPοἱ δὲ μαθηταὶ αὐτοῦTP] ἐπείνασαν καὶ ἤρξαντο τίλλειν στάχυας καὶ ἐσθίειν.

² [TPοἱ δὲ ΦαρισαῖοιTP] ἰδόντες εἶπαν αὐτῷ· ἰδοὺ [TPοἱ μαθηταί σουTP] ποιοῦσιν ὃ οὐκ ἔξεστιν ποιεῖν ἐν σαββάτῳ.

¹ [TMAt that timeTM] Jesus went through the grain fields on the Sabbath. And [TPhis disciplesTP] were hungry, and they began to pluck off heads of grain and eat them.

² But when [TPthe PhariseesTP] saw it, they said to him, "Behold, [TPyour disciplesTP] are doing what it is not permitted to do on the Sabbath!"

Matthew 12 opens with a rather generic temporal frame that helps to indicate that what follows is closely related in time but is a new pericope. Note that Jesus is the subject of the first clause, placed in the unmarked position following the verb. The action of the disciples is what precipitates the confrontation with the Pharisees. Both parties are introduced through topical frames. These topical changes could have been tracked easily enough by placing them in the unmarked position following the verb. The topical frame has the effect of promoting them, but not because they are the most important part of the clause. Their actions are most important. The topical frame in the speech of v. 2 also attracts extra attention, with even more attention attracted through the use of an attention-getter. The circumstantial frame[13] ἰδόντες in v. 2 clearly prioritizes the two actions described in the clause. The Pharisees' "seeing" sets the stage for the more important speech that follows.

Example 129 :: Romans 2:12

[TPὍσοι γὰρ **ἀνόμως** ἥμαρτον, TP] ἀνόμως **καὶ ἀπολοῦνται**,

καὶ [TPὅσοι **ἐν νόμῳ** ἥμαρτον,TP] διὰ νόμου **κριθήσονται·**

For [TPas many as have sinned without lawTP] **will also perish** without law,

and [TPas many as have sinned **under the law**TP] **will be judged** by the law.

---

13. See chapter 12.

The topical frames of v. 12 provide a significant aid in tracking who is doing what to whom. Although relative clauses such as this are fairly common, it is important to understand what is "going on under the hood," why it is that it achieves the rhetorical effects that it does. In this context, the use of topical frames is due not to a quick series of changes, but to the complexity of each subject that is introduced. Paul uses the topical frame in v. 12a to delineate a very specific group of people about whom he wants to comment. This topical frame is composed of a relative clause, with the object of its verb placed in position P2 for emphasis. Note how the emphasis in v. 12a sets the stage for a sharp contrast with the topic of v. 12b. The content of the frames is identical other than the emphasized objects. Contrast would have been present with or without the emphasis. Emphasizing the objects draws more attention to them and thus sharpens the contrast that was already present.

If a frame had not been used, it would have been more difficult to identify the subjects of these two clauses. Consider this default reconstruction:

ἀπολοῦνται γὰρ ἀνόμως ὅσοι ἀνόμως ἥμαρτον, καὶ κριθήσονται διὰ νόμου ὅσοι ἐν νόμῳ ἥμαρτον.[14]

Furthermore, since the default position for verbs is at the beginning of the clause, the primary means for unambiguously emphasizing them is to place them at the end of the clause.[15] Verse 12a uses an adverbial καί to signal what I refer to as *thematic addition*.[16] Thematic addition creates an explicit link between the added element and some corresponding element in the preceding context. In this case, ἀπολοῦνται is explicitly connected to ἥμαρτον ἀνόμως, since both actions are performed by the same subject. In other words, those who sin apart from the law will also have something else happen to them: they will perish apart from the law. Since the corresponding element that is thematically added is part of the subject, it needs to precede what is added to it. Otherwise the reader would not be able to easily identify the intended element.

The use of the topical frame in v. 12b is likely to maintain parallelism in the syntax, besides promoting the change of topic. Note that the action of the main verb is emphasized as well, as this is the new information that is added.

---

14. For examples of relative clauses that function as subjects but follow the main verb instead of preceding it, see Mark 3:10; Acts 13:48. In the vast majority of instances, relative clause subjects are introduced using a topical frame of reference, most likely to help the reader more easily process who is doing what to whom.

15. See chapter 13.

16. See chapter 16.

Based on the parallelism, the reader presupposes that those who sinned under the law will have something happen to them through the law.

10.2   Temporal Frames

Temporal frames occur frequently in both narrative and nonnarrative. In narrative, temporal frames are associated with discourse boundaries, such as changes of scene or pericope. Placing the temporal information at the beginning of the clause has the effect of attracting attention to it, in most cases establishing an explicit frame of reference for the clause that follows.[17] The same information could have been placed after the verb, but it would not have the same scene-setting effect. Many temporal frames are rather generic, simply communicating a discontinuity in time rather than specifying a particular point in time.

In nonnarrative, temporal frames often highlight switches from now to how things were or will be at some other point in time. Because of the linear nature of discourse, a writer cannot recount multiple events simultaneously. One event is recounted, and then there is a switch to the other one. Temporal frames can be used to indicate a resumption of another story or plot at some other point in time. In most cases, the temporal frames found in the Greek text are rendered as frames in English translations.

In this first example, a series of temporal frames sets the stage for the introduction of John the Baptist's ministry. The frames move from general to specific.

Example 130 :: Luke 3:1–3

1 [TM Ἐν ἔτει δὲ πεντεκαιδεκάτῳ τῆς ἡγεμονίας Τιβερίου Καίσαρος, ἡγεμονεύοντος Ποντίου Πιλάτου τῆς Ἰουδαίας, καὶ τετρααρχοῦντος τῆς Γαλιλαίας Ἡρῴδου, Φιλίππου δὲ τοῦ ἀδελφοῦ αὐτοῦ τετρααρχοῦντος τῆς Ἰτουραίας καὶ Τραχωνίτιδος χώρας, καὶ Λυσανίου τῆς Ἀβιληνῆς τετρααρχοῦντος, TM]

1 Now [TM in the fifteenth year of the reign of Tiberius Caesar, when Pontius Pilate was governor of Judea, and Herod was tetrarch of Galilee, and his brother Philip was tetrarch of the region of Iturea and Trachonitis, and Lysanias was tetrarch of Abilene, TM]

---

17. Remember that it is the status of the information that differentiates a frame of reference from emphasis. If the temporal information is the most salient element of what is newly asserted, it would be construed as receiving emphasis rather than creating a temporal frame of reference.

² [TMἐπὶ ἀρχιερέως Ἄννα καὶ Καϊάφα,ᵀᴹ] ἐγένετο ῥῆμα θεοῦ ἐπὶ Ἰωάννην τὸν Ζαχαρίου υἱὸν ἐν τῇ ἐρήμῳ.

² [TMin the time of the high priest Annas and Caiaphas,ᵀᴹ] the word of God came to John the son of Zechariah in the wilderness.

³ καὶ ἦλθεν εἰς πᾶσαν [τὴν] περίχωρον τοῦ Ἰορδάνου κηρύσσων βάπτισμα μετανοίας εἰς ἄφεσιν ἁμαρτιῶν.…

³ And he went into all the surrounding region of the Jordan, preaching a baptism of repentance for the forgiveness of sins.…

The prepositional phrase that begins v. 1 establishes a specific year in which the following event occurs. The circumstantial participial clauses may also be construed as part of this temporal frame of v. 1. This first verse establishes the time frame according to the political situation. There is another temporal frame at the beginning of v. 2 that establishes a setting with respect to the Jewish situation, stating who was high priest during this time. Although this extensive description indeed establishes a very specific temporal frame for what follows, it also has the effect of creating a buildup for the introduction of something important that follows: John's ministry. The effect in this case is twofold: setting a time for the events that follow, and providing a dramatic delay of John's introduction.

In the next example, the temporal frame accomplishes two tasks: updating the reference time for the events that follow, and highlighting a temporal discontinuity where it otherwise might have been missed.

Example 131 :: Mark 1:14

[TMΜετὰ δὲ τὸ παραδοθῆναι τὸν Ἰωάννηνᵀᴹ] ἦλθεν ὁ Ἰησοῦς εἰς τὴν Γαλιλαίαν κηρύσσων τὸ εὐαγγέλιον τοῦ θεοῦ

Now [TMafter John had been taken into custody, ᵀᴹ] Jesus went into Galilee proclaiming the gospel of God

Verse 12 describes Jesus' temptation in the wilderness, which is represented as happening immediately after his baptism. If the description of Jesus' preaching ministry immediately followed in v. 14 without updating the reference time of the narrative regarding the arrest of John, the reader likely would assume that there was a close temporal connection between Jesus' temptation and his preaching. The temporal frame links Jesus' preaching to the arrest of John the Baptist, with the frame making the reference time stand out more than it would have using the default order. Consider the following reconstruction of a default structure:

ἦλθεν δὲ ὁ Ἰησοῦς εἰς τὴν Γαλιλαίαν μετὰ τὸ παραδοθῆναι τὸν Ἰωάννην

Had the temporal information been placed at the end of the clause, it is unlikely that many Bibles would insert a break in the pericope before v. 14. Since a framing structure was used, it represents the temporal shift as though it was more significant than the default alternative. Temporal frames have the effect of making the "change" in time stand out more, helping readers to segment the discourse in their mental representation of it even though there is little other discontinuity in the context.

Temporal frames also play a significant role in the NT Epistles, enabling writers to clearly move back and forth in time to examine different aspects of theological concepts or events. Temporal frames of reference help the reader more easily process these switches.

Example 132 :: Romans 5:6, 8, 11

6 [TM"Ἔτι TM] γὰρ [TPΧριστὸςTP] ὄντων ἡμῶν ἀσθενῶν ἔτι [TMκατὰ καιρὸνTM] ὑπὲρ ἀσεβῶν ἀπέθανεν.

6 [TMYetTM] [TPChrist,TP] while we were still helpless, [TMat the proper timeTM] died **for the ungodly**.

8 συνίστησιν δὲ τὴν ἑαυτοῦ ἀγάπην εἰς ἡμᾶς ὁ θεός, ὅτι [TMἔτι ἁμαρτωλῶν ὄντων ἡμῶνTM] [TPΧριστὸςTP] ὑπὲρ ἡμῶν ἀπέθανεν.

8 but God demonstrates his own love for us, in that [TMwhile we were still sinners,TM] [TPChristTP] died **for us**.

11 οὐ μόνον δέ, ἀλλὰ καὶ καυχώμενοι ἐν τῷ θεῷ διὰ τοῦ κυρίου ἡμῶν Ἰησοῦ Χριστοῦ δι' οὗ [TMνῦνTM] τὴν καταλλαγὴν ἐλάβομεν.

11 And not only this, but also we are boasting in God through our Lord Jesus Christ, through whom we have [TMnowTM] received **the reconciliation**. [LEB, modified]

Verses 1–5 of the chapter describe the many benefits provided to believers through Christ's work on the cross, focusing on all that he accomplished. In v. 6, Paul transitions back in time to describe the state of affairs when Christ died for us. The adverb ἔτι sets a generic temporal frame, followed by the topical frame "Christ" to switch from the love of God in v. 5. The backgrounded genitive absolute participial clause also helps to establish a temporal frame. Finally, the frame "at the proper time" is used to recharacterize the time when we were helpless as the perfect time for the work of Christ. Paul has already driven home the point that we are saved by God's grace, but here he reminds us of how costly this was. Christ died not for those who were good, but "for the ungodly." This point is repeated in v. 8, again using the generic ἔτι as a temporal frame within the participial clause to stress that it is "while we were still sinners" that he died for us.

Another generic temporal frame in v. 11 reiterates this contrast between where we used to be before Christ and where we are now. It is clear from the context that the reconciliation came from the work of Christ, that it was not previously available. This temporal frame makes explicit what otherwise would have been implicit, that reconciliation is only "now" our experience. "Now" is not the most important part of the clause; the reconciliation that we receive is. The temporal frame makes sure that we keep everything in perspective, that we not "forget our roots," so to speak.

One finds the same kind of doubling back to an earlier time in order to make a point in the next example, from Hebrews.

Example 133 :: Hebrews 2:8

πάντα ὑπέταξας ὑποκάτω τῶν ποδῶν αὐτοῦ. [TMἐν τῷ γὰρ ὑποτάξαι [αὐτῷ] τὰ πάντα^TM] **οὐδὲν** ἀφῆκεν αὐτῷ ἀνυπότακτον. [TMΝῦν^TM] δὲ **οὔπω** ὁρῶμεν αὐτῷ τὰ πάντα ὑποτεταγμένα·	you subjected **all things** under his feet. For [TMin subjecting all things to him,^TM] he left **nothing** that was not subject to him. But [TMnow^TM] we do **not yet** see all things subjected to him,

Verse 8a makes very clear that "all things" were subjected under his feet. Verse 8b reiterates the time when all things were being subjected. At that time, "nothing" was left that was "not subject." The temporal frame allows the writer to make a statement about a very specific point in time. It also sets the stage for another switch to describe the way things are "now" in verse 8c; at this point in time, the subjecting of all things has not yet come to pass. Temporal frames allow the writer to clearly switch back and forth to different points in time by explicitly marking the switches to help readers properly process the transitions. This temporal information is not the most important in the clause (i.e., it is not newly asserted); instead, it establishes an explicit framework for reading the clause that follows. It provides a reference time to set the stage for the following statement.

Consider the series of temporal switches in the next example, 1 Pet 2:10. The comparison of how things used to be with how they are currently is inherently contrastive on the basis of the content alone. The use of temporal frames to effect these switches draws extra attention to the contrast, making it stand out all the more.

Example 134 :: 1 Peter 2:10

⁹ But you are a chosen race, a royal priesthood, a holy nation, a people for God's possession, so that you may proclaim the virtues of the one who called you out of darkness into his marvelous light,

οἵ [TMπότεTM] οὐ λαὸς [TMνῦνTM] δὲ λαὸς θεοῦ, οἱ οὐκ ἠλεημένοι [TMνῦνTM] δὲ ἐλεηθέντες.	who [TMonceTM] were not a people, but [TMnowTM] are the people of God, the ones who were not shown mercy, but [TMnowTM] are shown mercy.

The adverb πότε in v. 10a could likely have been omitted without causing confusion, as seen in v. 10c. Including this generic temporal element grounds what follows in a specific temporal frame and sets the stage for the switch in v. 10b. The back-and-forth switches dramatically highlight the before-and-after effects of belief in Christ. The temporal frames are not the most important part of the clauses; what took place at those times is most important.

10.3   Spatial Frames

Most spatial frames consist of a prepositional phrase placed in an initial position in the clause, Dik's P1. Placing information about place or location in an initial position has the effect of attracting more attention to it than it otherwise would have received in its default position at the end of the clause. When this information is nonfocal, the result is not emphasis, but establishing an explicit spatial frame of reference for what follows. The frame makes changes in place or location stand out more. Spatial frames are often found at boundaries within a discourse, such as between pericopes or scenes within a pericope.

This first example illustrates the use of a spatial frame to indicate a change in location from one place to another.

Example 135 :: Mark 13:9

Βλέπετε δὲ ὑμεῖς ἑαυτούς· παραδώσουσιν ὑμᾶς εἰς συνέδρια καὶ [SPεἰς συναγωγὰςSP] δαρήσεσθε	"But you, watch out for yourselves! They will hand you over to councils and you will be beaten [SPin the synagoguesSP]
καὶ [SPἐπὶ ἡγεμόνων καὶ βασιλέωνSP] σταθήσεσθε ἕνεκεν ἐμοῦ εἰς μαρτύριον αὐτοῖς.	and will have to stand [SPbefore governors and kingsSP] because of me, for a witness to them."

Jesus forewarns the disciples of what they can expect in their future ministry. The use of spatial frames in v. 9c and v. 9d helps ensure that the changes are tracked, making each of these statements stand out more starkly by highlighting the switch in location. Had the spatial information been placed at the end of the clause, the changes from councils to synagogues to before kings and governors would have been less pronounced. This is essentially how Luke's version relates Jesus' words:

Example 136 :: Luke 21:12

<table>
<tr>
<td>[TMΠρὸ δὲ τούτων πάντωνTM] ἐπιβαλοῦσιν ἐφ᾽ ὑμᾶς τὰς χεῖρας αὐτῶν καὶ διώξουσιν, παραδιδόντες εἰς τὰς συναγωγὰς καὶ φυλακάς, ἀπαγομένους ἐπὶ βασιλεῖς καὶ ἡγεμόνας ἕνεκεν τοῦ ὀνόματός μου·</td>
<td>"But [TMbefore all these things,TM] they will lay their hands on you and will persecute you, handing you over to the synagogues and prisons. You will be brought before kings and governors because of my name."</td>
</tr>
</table>

Notice that this version contains virtually the same content, but it structures the information differently from Mark's version. Luke's interest seems to be in the temporal sequence of these events rather than in the locations. Mark allows the events of v. 9 to be implicitly related to the events in v. 8: nation rising up against nation, earthquakes and famine. Luke, on the other hand, uses a generic temporal frame, πρὸ τούτων πάντων. Although it really does not provide specific information, it effectively segments the events that precede from the events that follow, breaking them into distinct yet related groups.

Mark's account segments the discourse at v. 9, but in a much more subtle way than in Luke. There is a change from third-person narration of the events to a second-person command to watch out. The differences in the Synoptic writers' information structure suggest differences in their communication objectives.

The next example, from Ephesians, illustrates the use of spatial frames in a figurative or theological sense rather than a physical change of location. Verse 12 establishes both a time ("at that time") and a location or state ("apart from Christ"). Notice that both phrases follow the main verb in an unmarked location. This information sets the stage for talking about what things are like "now in Christ Jesus."

Example 137 :: Ephesians 2:13

> ^{12} that you were at that time apart from Christ, alienated from the citizenship of Israel, and strangers to the covenants of promise, not having hope, and without God in the world.

$^{13[TM}$νυνὶ$^{TM]}$ δὲ $^{[SP}$ἐν Χριστῷ Ἰησοῦ$^{SP]}$ $^{[TP}$ὑμεῖς οἵ $^{[TM}$ποτε$^{TM]}$ ὄντες μακρὰν$^{TP]}$ ἐγενήθητε ἐγγὺς ἐν τῷ αἵματι τοῦ Χριστοῦ.	^{13}But $^{[TM}$now$^{TM]}$ $^{[SP}$in Christ Jesus$^{SP]}$ $^{[TP}$you, the ones who $^{[TM}$once$^{TM]}$ were far away, $^{TP]}$ have become near by the blood of Christ.

The two frames in v. 13 make the changes in time and location stand out, but not because they are the most important information. The fact that we have come near by the blood of Christ is most important; the spatial and temporal information provide explicit frames of reference for connecting what follows to what precedes.

The NT Epistles are full of spatial frames that specify theological states or positions rather than literal places, as in the next example. In Rom 1:16–17, Paul describes how the gospel is the power of God for salvation to all who believe, for in it the righteous of God is being revealed. Then he moves on to discuss the plight of the sinner living under conviction brought about by the law. In Rom 3, Paul reiterates that both the Jew and the Greek are under sin (v. 9), and in v. 20 that "by works of the law no human being will be justified in his sight" (ESV). All of this raises the question of how anyone, then, can be justified. The frames in v. 21 signal a significant shift from how things have been under the law to how they are now in light of the gospel.

Example 138 :: Romans 3:21

$^{[TM}$Νυνὶ$^{TM]}$ δὲ $^{[SP}$χωρὶς νόμου$^{SP]}$ **δικαιοσύνη θεοῦ** πεφανέρωται μαρτυρουμένη ὑπὸ τοῦ νόμου καὶ τῶν προφητῶν....	But $^{[TM}$now,$^{TM]}$ $^{[SP}$apart from the law,$^{SP]}$ **the righteousness of God** has been revealed, being testified about by the law and the prophets....

The temporal frame shifts from some previous time to our current state of affairs; the spatial frame provides a change from being under the law to apart from the law. The revelation of God's righteousness is the most important information in the clause; the framing information is knowable from the context. Placing this information in an unmarked position at the end of the clause would have communicated the same content, but without creating an explicit frame of reference for the main clause. The two frames attract attention to the changes, accentuating the discontinuity of time and status. Every major translation places some kind of break at v. 21. The way that Paul has chosen to structure his information clearly highlights the discontinuity that was already present, based on the changes of time and situation.

The next example contains a corresponding pair of point/counterpoint sets. The use of the spatial frames helps to tighten the connection as well as to sharpen the contrast.

Example 139 :: Matthew 23:27–28

27 Οὐαὶ ὑμῖν, γραμματεῖς καὶ Φαρισαῖοι ὑποκριταί, ὅτι παρομοιάζετε τάφοις κεκονιαμένοις, ‹✘οἵτινες [SPἔξωθενSP] μὲν φαίνονται ὡραῖοι,✘› ‹✔[SPἔσωθενSP] δὲ γέμουσιν ὀστέων νεκρῶν καὶ πάσης ἀκαθαρσίας.✔›

28 οὕτως [TPκαὶ ὑμεῖςTP] ‹✘[SPἔξωθενSP] μὲν φαίνεσθε τοῖς ἀνθρώποις δίκαιοι,✘› ‹✔[SPἔσωθενSP] δέ ἐστε μεστοὶ ὑποκρίσεως καὶ ἀνομίας.✔›

27 "Woe to you, scribes and Pharisees—hypocrites!—because you are like whitewashed tombs ‹✘which [SPon the outsideSP] appear beautiful,✘› ‹✔but [SPon the insideSP] are full of the bones of the dead and of everything unclean!✔›

28 In the same way, ‹✘[SPon the outsideSP] [TPyou alsoTP] appear righteous to people,✘› ‹✔but [SPinsideSP] you are full of hypocrisy and lawlessness."✔›

Jesus talks about two aspects of whitewashed tombs, correlating them to comparable aspects of the religious leaders. The antonyms ἔξωθεν and ἔσωθεν highlight the semantic contrast present in the context, even without the use of frames. The frames simply accentuate the contrast that was already present. The use of οὕτως in v. 28 explicitly directs the reader in how to correlate what follows with what precedes; the parallelism in syntax and content make the intended connection perfectly clear. The most important information in each clause is not the location, but rather the state of affairs in the location.

The next example illustrates the figurative use of a generic prepositional phrase to create a distinction, in this case a prioritization by placing one thing "above" the others.

Example 140 :: 1 Peter 4:8

7 Now the end of all things draws near. Therefore be self-controlled and sober-minded for your prayers.

8 [SPπρὸ πάντων SP] τὴν εἰς ἑαυτοὺς   8 [SP Above all, SP] keep **your love**
ἀγάπην ἐκτενῆ ἔχοντες, ὅτι ἀγάπη   **for one another constant,** because
καλύπτει πλῆθος ἁμαρτιῶν.   love covers a large number of sins.

Verse 7 lays a foundation for the figurative spatial frame of v. 8. The end of all things drawing near calls for a certain response: self-control and sober-mindedness. These imperatives are elaborated upon by way of a participial clause describing an overarching quality that we should have. This quality is prioritized through the use of a figurative spatial frame, πρὸ πάντων, indicating that it takes precedence over everything else. A rationale is provided in the following ὅτι clause: love covers a multitude of sins. The use of a participle for ἔχοντες indicates that it is not on par with the imperatives that precede it.[18] These are the main verbs of the sentence, not ἔχοντες. However, the use of the spatial frame clearly indicates the importance of having a fervent love. The use of the participle to elaborate the imperatives, versus making ἔχοντες another imperative, prioritizes the action. The main points of the sentence are the imperatival actions, actions that necessitate having a fervent love as they are carried out.

Summary

Topical, temporal, and spatial information may be found at both the beginning and end of clauses in Koiné Greek. Porter has noted the meaningful difference between placing the subject before the verb versus after it.[19] Diessel noted a similar difference regarding the placement of adverbials, as does Wallace.[20] These observations are consistent with the claims of Simon Dik regarding the placement of certain clause components in what he refers to as position P1. Placing nonfocal information in this clause-initial position has the effect of establishing an explicit frame of reference for the clause that follows. It does not result in emphasis. By definition, emphasis refers to taking what was already most important in a clause and placing it in Dik's P2 at the beginning of the clause.

---

18. The LEB obscures this, translating the elaborating participle as another imperative, as does the NASB: "Above all, keep fervent in your love for one another, because love covers a multitude of sins." The grammatical distinction in Greek indicates a functional distinction in the actions; they are not all of equal importance. See chapter 12.

19. Porter, *Idioms*, 296; cf. Levinsohn, *Discourse Features*, 29–30.

20. Diessel, "Competing Motivations," 459; cf. Daniel B. Wallace, *Greek Grammar beyond the Basics: An Exegetical Syntax of the New Testament* (Grand Rapids: Zondervan, 1999), 636, 642.

Frames of reference are used to highlight the introduction of a new topic or center of interest in the discourse. They are also used to attract attention to a discontinuity in the discourse in order to help the reader/hearer properly process it. Contrast is not created by the use of frames of reference, though it may increase it. Contrast is derived from the semantics of the context; it is either present in the context or not. Devices like frames of reference or particles like ἀλλά can serve to make what was already present stand out even more.

The discussion of frames of reference continues in the next chapter.

11

FRAMING DEVICES (2)

This chapter introduces three more kinds of frames of reference, distinguished by the type of information placed in Dik's clause-initial P1 position (see §9.2.7). Recall the discussion from the introduction of chapter 10 that there are a number of factors influencing placement of adverbial subordinate clauses either before or after the main clause they modify. Adverbial clauses play such an important role in the processing of main clauses that certain kinds of adverbials almost always occur at the beginning of the clause.

Statistically speaking, it is more common for conditional clauses to occur at the beginning of the clause than at the end. Nonetheless, placing them in the initial position still accomplishes the same framing function as fronting adverbials that commonly occur at the end (e.g., reason/result clauses). The clause-initial adverbials are still considered to be in position P1, regardless of their distributional frequency.

It is not the statistical frequency or infrequency that makes the initial placement of adverbials special, but the cognitive processing function that they accomplish in this position. In each case, the nonfocal element provides an explicit frame of reference for the clause that follows. It is not the most important part of the clause (i.e., focal), instead it sets the stage for the clause that follows by establishing a specific state of affairs or context for relating the clause that follows to the previous context.

11.1 Conditional Frames

Conditional frames of reference are found only in the epistolary writings and in the reported speeches of narrative. There are only four possible instances in narrative proper.[1] They are graphically identified in the examples using this superscripted abbreviation: [CE], which means *conditional* or *exceptive* frame. Conditional frames are introduced by the conditional particles ἐάν or εἰ. They establish a specific condition that must be met before the main clause that follows holds true. In most cases, conditions precede the main clause due to their importance to processing. When they are placed after the main clause, some other marker will indicate that a condition follows. Positioning the condition as a frame of reference highlights the contingency of the main clause, which otherwise might have sounded like an affirmation until the condition or exception was read at the end. Thus, the semantic importance of the condition to the proper processing of the main clause is the primary motivation for its initial placement.

The opening chapter of 1 John has a series of conditional frames that allow the writer to quickly switch from one state of affairs to another. Each clause, by changing the condition for the main clause that follows, provides a new perspective on what it means to have fellowship with Jesus. There is noticeable contrast between the clauses based on the semantics of the content, but it is heightened through the use of frames to juxtapose opposite conditions with their correlating consequences.

Example 141 :: 1 John 1:6–10

6 [CE]Ἐὰν εἴπωμεν ὅτι κοινωνίαν ἔχομεν μετ' αὐτοῦ καὶ ἐν τῷ σκότει περιπατῶμεν,[CE] ψευδόμεθα καὶ οὐ ποιοῦμεν τὴν ἀλήθειαν·

6 [CE]If we say that we have fellowship with him and walk in the darkness,[CE] we lie and do not practice the truth.

7 [CE]ἐὰν δὲ ἐν τῷ φωτὶ περιπατῶμεν ὡς αὐτός ἐστιν ἐν τῷ φωτί,[CE] κοινωνίαν ἔχομεν μετ' ἀλλήλων καὶ τὸ αἷμα Ἰησοῦ τοῦ υἱοῦ αὐτοῦ καθαρίζει ἡμᾶς ἀπὸ πάσης ἁμαρτίας.

7 But [CE]if we walk in the light as he is in the light,[CE] we have fellowship with one another, and the blood of Jesus his Son cleanses us from all sin.

8 [CE]ἐὰν εἴπωμεν ὅτι ἁμαρτίαν οὐκ ἔχομεν,[CE] ἑαυτοὺς πλανῶμεν καὶ ἡ ἀλήθεια οὐκ ἔστιν ἐν ἡμῖν.

8 [CE]If we say that we do not have sin,[CE] we deceive ourselves and the truth is not in us.

---

1. Conditional frames are found in narrative asides in Mark 7:3–4 (2x) and John 21:25. Acts 20:16 contains a conditional frame fronted with respect to an infinitival complement of the main verb, but not preceding the main verb.

9 [CE ἐὰν ὁμολογῶμεν τὰς ἁμαρτίας ἡμῶν,CE] πιστός ἐστιν καὶ δίκαιος, ἵνα ἀφῇ ἡμῖν τὰς ἁμαρτίας καὶ καθαρίσῃ ἡμᾶς ἀπὸ πάσης ἀδικίας.

9 [CEIf we confess our sins,CE] he is faithful and just,so that he will forgive us our sins and will cleanse us from all unrighteousness.

10 [CE ἐὰν εἴπωμεν ὅτι οὐχ ἡμαρτή- καμεν,CE] ψεύστην ποιοῦμεν αὐτὸν καὶ ὁ λόγος αὐτοῦ οὐκ ἔστιν ἐν ἡμῖν.

10 [CEIf we say that we have not sinned,CE] we make him a liar, and his word is not in us.

Each conditional frame of reference provides a state of affairs for which the main clause applies. The prominence assigned to the condition alerts the reader that this must hold true before the main proposition holds true. Below is an alternate rendering of v. 6, based on placing the condition at the end of the main clause. Note the use of "only" to signal that something more is needed to fully process the main clause:

We only lie and do not practice the truth if we say that we have fellowship with him and walk in the darkness.

There may be other contexts where we might lie and not practice the truth, but the writer is focusing on only one of them. This particular context has two components: saying that we have fellowship and not practicing the truth. As we see in v. 7, doing what we say we are doing makes all of the difference in the world.

Verse 8 establishes that there is no room for denying that we have sin. This raises the question of how we should respond to sin in light of the fact that it is universal. Verse 9 provides the answer using another conditional frame. This same content could have been stated using

- an unmarked structure: "Confess your sins in order that he would forgive them"; or
- two main clauses: "Confess your sins, and he will forgive them."

Instead, we find that the main clause states God's qualities of faithfulness and justice. In the NRSV, the main clause is translated as though it is a relative clause and the ἵνα clause as though it were the main clause: "If we confess our sins, he who is faithful and just will forgive us our sins and cleanse us from all unrighteousness." The focus of attention in the main clause of v. 9 is on God's qualities; the rest of the information is in subordinate clauses. If the fronted condition is met, forgiveness and cleansing will follow.

The conditional frame in v. 10 allows the writer to examine the corollary of confession: saying that we have not sinned. Although this statement is similar to the one in v. 8, there is a shift from what it means for us to what it means to God. Making such a claim is indistinguishable from calling God a liar. The parallel syntax and wording of vv. 6, 8, and 10 help to insure that the reader connects these verses. The parallelism draws attention to the differences because the preceding content is still fresh in the reader's mind.

In Rom 8:11–12, Paul states that we are not obligated to live according to the flesh now that the Spirit has made us alive. Verse 13 contrasts the two alternatives, establishing explicit states of affairs for the main clauses that follow using conditional frames.

Example 142 :: Romans 8:13

[CEεἰ γὰρ κατὰ σάρκα ζῆτε,CE] μέλλετε ἀποθνῄσκειν· [CEεἰ δὲ πνεύματι τὰς πράξεις τοῦ σώματος θανατοῦτε,CE] ζήσεσθε.

For [CEif you live according to the flesh,CE] you are going to die, but [CEif by the Spirit you put to death the deeds of the body,CE] you will live.

Paul could have used a topical frame to state the principle: "[TPThe one living according to the fleshTP] will die…." Doing so would have rendered it an impersonal statement instead of the personal call to decision found in the canonical version.

Unlike the example from 1 John 1, Paul changes the verbs in the two frames rather than maintaining a parallelism of "living in the flesh" versus "living in the Spirit." The first frame focuses on a way of living that leads to death, the second on a putting to death that leads to life. In other words, there is parallel syntax without an accompanying parallelism of the content. This has the effect of sharpening the contrast by breaking from the expected parallelism.

There is a quotation from Ps 95:7 repeated several times in Hebrews that uses a condition to establish an explicit frame of reference for what follows.

Example 143 :: Hebrews 3:7

7 Διό, καθὼς λέγει τὸ πνεῦμα τὸ ἅγιον· [TMσήμερονTM] [CEἐὰν τῆς φωνῆς αὐτοῦ ἀκούσητε,CE]

7 Therefore, just as the Holy Spirit says, [TM"Today, TM] [CEif you hear his voice,CE]

8 μὴ σκληρύνητε τὰς καρδίας ὑμῶν ὡς ἐν τῷ παραπικρασμῷκατὰ τὴν ἡμέραν τοῦ πειρασμοῦ ἐν τῇ ἐρήμῳ,

8 do not harden your hearts as in the rebellion, in the day of testing in the wilderness,

"Today" establishes a temporal frame of reference for the clause that follows, while the conditional frame establishes an explicit state of affairs. These
frames are not the most important information in the clause; "do not harden
your hearts" is. The writer wants to focus on a specific context in which hearts
should not be hardened: hearing God's voice. There may be a time when hardening is appropriate, but the conditional frame constrains the main clause that
follows to be read in the specific context of the condition.

A complex conditional frame introduces a very involved state of affairs in
James 2 that is finally commented on in v. 4.

Example 144 :: James 2:2–4

¹ My brothers, do not hold your faith in our glorious Lord Jesus Christ
with partiality.

² [CEἐὰν γὰρ εἰσέλθῃ εἰς συναγω-γὴν ὑμῶν ἀνὴρ χρυσοδακτύλιος ἐν ἐσθῆτι λαμπρᾷ,	² For [CEif someone enters into your assembly in fine clothing with a gold ring on his finger,
εἰσέλθῃ δὲ καὶ πτωχὸς ἐν ῥυπαρᾷ ἐσθῆτι,	and a poor person in filthy cloth-ing also enters,
³ ἐπιβλέψητε δὲ ἐπὶ τὸν φοροῦντα τὴν ἐσθῆτα τὴν λαμπρὰν καὶ εἴπητε· σὺ κάθου ὧδε καλῶς,	³ and you look favorably on the one wearing the fine clothing and you say, "Be seated here in a good place,"
καὶ τῷ πτωχῷ εἴπητε· σὺ στῆθι ἐκεῖ ἢ κάθου ὑπὸ τὸ ὑποπόδιόν μου,CE]	and to the poor person you say, "You stand there or be seated by my footstool,"CE]
⁴ οὐ διεκρίθητε ἐν ἑαυτοῖς καὶ ἐγένεσθε κριταὶ διαλογισμῶν πονηρῶν;	⁴ have you not made distinctions among yourselves and become judges with evil thoughts?

From a grammatical point of view, James uses the various conditional clauses
of the frame to make sure that there is no room to miss his point. Had he
only mentioned the response to the poor person or to the rich person,
his point about making distinctions would not have been nearly as clear.
Similarly, if the question "Are you not making distinctions… ?" came first,
followed by the conditional clauses, the overall proposition would not be
nearly as compelling. Placing the conditional clauses at the end of the main
clause could imply that they are the new information, rather than making

distinctions.[2] This frame is long and complex enough that the NIV breaks the complex clause of vv. 2–4 into several parts as main clauses rather than maintaining the subordination found in Greek. However this translation strategy fundamentally changes the buildup found in the Greek proposition.

James's goal is to help the reader realize that behaving along the lines of the scenario in the conditional frame is indeed showing partiality and not something else. This command is clearly laid out in v. 1 and is practically illustrated in vv. 2–4 to make sure that no one misses the point. The use of devices like thematic addition at the end of v. 2 helps tighten the connections already present due to the contrastive parallels drawn between the rich person and the poor person.

In some instances, what we would consider an exceptive clause in English functions as a frame, introduced by εἰ μή. These are infrequent, and they are handled as a conditional frame based on the presence of the Greek conditional particle.[3] They have the same effect of constraining the main clause that follows to be processed in light of the exceptive statement, attracting extra attention to it.

---

2. In Mark 9:42, for example, it is said that anyone who causes one of the little ones who believe in Jesus to sin would be better off with something else, which is disclosed in a pair of conditions at the end of the clause: being tethered to a millstone and cast into the sea. In v. 43, the condition functions as a frame, and it is not the most important information in the clause; the cutting off of the hand is most important.

42 Καὶ [TPὃς ἂν σκανδαλίσῃ ἕνα τῶν μικρῶν τούτων τῶν πιστευόντων [εἰς ἐμέ],TP] καλόν ἐστιν αὐτῷ μᾶλλον εἰ περίκειται μύλος ὀνικὸς περὶ τὸν τράχηλον αὐτοῦ καὶ βέβληται εἰς τὴν θάλασσαν.	42 "And [TPwhoever causes one of these little ones who believe in me to sin,TP] it is better for him if instead a large millstone is placed around his neck and he is thrown into the sea.
43 Καὶ [CEἐὰν σκανδαλίζῃ σε ἡ χείρ σου,CE] ἀπόκοψον αὐτήν· καλόν ἐστίν σε κυλλὸν εἰσελθεῖν εἰς τὴν ζωὴν ἢ τὰς δύο χεῖρας ἔχοντα ἀπελθεῖν εἰς τὴν γέενναν, εἰς τὸ πῦρ τὸ ἄσβεστον.	43 And [CEif your hand causes you to sin,CE] cut it off! It is better for you to enter into life crippled than, having two hands, to go into hell—into the unquenchable fire!"

The point to be made in v. 42 is that sometimes conditions are part of what is newly asserted (i.e., focal), hence the placement at the end of the clause as predicted by natural information flow (see §9.2.4).

3. Exceptive clauses typically follow a negated clause, providing an exception from the set of negated items. The net result is to create a point/counterpoint set, where the exceptive clause introduces the highlighted point. See chapter 4.

Example 145 :: Matthew 24:22

καὶ ^{[CE}εἰ μὴ ἐκολοβώθησαν αἱ ἡμέραι ἐκεῖναι,^{CE]} οὐκ ἂν ἐσώθη πᾶσα σάρξ· διὰ δὲ τοὺς ἐκλεκτοὺς κολοβωθήσονται αἱ ἡμέραι ἐκεῖναι.	"And ^{[CE}unless those days had been shortened,^{CE]} no human being would be saved. But for the sake of the elect, those days will be shortened."

Although the collocation εἰ μή might be translated into English idiomatically as "unless" or "except," it is simply a negated conditional clause that has a pragmatic effect comparable to the other conditional frames that we have looked at. No one would have been saved if something (shortened days) had not happened. Placing the subordinate clause in an initial position does not mean that it is the most important part of the clause; what is most important is no human being saved. The prominence added to the condition establishes an explicit frame of reference for processing the following clause. This claim about not saving any flesh is meant for a particular context, specified by the conditional frame.

Other exceptive frames are found in Matt 24:22; Mark 8:14; John 9:33; 15:22, 24; 18:30; Rom 9:29.

11.2 Comparative Frames

Comparative frames of reference establish a basis against which something in the main clause is compared. The comparison typically describes the manner in which the main action should be done, with the frame setting the stage for what follows. As with other kinds of frames, the fronted adverbial is not the most important part of the clause; it simply provides the basis of comparison. The basis stands out, but not for the sake of emphasis. The action or the actor(s) of the main clause is generally what is most important.

Jesus' admonition about judging provides a good example of how a comparative frame functions to highlight a key idea. The call is not to avoid judging, but to judge in the way that you would want to be judged—that is, equitably.

Example 146 :: Matthew 7:2

¹ "Do not judge, so that you will not be judged."

² ^{[CP}ἐν ᾧ γὰρ κρίματι κρίνετε^{CP]} κριθήσεσθε, καὶ ^{[CP}ἐν ᾧ μέτρῳ	² "For ^{[CP}by what judgment you judge,^{CP]} you will be judged, and ^{[CP}by

μετρεῖτε^{CP]} μετρηθήσεται ὑμῖν.   what measure you measure out,[CP] it will be measured out to you."

The action of the main clause is the focus of attention. The comparative frame presents the manner in which the main action should be done by establishing it as the basis for the clause that follows. We probably would accomplish this kind of task most naturally in English by using a rhetorical question: "You know how you judge other people? That is the way you will be judged. You know the measure that you use for others? That is what will be used for you." Thus there is a bit of a mismatch between Greek and English here in terms of preference, but it can be easily bridged in exposition through using comparable constructions like rhetorical questions. Both frames and rhetorical questions can accomplish the task of activating a specific state of affairs in our mental representations of the discourse. The task accomplished is what matters, not the specific device used in one language versus another.

Remember that since the basis of comparison is not newly asserted information, there is no emphasis on the manner. The frame simply provides the basis of comparison for the clause that follows. The fact that it will happen to you is the main point Matt 7:2. The frame of reference activates the information about which a comment will be made. Had the clause been phrased with the prepositional phrases in an unmarked position at the end of the clause, it would likely have been understood to be the new information of the clause rather than a basis of comparison. Providing the basis of comparison in the frame of reference draws attention to it, indicating that the main clause that follows is focal.

Luke's version of the "golden rule" provides another illustration of a comparative frame that draws attention to the basis of comparison.

Example 147 :: Luke 6:31

Καὶ [CPκαθὼς θέλετε ἵνα ποιῶσιν   And [CPjust as you want people to
ὑμῖν οἱ ἄνθρωποι^{CP]} ποιεῖτε αὐτοῖς   do to you,[CP] do the same to them.
ὁμοίως.

Jesus' goal is to get people to act, and the manner of the action is defined by how you want to be treated. The focal information of the main clause is "[you] do the same." The framed material draws attention to the manner in which this action is to be carried out. Again, a rhetorical question accomplishes the same task rather naturally in English: "[Do] you know how you want others to treat you? Treat them in that same manner." Instead of waiting for people to be kind and courteous to you, followers of Jesus should be the initiators. In other words, stop waiting for others to be kind or nice to you and start doing it yourself! The manner of the action is not the most important part of the clause; it is you doing it. Placing the basis of comparison in a frame of reference avoids confusion over what is most important in the main clause.

The next example illustrates the combination of several devices to make a single point.

Example 148 :: 1 John 2:5b–6

5b ⟨→ἐν τούτῳ→⟩ γινώσκομεν ὅτι ἐν αὐτῷ ἐσμεν.	5b ⟨→By this→⟩ we know that we are in him.
6 ⟨⊙ [TPὁ λέγων ἐν αὐτῷ μένειν TP] ὀφείλει [CPκαθὼς ἐκεῖνος περιεπάτησεν CP] καὶ αὐτὸς [οὕτως] περιπατεῖν.⊙⟩	6 ⟨⊙ [TPThe one who says that he resides in him TP] ought also to walk in this way: [CPjust as that one walked. CP] ⊙⟩

Verses 5–6 are fairly complex, with the comparative frame occurring in the infinitival clause of v. 6. The forward-pointing reference in v. 5 draws extra attention to the litmus test for knowing that "we are in him." The one who claims to reside in him is to walk in a particular way. This could have been phrased where the manner was emphasized: "You ought to walk *as that one walked*."[4] Instead, the basis of comparison provides a frame of reference for the clause that follows, focusing attention on *our* walking instead of *his* walking. His walking is important, but only as it sets the standard for ours.[5] Just as that one walked, so also the one claiming to reside in him ought to walk. The thematic addition provided by adverbial καί strengthens the link back to Jesus. It would have been much simpler to state, "The one claiming to reside in him ought to walk just as he walked," without the frame and without thematic addition. Doing so would have placed the basis of the comparison in the default position for new, focal information, potentially creating confusion over the writer's intended focus. In its canonical form, the frame sets the stage for the main clause, keeping attention on our walking instead of his.

---

4. The subject ἐκεῖνος does receive emphasis, but the scope of the emphasis is limited to the subordinate comparative clause. The subject of the main clause, καὶ αὐτός, receives primary emphasis (see chapter 13).

5. Use of the "far" demonstrative ἐκεῖνος provides further confirmation that the central interest here is not Jesus: that is, he is athematic. See chapter 18.

In the next example, Paul uses two frames to establish a basis of comparison for describing his ministry: "according to the grace given to him" and "as a skilled master builder."

Example 149 :: 1 Corinthians 3:10

[CPΚατὰ τὴν χάριν τοῦ θεοῦ τὴν δοθεῖσάν μοιCP] [CPὡς σοφὸς ἀρχιτέκτωνCP] θεμέλιον ἔθηκα, ἄλλος δὲ ἐποικοδομεῖ. ἕκαστος δὲ βλεπέτω πῶς ἐποικοδομεῖ.	[CPAccording to the grace of God given to me,CP] [CPlike a skilled master builderCP] I laid a foundation,and another is building upon it. But each one must direct his attention to how he is building upon it.

The first comparative frame establishes that whatever action follows was not done in his own strength or ability, but in accordance with the grace that he has received from God. The second frame, ὡς σοφὸς ἀρχιτέκτων, establishes that whatever action follows is the work not of a novice, but of a seasoned veteran. Both frames ground Paul's claims about his ministry.

His point here is that he intended only to lay the foundation, not build the whole building. The latter is the work of those who come after him. He built the foundation and only the foundation; he did this empowered by grace and experience. The two frames provide the setting for his claim regarding laying a foundation. His qualifications are not the most important thing in this context; the foundation he laid is most important.

The last example of a comparative frame is very complex, qualified using a point/counterpoint set. Paul's primary point is to encourage the Philippians to work out their salvation in a particular way: with fear and trembling. To set the stage for this, the comparative frame describes the manner in which this should be done.

Example 150 :: Philippians 2:12

Ὥστε, ἀγαπητοί μου, [CPκαθὼς πάντοτε ὑπηκούσατε,	Therefore my dear friends, [CPjust as you have always obeyed,
⟨✗μὴ ὡς ἐν τῇ παρουσίᾳ μου μόνον✗⟩	⟨✗not as in my presence only✗⟩
ἀλλὰ ⟨✓νῦν πολλῷ μᾶλλον ἐν τῇ ἀπουσίᾳ μου,✓⟩ CP]	but ⟨✓now much more in my absence,✓⟩ CP]

μετὰ φόβου καὶ τρόμου τὴν ἑαυτῶν σωτηρίαν κατεργάζεσθε·	work out your own salvation **with fear and trembling**.

Note that "fear and trembling" also describes a manner, but it receives emphasis. The manner in which they have always obeyed lays the groundwork, creating the expectation that they will obey this newest command just as they have always obeyed the other things asked of them.

The point/counterpoint set elaborates that their obedience was carried out not only under Paul's watchful eye, but also in his absence. The frame draws attention to the basis against which the following action should be done, but without elevating it to the status of emphasis. The way they have always obeyed is well known to them, indicating that the information fills Dik's P1 position. "With fear and trembling" is the manner that receives emphasis in P2. This example highlights the importance of determining the information status of each clause component. Not every comparative basis establishes a frame. Frames are distinguished from emphasis based on whether the information is presupposed/knowable or newly asserted (see §9.2).

11.3   Reason/Result Frames

Reason/result frames are relatively infrequent, but they deserve some attention. They can be prepositional phrases that reiterate a proposition from the preceding context using a pronoun (e.g., διὰ τοῦτο); they can also be subordinate clauses introduced by ὅτι or ἵνα. This kind of adverbial clause prototypically is found at the end of the main clause. As with the other frames, placing the information in a position of prominence creates an explicit frame of reference for the clause that follows based on its status as known or knowable. It provides the reason for or result of the main proposition that follows; it draws attention to the rationale or objective.

Example 151 :: Matthew 13:6

ἡλίου δὲ ἀνατείλαντος ἐκαυματίσθη καὶ [RRδιὰ τὸ μὴ ἔχειν ῥίζανRR] ἐξηράνθη.	"But when the sun rose it was scorched, and [RRbecause it did not have enough root,RR] it withered."

In Matthew's account of the parable of the sower, the reason that the plant withered provides the basis for relating the preceding action to what follows. The implication is that if there had been roots, the withering would not have taken place. If the reason had been placed in the expected position at the end of the clause, it could have been understood to be focal (i.e., most important). In the canonical form, placing reason information in a frame ensures that the focus of the main clause is clearly on withering.

Similarly, Mark's parallel account in 4:6 also uses a reason/result frame.

Example 152 :: Mark 4:6

καὶ [TMὅτε ἀνέτειλεν ὁ ἥλιοςTM] ἐκαυματίσθη καὶ [CPδιὰ τὸ μὴ ἔχειν ῥίζανCP] ἐξηράνθη.	"And [TMwhen the sun roseTM] it was scorched, and [CPbecause it did not have enough root,CP] it withered."

Note that the activity of the sun is portrayed as a temporal frame rather than backgrounded in a circumstantial frame as in Matt 13:6. Both have a similar effect of establishing context, but each uses a different means of structuring the information. In both cases, the seed remains the center of interest, not the sun.

The reason/result frame in the parable of the persistent widow and the judge comes near the end of a very complex clause, just before the main proposition of granting her justice.

Example 153 :: Luke 18:4–5

4 καὶ οὐκ ἤθελεν ἐπὶ χρόνον. [TMμετὰ δὲ ταῦταTM] εἶπεν ἐν ἑαυτῷ· [CEεἰ καὶ τὸν θεὸν οὐ φοβοῦμαι οὐδὲ ἄνθρωπον ἐντρέπομαι,CE]	4 "And he was not willing for a time, but [TMafter these thingsTM] he said to himself, [CE'Even if I do not fear God or respect people,CE]
5 [RRδιά γε τὸ παρέχειν μοι κόπον τὴν χήραν ταύτηνRR] ἐκδικήσω αὐτήν, ἵνα μὴ εἰς τέλος ἐρχομένη ὑπωπιάζῃ με.	5 yet [RRbecause this widow is causing trouble for me,RR] I will grant her justice, so that she does not wear me down in the end by her coming back!'"

The statement that the judge was not willing "for a time" creates the possibility that he would be willing at some point. The generic "after these things" moves forward to some later time, perhaps the point when he will be willing to hear the widow's case.

There are two frames that establish the states of affairs for the main clause, ἐκδικήσω αὐτήν. The first is a conditional frame that establishes what functions as a concession. In other words, although it is true that the judge neither fears God nor respects people, there is something that will motivate him to make an unexpected change. The reason/result frame describes what brings about this change: wanting to get this widow to stop bothering him.[6] The desired result follows the main clause, introduced by ἵνα. The reason for his granting her justice is to get her to stop bothering him, in the hope that she will not wear him out.

An added effect of using frames for so much of the information in this clause is to delay learning what exactly the judge will do, creating suspense. The reason/result frame also makes clear that his changed attitude is motivated not by some newly found righteousness or repentance, but by the selfish motivation of getting her off of his back.

In the next example, the reason is placed in a frame of reference apparently to avoid it being misunderstood to be the most important information in the main clause.

Example 154 :: John 8:45

[44] "You are of your father the devil, and you want to do the desires of your father! That one was a murderer from the beginning, and does not stand firm in the truth, because truth is not in him. Whenever he speaks the lie, he speaks from his own nature, because he is a liar and the father of lies."

[45] [TPἐγὼTP] δὲ [RRὅτι **τὴν ἀλή-θειαν** λέγω,RR] **οὐ πιστεύετέ** μοι.	[45] "But [RRbecause [TPITP] am telling **the truth**,RR] **you do not believe** me."

Jesus contrasts the words and actions of the religious leaders with his own. He has accused them of following the desires of their father, the devil, whom Jesus characterizes as a murderer and liar. He switches from them to himself in v. 45, using a topical frame in combination with the development marker δέ.

If the ὅτι-clause had been placed at the end of the main clause, it likely would have been read as the most important part of the clause. In other words, they are not believing Jesus for some particular reason. This is not the case. If someone is speaking the truth, the expectation is that the speaker will be believed. This is not the case with the Pharisees.

---

6. See the discussion of referential indefinites/contemptuous usage of demonstrative pronouns in chapter 18.

Placing the ὅτι-clause in a frame effectively changes the presupposition of the clause. The fact that Jesus is telling the truth presupposes some kind of response, most likely belief. Instead of belief, their response is unbelief. In v. 47b, Jesus clearly states why they do not listen to him, highlighting it with a forward-pointing reference and target: they are not of God.

Another reason/result frame is found in the introduction of the letter from the Jerusalem council to the new Gentile believers, making for a very complex clause.

Example 155 :: Acts 15:24–25

24 [RR'Επειδὴ ἠκούσαμεν ὅτι τινὲς ἐξ ἡμῶν [ἐξελθόντες] ἐτάραξαν ὑμᾶς λόγοις	24 [RR"Because we have heard that some have gone out from among us—to whom we gave no orders—
ἀνασκευάζοντες τὰς ψυχὰς ὑμῶν οἷς οὐ διεστειλάμεθα,RR]	and have thrown you into confusion by words upsetting your minds,RR]
25 ἔδοξεν ἡμῖν γενομένοις ὁμο-θυμαδὸν ἐκλεξαμένοις ἄνδρας πέμψαι πρὸς ὑμᾶς σὺν τοῖς ἀγαπητοῖς ἡμῶν Βαρναβᾷ καὶ Παύλῳ,....	25 it seemed best to us, having reached a unanimous decision, and having chosen men, to send them to you together with our dear friends Barnabas and Paul...."

The main proposition of this complex clause is "it seemed best to send...." All of the rest is either framing information or elaboration. The reason/result frame of v. 24 provides the rationale for the council's action. They had heard that some from Jerusalem had confused the believers. This confusion is elaborated as "upsetting your minds." The apostles distance themselves from the troublemakers, characterizing them as not having been given orders.

The main verb of the sentence, ἔδοξεν, is actually a helping verb, expecting an infinitive to complete the action. This infinitive, πέμψαι, is preceded by two circumstantial frames that set the stage for this action, backgrounding it so that "to send" is marked as more important than "having reached" or "having chosen." Although the complexity of the grammar may look like a hopeless mess to some, each grammatical decision has exegetical implications. The complexity evinces a careful crafting of the discourse that is worthy of our attention.

The final example, from Galatians, also occurs in a rather complex setting.

Example 156 :: Galatians 2:4–5

⁴ [RRδιὰ δὲ τοὺς παρεισάκτους ψευδαδέλφους, οἵτινες παρεισῆλθον κατασκοπῆσαι τὴν ἐλευθερίαν ἡμῶν ἣν ἔχομεν ἐν Χριστῷ Ἰησοῦ, ἵνα ἡμᾶς καταδουλώσουσιν,RR]

⁴ [RRNow this was because of the false brothers secretly brought in, who slipped in to spy out our freedom that we have in Christ Jesus, in order that they might enslave us,RR]

⁵ οἷς οὐδὲ πρὸς ὥραν εἴξαμεν τῇ ὑποταγῇ, ἵνα ἡ ἀλήθεια τοῦ εὐαγγελίου διαμείνῃ πρὸς ὑμᾶς.

⁵ to whom not even for an hour did we yield in subjection, in order that the truth of the gospel might remain continually with you.

The main proposition here is that they did not submit for even an hour. The prepositional phrase of v. 4 explains why they did not submit. This reason/ result frame introduces the participants to whom Paul and Timothy did not submit. The intention of this infiltration by outsiders is also introduced in the frame: to enslave Paul and Timothy. The statement about not submitting is framed by both the nature and the intentions of the false brothers. Paul had already submitted his gospel to those who were influential (see Gal. 2:2), and they had required no modification of it. Placing this information in a frame marks it as the primary basis for the action that follows; it dispels the possibility that Paul is simply resisting godly authority, an act that is not noble but rather is reprehensible. Since the frame also introduces these false brothers, the entire sentence would need to be restructured in order to avoid using a frame of some kind. The reason frame allows Paul to introduce a very complex state of affairs while at the same time keeping primary attention focused in the main idea: not yielding for even an hour.

Summary

This chapter has described the discourse functions of conditional, comparative, and reason/result frames. There are a variety of factors that influence the placement of adverbial clause elements. In the case of conditionals, their importance for properly processing the main clause makes it difficult to place them anywhere other than the beginning. Comparative adverbials are found at both the beginning and the end. Reason/result adverbials most often come at the end.

Despite the various motivating factors, placing these adverbials at the beginning of a clause can still create an explicit frame of reference for the clause that follows. Remember that the status of the information—whether it is newly asserted versus known/knowable—is the determining factor in differentiating a frame of reference from emphasis. It is not the statistical distribution that determines such things; it is status and function of the adverbial in the specific discourse context.

Conditional frames alert the reader that the main proposition is conditioned upon some criteria being met. Reason/result frames are often motivated by the desire to indicate that this information is not the most important in the main clause. Although semantic and typological constraints influence the placement of these adverbial elements, they share a common function within the discourse, consistent with Dik's claims regarding position P1.

CIRCUMSTANTIAL FRAMES

This chapter focuses on what have been called *predicate* participles[1] or *adverbial* participles.[2] Specifically, I am referring to anarthrous participles (those that lack the article) that are functioning as the predicating verb in a dependent clause. I maintain that participles do not function as a verb in an independent clause; instead, they depend upon a main clause in some way, no matter how loosely. As Moule states, "The ruling consideration in interpreting participles is that they express something which is dependent on the main verb, or a pendant to it."[3]

The participle is used much more widely and diversely in Greek than in English. It is the workhorse of the Greek verbal system, with participles being used for more actions than would be acceptable in English. This mismatch in usage has significantly impacted the participle's grammatical description. Remember, our goal is to understand the Greek usage first, and only then should we worry about translation. The participle is one of those areas where it is imperative to think about Greek *as Greek*.

Greek writers quite regularly use participles in extended chains, either to establish states of affairs or to elaborate upon what is practically meant by the main action of the clause. In practical terms, Greek writers could accomplish in a single sentence what would take us in English a paragraph or more. In this way, the Greek participle often operates at a more important level of the discourse than does an English participle. The discourse function of the par-

---

1. Stanley E. Porter, *Idioms of the Greek New Testament* (2nd ed.; Sheffield: Sheffield Academic, 1999), 183.

2. Daniel B. Wallace, *Greek Grammar beyond the Basics: An Exegetical Syntax of the New Testament* (Grand Rapids: Zondervan, 1999), 622.

3. C. F. D. Moule, *An Idiom Book of New Testament Greek* (Cambridge: Cambridge University Press, 1959), 99.

ticiple in each language is drastically different, even though theoretically they are grammatical counterparts.

We might be tempted to think of the participial action as unimportant, but that is not the case. It is simply a matter of prioritization, with finite verbs being used for more central action or activity. Think about the English paragraph, how there is typically one action that has more significance than the others in the paragraph. Not every action is equally important, and participles provide the grammatical means of explicitly marking this. The Greek participle allows the writer to make one finite verb (e.g., indicative or imperative) central to the entire sentence by rendering the rest of the actions as participles.

Translation into English has done much to influence our understanding the Greek participle. Translators often prefer to render complex chains of Greek participles using finite verb forms in coordinate or paratactic relations (e.g., using "and" or "but").[4] Alternatively, we might prefer to use subordinate clauses to specify the exact hypotactic relations of the participial action to that of the main verb.[5] Perhaps it is for this reason that descriptions of the participle often map it to a hypotactic or paratactic relation in English rather than maintaining the relative relational ambiguity of the participle to the main verbal action. Although most grammarians note the ambiguity of the basic participial form, many attempt to obviate this by categorizing participles according to elaborate systems of classification.[6] Rather than try to add to such classification, my goal is to provide a unified explanation of the participle's function in Greek discourse by understanding the choices associated with its usage. In other words, the choice to use a participle represents the choice not to use another verb form.

---

4. For example, Dana and Mantey state regarding the circumstantial participle, "Here the English participle fails to extend its use sufficiently to take care of the entire force of the Greek participle, and at the same time it is doubtful if a separate clause is an exact translation. It is one of those idioms which have no exact parallel in English" (H. E. Dana and Julius R. Mantey, *A Manual Grammar of the Greek New Testament* [New York: Macmillan, 1968], 229).

5. Young states, "The particular way they modify the verb is not grammaticalized in Greek; that is, the adverbial force is not indicated by the grammar" (Richard A. Young, *Intermediate New Testament Greek: A Linguistic and Exegetical Approach* [Nashville: Broadman & Holman, 1994], 152).

6. Hadley and Allen state, "It must be remembered that the Greek participle, while it stands in all these relations, does not express them definitely and distinctly. Hence the different uses run into each other, and cases occur in which more than one might be assigned" (James Hadley and Frederic De Forest Allen, *Greek Grammar for Schools and Colleges* [London: Macmillan, 1884], 303).

The most important thing to understand about participles is the idea of *prioritization of the action*. The use of a participle to grammaticalize an action represents the choice not to use a finite verb form (e.g., indicative or imperative mood), whether connected through coordination or subordination. Participles are not finite verbs, and the choice to use one should be respected in our exegesis. Bear in mind also that the Greek participle may be operating at a level of the discourse comparable to an English finite verb, particularly in long chains. From an exegetical standpoint, the key point to understand is the use of participles to prioritize the action within the complex. The finite action is the most prominent one, with participles playing a supporting role. Regardless of how we might translate Greek participles into English, in Greek they function to explicitly prioritize the action.

12.1   Conventional Explanation

Greek participles traditionally have been divided into two basic functions: adjectival and adverbial. The adjectival ones function as substantives or directly modify substantives, and often they take the article. Adverbial (or verbal) participles modify a verb, typically by specifying some kind of dependent action, and they are anarthrous. These adverbial participles are then subdivided variously by different grammarians. In constructions like periphrastics or those using complementary participles, the participles are a required part of the clause that cannot be removed without substantially altering the meaning.[7] The remaining usage is often subdivided into supplementary and circumstantial participles. In both instances, the verbal action of the participle relates to the main action of the clause in some way, even if there is no specific syntactic dependence, as in a "genitive absolute" construction. This final group of participles is our focus.

First, there is a widespread acknowledgment that participles are not independent finite verbs, even though they appear at times to function independently. Regardless of the postulated finite-like categories, grammarians hedge any claims by noting that these participles are dependent on the main action of the clause in some way. Porter notes this dependence on the main verb even in absolute or "independent" usage, defining it as "a participle not directly dependent upon a finite verb or any other structure but clearly linked

---

7. Robertson notes that if the participle is removed from such a construction, "the sentence bleeds" (A. T. Robertson, *A Grammar of the Greek New Testament in the Light of Historical Research* [1919; repr., Bellingham, Wash.: Logos, 2006], 1124). Cf. Porter, *Idioms*, 45–46, 192–93; Wallace, *Greek Grammar*, 646–50.

in some way."[8] Similarly, although Wallace posits an independent usage, he finds it largely restricted in distribution. After positing its existence, he states, "By way of conclusion on the independent participle (both imperative and indicative), we wholeheartedly affirm the sober assessment by Brooks and Winbery: *'Certainly no participle should be explained as an independent participle if there is any other way to explain it.'*"[9] The mismatch in usage compared to English leads some to view the participle as at times finite and independent in spite of the recognition that it nearly always proves otherwise.

Winer is the notable exception, claiming that "in almost all these N.T. passages we either find amongst the preceding or following words a finite verb to which the partic[iple] is annexed (and in this case we must not allow the ordinary punctuation of the text to embarrass us), or else we have an example of anacoluthon, the writer having lost sight of the construction with which he commenced the sentence."[10] He cites numerous examples where the connections to finite verbs stretch over several verses, either before or after the participle—for example, 2 Cor 8:18–20; Eph 5:21; Heb 7:2. Regarding Eph. 5:21, he states, "ὑποτασσόμενοι is certainly attached to the principal verb πληροῦσθε ἐν πν[εύματι], like the other participles in verses 19, 20, and must not be taken … for an imperative."[11] The solution to many of these issues lies in considering the function of the participle within the larger discourse, even across verse boundaries.

In addition to the caveats about dependence, there is also widespread acknowledgment that more specific verb forms were available that could have more explicitly specified the relation of the participial action to the main verb on which it depends. In other words, if a writer had wanted to be more specific about the relation to the main action, there were plenty of options more specific than a participle. Funk makes this point commenting on circumstantial participles:

> For this construction, two finite verbs connected by καί would serve equally well, since the participle of attendant circumstance does not specify the relation between the action of the main verb and the attendant circumstance.[12]

---

8. Porter, *Idioms*, 184.

9. Wallace, *Greek Grammar*, 653.

10. G. B. Winer, *A Treatise on the Grammar of New Testament Greek* (trans. and rev. W. F. Moulton; 3rd ed.; Edinburgh: T & T Clark, 1882), 440–41.

11. Ibid., 441. He continues, "The following words αἱ γυναῖκες κ.τ.λ. (ver. 22) are then annexed without any verb of their own … as a further exposition of this ὑποτασσόμενοι" (ibid., 441–42).

12. Robert W. Funk, *A Beginning-Intermediate Grammar of Hellenistic Greek* (2nd ed.; 3 vols.; SBLSBS 2; Missoula, Mont.: Scholars, 1973), §846.8.

The Greek circumstantial participle is therefore a less precise form of expression than corresponding subordinate clauses of time, condition, concession, etc.[13]

MHT makes a similar observation regarding participles of means, manner, and so forth:

> These analogies are only adduced to show that the use of the participle always lay ready to hand, with or without the auxiliary verb, and was a natural resource whenever the ordinary indicative (or, less often, imperative) was for any cause set aside.[14]

Robertson makes the same point in the form of a warning:

> In itself, it must be distinctly noted, the participle does not express time, manner, cause, purpose, condition or concession. These ideas are not in the participle, but are merely suggested by the context, if at all, or occasionally by a particle like ἅμα, εὐθύς, καίπερ, ποτέ, νῦν, ὡς. There is no necessity for one to use the circumstantial participle. If he wishes a more precise note of time, cause, condition, purpose, etc., the various subordinate clauses (and the infinitive) are at his command, besides the co-ordinate clauses.[15]

Wallace devotes the most time into subcategorizing verbal participles, acknowledging at various points the overlap or ambiguity that exists in the classification. After describing all of these categories, he concludes with the following caveat: "Yet it should be stressed that the participle in itself means none of these ideas."[16] These comments make clear that the concepts of means, manner, condition, and time are not part of the semantic meaning of the participle; they are part of the semantics of the context. These concepts or relations (theoretically) would have been present whether a participle or a finite form had been used. In their absence, these relations are left implicit.

---

13. Ibid., §845.

14. MHT 1:224.

15. Robertson, *Grammar*, 1124. BDF affirms this, stating, "The logical relation of the circumstantial participle to the rest of the sentence is not expressed by the participle itself (apart from the future participle), but is to be deduced from the context; it can be made clear, however, by the addition of certain particles. Other more extended but more precise constructions are available for the same purpose: prepositional phrases, conditional, causal, temporal clauses, etc., and finally the grammatical coordination of two or more verbs" (BDF §417). Cf. MHT 3:153.

16. Wallace, *Greek Grammar*, 638.

The preoccupation with classification for the sake of translation has done much to distract attention from understanding the discourse function of the Greek participle. It is as though exegetes would have preferred a hypotactic or paratactic marker that makes explicit the relation of the participle to the main action. However, participles leave such relations implicit. Had a writer wanted to make them explicit, ample remedies were available. The exegetical significance of this choice to use a particle instead of a finite form must not be overlooked. The propensity to assign classifications to the kind of participle seems driven by a desire to address the mismatch in usage between Greek and English by minimizing or eliminating it.

So far, I have drawn two conclusions from the grammatical discussions:

- the choice to use a participle to grammaticalize an action represents the choice to use a verb form that is less specific than a finite verb, whether in paratactic or hypotactic relation;
- the verbal participle does not explicitly specify the grammatical categories assigned to it, and this fact is widely acknowledged.

Most every grammarian acknowledges the fact that choosing a participle means not choosing a more explicit form, but little attention is given to why a writer would use a participle instead of a more explicit alternative.

The notable exception to this is Wallace, though he seems to limit its application to circumstantials. Regarding the circumstantial participle, he notes,

> The relative semantic weight in such constructions is that *a greater emphasis is placed on the action of the main verb than on the participle.* That is, the participle is something of a prerequisite before the action of the main verb can occur.[17]

In other words, the net result of choosing a participle over a finite verb is to have the main verbal action of the clause receive primary attention. Had two finite verbs been used, attention would have been equally split between the two. In this case, judgments about the importance of one action relative to the other would have been based on content and context. This observation provides our point of departure to a discourse-based explanation of the function of Greek adverbial participles.

---

17. Wallace, *Greek Grammar*, 642–43.

12.2   Discourse Explanation

To begin with, there is a meaningful distinction to be made between adverbial participles that precede the verb of the main clause and those that follow the main clause. Levinsohn claims,

> Anarthrous[18] participial clauses that *precede* their nuclear [i.e., main] clause present information that is backgrounded. This means that the information they convey is of secondary importance vis-à-vis that of the nuclear clause. This claim does not hold for anarthrous participial clauses that follow their nuclear clauses.[19]

Despite the various claims about the function of adverbial participles (e.g., manner, time, cause, purpose), the ones that precede the main clause share a unified function. The use of the participle represents the choice not to use a finite verb.

Since the participle is dependent upon the main verb to supply the information that it does not encode on its own (e.g., mood), the participle does not obtain the same status as a finite verb.[20] This means that the participle plays a supporting role to the main verb, and the role differs depending upon the placement of the participle with respect to the main verb. Those that precede the main verb have the effect of backgrounding the action of the participle, indicating that it is less important than the main verbal action.

I will discuss three different kinds of circumstantial frames in the coming sections, differentiated by their morphological case. All circumstantial frames play essentially the same role of backgrounding what could potentially have been main action. The differences in the cases correspond to the different roles played by the subject of the participle compared to the main clause.

---

18. That is, lacking the article.

19. Stephen H. Levinsohn, *Discourse Features of New Testament Greek: A Coursebook on the Information Structure of New Testament Greek* (2nd ed.; Dallas: SIL International), 183.

20. Wallace states, "The attendant circumstance participle is used to communicate an action that, in some sense, is coordinate with the finite verb. In this respect it is not dependent, for it is translated like a verb. Yet it is still dependent *semantically*, because it cannot exist without the main verb. It is translated as a finite verb connected to the main verb by *and*. The participle then, in effect, 'piggy-backs' on the mood of the main verb" (*Greek Grammar*, 640). Regardless of the translation, note that they are indeed dependent grammatically and thus not coordinate. To overlook this point is to miss the distinction between using a participle rather than a finite verb form that is truly coordinate. How best to translate the participle into English is a different matter altogether from understanding its exegetical significance in Greek.

- If the subject of the participle is also the subject of the main clause, a nominative form typically is used.
- If the subject of the participle plays a nonsubject role in the main clause (i.e., in the dative, accusative, or genitive case), then the participle and its subject typically will agree in case with the other reference to the same participant in the main clause.
- If the subject of the participle is not involved at all in the main clause, a genitive form will be used for both the subject and the participle. This is generally called a "genitive absolute."

The genitive absolute signals the reader not to expect the subject of the participle to be involved in the main clause, whereas the other forms do not carry this expectation.[21]

12.3   Application

Circumstantial frames are composed of circumstantial participial clauses placed before the verb of the main clause. Circumstantial frames set the stage for the main action that follows, but the action is backgrounded with respect to the main action rather than made prominent. These actions are ones that could have been main clauses in their own right. Instead, the writer chose to make them play "second fiddle" to the main action rather than being on an even par with them. Below, circumstantial frames are identified in the examples using shaded text to graphically signify their backgrounding effect.

12.3.1   Nominative Circumstantial Frames

Nominative circumstantial frames refer to adverbial participial clauses that precede the main verb and are inflected in the nominative case. The nominative case creates the expectation that the subject of the participle will also be the subject of the main clause. The next example uses participles both before and after the main verb, allowing us to see the difference in function. The shaded text identifies the backgrounded circumstantial frames.

---

21. Levinsohn describes the genitive absolute (GA) as a "switch reference" marker, similar in function to those found in many languages around the world. He states, "Healey and Healey ... found that, out of the 313 New Testament occurrences of the GA that they identified, only three or four did not strictly obey the rule that there be a change of subject between the GA and the nuclear clause. Even the apparent exceptions show changes consistent with the behavior of switch-reference markers in other languages" (*Discourse Features*, 182).

Example 157 :: Matthew 28:17–20

¹⁷ καὶ ἰδόντες αὐτὸν προσεκύ-νησαν, οἱ δὲ ἐδίστασαν.

¹⁷ And when they saw him, they worshiped him, but some doubted.

¹⁸ καὶ προσελθὼν ὁ Ἰησοῦς ἐλάλη-σεν αὐτοῖς λέγων· ἐδόθη μοι πᾶσα ἐξουσία ἐν οὐρανῷ καὶ ἐπὶ [τῆς] γῆς.

¹⁸ And Jesus approached and spoke to them, saying, "All author-ity in heaven and on earth has been given to me.

¹⁹ πορευθέντες οὖν μαθητεύσατε πάντα τὰ ἔθνη, βαπτίζοντες αὐτοὺς εἰς τὸ ὄνομα τοῦ πατρὸς καὶ τοῦ υἱοῦ καὶ τοῦ ἁγίου πνεύματος,

¹⁹ Therefore, go and make disciples of all the nations, *baptizing* them in the name of the Father and of the Son and of the Holy Spirit,

²⁰ διδάσκοντες αὐτοὺς τηρεῖν πάντα ὅσα ἐνετειλάμην ὑμῖν· καὶ ἰδοὺ ἐγὼ μεθ᾽ ὑμῶν εἰμι πάσας τὰς ἡμέρας ἕως τῆς συντελείας τοῦ αἰῶνος.

²⁰ *teaching* them to observe every-thing I have commanded you, and behold, I am with you all the days until the end of the age."

The narrative portions of vv. 17–18 contain several different actions. The use of participles to create circumstantial frames has the effect of prioritizing the relative importance of the actions for the reader. The finite verbs in the indicative and imperative moods stand out more than the participial action because of the grammatical dependence of the participles on these verbs. In v. 17, three things happened: they saw him, they worshiped him, and some doubted. In the first part of the verse, the use of the participle backgrounds the action of seeing, indicating that worshiping him is the main action. The writer communicates both actions, but use of the participle backgrounds the action of seeing, keeping the spotlight on the worshiping.

The same principle of backgrounding is at work in v. 18, where Jesus' approach is marked as less important than what he says. Both actions needed to be communicated, but using indicative verbs for both would have por-trayed the two as being equally important.

Within Jesus' speech in v. 19, the actions of going and of making disci-ples are stated, but they are prioritized using a circumstantial frame. If Greek imperatives were used for both actions (as in most English translations), it would have introduced ambiguity about which of the two was more impor-tant to the speaker. The participle backgrounds the action of going, relegating it to a supportive role and thereby keeping attention focused on the main action of the sentence.

The command to make disciples is elaborated by a pair of participial clauses, marked in the example by italics. These clauses practically describe what is meant by "make disciples." It looks like "baptizing them ..." and "teaching them to observe...." Rather than introducing circumstances associated with the main action, the participles that follow elaborate the main action.

The next example uses circumstantial frames to set the stage for the main action. Had main verbs been used for all of these actions, the story would have seemed longer because each action would be portrayed as a separate event. Using participles for some of the action has the effect of condensing and prioritizing the action.

Example 158 :: Luke 5:2–5

² καὶ εἶδεν δύο πλοῖα ἑστῶτα παρὰ τὴν λίμνην· οἱ δὲ ἁλιεῖς ἀπ᾽ αὐτῶν ἀποβάντες ἔπλυνον τὰ δίκτυα.	² and he saw two boats there beside the lake, but the fishermen had gotten out of them and were washing their nets.
³ ἐμβὰς δὲ εἰς ἓν τῶν πλοίων, ὃ ἦν Σίμωνος, ἠρώτησεν αὐτὸν ἀπὸ τῆς γῆς ἐπαναγαγεῖν ὀλίγον·	³ And he got into one of the boats, which was Simon's, and asked him to put out from the land a little.
καθίσας δὲ ἐκ τοῦ πλοίου ἐδίδασκεν τοὺς ὄχλους.	And he sat down and began to teach the crowds from the boat.
⁴ Ὡς δὲ ἐπαύσατο λαλῶν, εἶπεν πρὸς τὸν Σίμωνα· ἐπανάγαγε εἰς τὸ βάθος καὶ χαλάσατε τὰ δίκτυα ὑμῶν εἰς ἄγραν.	⁴ And when he stopped speaking, he said to Simon, "Put out into the deep water and let down your nets for a catch."
⁵ καὶ ἀποκριθεὶς Σίμων εἶπεν· ἐπιστάτα, δι᾽ ὅλης νυκτὸς κοπιάσαντες οὐδὲν ἐλάβομεν· ἐπὶ δὲ τῷ ῥήματί σου χαλάσω τὰ δίκτυα.	⁵ And Simon answered and said, "Master, although we worked hard through the whole night, we caught nothing. But at your word I will let down the nets."

Verse 2b contains two actions: getting out of the boat and washing the nets. Circumstantial frames condense what could have been portrayed as two events into one, with the first backgrounded with respect to the second. The same holds true in v. 3, where getting into the boat and sitting down are backgrounded compared to the main actions of asking to put the boat out and teaching. The participles not only background the action, but also condense it by subordinating less important actions under main events. Finally, in v. 5, the participial clause describes how they had worked "through the whole night." Peter's main point is that they caught "nothing"; the circumstantial frame simply sets the stage for the claim that follows.

This next example, from 1 Peter, uses circumstantial frames to set the stage for how believers are to conduct themselves.

Example 159 :: 1 Peter 1:14–15

14 [CPὡς τέκνα ὑπακοῆςCP] ‹✗μὴ συσχηματιζόμενοι ταῖς πρότερον ἐν τῇ ἀγνοίᾳ ὑμῶν ἐπιθυμίαις✗›	14 [CPAs obedient children,CP] ‹✗do not be conformed to the former desires you used to conform to in your ignorance,✗›
15 ἀλλὰ ‹✓κατὰ τὸν καλέσαντα ὑμᾶς ἅγιον✓› [TPκαὶ αὐτοὶTP] ἅγιοι ἐν πάσῃ ἀναστροφῇ γενήθητε,	15 but ‹✓as the one who called you is holy,✓› [TPyou yourselvesTP] be **holy in all your conduct,**

The main idea of the sentence is that all their conduct is to be done in holiness. The point/counterpoint set in the circumstantial frame sets the stage while keeping attention focused on the main action. Most English translations render v. 14 as an imperative. Although English may prefer not to use participles in this way, one must not overlook the exegetical significance of the circumstantial frame. There is only one main idea in this sentence, not two or three. The writer's choice to use a participle rather than an imperative represents the choice to background one action in order to ensure that attention remains on the one primary action of the sentence. The point/counterpoint information is important, but it is secondary to the one finite verb of the larger complex.

The next example is taken from Acts, where word of Philip's ministry in Samaria reaches the apostles in Jerusalem.

Example 160 :: Acts 8:14–15

14 Ἀκούσαντες δὲ οἱ ἐν Ἱεροσολύμοις ἀπόστολοι ὅτι δέδεκται ἡ Σαμάρεια τὸν λόγον τοῦ θεοῦ, ἀπέστειλαν πρὸς αὐτοὺς Πέτρον καὶ Ἰωάννην,	14 Now when the apostles in Jerusalem heard that Samaria had accepted the word of God, they sent Peter and John to them,
15 οἵτινες καταβάντες προσηύξαντο περὶ αὐτῶν ὅπως λάβωσιν πνεῦμα ἅγιον·	15 who went down and prayed for them so that they would receive the Holy Spirit.

There are only two main actions in these sentences: sending Peter and John and praying for the new believers. Using circumstantial frames for the other actions allows them to be included in such a way as not to detract attention from the main events. These actions are backgrounded, setting the stage for the more important finite verbs that follow. If indicative verbs had been used for all of the actions, then the actions of hearing and going would have been portrayed as events of equal importance to those of sending and praying. Use of the circumstantial frames prioritizes the actions by backgrounding the less important ones.

Example 161 :: Matthew 11:2–3

² [TP Ὁ δὲ Ἰωάννης TP] ἀκούσας ἐν τῷ δεσμωτηρίῳ τὰ ἔργα τοῦ Χριστοῦ πέμψας διὰ τῶν μαθητῶν αὐτοῦ	² Now when [TP John TP] heard in prison the deeds of Christ, he sent word by his disciples
³ εἶπεν αὐτῷ· **σὺ** εἶ ὁ ἐρχόμενος ἢ **ἕτερον** προσδοκῶμεν;	³ and said to him, "Are **you** the one who is to come, or should we look for **another?**"

In this example, there has just been a switch from following the ministry of Jesus to following the ministry of John. The use of circumstantial clauses provides the reader a specific frame of reference within which to process John's questions to Jesus. He is not asking them in a vacuum, but rather in response to hearing about Jesus' ministry. The second participial clause lets us know that this questioning is happening indirectly, not with John meeting Jesus in person. As in the other cases, the participles background the action, indicating that what is said (v. 3) is the most important action in the sentence.

This last nominative example is actually the longest chain found in the NT. The effect is to establish a very complex state of affairs as efficiently as possible, while at the same time keeping attention focused on the main action of "touching."

Example 162 :: Mark 5:25–27

²⁵ Καὶ [TP γυνὴ TP] οὖσα ἐν ῥύσει αἵματος δώδεκα ἔτη	²⁵ And there was [TP a woman TP] who was suffering from hemorrhages twelve years.
²⁶ καὶ πολλὰ παθοῦσα ὑπὸ πολλῶν ἰατρῶν	²⁶ And she had endured many things under many physicians,

καὶ δαπανήσασα τὰ παρ᾽ αὑτῆς πάντα	and had spent all that she had
καὶ μηδὲν ὠφεληθεῖσα	and had received no help at all,
ἀλλὰ μᾶλλον εἰς τὸ χεῖρον ἐλθοῦσα,	but instead became worse.
²⁷ ἀκούσασα περὶ τοῦ Ἰησοῦ,	²⁷ When she heard about Jesus,
ἐλθοῦσα ἐν τῷ ὄχλῳ ὄπισθεν ἥψατο τοῦ ἱματίου αὐτοῦ·	she came up in the crowd behind him and touched his cloak,

A comparison of Mark's version to the other Synoptic accounts shows that the latter are more abbreviated, without as much detail and without as many participles. In Mark's gospel, the use of circumstantial frames for so much of the background information ensures that the final action, her touching Jesus' cloak, is clearly marked as the most important in the sentence. Using indicative verb forms for the circumstantial information would have significantly multiplied the number of main events in this story. It also would have obscured which action the writer viewed as most important. The choice to use so many participles has exegetical significance.

There is additional support for construing the touching as the most important action in this sentence. In v. 30, the same use of circumstantial frames focuses attention on Jesus' question about who touched him.

Example 163 :: Mark 5:30

| καὶ εὐθὺς [TPὁ Ἰησοῦς TP] ἐπιγνοὺς ἐν ἑαυτῷ τὴν ἐξ αὐτοῦ δύναμιν ἐξελθοῦσαν | And immediately [TPJesus,TP] perceiving in himself that power had gone out from himself, |
| ἐπιστραφεὶς ἐν τῷ ὄχλῳ ἔλεγεν· τίς μου ἥψατο τῶν ἱματίων; | turned around in the crowd and said, "Who touched my clothing?" |

Using indicative verbs for the action of perceiving and turning would have made all of the actions appear equally important. Backgrounding the first two allows the circumstantial frame of reference to be established without obscuring which action is most important.

12.3.2   Genitive Circumstantial Frames

Genitive circumstantial frames play substantially the same role of backgrounding the action as observed with the nominative ones.[22] The primary difference is that the subject of the genitive circumstantial typically is not involved in any other way within the main clause; in other words, they are not the subject, direct object, or indirect object of the main clause. Fuller states,

> The function of the form of participle and noun/pronoun in the Genitive (without any other formal cause, such as a preposition) is to draw the reader's attention to certain information in a more detached way than other circumstantial participles.... The information in the GA [genitive absolute] acts as a frame in which to interpret the information of the main clause, or of an even larger discourse.[23]

Oftentimes they are temporal in nature (e.g., describing the rising or setting of the sun), but without signaling the same kind of discontinuity as a temporal frame of reference. Instead, genitive circumstantials describe the state of affairs in which the main action occurred. This implies that there is relative continuity between what follows and the preceding state of affairs.

Example 164 :: Luke 4:40a, 42

40a Δύνοντος δὲ τοῦ ἡλίου [TPἅπαντες ὅσοι εἶχον ἀσθενοῦντας νόσοις ποικίλαις TP] ἤγαγον αὐτοὺς πρὸς αὐτόν·

40a Now as the sun was setting, [TPall who had those who were sick with various diseases TP] brought them to him,

42 Γενομένης δὲ ἡμέρας ἐξελθὼν ἐπορεύθη εἰς ἔρημον τόπον· καὶ οἱ ὄχλοι ἐπεζήτουν αὐτὸν καὶ ἦλθον ἕως αὐτοῦ καὶ κατεῖχον αὐτὸν τοῦ μὴ πορεύεσθαι ἀπ᾽ αὐτῶν.

42 And when it was day, he departed and went to an isolated place. And the crowds were seeking him, and came to him and were trying to prevent him from departing from them.

The genitive circumstantial at the beginning of v. 40 provides temporal transition from the healing of Simon's mother-in-law to the account of Jesus healing the masses, indicating that a change in time has occurred. It provides a generic

---

22. What I am calling "genitive circumstantial frames" are typically referred to as "genitives absolute." There is disagreement about the appropriateness of this term in some cases because the participial clause at times is not absolutely independent (e.g., Matt 1:20; 18:25; Mark 9:28). See Robertson, *Grammar*, 513–14.

23. Lois K. Fuller, "The 'Genitive Absolute' in New Testament/Hellenistic Greek: A Proposal for Clearer Understanding," *JGChJ* 3 (2006): 151.

temporal shift but otherwise maintains continuity of participants and location.

The same holds true for v. 42, where a genitive circumstantial frame marks the transition from Jesus casting out a demon to going off to an isolated place to pray. The specific shift in time is not important, but rather indicates something more generic. These temporal transitions serve to segment the discourse into smaller chunks, even though they are otherwise closely related. Placing the same information in a temporal frame of reference would have signaled a greater discontinuity in the context in either case. These kinds of temporal circumstantial frames update the reference time of the narrative in a context of relative continuity, but without going so far as creating a new pericope. The subject of the participial clause is not involved in the main clause that follows, so an *absolute* form is used to signal this to the reader.

The next example, taken from the parable of the sower, illustrates how genitive circumstantial frames are used to describe action performed by a participant that does not play a role in the main clause.

Example 165 :: Matthew 13:19

[LD [TPπαντὸςTP] ἀκούοντος τὸν λόγον τῆς βασιλείας

καὶ μὴ συνιέντος ἔρχεται ὁ πονηρὸς καὶ ἁρπάζει τὸ ἐσπαρμένον ἐν τῇ καρδίᾳ αὐτοῦ,LD] [TPοὗτόςTP] ἐστιν ὁ παρὰ τὴν ὁδὸν σπαρείς.

[LD"When [TPanyoneTP] hears the word about the kingdom

and does not understand it, the evil one comes and snatches away what was sown in his heart.LD] This is what was sown on the side of the path."

The genitive circumstantial frame is used to introduce the participant from whom the evil one comes and snatches away the word that was sown. Other than possessing the heart in which the word was placed, this participant is not involved in the main clause. Verse 19 in turn introduces the seed that will be commented on in the last part of the verse. The interest of the main clause of the sentence focuses on which seed is being referred to. In the left-dislocation,[24] the main interest is on what the evil one does to the seed. The genitive circumstantial here signals the reader that the subject of the participle will not play a significant role in the main clause.[25]

---

24. See chapter 14.

25. Whether one construes the participial clause as a genitive absolute or not, the reference in the main clause (αὐτοῦ) agrees in case and number with that in the participial clause.

Levinsohn claims that at times the genitive absolute is used to attract attention to significant switches from one group of participants to another.

> Now, a construction that indicates switch reference provides a natural way of highlighting the introduction to an existing scene of participants who perform significant actions that change the direction of the story, etc. This is because, when the GA [genitive absolute] has the *same* subject as the *previous* clause, the scene is set for a *different* participant to be the subject of the nuclear clause. The employment of the GA with the same subject as the previous clause thus gives natural prominence to the event described in the following nuclear [i.e., main] clause.[26]

The next two examples illustrate this kind of usage, where it essentially functions as tail-head linkage (♋),[27] reiterating content from the preceding context as a circumstantial frame of reference for the main clause that follows.

Example 166 :: Matthew 2:1

1:24 And Joseph, when he woke up from sleep, did as the angel of the Lord commanded him, and he took his wife 25 and did not have sexual relations with her until she gave birth to a son. And he called his name Jesus.

2:1 ‹♋[TP Τοῦ δὲ Ἰησοῦ TP] γεννη-θέντος ἐν Βηθλέεμ τῆς Ἰουδαίας ἐν ἡμέραις Ἡρῴδου τοῦ βασιλέως,♋› ἰδοὺ **μάγοι ἀπὸ ἀνατολῶν** παρεγένοντο εἰς Ἱεροσόλυμα

2:1 Now ‹♋after [TP Jesus TP] was born in Bethlehem of Judea in the days of Herod the king,♋› behold, **wise men from the east** came to Jerusalem,

The preceding verses from chapter 1 describe how Joseph did not have sexual relations with Mary until after the birth of Jesus. Verse 1 of chapter 2 reiterates the birth of Jesus but adds the location and political circumstances in which he was born. This is followed by an attention-getter and the introduction of the wise men from the east. Their arrival is significant in that their visit to Herod (and Jesus) leads to Herod's slaughter of the innocents. Their arrival moves

---

26. Levinsohn, *Discourse Features*, 182. Tail-head linkage is also found using nominative circumstantial frames, not just genitives (e.g., Matt 2:9; Luke 18:22, 23, 24; John 9:6; 18:1; Acts 7:60; 2 Cor 10:12; Rev 1:12). The effect that Levinsohn describes might be better explained as a pragmatic effect of the tail-head linkage, which often takes the form of a genitive absolute, as opposed to a special use associated with the genitive absolute construction itself.

27. See chapter 8.

the story forward to the next major series of events. However, Jesus does not play a role in the main clause, hence the use of a genitive circumstantial frame.

Example 167 :: Luke 9:34

‹☉[TPταῦταTP] δὲ [TPαὐτοῦTP] λέγοντος☉› ἐγένετο νεφέλη καὶ ἐπεσκίαζεν αὐτούς· ἐφοβήθησαν δὲ ἐν τῷ εἰσελθεῖν αὐτοὺς εἰς τὴν νεφέλην.	And ‹☉while [TPheTP] was saying [TPthese things,TP]☉› a cloud came and overshadowed them, and they were afraid as they entered into the cloud.

Once again the genitive circumstantial frame is used to reiterate a portion of the preceding discourse, in this case Peter's curious suggestion to build tabernacles for Jesus, Moses, and Elijah at the transfiguration. Immediately after the cloud overshadows them, a voice from heaven affirms Jesus' status as the Son of God. The default expectation is that the appearance of the cloud comes just after Peter's statement, since the two events are recounted one after another. There is no intervening event to make the reader expect otherwise. The repetition of the redundant information in the genitive circumstantial effectively slows the narrative and adds some measure of suspense. Use of the genitive participle is to be expected because Peter plays no role in the main clause.

The next examples, from Acts, are instances of tail-head linkage, serving to slow the narrative down and highlight the introduction of the new participants.

Example 168 :: Acts 10:9

[7] And when the angel who spoke to him departed, he summoned two of the household slaves and a devout soldier from those who attended him, [8] and after he had explained everything to them, he sent them to Joppa.

[9] [TPΤῇ δὲ ἐπαύριον,TP] ‹☉ὁδοιπορούντων ἐκείνων καὶ τῇ πόλει ἐγγιζόντων,☉› ἀνέβη Πέτρος ἐπὶ τὸ δῶμα προσεύξασθαι περὶ ὥραν ἕκτην.	[9] And [TPthe next day,TP] ‹☉as they were on their way and approaching the city,☉› Peter went up on the housetop to pray at about the sixth hour.

This example is taken from the story of Cornelius sending for Peter to come and preach the gospel to him and his household. His two servants are first introduced in v. 7, and they are the subject of the genitive circumstantial frame. The repetition of the information from v. 8 effectively slows down the pace of the narrative in anticipation of a significant event that follows. It also connects the new, seemingly unrelated incidents back to the preceding discourse. The same kind of repetition is found again in v. 19.

Example 169 :: Acts 10:19

¹⁷ Now while Peter was greatly perplexed within himself as to what the vision that he had seen might be, behold, the men who had been sent by Cornelius, having found the house of Simon by asking around, stood at the gate. ¹⁸ And they called out and asked if Simon who was also called Peter was staying there as a guest.

¹⁹ ‹↻Τοῦ δὲ Πέτρου διενθυμουμένου περὶ τοῦ ὁράματος↻› εἶπεν [αὐτῷ] τὸ πνεῦμα· ἰδοὺ ἄνδρες τρεῖς ζητοῦντές σε,	¹⁹ And ‹↻while Peter was reflecting about the vision,↻› the Spirit said to him, "Behold, three men are looking for you."

We were already told in a temporal frame at the beginning of v. 17 that Peter was perplexed about his vision, which is followed by the arrival of Cornelius's men at the house where Peter was staying. The genitive circumstantial has the effect of switching back to the scene with Peter on the roof from the one at the front gate. Since there is a switch in subjects from Peter to the Spirit, the genitive form signals that Peter is not a primary participant in the main clause, creating the expectation of a different subject. A dative circumstantial clause could have been used, to agree with the main clause reference to Peter (i.e., αὐτῷ). Both NA²⁷ and UBS⁴ place αὐτῷ in brackets. The use of the genitive form could support the argument for omitting this pronoun.

Another genitive circumstantial creating tail-head linkage is found in v. 44, with the effect of highlighting the outpouring of the Holy Spirit directly on believers. This is the first instance of a direct outpouring without a laying on of hands since Acts 2. Verse 44 is preceded by Peter's speech to Cornelius and his household.

Example 170 :: Acts 10:44

‹↻Ἔτι λαλοῦντος τοῦ Πέτρου τὰ ῥήματα ταῦτα↻› ἐπέπεσεν τὸ πνεῦμα τὸ ἅγιον ἐπὶ πάντας τοὺς ἀκούοντας τὸν λόγον.	‹↻While Peter was still speaking these words,↻› the Holy Spirit fell on all those who were listening to the message.

The repetition closely connects the speech with the event that follows, highlighting this special outpouring. It attracts attention to the very first believers besides the apostles to directly receive the Spirit without the laying on of hands: Gentiles, not Jews.

12.3.3   Dative and Accusative Circumstantial Frames

There are only fourteen instances of circumstantial frames that are neither nominative nor genitive. The subject of these participial clauses plays some role in the main clause other than the subject. The case of the participial clause agrees with the reference to the participant in the main clause.[28]

In the first example, a dative circumstantial records Jesus moving into a boat.

Example 171 :: Matthew 8:23

Καὶ ἐμβάντι αὐτῷ εἰς τὸ πλοῖον ἠκολούθησαν αὐτῷ οἱ μαθηταὶ αὐτοῦ.	And as he got into the boat, his disciples followed him.

The frame has the same function of establishing the circumstantial state of affairs for the main clause that follows, and the case of the participle matches the reference to the participant in the main clause. The circumstantial action is still backgrounded with respect to the main clause action. The change in case from nominative or genitive can be attributed to cognitive processing. The case agreement helps the reader connect the circumstantial frame with the subsequent reference to the same participant in the main clause.

In the following example, Jesus has just crossed the lake to where he meets the Gerasene demoniac.

Example 172 :: Luke 8:27a

ἐξελθόντι δὲ αὐτῷ ἐπὶ τὴν γῆν ὑπήντησεν ἀνήρ τις ἐκ τῆς πόλεως ἔχων δαιμόνια	And as he got out on the land, a certain man from the town met him who had demons

The subject in v. 26 is Jesus along with the disciples. The circumstantial frame focuses attention back on Jesus, but not because he is the subject of the main clause. Instead, it sets the stage for his interaction with the demon-possessed

---

28. At times, the genitive circumstantial is used instead of the dative or accusative, even where the case of the participant in the main clause is not genitive (e.g., Acts 4:1, where the main clause reference to Peter and John is in the dative case).

man. This frame helps to set the stage for the meeting that follows by back-grounding Jesus' departure from the boat, keeping attention focused on the main action of the sentence.

In this final example, a circumstantial frame is used to set the stage for an infinitive that completes the action of the main verb.

Example 173 :: Acts 6:2

προσκαλεσάμενοι δὲ οἱ δώδεκα τὸ πλῆθος τῶν μαθητῶν εἶπαν·	So the twelve summoned the community of disciples and said,
οὐκ ἀρεστόν ἐστιν ἡμᾶς κατα-λείψαντας τὸν λόγον τοῦ θεοῦ διακονεῖν τραπέζαις.	"It is not desirable that we neglect the word of God to serve tables."

The frame allows reference to be made to what is desirable (attending to God's word) while keeping attention focused on what is not desirable: waiting on tables. Both neglecting the word of God and waiting on tables are undesirable. Attention is focused on what is distracting the apostles from what they ought to be doing.

All circumstantial frames have the same basic pragmatic effect: back-grounding the action that they describe with respect to the main action of the clause. The writer could have used a finite verb to convey the same infor-mation. These frames help to prioritize the importance of action in a clause by pushing the less important action into the background. The case of the circumstantial frame depends upon the relationship of the participle's subject to its role in the main clause.

12.3.4   Adverbial Participles Following the Main Verb

Participles that follow the main verb have a somewhat different effect from those that precede it, in that they elaborate the action of the main verb, often providing more specific explanation of what is meant by the main action. In most cases, they practically spell out what the main action looks like. These participles have nearly the same function as their counterparts in English, and thus they are much easier to maintain in translation than circumstantial participles.

These elaborating participles prioritize action in a manner similar to cir-cumstantial participles, presenting action that is less salient than the finite verbs. They differ from circumstantial participles in that the participial action directly modifies the main verbal action. Rather than offering a distinct action in its own right, the participle relegates its action to supporting the main action. By using a participle rather than a finite verb, the writer places its action under the umbrella of the main verb, typically adding more detail or elaboration to the main verb.

This first example recounts how Jesus was going about Galilee, and this basic action is elaborated in three participial clauses that follow.

Example 174 :: Matthew 4:23

Καὶ περιῆγεν ἐν ὅλῃ τῇ Γαλιλαίᾳ	And he went around through all of Galilee,
διδάσκων ἐν ταῖς συναγωγαῖς αὐτῶν	*teaching* in their synagogues
καὶ *κηρύσσων* τὸ εὐαγγέλιον τῆς βασιλείας	and *proclaiming* the good news of the kingdom
καὶ *θεραπεύων* πᾶσαν νόσον καὶ πᾶσαν μαλακίαν ἐν τῷ λαῷ.	and *healing* every disease and every sickness among the people.

The writer could have made all of the actions main events through the use of indicative verbs instead of participles (i.e., "He went … and taught in their synagogues and proclaimed … and healed …"). The participles elaborate upon what his going around looked like, and they portray the various actions as being somehow related rather than independent of one another.

Levinsohn claims that the exhortations conveyed by participles that follow imperatives "are at least as important as the imperative itself."[29] This may well be true, but the choice not to use an imperative has the effect of linking the participial action back to one main imperative rather than having it stand on its own as a separate command. These participles often describe in more detail what is entailed by the main verb, elaborating on it without elevating the participial action to the same level of salience as the main verb. Judgments about the importance of the elaboration are based on context, but the choice to use a dependent verb form has the effect of linking this action to the main verb rather than having it stand as a distinctly independent action.

In Rom 12 there is a string of participles that elaborate a general concept introduced in a verbless clause. The elaborating function of the adverbial participle following the main clause illustrates well this usage.

---

29. Stephen H. Levinsohn, *Self-Instruction Materials on Non-narrative Discourse Analysis* (Dallas: SIL International, 2008), 36.

Example 175 :: Romans 12:9–13

⁹ Ἡ ἀγάπη ἀνυπόκριτος.	⁹ Love must be without hypocrisy.
ἀποστυγοῦντες τὸ πονηρόν,	*Abhor* what is evil;
κολλώμενοι τῷ ἀγαθῷ,	*be attached* to what is good,
¹⁰ τῇ φιλαδελφίᾳ εἰς ἀλλήλους φιλόστοργοι,	¹⁰ *being devoted* to one another in brotherly love,
τῇ τιμῇ ἀλλήλους *προηγούμενοι,*	*esteeming* one another more highly in honor,
¹¹ τῇ σπουδῇ μὴ *ὀκνηροί,*	¹¹ not *lagging* in diligence,
τῷ πνεύματι *ζέοντες,*	being enthusiastic in spirit,
τῷ κυρίῳ *δουλεύοντες,*	*serving* the Lord,
¹² τῇ ἐλπίδι *χαίροντες,*	¹² *rejoicing* in hope,
τῇ θλίψει *ὑπομένοντες,*	*enduring* in affliction,
τῇ προσευχῇ *προσκαρτεροῦντες,*	*being devoted* to prayer,
¹³ ταῖς χρείαις τῶν ἁγίων *κοινωνοῦντες,*	¹³ *contributing* to the needs of the saints,
τὴν φιλοξενίαν *διώκοντες.*	*pursuing* hospitality.

Sanday and Headlam observe that in vv. 9–21, "ἀγάπη is the ruling thought, but the Apostle does not allow himself to be confined and pours forth directions as to the moral and spiritual life which crowd into his mind."[30] Thus, the big idea is stated in the verbless clause, while the elaboration of this idea is carried out with participles, not finite verb forms. Achtemeier makes a similar point: "Paul simply declares, 'love is not hypocritical' and then draws implications for Christian interaction from that fact. Those implications are what Paul then states in verses 9b–13; they all demonstrate unhypocritical love in action."[31] Thus, the main clause states the main idea, while the participles indicate the subordinate role of the information that they communicate.[32]

---

30. William Sanday and Arthur C. Headlam, *A Critical and Exegetical Commentary on the Epistle of the Romans* (3rd ed.; ICC; Edinburgh: T & T Clark, 1897), 360.

31. Paul J. Achtemeier, *Romans* (IBC; Atlanta: John Knox, 1985), 198.

32. Dunn states, "Vv 9–13 run together structurally, the implied imperative of the initial call for love expanded in a series of participial clauses" (James D. G. Dunn, *Romans 9–16* [WBC 38B; Dallas: Word, 2002], 737).

Many want to take the verbless clause of v. 9 as an imperative, as well as some participles (e.g., LEB, NASB). This option was available to Paul, and doing so would have made all of the ideas equally important rather than subordinated under the general heading of love being unhypocritical.

It is important to respect the grammatical choices that the writers made in communicating Scripture, regardless of how we might need to translate them into English. We find a nearly identical structure later in the same chapter in vv. 14–16a and 16b–19. The main clauses introducing the elaborating participles use imperatives rather than a verbless clause to encode the action. The elaborating participles, shown in italics, still practically illustrate what is meant by the action of the main sentence.

Example 176 :: Romans 12:14–19

¹⁴ εὐλογεῖτε τοὺς διώκοντας [ὑμᾶς],	¹⁴ Bless those who persecute you,
⟨✔εὐλογεῖτε✔⟩ καὶ ⟨✘μὴ καταρᾶσθε.✘⟩	⟨✔bless✔⟩ and ⟨✘do not curse them.✘⟩
¹⁵ χαίρειν μετὰ χαιρόντων, κλαίειν μετὰ κλαιόντων.	¹⁵ Rejoice with those who rejoice; weep with those who weep.
¹⁶ τὸ αὐτὸ εἰς ἀλλήλους *φρονοῦντες,*	¹⁶ *Think* the same thing toward one another;
⟨✘μὴ τὰ ὑψηλὰ *φρονοῦντες*✘⟩	⟨✘do not *think* arrogantly,✘⟩
ἀλλὰ ⟨✔τοῖς ταπεινοῖς *συναπαγόμενοι.*✔⟩	but ⟨✔*associate* with the lowly.✔⟩
μὴ γίνεσθε φρόνιμοι παρ’ ἑαυτοῖς.	Do not be wise in your own sight.
¹⁷ μηδενὶ κακὸν ἀντὶ κακοῦ *ἀποδιδόντες,*	¹⁷ *Pay back* no one evil for evil.
προνοούμενοι καλὰ ἐνώπιον πάντων ἀνθρώπων·	*Take thought* for what is good in the sight of all people.
¹⁸ [CEεἰ δυνατὸν τὸ ἐξ ὑμῶν,CE] μετὰ πάντων ἀνθρώπων *εἰρηνεύοντες·*	¹⁸ [CEIf it is possible on your part,CE] *be at peace* with all people.
¹⁹ ⟨✘μὴ ἑαυτοὺς *ἐκδικοῦντες,* ἀγαπητοί,✘⟩	¹⁹ ⟨✘*Do* not *take revenge* yourselves, dear friends,✘⟩
ἀλλὰ ⟨✔δότε τόπον τῇ ὀργῇ,✔⟩	but ⟨✔give place to God's wrath,✔⟩
γέγραπται γάρ· ἐμοὶ ἐκδίκησις, ἐγὼ ἀνταποδώσω, λέγει κύριος.	for it is written, "Vengeance is mine, I will repay," says the Lord.

Another example of an extended chain of participles that is often claimed to be "imperatival"[33] is found in Eph 5. I contend that these participles play the same elaborating role as in Rom 12, practically illustrating what it looks like to be filled with the Spirit.[34]

Example 177 :: Ephesians 5:17–22

[17] διὰ τοῦτο ⟨✗μὴ γίνεσθε ἄφρονες,✗⟩	[17] Because of this ⟨✗do not become foolish,✗⟩
ἀλλὰ ⟨✔συνίετε τί τὸ θέλημα τοῦ κυρίου.✔⟩	but ⟨✔understand what the will of the Lord is.✔⟩
[18] καὶ ⟨✗μὴ μεθύσκεσθε οἴνῳ,✗⟩ ἐν ᾧ ἐστιν ἀσωτία,	[18] And ⟨✗do not be drunk with wine✗⟩ (in which is dissipation),
ἀλλὰ ⟨✔πληροῦσθε ἐν πνεύματι,✔⟩	but ⟨✔be filled by the Spirit,✔⟩
[19] λαλοῦντες ἑαυτοῖς [ἐν] ψαλμοῖς καὶ ὕμνοις καὶ ᾠδαῖς πνευματικαῖς,	[19] *speaking* to one another in psalms and hymns and spiritual songs,
ᾄδοντες καὶ ψάλλοντες τῇ καρδίᾳ ὑμῶν τῷ κυρίῳ,	*singing* and *singing praise* in your heart to the Lord,
[20] εὐχαριστοῦντες πάντοτε ὑπὲρ πάντων ἐν ὀνόματι τοῦ κυρίου ἡμῶν Ἰησοῦ Χριστοῦ τῷ θεῷ καὶ πατρί.	[20] *giving thanks* always for all things in the name of our Lord Jesus Christ to the God and Father,
[21] Ὑποτασσόμενοι ἀλλήλοις ἐν φόβῳ Χριστοῦ,	[21] *being subject* to one another out of reverence for Christ
[22] αἱ γυναῖκες τοῖς ἰδίοις ἀνδράσιν ὡς τῷ κυρίῳ,	[22] —wives to their own husbands as to the Lord,

There is a series of commands given in vv. 17–18, each paired with another in the form of a point/counterpoint set. Verse 19 begins a chain of participles that elaborate what it practically looks like to be filled with the Spirit: it looks like speaking to one another in song, like singing and making melody to the Lord, and like submitting to one another. I understand v. 22 to be elaborating

---

33. That is, the participles should be understood to function as imperatives.

34. For a discussion against viewing these participles as imperatival, see Wallace, *Greek Grammar*, 638–39.

on v. 21, since it lacks a verb and is thus logically dependent on v. 21. Thus, the chain of participles elaborates on the imperative of v. 18b, while the verbless clause of v. 22 elaborates on the content of v. 21, illustrating what it practically looks like to submit to one another.[35]

To infer an imperative in v. 22 is an interpretation, unsubstantiated by the grammar. The main command is "be filled by the Spirit," and there is not another until v. 25: "husbands, love your wives." The statements to wives regarding submission are illustrating mutual submission, not singling women out. The section on submission is grammatically subordinated to the command of v. 18b.[36]

In 1 Pet 3:8–9, there is another verbless clause that describes five qualities that everyone should have. These qualities are then elaborated in two complex participial clauses in v. 9. These participles collectively form a point/counterpoint set.

Example 178 :: 1 Peter 3:8–9

[8] Τὸ δὲ τέλος πάντες ὁμόφρονες, συμπαθεῖς, φιλάδελφοι, εὔσπλαγχνοι, ταπεινόφρονες,	[8] And finally, all of you be harmonious, sympathetic, showing mutual affection, compassionate, humble,
[9] ⟨✗μὴ *ἀποδιδόντες* κακὸν ἀντὶ κακοῦ ἢ λοιδορίαν ἀντὶ λοιδορίας,✗⟩	[9] ⟨✗not *repaying* evil for evil or insult for insult,✗⟩
⟨✓τοὐναντίον δὲ *εὐλογοῦντες*✓⟩ ὅτι εἰς τοῦτο ἐκλήθητε ἵνα εὐλογίαν κληρονομήσητε.	but ⟨✓on the other hand *blessing* others,✓⟩ because for this reason you were called, so that you could inherit a blessing.

---

35. Winer states, "ὑποτασσόμενοι is certainly attached to the principal verb πληροῦσθε ἐν πνεύματι, like the other participles in verses 19, 20, and must not be taken … for an imperative…" He continues, "the following words Αἱ γυναῖκες κ.τ.λ. (ver. 22) are then annexed without any verb of their own … as a further exposition of this ὑποτασσόμενοι" (G. B. Winer, *A Treatise on the Grammar of New Testament Greek* (trans. and rev. W. F. Moulton; 3rd ed.; Edinburgh: T & T Clark, 1882), 441–42).

36. For a singling out of women regarding submission, see 1 Pet 3:1. Note that there too the verb of v. 1 is a participle, linking back to the imperative of 2:13 to address the same thought to a new constituency group. The same holds true for the section addressing slaves in 2:18. I construe the use of participles in vv. 13, 18 as a grammatical strategy for linking back to the previous argument following a supportive aside in vv. 21–25.

The first elaboration has two components, evil and insult, that are not to be repaid; the second elaboration has two subpoints that provide the reason for blessing others and the result of blessing others. The writer could have just as easily encoded the participles of v. 9 as imperatives, but this would have created a chain of three commands instead of one that is elaborated in two parts. Using three imperatives would have restructured this entire section of the discourse.

Suggested Reading

Blass, F., A. Debrunner, and R. W. Funk. *A Greek Grammar of the New Testament and Other Early Christian Literature.* §417.

Cox, Steven L. "Are Genitive Absolutes Always Absolute?"

Fuller, Lois K. "The 'Genitive Absolute' in New Testament/Hellenistic Greek: A Proposal for Clearer Understanding."

Funk, Robert W. *A Beginning-Intermediate Grammar of Hellenistic Greek.* §§845–46.

Levinsohn, Stephen H. *Discourse Features of New Testament Greek: A Coursebook on the Information Structure of New Testament Greek.* 193–202.

MHT 3:153–58.

Porter, Stanley E. *Idioms of the Greek New Testament.* 183–86.

Robertson, A. T. *A Grammar of the Greek New Testament in the Light of Historical Research.* 512–13, 1124–41.

Wallace, Daniel B. *Greek Grammar beyond the Basics: An Exegetical Syntax of the New Testament.* 621–55.

Winer, G. B. *A Treatise on the Grammar of New Testament Greek.* 440–44.

EMPHASIS

This chapter provides an overview of the ways emphasis can be signaled in the Greek NT. Let me make it clear from the outset that what most grammarians mean by *emphasis* is quite different from my use of the term here. I define *emphasis* as taking what was already the most important part of a clause and placing it in a position of prominence in order to attract even more attention to it. The key element of this definition is "what was already the most important." NT grammarians tend to use *emphasis* to refer to most any kind of prominence, essentially as a synonym. The concern here is the process of drawing extra attention to what was already the most important information in a given context.

13.1   Conventional Explanation

Recall Callow's definition of prominence as "any device whatever which gives certain events, participants, or objects more significance than others in the same context."[1] A cursory review of Greek grammars and commentaries reveals that the term *emphasis* is used in much the same sense as Callow's *prominence*.

However, much of the reference to emphasis does indeed center on word order. In the case of BDF, there is a tendency to associate emphasis with a specific position in the clause, typically the initial position: "Any emphasis on an element in the sentence causes that element to be moved forward."[2] In the

---

1. Kathleen Callow, *Discourse Considerations in Translating the Word of God* (Grand Rapids: Zondervan, 1974), 50.
2. BDF §472(2).

case of Robertson, he seems to view other factors determining emphasis, but he does not provide much in the way of specifics:

> This is one of the ruling ideas in the order of words. This emphasis may be at the end as well as at the beginning of the sentence, or even in the middle in case of antithesis. The emphasis consists in removing a word from its usual position to an unusual one.[3]

Most grammarians tend to merge what I refer to as "frames of reference" with "emphasis" in such discussions, yet they make remarks that seem to confirm some level of differentiation between the two. Consider Porter's discussion of subject placement and the pragmatic effects that it achieves.

> The expressed subject is often used as a form of topic marker or shifter (in a "topic and comment sequence"), and is appropriately placed first to signal this semantic function.... The subject gives new or emphatic information and the predicate elucidates it.[4]

Although he uses the term "emphasis," he seems to view it more as contrastive or switching. He continues,

> When the subject is placed in the second or third position in the clause (i.e., after the predicate and/or complement), its markedness or emphasis apparently decreases. The reason for this is related to the linear structure of NT Greek, in which the first position is reserved for the most important element. Moving the subject to a subsidiary position, however, *does not necessarily elevate another element in the clause to a position of prominence.* Placing, for example, the predicate (the basic structural element) first or the complement first does not necessarily draw attention to either element, since the resulting pattern is very similar to the two basic clause structure patterns. This movement of clause elements does decrease the importance of the subject, however, relegating it to a secondary position as a topic marker.[5]

Porter associates emphasis with the initial position, especially when the subject is placed there, yet placing the predicate or complement there may not result in emphasis. As with Robertson, it is as though he knows it when he sees it, but the principles governing his judgments are vague.

---

3. A. T. Robertson, *A Grammar of the Greek New Testament in the Light of Historical Research* (1919; repr., Bellingham, Wash.: Logos, 2006), 417.

4. Stanley E. Porter, *Idioms of the Greek New Testament* (2nd ed.; Sheffield: Sheffield Academic, 1999), 295.

5. Ibid., 296 (italics added).

There is also a propensity to claim that personal pronouns are a signal of emphasis, as illustrated from Wallace's discussion:

> The nominative personal pronoun is most commonly used for emphasis. The emphasis may involve some sort of *contrast*. In such instances, two subjects are normally in view, though one might be only implied. This contrast is either of kind (antithetical) or degree (comparison). For example, in "He washed and she dried," the contrast is comparative (both people doing the dishes). In the sentence "He slept and she worked," the contrast is antithetical.[6]

His examples contain what is called a "double-difference contrast," where two sets of like things are juxtaposed (i.e., he/she and washed/dried or slept/worked). In both examples, the pronominal subjects receive prominence (expressed by secondary intonational stress in English) because they function as topical frames of reference. The most important part of the clause is what each of them does. This is where the strongest contrast exists, and it would have been present with or without the use of frames or emphasis. The use of the frames strengthens the connection between the two actions of washing versus drying, or sleeping versus working. The grammarians are correct to assign significance to the presence of redundant personal pronouns; however, a better explanation is needed to account for the varying effects that they achieve.

13.2   Discourse Explanation

Chapter 9 introduced information structuring principles. There I noted two basic reasons for moving a clause component to a position of prominence: to establish an explicit frame of reference for the clause that follows (i.e., what is traditionally referred to as *contrast*), and to emphasize what was already the most important element of the clause. We now focus in more detail on understanding the latter of these two phenomena.

Virtually every sentence contains some kind of information that is newly asserted. This information represents the reason the speaker is saying what he or she is saying; it is the point of the communication. This information might be brand new to the hearer; it may provide some new connection or relationship to what was already known or established. This new information, which represents the point of the utterance, was referred to as the *focus* of the clause (see §9.2.5). By definition, focal information is the most important part of the

---

6. Daniel B. Wallace, *Greek Grammar beyond the Basics: An Exegetical Syntax of the New Testament* (Grand Rapids: Zondervan, 1999), 321.

clause. Its importance is based solely upon its contribution to the context, not its position in the clause. Typically, focal information is placed as close to the end of the clause as possible, in Greek, English, and many other languages.[7]

There are times when the writer wants to attract extra attention to what is already the most important part of the clause. Attracting extra attention to what was already most important is what I refer to as *emphasis*. This is a much narrower definition than is found in NT grammars; hence there is overlap between the two. The primary way that emphasis is communicated in Koiné Greek is through restructuring the information of the clause to place the focal information in a specially marked position.[8] The emphasized information stands out more because the expected ordering of the clause has been violated.

All of the instances of emphasis established on the basis of information structure are labeled in the *LDGNT* with the terms "main clause emphasis" or "subordinate clause emphasis." This label signifies that the clause element has been placed in a non-default position within its clause. In the case of "main clause emphasis," the emphasized element is the most important element on that level of the outline. The term "subordinate clause emphasis" identifies an element placed in marked focus within a subordinate clause that precedes the main clause. This element is the most important part of the subordinate clause only, not the main clause. The only difference between the main- and subordinate-clause emphases is the scope of the emphasis. The scope of main-clause emphasis extends over the entire clause on that particular level of the outline. Subordinate-clause emphasis extends only over the subordinate clause in which it occurs, not over the main clause to which it is subordinated.

There are other means of establishing emphasis. Levinsohn notes that when a long or complex clause component is emphasized, only the most important part of the component will be placed in the position of prominence.[9] Since the information is newly asserted and thus focal, the position corresponds with what Dik's P2 position. The rest of the component is placed in its default position in the clause. There is a practical limit to the complexity allowed in this position. Moving only part of a component may avoid causing confusion for the reader in cases where the component is long or complex. It

---

7. Cf. Comrie's principle of Natural Information Flow (Bernard Comrie, *Language Universals and Linguistic Typology: Syntax and Morphology* [Chicago: University of Chicago Press, 1989], 127–28).

8. More specifically, this refers to marked focus, removing the focal information from its default position and placing it in a marked position, Dik's P2 position (see §9.2.6).

9. See Stephen H. Levinsohn, *Discourse Features of New Testament Greek: A Coursebook on the Information Structure of New Testament Greek* (2nd ed.; Dallas: SIL International), 57–61.

may also be motivated by the desire to single out the most important part of the clause for special attention.[10]

Even though one part is specially singled out, the whole component receives some measure of emphasis. Moving only the one part singles out that part. The rest of the emphasized clause element is identified by the label "main clause emphasis-other" in the *LDGNT*. This allows for distinguishing newly asserted components that receive emphasis from those associated with the emphasized component. Both will be graphically indicated using bold text.

Another means of assigning emphasis through association with an emphasized element is the use of point/counterpoint sets. Many counterpoints are established by negating one clause element in order to set the stage for a more important element that corrects or replaces it. The point that replaces the counterpoint is often part of the same clause. By virtue of the fact that it replaces an emphasized element, the replacement point receives emphasis just as the counterpoint element. The counterpoint functions as a foil for the point that follows, attracting more attention to it than it would otherwise have received without the counterpoint.

Now let's move on to consider some examples, beginning with main-clause emphasis. These will be followed by instances of discontinuous components, where only one part of a component is moved to the position of prominence.

13.3   Application

In Rom 1:16, Paul claims that he is not ashamed of the gospel, and he follows this with supporting statements that emphasize the most important parts of the newly asserted information. Part of the predicate of v. 16b is placed in a marked position to emphasize the basis for not being ashamed of the gospel.

Example 179 :: Romans 1:16–17

[16] Οὐ γὰρ ἐπαισχύνομαι τὸ εὐαγγέλιον,	[16] For I am not ashamed of the gospel,
δύναμις γὰρ **θεοῦ** ἐστιν εἰς σωτηρίαν παντὶ τῷ πιστεύοντι, Ἰουδαίῳ τε πρῶτον καὶ Ἕλληνι.	for it is **the power of God** for salvation to everyone who believes, to the Jew first and also to the Greek.

---

10. In the latter case, this most important part of the component is called the "dominant focal element."

¹⁷ **δικαιοσύνη** γὰρ **θεοῦ** ἐν αὐτῷ ἀποκαλύπτεται ἐκ πίστεως εἰς πίστιν, καθὼς γέγραπται·	¹⁷ For **the righteousness of God** is revealed in it from faith to faith, just as it is written,
[TPὁ δὲ δίκαιος^TP] **ἐκ πίστεως** ζήσεται.	"But [TPthe one who is righteous^TP] **by faith** will live."

The clause presupposes that the gospel is something for everyone who believes, but it is a matter of what. It is not just the "good news," but also the "power of God" for salvation to all who believe. "Power of God" is the most important part of the clause, regardless of where it is placed. Placing what was already most important in a position of prominence has the effect of adding emphasis. Similarly in v. 17, the clause presupposes that something is revealed in the gospel: "the righteousness of God." This is not a contrastive subject or topical frame of reference. The subject fills in the blank of the proposition.

In both cases, the emphasized element would be the most important information regardless of whether it was placed in a marked position or not. Information status is based on contribution to the discourse context, not on the position in the clause. The same information could have been structured with the most important information as close to the end of the clause as possible.

ἀποκαλύπτεται γὰρ ἐν αὐτῷ δικαιοσύνη θεοῦ ἐκ πίστεως εἰς πίστιν.…
For the righteousness of God is revealed in it from faith to faith.…

Placing δικαιοσύνη θεοῦ in a marked position has the effect of attracting even more attention to it due to its importance in the context.

In the final sentence of v. 17, it is presupposed that the righteous will live by something. Paul cites this text from Hab 2:4 as a means of reinforcing his claim regarding the importance of faith in the first part of the verse. Faith is the mode by which the righteousness of God is revealed. This quotation supports the notion that faith is the thing by which the righteous will live, as opposed to by some other resource.[11]

The first exhortation from James provides the next example of emphasis. The reader is called to consider it something when something else happens, but the something else is reserved for a subordinate clause.

---

11. In the Hebrew text of this quotation, "faith" is also placed in position P2, indicating that it was to receive emphasis just as rendered in the Greek of Rom 1.

Example 180 :: James 1:2

Πᾶσαν χαρὰν ἡγήσασθε, ἀδελφοί μου, ὅταν **πειρασμοῖς** περιπέσητε **ποικίλοις**.…	Consider it **all joy**, my brothers, whenever you encounter **various trials**.…

"All joy" is to be the response when trials come, made clear by the positioning of this component and its information status. The vocative ἀδελφοί μου adds little semantic information, but it has the effect of further delaying what it is that the addressees are to consider all joy.[12] Rather than considering some obviously positive thing to be all joy, encountering trials should be the object of joy. Only the most salient part of the noun phrase πειρασμοῖς ποικίλοις is moved within the subordinate clause, so the remainder is found in its default position following the verb. This remainder is labeled "main clause emphasis-other" in the *LDGNT*.

The scope of the emphasis on πειρασμοῖς ποικίλοις extends only over the subordinate clause ὅταν πειρασμοῖς περιπέσητε ποικίλοις, not over the sentence to which it is subordinated. The scope of emphasis on πᾶσαν χαρὰν extends over the entire sentence and represents the main point of the clause. We need to know about encountering trials of various kinds in order to know how to respond to them—that is, considering them "all joy." Within the subordinate clause, "trials" receives emphasis to draw attention to something that most would not consider a joy.

Example 181 :: Matthew 7:9–10

[9] ἢ [TPτίς ἐστιν ἐξ ὑμῶν ἄνθρωπος, ὃν αἰτήσει ὁ υἱὸς αὐτοῦ ἄρτον,TP] μὴ **λίθον** ἐπιδώσει αὐτῷ;	[9] "Or [TPwhat man is there among you, if his son will ask him for bread, TP] will give him **a stone**?
[10] ἢ **καὶ ἰχθὺν** αἰτήσει, μὴ **ὄφιν** ἐπιδώσει αὐτῷ;	[10] Or also if he will ask for **a fish**, will give him **a snake**?"

This statement by Jesus begins by introducing a very specific kind of person in order to comment about that person. The comment concerns what the man will give to his son. Greek negative particles may be positioned before clause components other than verbs. They still negate the entire proposition in declarative statements, but they can serve as a marker of emphasis. In this

---

12. For a discussion of redundant forms of address, see §5.4.1.

case, vv. 9–10 are rhetorical questions, expecting a negative reply; that is, "What kind of man among you would do this? None of you."

Emphasis is added to the object that this hypothetical person might give to his son. In v. 9, "a stone" receives emphasis in order to set the stage for the following clauses. The point is going to be made in v. 11 that our heavenly Father is far more capable than human fathers of giving good things to those who ask him. Even these imperfect fathers can give better gifts than stones. By emphasizing the unlikely things that a father might give, it drives home the point that they can give much better gifts than these. If this is true, how much better then are the gifts from above.

In v. 10, the newly requested object receives emphasis, and thematic addition is applied through the use of an adverbial καί to explicitly link "fish" with its counterpart "bread" from the preceding clause.[13] There are two switches in this verse, but the actions of asking and giving remain unchanged. Both of the switched items receive emphasis, which helps the reader recognize the changes. It also strengthens the connection to the preceding verse, besides that achieved by the thematic addition. However, vv. 9–10 serve as staging for the main point that comes in v. 11. Verse 12 provides an application about asking and receiving, introduced by the inferential particle οὖν.

Example 182 :: Matthew 7:12

[11] "Therefore if you, although you are evil, know how to give good gifts to your children, how much more will your Father who is in heaven give good things to those who ask him?"

[12] [LD]Πάντα οὖν ὅσα ἐὰν θέλητε ἵνα ποιῶσιν ὑμῖν οἱ ἄνθρωποι,[LD] [TPοὕτως[TP] **καὶ ὑμεῖς** ποιεῖτε αὐτοῖς· οὗτος γάρ ἐστιν ὁ νόμος καὶ οἱ προφῆται.	[12] [LD]"Therefore in all things, whatever you want that people should do to you,[LD] [TPthus[TP] **also you** do to them. For this is the law and the prophets."

As in v. 9, there is a very complex state of affairs that is introduced in v. 12 in order to make a rather simple comment about it.

The left-dislocation is used in Greek in much the same way adults use a rhetorical question in colloquial English. The point of the dislocation is to introduce a concept in order to make a comment about it. Here is a paraphrase of the verse: "You know how you want others to treat you? In that same way, you also do to them." Thus, "Instead of waiting for people to treat you the

---

13. See chapter 16.

way you want, get out there and do it." The thematic addition explicitly connects you to the people who might do things for you. The fundamental point of the verse is to reverse the roles, to call people to be doing instead of looking to others to do it. Emphasizing ὑμεῖς and using thematic addition make this a very powerful call to action.

Galatians 4 contrasts the plights of Isaac and Ishmael by virtue of their respective mother's status. Paul concludes that we are children of the free woman, not the slave. This idea of freedom, introduced in the preceding chapter, is now emphasized in 5:1 as the goal or purpose for which Christ has set us free, as opposed to some other possible purpose.

Example 183 :: Galatians 5:1

Τῇ ἐλευθερίᾳ ἡμᾶς Χριστὸς ἠλευθέρωσεν· στήκετε οὖν καὶ **μὴ πάλιν** ζυγῷ δουλείας **ἐνέχεσθε**.	For **freedom** Christ has set us free. Stand firm, therefore, and **do not be subject again** to a yoke of slavery.

In light of this fact, we are to stand firm. There is one other response that is commanded. Earlier in the letter Paul makes the point that the Galatians were in subjection and slavery to "those that by nature are not gods (4:8 ESV). He asks in 4:9 whether they want to be enslaved again to these things. In light of being called to freedom, there are to be two responses: standing firm and not again being subject. The most important part of the verb component is emphasized, while the balance of it is found in the only position that can assign emphasis to the verb: the end of the clause. The Galatians have been subject before; they are not to let it happen again. The use of emphasis serves to reinforce key ideas as the writer transitions from the OT example to its practical application in the believer's life in chapter 5.

Example 184 :: Philippians 2:2–4

2 ⟨◻πληρώσατέ μου τὴν χαρὰν◻⟩ ἵνα **τὸ αὐτὸ** φρονῆτε, τὴν αὐτὴν ἀγάπην ἔχοντες, σύμψυχοι, **τὸ ἓν** φρονοῦντες,	2 ⟨◻complete my joy,◻⟩ so that you are **in agreement**, having the same love, united in spirit, having **one purpose**.
3 ⟨✗μηδὲν κατ' ἐριθείαν μηδὲ κατὰ κενοδοξίαν✗⟩	3 ⟨✗Do nothing according to selfish ambition or according to empty conceit,✗⟩

ἀλλὰ ‹✔ [TPτῇ ταπεινοφροσύνῃTP] ἀλλήλους ἡγούμενοι ὑπερέχοντας ἑαυτῶν,✔›	but ‹✔ [TPin humilityTP] considering **one another** better than yourselves,✔›
⁴ ‹✗μὴ τὰ ἑαυτῶν ἕκαστος σκοποῦντες✗›	⁴ ‹✗each one of you not looking out for **his own interests,**✗›
ἀλλὰ ‹✔[καὶ] τὰ ἑτέρων ἕκαστοι.✔›	but ‹✔**also** each of you looking out **for the interests of others.**✔›

Technically, the main clause of v. 2 functions as a metacomment, serving to highlight the key proposition that follows: thinking the same thing. It is presupposed that they are to think something, and the answer is emphasized. This whole passage focuses on unity and being like-minded. Emphasizing this in the main proposition sets the stage for different aspects of the same idea to be elaborated on in the balance of vv. 2–4.

The elaborating participles describe what kinds of things that the writer wants them to have, to think, and to consider. Regarding what they should have, it is "the same love" as opposed to something else, united in spirit. They are to think in a certain way, in "one/the same" way, further reinforcing the themes of unity and like-mindedness. Two counterpoints provide a backdrop for the next elaboration. Rather than doing things out of selfish ambition or empty conceit, they should make humility the basis for acting.

"In humility" provides a frame of reference for the clause that follows, calling the believers to give consideration to something in humility. In keeping with the overall theme, the consideration is to be "of others" rather than of themselves, considering them better than themselves. Another point/counterpoint set uses emphasis to expand on this thought. It is not only "his own" interests that each one should be looking out for, but also "those of others." The use of thematic addition strengthens the connection between one's own interests and those of others. It also provides an indication that looking to the interests of others does not mean that looking after one's own interests is illegitimate; rather, personal interests are not to be looked after to the exclusion of others. The key point in this passage is unity and like-mindedness. There is no place for selfishness or conceit. One natural way of considering others above yourself is to look to their interests above your own.

The content of the following verse is the proposition for which John 3:16 provides support. "God so loving the world" is not the primary proposition in Jesus' argument. Instead, 3:16 provides the rationale for why the Son of Man was lifted up.

Example 185 :: John 3:14

Καὶ [LDκαθὼς [TPΜωϋσῆςTP] ὕψωσεν τὸν ὄφιν ἐν τῇ ἐρήμῳ,LD] [CPοὕτωςCP] **ὑψωθῆναι** δεῖ **τὸν υἱὸν τοῦ ἀνθρώπου.**…	"And [LDjust as [TPMosesTP] lifted up the snake in the wilderness,LD] [CPthusCP] it is necessary that **the Son of Man be lifted up.**…"

Verse 14 recalls the incident in the wilderness where those who had been bitten by the fiery serpents could be healed by looking on the serpent that Moses had placed on the stick. This incident provides the basis of comparison for what was about to happen to the Son of Man. The comparative frame of reference establishes the basis against which something else will be compared. The infinitival clause, ὑψωθῆναι τὸν υἱὸν τοῦ ἀνθρώπου, is subordinated to the main verb, δεῖ. Due to its complexity, only the most important portion of the subordinate clause is placed in position P2, but the whole component receives emphasis. Leaving the "the Son of Man" at the very end of the main clause delays the disclosure of exactly who else needs to be lifted up. Structured as it is, all of the information in the clause is well identified except for the identity of the second object to be lifted up. Placing the complement of δεῖ in a marked position ensures that it receives extra attention.

The next example illustrates the distinction between emphasis within the main clause compared to within a fronted subordinate clause in terms of emphasis. The scope of the emphasis in the topical frame of reference is limited to the frame itself and does not extend over the main clause.

Example 186 :: Galatians 3:9–10a

9 ὥστε [TPοἱ ἐκ πίστεωςTP] εὐλογοῦνται σὺν τῷ πιστῷ Ἀβραάμ.	9 So then, [TPthe ones who have faithTP] are blessed together with Abraham who believed.
10 [TPῬσοι γὰρ **ἐξ ἔργων νόμου** εἰσίν,TP] **ὑπὸ κατάραν** εἰσίν·	10 For [TPas many as are of the works of the lawTP] are under a curse,

The topical frame in each verse introduces a specific group of people. The key characteristic that distinguishes them is emphasized, highlighting the contrast between the ones who have faith mentioned in v. 9 and those who are of works of the law. The contrast between these groups is inherently part of the context, present in the content with or without the use of emphasis. Adding emphasis simply highlights the contrast, making sure that the reader catches the important switch from one group to another. The use of topical frames of reference in v. 9 and v. 10 also heightens the contrast.

Once the topic is switched from those of faith to those who are of works, the comment about their plight also contrasts with those in v. 9. The emphasis sharpens this contrast and reinforces the very different prospects facing these groups. Rather than being blessed along with Abraham, they are "under a curse," a contention that is supported with a quotation from Deut 27:26 at the end of v. 10. The similarity of the content between v. 9 and v. 10 calls for comparison. The most important differences between these propositions receive emphasis to highlight the key elements.

Key ideas very frequently receive emphasis in the Johannine Epistles, as seen in the following example from 1 John 1. The writer is interested in particular aspects of particular things, and by placing the newly asserted information in a marked position in its respective clause, he ensures that these things are not missed.

Example 187 :: 1 John 1:6–8

6 [CE'Εὰν εἴπωμεν ὅτι **κοινωνίαν** ἔχομεν μετ' αὐτοῦ καὶ **ἐν τῷ σκότει** περιπατῶμεν,CE] ψευδόμεθα καὶ οὐ ποιοῦμεν τὴν ἀλήθειαν·

6 [CEIf we say that we have **fellowship** with him and walk **in the darkness**,CE] we lie and do not practice the truth.

7 [CEἐὰν δὲ **ἐν τῷ φωτὶ** περιπατῶμεν ὡς **αὐτός** ἐστιν ἐν τῷ φωτί,CE] **κοινωνίαν** ἔχομεν μετ' ἀλλήλων

7 But [CEif we walk **in the light** as **he** is in the light,CE] we have **fellowship** with one another,

καὶ [TPτὸ αἷμα Ἰησοῦ τοῦ υἱοῦ αὐτοῦTP] καθαρίζει ἡμᾶς ἀπὸ πάσης ἁμαρτίας.

and [TPthe blood of Jesus his SonTP] cleanses us from all sin.

8 [CEἐὰν εἴπωμεν ὅτι ἁμαρτίαν **οὐκ ἔχομεν**,CE] ἑαυτοὺς **πλανῶμεν**

8 [CEIf we say that **we do not have** sin,CE] **we deceive** ourselves

καὶ [TPἡ ἀλήθειαTP] οὐκ ἔστιν ἐν ἡμῖν.

and [TPthe truthTP] is not in us.

In v. 6, two elements are emphasized in the conditional frame. The comment of the main clause is conditioned on specific criteria being met. The first one is saying that we have "fellowship" with him, as opposed to something else. The second is walking "in the darkness," which will be contrasted with walking "in the light" in v. 7. The net results of meeting this condition are lying and not practicing the truth. There is no way to be walking in the darkness and still have fellowship with God.

This claim of v. 6 is reinforced in v. 7 by a restatement of the same basic proposition. The writer is not interested just in being "in the light" as opposed to being in the darkness, but with being in the light in a particular way. He focuses on being in the light as "he" (Jesus) is in the light; this is the benchmark to measure against. If this condition is met, the net result is having "fellowship," the thing that was claimed and denied in the preceding clause. There is no hope for fellowship with God if we are in the darkness. Even being in the light may not be sufficient. The benchmark for what qualifies as being in the light is the way Jesus is in the light. Then and only then will we find fellowship, but in this case "with one another."

In v. 8, the verb receives emphasis instead of some other component of the clause. Since the verb normally occurs at the beginning of the clause, fronting it for the sake of emphasis would not stand out as marked; there would be no way of telling whether it is being emphasized or not. The way this problem is handled in verb-initial languages like Greek is to use the final position of the clause as the position of emphasis for the verb.[14]

Moving the negative particle from the initial position in the clause and placing it before a clause element is another way of marking emphasis.[15] Note that it is placed just before the verb at the end of the clause. The entire proposition is still negated. The movement of the negator serves to reinforce where the emphasis is being placed: on the verb. We might say all kinds of things about sin, but the writer is interested in commenting on a specific situation: saying that we "do not have" sin. The net result, much like thinking that we can have fellowship with God while walking in the darkness, is to deceive ourselves and not have the truth in us. In both the subordinate clause of the conditional frame and the main clause of v. 9, the verbal action is the most important information. Placing the verb in the special P2 position at the end of the clause has the effect of emphasizing the action.[16]

---

14. This may be what Robertson is referring to when he states, "This emphasis may be at *the end* as well as at the beginning of the sentence, or even in the middle in case of antithesis" (*Grammar*, 417 [italics added]).

15. See Steven E. Runge, "Teaching Them What NOT to Do: The Nuances of Negation in the Greek New Testament" (paper presented at the annual meeting of the Evangelical Theology Society, San Diego, Calif., 13–16 November 2007).

16. There are other times where the verb occurs in the final position and does not receive emphasis, as is the case when the other clause components have been fronted for other reasons. This leads to the verb being the only clause component left following the P1/P2 elements at the beginning of the clause. Judgments regarding emphasis are based upon the difference between what is presupposed and what is newly asserted in the context; it is

In the next example, the negative particle is a marker of emphasis in a series of counterpoints that culminate in a positive point at the end of the clause.

Example 188 :: Galatians 1:1

Παῦλος ἀπόστολος	Paul, an apostle
⟨✗οὐκ **ἀπ' ἀνθρώπων**✗⟩	⟨✗not **from men**✗⟩
⟨✗οὐδὲ **δι' ἀνθρώπου**✗⟩	⟨✗nor **by men**✗⟩
ἀλλὰ ⟨✓διὰ Ἰησοῦ Χριστοῦ✓⟩	but ⟨✓through Jesus Christ✓⟩
καὶ ⟨✓θεοῦ πατρὸς τοῦ ἐγείραντος αὐτὸν ἐκ νεκρῶν....✓⟩	and ⟨✓God the Father who raised him from the dead....✓⟩

By negating these means by which he might possibly have gained his apostleship, Paul dismisses any incorrect notions. At the same time, he builds anticipation for the actual basis of his apostleship. The negated alternatives play a significant role in the following discourse as Paul addresses criticisms about his ministry. The emphasis in the counterpoints is marked by the position of the negative particles; the emphasis in the point is determined by its role in replacing the negated alternatives.

Matthew 6:24 begins and ends by focusing on something that is not possible. In the first clause of the verse, the subject alone is negated through the use of a negative adjective. Attention is focused on the ability to serve something, which is described in a subordinate infinitival clause. Within this subordinate clause, the object that is served is emphasized.

Example 189 :: Matthew 6:24

[TPΟὐδεὶςTP] δύναται **δυσὶ κυρίοις** δουλεύειν·	"[TPNo oneTP] is able to serve **two masters.**
ἢ γὰρ τὸν ἕνα **μισήσει** καὶ τὸν ἕτερον **ἀγαπήσει**,	For either **he will hate** the one and **love** the other,
ἢ ἑνὸς **ἀνθέξεται** καὶ τοῦ ἑτέρου **καταφρονήσει**.	or **he will be devoted** to one and **despise** the other.

---

not simply the position of the clause components. The principles of information structure are principles, not rules. They must be employed as such.

| οὐ δύνασθε **θεῷ** δουλεύειν καὶ **μαμωνᾷ**. | You are not able to serve **God** and **money**." |

In the first clause of the verse, "two masters" is placed in position P2 within the infinitival clause δουλεύειν δυσὶ κυρίοις to set the stage for the argument that follows. The first clause introduces the principle that will be considered. The following clauses affirm this principle using specific masters.

In the second clause of the verse, two different actions are ascribed to the person trying to serve the two masters. One master "he will hate," the other master "he will love"; the actions are marked as receiving emphasis by virtue of their position at the end of their respective clause, since they are focal information. The same holds true for the third clause; both "be devoted" and "despise" are focal and are placed in the P2 position for verbs.

The final clause provides a summary of the preceding section by reiterating the first proposition of the verse with more detail. Rather than generically referring to two masters, the text gives emphasis to the actual masters that Jesus has in mind. "God" receives emphasis based on its marked location, and it alone is fronted probably because it is the more important of the two. "Money" receives emphasis by virtue of its relation to its fronted counterpart, but is the less important of the two. Structured in this way, serving God is portrayed as the preferred master compared to money.

The proposition of Eph 2:8 serves to strengthen and support the content of vv. 6–7 while at the same time renewing the proposition introduced in v. 5.

Example 190 :: Ephesians 2:8–9

[8] **Τῇ** γὰρ **χάριτί** ἐστε σεσῳσμένοι διὰ πίστεως·	[8] For **by grace** you are saved through faith,
καὶ τοῦτο ⟨✗οὐκ **ἐξ ὑμῶν**,✗⟩ ⟨✓**θεοῦ τὸ δῶρον**·✓⟩	and this is ⟨✗not **from yourselves**,✗⟩ ⟨✓it is **the gift of God**;✓⟩
[9] ⟨✗οὐκ **ἐξ ἔργων**,✗⟩ ἵνα μή **τις** καυχήσηται.	[9] ⟨✗it is not **from works**,✗⟩ so that **no one** can boast.

In v. 8, "grace" is emphasized as the basis for salvation, as opposed to works or something else. The claims of v. 8 reiterate a proposition first introduced at the end of v. 5:

καὶ ὄντας ἡμᾶς νεκροὺς τοῖς παραπτώμασιν συνεζωοποίησεν τῷ Χριστῷ, — **χάριτί** ἐστε σεσῳσμένοι....	and we being dead in trespasses, he made us alive together with Christ (**by grace** you are saved)....

The second clause of v. 8 describes how it is that this salvation comes about by describing how it does not come about. The point of the point/counterpoint set is bracketed on both sides by negated counterpoints. Both the point and the counterpoints focus on the implications of being saved "by grace" rather than on some other basis. If it is "by grace," then it cannot be "from yourselves" or "from works." Instead, the grace is "the gift of God," in order that "no one" would be able to boast.

The emphasis in the first clause of v. 8 is determined by the positioning at the beginning of the clause. In the point/counterpoint set, the emphasis is determined by the placement of the negative particle and the relation of the point as a replacement of the counterpoints. Within the subordinate clause of v. 9, τις receives emphasis based on the location of the negative particle.

The same propositional content could have been related without the use of emphasis, as in the following: "You have been saved by grace, and this is a gift of God, [not of yourselves or of works,] that you would not be able to boast." A truly flat version of this verse would likely omit the counterpoints, as they serve only to highlight the point.

Summary

Most every clause contains some newly asserted information that the writer or speaker wants you to know. This information is the most important part, regardless of its location in the clause. If it is particularly important, the writer has the option of taking what was already most important and attracting extra attention to it. This process of attracting extra attention has the effect of emphasizing the new information. Emphasis is most often conveyed in Greek by reordering the structure of the clause to place the element to be emphasized in position P2. Since the unmarked position of verbs is at the beginning of the clause, the P2 position for them is at the end of the clause. Other factors, such as the pragmatic movement of the negative particle and rhetorical structures like point/counterpoint sets can also serve as markers of emphasis.

Suggested Reading

Bailey, Nicholas A. "Thetic Constructions in Koiné Greek."

Butler, Christopher C. "Focusing on Focus: A Comparison of Functional Grammar, Role and Reference Grammar and Systemic Functional Grammar."

Delin, J. *The Focus Structure of It-Clefts.*

Lambrecht, Knud. *Information Structure and Sentence Form: Topic, Focus, and the Mental Representations of Discourse Referents.*

Levinsohn, Stephen H. *Discourse Features of New Testament Greek: A Coursebook on the Information Structure of New Testament Greek.* 29–68.

Pavey, Emma. "An Analysis of *It*-Clefts within a Role and Reference Grammar Framework."

Runge, Steven E. "Relative Saliency and Information Structure in Mark's Parable of the Sower."

——. "Teaching Them What NOT to Do: The Nuances of Negation in the Greek New Testament."

14
LEFT-DISLOCATIONS

14.1 Conventional Explanation

Left-dislocations have been referred to by NT grammarians variously as cleft constructions,[1] hanging nominatives,[2] pendent nominatives,[3] *casus pendens*,[4] and independent nominatives.[5] Wallace associates the use of this construction with either emotion or emphasis. Young also associates the construction with emphasis: "A cleft construction is a focusing device that highlights information at the beginning of a sentence that is repeated later in the same sentence."[6] Porter too correlates the construction with highlighting: "This construction quite possibly is used to draw attention to an item in the main clause which would be otherwise overlooked," or alternatively it "may also serve as a topic marker or shifter which does not become grammatically entangled in the main construction."[7]

These descriptions associate an effect with the usage, but they say little about what constrains it or what brings about the various effects. Why is this construction sometimes used and other times not? Is it always optional and therefore emphatic? Does the construction accomplish some discourse

---

1. Richard A. Young, *Intermediate New Testament Greek: A Linguistic and Exegetical Approach* (Nashville: Broadman & Holman, 1994), 15.

2. Ibid.

3. Daniel B. Wallace, *Greek Grammar beyond the Basics: An Exegetical Syntax of the New Testament* (Grand Rapids: Zondervan, 1999), 52.

4. BDF §466(2).

5. Stanley E. Porter, *Idioms of the Greek New Testament* (2nd ed.; Sheffield: Sheffield Academic, 1999), 85–86.

6. Young, *Intermediate New Testament Greek*, 15.

7. Porter, *Idioms*, 86.

function other than emphasis? Are there contexts where it is required? The following description will tackle these issues, beginning with constraints on the introduction of new entities to the discourse.

14.2   Linguistic Explanation

There is a significant cognitive constraint on the introduction of new entities to the discourse, posited by Chafe.[8] He claims that there is a cross-linguistic preference to introduce only "one new concept at a time," which has been confirmed by others.[9] This constraint is manifested in two common constructions: presentational clauses and topic/comment clauses.[10]

Example 191

Presentational clause
There is a guy from the office. He asked me.…

Topic/comment clause
I know a guy from the office. He asked me.…

In both instances the brand new entity is introduced as the complement/object of the verb. The presentational clause uses a "dummy subject" to predicate the existence of the new entity, hence the whole clause is said to present brand new information. The subject of the topic/comment is by definition at least cognitively accessible, typically already active in the discourse.

---

8. Wallace L. Chafe, "Cognitive Constraints on Information Flow," in *Coherence and Grounding in Discourse* (ed. Russel S. Tomlin; Amsterdam: John Benjamins, 1987), 21–51. For a more complete overview of the constraints on introducing new participants to the discourse, see Steven E. Runge, "A Discourse-Functional Description of Participant Reference in Biblical Hebrew Narrative" (D.Litt. diss., University of Stellenbosch, 2007), 35–44, 109–12.

9. Lambrecht's discussion of the principle of separation of role and reference (Knud Lambrecht, *Information Structure and Sentence Form: Topic, Focus, and the Mental Representations of Discourse Referents* [CSL 71; Cambridge: Cambridge University Press, 1996], 184–91); Chafe's "activate only one new concept at a time" ("Cognitive Constraints," 31–32); Givón's "one new unit per proposition" (Talmy Givón, *Syntax: A Functional-Typological Introduction*, vol. 1 [Amsterdam: John Benjamins, 1984], 258–63).

10. There are three basic types of sentence articulation (i.e., pragmatic structures), each of which accomplishes a different pragmatic function. The third is focus-presupposition. See Avery Andrews, "The Major Functions of the Noun Phrase" in *Clause Structure* (vol. 1 of *Language Typology and Syntactic Description*; ed. Timothy Shopen; Cambridge: Cambridge University Press, 1985), 77–80; Lambrecht, *Information Structure*, 117–27.

Discourse referents that are already established, or that are cognitively accessible from the context, are not bound by this "one new concept at a time" constraint.[11] In other words, if an entity is accessible from the preceding discourse, via a cognitive schema[12] or from general knowledge of the world, it may acceptably function as the topic of a clause.[13] These are the basic cognitive principles constraining the acceptability of topics. Brand new entities (i.e., future topics) may be introduced into the discourse by way of a presentational construction or as the comment of a topic/comment construction.

Languages tend to be very efficient. As with most constraints, there are usually shortcuts that allow speakers to more efficiently accomplish their objectives. This holds true for the introduction of brand new participants. The shortcut is to syntactically detach the new entity from the main part of the clause. By introducing it outside the main clause, it can acceptably function as the topic while still honoring Chafe's "one new concept" constraint. In order to help the reader make the connection between the dislocated entity and its function in the main clause that follows, the detached element is reiterated in the main clause by way of a pronoun or generic reference of some kind that refers back to the detached element. Prototypically, the pronominal trace is placed in the normal clause position of the dislocated component.

This detachment construction is typically referred to by linguists as a *dislocation* and by grammarians as a *pendens* construction. This chapter focuses on *left*-dislocations, where the new entity is dislocated to the beginning of the clause and then resumed in the main clause through the use of a pronominal trace.

Foley and Van Valin state, "The primary functions of these constructions are to introduce new participants into a discourse or to reintroduce a referent which was previously introduced but which has not been mentioned in the immediately preceding discourse."[14] An example that they cite includes a list of items, one of which is resumed as the topic after the list is introduced. The effect is to promote one of the previously mentioned entities as the next primary topic of the discourse.

Lambrecht offers a similar analysis. Although presentational constructions are the standard means of promoting a topic from nonactive (brand new,

---

11. Robert A. Dooley and Stephen H. Levinsohn, *Analyzing Discourse: A Manual of Basic Concepts* (Dallas: SIL International, 2001), 57.

12. For example, mentioning "the temple in Jerusalem" activates a host of entities associated with it, such as priests, the holy of holies, and offerings and sacrifices.

13. See Runge. "Discourse-Functional Description," 108–20.

14. William A. Foley and Robert D. Van Valin Jr., "Information Packaging in the Clause," in *Clause Structure* (vol. 1 of *Language Typology and Syntactic Description*; ed. Timothy Shopen; Cambridge: Cambridge University Press, 1985), 356.

unused, or accessible) to active in the hearer's mental representation of the discourse,[15] left-dislocation constructions are reserved for topic-announcing or topic-shifting contexts.[16]

It should be noted that left-dislocations are used much more extensively in the Greek NT than in colloquial English and that English usage at times influences the description of the Greek usage. Left-dislocation in English is often associated with adolescent speech or with a poorly organized utterance.[17] English speakers find rhetorical questions a much more acceptable means of detaching a new topic from the comment about it.

Example 192

> **Left-dislocation**
> "That guy from the office I mentioned, well he asked...."
>
> **Rhetorical question**
> "Remember that guy from the office I mentioned? Well he asked...."

Generally speaking, left-dislocations serve to streamline the introduction of an entity into the discourse. They have the effect of either announcing or shifting the topic of the clause that follows. This attracts more attention to the topic than it would have otherwise received with one of the more conventional methods. Where the topic needs to be activated from scratch, left-dislocations serve a necessary function, activating the entity into the discourse.

There are two significant departures from the expected linguistic norms observed in the usage of left-dislocations in the Greek NT. First, the construc-

---

15. Lambrecht, *Information Structure,* 176.

16. Ibid., 204.

17. For example, Wallace (*Greek Grammar,* 52) associates left-dislocations with "primitive speech" like that used by unsophisticated speakers, or as representing awkward communication. Lambrecht notes, "Detachment constructions are often considered substandard or at least inappropriate in formal registers. This is no doubt a consequence of the fact that the canonical sentence type, in which the subject is a full lexical NP in argument position, has traditionally served as the basic model of sentence structure.... In order to accommodate the functional need for NP detachment, written languages often resort to constructions of the *as-for* type..., which are detachment constructions in disguise.... As is often the case in normative grammar, syntactic irregularity and semantic opacity are more readily tolerated than transparent violations of canonical structures" (*Information Structure,* 182). He notes that the "as for ..." construction is both syntactically irregular and semantically opaque. Furthermore, English speakers tend to use rhetorical questions as an alternative strategy to left-dislocations. These factors may be what lead Wallace to associate left-dislocation with adolescent speech.

tion frequently is used to introduce entities that are already accessible to the reader—that is, entities simple enough to be introduced by more standard conventions. Use of a left-dislocation in such cases represents overkill, serving the rhetorical purpose of topic promotion.

The second departure from the expected norm is related to the first. In over 80 percent of the instances of left-dislocation in the Greek NT, the pronominal trace is placed in a marked position at the beginning of the clause. The reason for this is either to place the new entity in *marked focus* for the sake of emphasis[18] or to create a frame of reference for the clause that follows (i.e., topicalization).[19]

There are two basic uses of left-dislocations observed in the Greek NT:

- streamlining the introduction of a complex entity into one clause instead of two;
- thematically highlighting the introduction of an entity because of its significance to the discourse.

In many cases, one cannot draw a binary either/or distinction between these functions. Both factors may motivate the usage in a given context. Fundamentally, use of the construction adds prominence to the entity. The status of the information and the location of the pronominal element are the determining factors regarding thematic highlighting.

In some instances, the pronominal trace referring back to the introduced entity is placed in the expected syntactic position of the constituent following the main verb, serving as a placeholder referring back to the dislocated element. Although this type of usage is predominant in other languages, less than 20 percent of the NT usage conforms to this expectation.

In the vast majority of cases, the resumptive element is found in the clause initial positions of P1 or P2. I attribute this deviation from the norm to two factors:

Processing. The entity introduced is so long or complex as to obscure the transition from the dislocation to the main clause. Placing the pronoun in position P1 as a frame of reference marks this transition, making it easier for the reader/hearer to properly process the discourse.

Thematic highlighting/Rhetoric. When a device is not needed for semantic or processing reasons, it typically plays the pragmatic function of highlighting. In this case, the entity or concept to which the pronoun refers is thematically highlighted.

---

18. See chapter 13.
19. See chapters 9–12.

There is a very specific hierarchy of how these devices are interpreted by readers and hearers, based on how humans are wired to process discontinuity. I described this hierarchy in §6.2 in reference to the multiple functions of the historical present.[20]

Figure 6 :: Processing hierarchy

Discourse-Pragmatic Function

which entails

Processing Function

which entails

Semantic Function

In the case of left-dislocations, the resumptive pronoun plays a semantic role by referring back to the newly introduced entity. In the cases where the entity is long or complex, the pronoun may be placed in position P1 as a processing aid, signaling the end of the dislocation and the beginning of the main clause. In a number of instances the clauses with the pronoun in a marked position are simple enough that there is no semantic or processing need for the pronoun. In such cases, it accomplishes a discourse-pragmatic function of highlighting the newly introduced entity. Whereas the forward-pointing devices highlighted a following event or speech, the referent of the pronoun receives the highlighting. In this way, the highlighting is thematic rather than forward-pointing. The newly introduced entity itself is given prominence, not the event or speech. The pronoun still serves a semantic function and still serves a processing function, but it also does something more. The fact that it is redundant is what brings about this effect; it is not a semantic meaning of the dislocation structure itself.

Pronouns always play a semantic role. They may not be semantically required, but they still communicate semantic content. We saw this to be the case with forward-pointing references in chapter 3. When the reference is not semantically required, it is construed as accomplishing something more. The redundant usage is next expected to be serving a processing function, drawing the reader's attention to a discontinuity in the discourse. In this case, it is the transition between the dislocation and the main clause. It still serves a semantic function, but it serves a processing function as well. The discontinuity was

---

20. See Runge, "Discourse-Functional Description," 39.

already present. The discourse device has the effect of accentuating what was already there, making it stand out more.

In much of the NT usage the entity introduced is simple enough that using a standard frame of reference would suffice, as described in chapters 10–11. Although the pronoun is redundant, it still accomplishes a significant discourse function. In fact, it is precisely because it is redundant that it accomplishes this function, as shown in the processing hierarchy. The net result is that left-dislocations have become a stylized rhetorical device by the Koiné period, likely based on the usage by rhetoricians during the Classical period. The contexts in which they are predominantly used bear this out. This stylistic development explains the preponderant placement of resumptive pronouns in P1/P2 rather than placing them after the verb, as more widely attested in other languages.

14.3   Application

14.3.1   Streamlining the Introduction of New Participants

This section presents examples of left-dislocations employed for the primary task of streamlining the introduction of an entity to the discourse. These first examples illustrate the basic linguistic function of left-dislocations, with the resumptive pronoun following the main verb.

In the first example, "the one who causes one of these little ones …" is introduced in the left-dislocation, and a comment is made about this entity in the main clause. The pronoun αὐτῷ refers back to the dislocation, occurring in an unmarked position following the verb of the main clause. The bracketed, superscripted "LD" ([LDsample textLD]) denotes the beginning and end of the left-dislocation.

Example 193 :: Matthew 18:6

[LDὍς δ' ἂν σκανδαλίσῃ ἕνα τῶν μικρῶν τούτων τῶν πιστευόντων εἰς ἐμέ,LD] συμφέρει αὐτῷ ἵνα κρεμασθῇ μύλος ὀνικὸς περὶ τὸν τράχηλον αὐτοῦ καὶ καταποντισθῇ ἐν τῷ πελάγει τῆς θαλάσσης.	"But [LDwhoever causes one of these little ones who believe in me to sin,LD] it would be better for him that a large millstone be hung around his neck and he be drowned in the depths of the sea."

The Synoptic parallel from Mark 9:42 uses the same structure, reiterating the dislocated entity following the main verb. In contrast, Luke conveys the same propositional content using two clauses, thus avoiding the use of left-dislocation.

Example 194 :: Luke 17:1–2

¹ Εἶπεν δὲ πρὸς τοὺς μαθητὰς αὐτοῦ· **ἀνένδεκτόν** ἐστιν τοῦ τὰ σκάνδαλα μὴ **ἐλθεῖν**,	¹ And he said to his disciples, "It is **impossible** for causes for stumbling **not to come**,
πλὴν οὐαὶ δι᾽ οὗ ἔρχεται·	but woe to him through whom they come!
² λυσιτελεῖ αὐτῷ εἰ [TPλίθος μυλικὸς TP] περίκειται περὶ τὸν τράχηλον αὐτοῦ καὶ ἔρριπται εἰς τὴν θάλασσαν ἢ ἵνα σκανδαλίσῃ τῶν μικρῶν τούτων ἕνα.	² It would be better for him if a [TPmillstone TP] is placed around his neck and he is thrown into the sea than that he causes one of these little ones to sin."

The second clause of v. 1 introduces the one causing others to stumble, stating that it is impossible for him not to come. The statement about it "being better for him" begins in v. 2. There are some differences in the content between Luke and Matthew, most notably Luke's comment about the impossibility of avoiding their coming. Matthew's briefer account uses a shortcut to introduce an entity comparable to that in Mark, thereby avoiding the need for multiple clauses. All three versions communicate largely the same propositional content, but Luke gets there using a different strategy.

The left-dislocated entity in the next example is introduced in a rather complex relative clause and then reiterated in the main clause by way of a personal pronoun. The pronoun is found in an unmarked position following the verb. This hypothetical person has not previously been mentioned in the discourse.

Example 195 :: Mark 11:23

⟨!ἀμὴν!⟩ ⟨🏳λέγω ὑμῖν🏳⟩ ὅτι [LDὃς ἂν εἴπῃ τῷ ὄρει τούτῳ· ἄρθητι καὶ βλήθητι εἰς τὴν θάλασσαν, καὶ ⟨✗μὴ διακριθῇ ἐν τῇ καρδίᾳ αὐτοῦ✗⟩ ἀλλὰ ⟨✓πιστεύῃ ὅτι ὃ λαλεῖ γίνεται,✓⟩LD] ἔσται αὐτῷ.	⟨!"Truly!⟩ ⟨🏳I say to you🏳⟩ that [LDwhoever says to this mountain, 'Be lifted up and thrown into the sea!' and ⟨✗does not doubt in his heart,✗⟩ but ⟨✓believes that what he says will happen,✓⟩LD] it will be done for him."

This kind of usage is not preferred in proper Koiné Greek, but nonetheless it follows the parameters expected from cross-linguistic usage. Interestingly, Matthew's version of this saying presents the same propositional content through the use of a conditional frame of reference, thereby avoiding Mark's nonpreferred usage of the construction. Rather than predicating the existence of a hypothetical entity, the same propositional content is communicated in the second person, with the disciples as the subject.

Example 196 :: Matthew 21:21

ἀποκριθεὶς δὲ ὁ Ἰησοῦς εἶπεν αὐτοῖς· ‹!ἀμὴν!› ‹🗔λέγω ὑμῖν,🗔› [CEἐὰν ἔχητε πίστιν καὶ μὴ δια-κριθῆτε,CE] ‹✗οὐ μόνον τὸ τῆς συκῆς ποιήσετε,✗›	And Jesus answered and said to them, ‹!"Truly!› ‹🗔I say to you,🗔› [CEif you have faith and do not doubt,CE] ‹✗you will do **not only what was done to the fig tree,✗›**
ἀλλὰ ‹✓[CEκἂν τῷ ὄρει τούτῳ εἴπητε· ἄρθητι καὶ βλήθητι εἰς τὴν θάλασσαν,CE] γενήσεται·✓›	but ‹✓even [CEif you say to this mountain, 'Be lifted up and thrown into the sea,'CE] it will happen!"✓›

Using the second person avoids the need to introduce a hypothetical entity, besides more specifically focusing the application on the hearers. Again, we see the same propositional content presented in two different ways. The choice to apply the saying to a hypothetical entity necessitated the introduction of this entity. The left-dislocation provides an efficient means of making such an introduction in a single clause.

The next example illustrates the use of left-dislocation in a context where the entity introduced may not be complex enough to require dislocation. Matthew and Luke use left-dislocations to introduce the entity.

Example 197 :: Matthew 12:32

καὶ [LDὃς ἐὰν εἴπῃ λόγον κατὰ τοῦ υἱοῦ τοῦ ἀνθρώπου,LD] ἀφεθήσεται αὐτῷ·	"And [LDwhoever speaks a word against the Son of Man,LD] it will be forgiven him.
[LDὃς δ' ἂν εἴπῃ κατὰ τοῦ πνεύματος τοῦ ἁγίου,LD] οὐκ ἀφεθήσεται αὐτῷ οὔτε ἐν τούτῳ τῷ αἰῶνι οὔτε ἐν τῷ μέλλοντι.	But [LDwhoever speaks against the Holy Spirit,LD] it will not be forgiven him either in this age or in the coming one!"

Luke 12:10 conveys virtually the same content but uses a future indicative verb versus the subjunctive form found in Matthew. In contrast, Mark's version omits the pronominal trace, turning the potentially dislocated entity into a

simple topical frame of reference. Mark also uses a point/counterpoint set to drive home the lack of forgiveness that the blasphemer can expect.

Example 198 :: Mark 3:29

[TPὃς δ' ἂν βλασφημήσῃ εἰς τὸ πνεῦμα τὸ ἅγιον,TP] ⟨✗οὐκ ἔχει ἄφεσιν εἰς τὸν αἰῶνα,✗⟩ ἀλλὰ ⟨✓ἔνοχός ἐστιν αἰωνίου ἁμαρτήματος.✓⟩

"But [TPwhoever blasphemes against the Holy SpiritTP] ⟨✗does not have forgiveness forever,✗⟩ but ⟨✓is guilty of an eternal sin"….✓⟩

By definition, a left-dislocation requires a resumptive reference somewhere in the main clause. Mark's version is slightly more difficult to process, since the entity that is activated is fairly complex.

These different versions illustrate that cognitive processing considerations are judgments rather than hard-and-fast rules. The sayings in Matthew and Luke represent a more conservative judgment regarding the accessibility of the new entity and its impact on the overall processing of the clause. Mark's version exhibits a greater confidence in the reader's ability to process the nondetached introduction. There is no indication of variants in the NA[27] apparatus to dispute the inclusion or exclusion of the pronominal traces in these passages.

Left-dislocations are frequently used outside of the Gospels to introduce hypothetical entities to make the writer's point, as illustrated in the following example from James.

Example 199 :: James 4:17

[LDεἰδότι οὖν καλὸν ποιεῖν καὶ μὴ ποιοῦντι,LD] ἁμαρτία αὐτῷ ἐστιν.

Therefore, [LDto the one who knows to do good and does not do it,LD] to him it is sin.

The comment made about "the one knowing the good to do and not doing it" is very simple in comparison to topic to which it applies. The same propositional content could have been communicated by way of a conditional frame of reference and use of the second person, as was illustrated in example 196:

"If you know the good you are to do and you do not do it, it is sin."
or
"It is sin. if you know the good you are to do and do not do it."

However, the choice to use a hypothetical third-person entity brings with it the need for the introduction of this entity. The left-dislocation efficiently accomplishes this introduction without resorting to two clauses.

Other examples of left-dislocations that place the pronominal trace in an unmarked position following the verb are Matt 4:16; 10:11; 12:18, 36; 20:23; 21:41, 44; 27:40; Mark 3:17; 4:25a, 25b; 8:38; 9:42; 15:29; Luke 6:31, 47; 8:18a, 18b; 12:10, 48; 20:18; John 1:12; 7:38; 15:2; 17:2; Acts 7:40; 11:29; 15:38; Rom 4:5; 1 Cor 7:8; 13; 11:14, 15; 2 Cor 7:6; Gal 6:7; 1 Thess 3:12; 1 Tim 6:17; James 3:13; 2 Pet 3:16; 1 John 2:5, 24, 27; 3:17; Rev 2:7, 17, 26; 3:12; 6:4, 8. In each case, a new entity is introduced into the discourse by a dislocation construction. This construction efficiently introduces new or complex entities into the discourse.

The instances where the pronominal trace occurs in an unmarked position in the clause represent the minority of left-dislocations found in the Greek NT. Far more frequently the resumptive pronoun is observed in a marked position at the beginning of the clause.

14.3.2   Processing Function

This next section describes the placement of the resumptive pronoun in a frame of reference for processing reasons. [21] The entity introduced in the dislocation is complex enough that there might be confusion over where the dislocation ends and the main clause begins. Placing the pronominal element in a frame of reference marks this transition, making it easier for the reader to recognize and process by making the discontinuity stand out. Placing the pronoun in a marked position can also have a rhetorical effect (see §14.3.3).

Left-dislocations are most often used in the Greek NT to introduce new *topical* entities. A very complex entity with a point/counterpoint set is found in James 1:25. The writer is not interested merely in the one who looks intently at the law, but in the one who responds to it in a specific way. A point/counterpoint set highlights the key details:

Example 200 :: James 1:25

[LDὁ δὲ παρακύψας εἰς νόμον τέλειον τὸν τῆς ἐλευθερίας καὶ παραμείνας, ⟨✗οὐκ **ἀκροατὴς ἐπιλησμονῆς** γενόμενος✗⟩ ἀλλὰ ⟨✓**ποιητὴς ἔργου**,✓⟩LD] [TPοὗτοςTP] **μακάριος ἐν τῇ ποιήσει αὐτοῦ** ἔσται.

But [LDthe one who looks into the perfect law of liberty and continues to do it, ⟨✗not being **a forgetful hearer**✗⟩ but ⟨✓**a doer who acts**,✓⟩LD] [TPthis oneTP] will be **blessed in what he does**.

---

21. See chapters 9–11.

The entity introduced in v. 25 stands in juxtaposition with one introduced more simply in vv. 23–24. There, a left-dislocation is also used, but the "looking into the law" and "the response" are part of the comment made about the dislocated entity rather than being part of the introduction.

Example 201 :: James 1:23–24

23 ὅτι [LDεἴ τις **ἀκροατὴς λόγου** ἐστὶν καὶ οὐ **ποιητής,**LD] [TPοὗτοςTP] ἔοικεν ἀνδρὶ κατανοοῦντι τὸ πρόσωπον τῆς γενέσεως αὐτοῦ ἐν ἐσόπτρῳ·

24 κατενόησεν γὰρ ἑαυτὸν καὶ ἀπελήλυθεν καὶ εὐθέως ἐπελάθετο **ὁποῖος** ἦν.

23 because [LDif anyone is **a hearer of the message** and not **a doer,**LD] [TPthis oneTP] is like someone staring at his own face in a mirror,

24 for he looks at himself and goes away and immediately forgets **what sort of person** he was.

The complexity of the dislocation in v. 25 is acceptable ostensibly because so much of the content is already familiar from the preceding context. The entity of v. 25 represents a repackaging of the same information from vv. 23–24 to create a contrastive counterpart. The most important part of v. 25 is not the complex entity, but rather the comment about him. The one who meets these criteria is "blessed in what he does," which receives emphasis in the main clause. The left-dislocation efficiently introduces the complex entity, and the resumption in a frame of reference signals to the reader the end of the dislocation and the beginning of the main clause.

This next example illustrates the use of a left-dislocation to provide a temporal frame for the clause that follows.

Example 202 :: Matthew 21:1

Καὶ [LDὅτε ἤγγισαν εἰς Ἱεροσόλυμα καὶ ἦλθον εἰς Βηθφαγὴ εἰς τὸ ὄρος τῶν ἐλαιῶν,LD] [TMτότεTM] [TPἸησοῦςTP] ἀπέστειλεν δύο μαθητὰς

And [LDwhen they drew near to Jerusalem and came to Bethphage at the Mount of Olives,LD] [TMthenTM] [TPJesusTP] sent two disciples,

This temporal frame is fairly complex, with two clauses and prepositional phrases, so one might claim that use of the left-dislocation here is motivated by cognitive constraints. The pro-adverb[22] τότε explicitly signals the end of

---

22. "A pro-adverb is a pro-form that substitutes for an adverb or other expression

the dislocation and the beginning of the main clause. The fronted topical frame of reference may be another factor influencing the reiteration of the information using τότε.

The Synoptic parallels use simple frames of reference, without dislocation. In Mark 11:1, a slightly less complex temporal frame is used to communicate the same propositional content, but without using τότε.

Example 203 :: Mark 11:1

Καὶ [TMὅτε ‹⊘ἐγγίζουσιν⊘› εἰς Ἱεροσόλυμα εἰς Βηθφαγὴ καὶ Βηθανίαν πρὸς τὸ ὄρος τῶν ἐλαιῶν,TM] ‹⊘ἀποστέλλει⊘› δύο τῶν μαθητῶν αὐτοῦ....	And [TMwhen ‹⊘they came near⊘› to Jerusalem, to Bethphage and Bethany at the Mount of Olives,TM] ‹⊘he sent⊘› two of his disciples....

Mark's version lacks the second verb of motion, ἦλθον, and uses historical presents both in the temporal frame and in the main clause. There is no fronted topical frame of reference in the main clause, though there are three prepositional phrases compared to Matthew's two. It appears to be a judgment call by the writer that the construction did not warrant the extra processing aid of a resumptive pro-adverb. Luke's version in 19:29 uses καὶ ἐγένετο to introduce the temporal frame, which I understand to be introducing the entire complex clause.

Example 204 :: Luke 19:29

Καὶ ἐγένετο [TMὡς ἤγγισεν εἰς Βηθφαγὴ καὶ Βηθανίαν πρὸς τὸ ὄρος τὸ καλούμενον Ἐλαιῶν,TM] ἀπέστειλεν δύο τῶν μαθητῶν	And it happened that [TMwhen he drew near to Bethphage and Bethany, to the hill called the Mount of Olives,TM] he sent two of the disciples,

As in Mark's version, there are no frames of reference at the beginning of the main clause, and there is only one main verb in the dislocation. There is one less prepositional phrase in Luke compared to Mark, another simplification. The lack of fronted items in the main clause and the lack of a resumptive pro-adverb make for an uninterrupted flow in the text. This results in Luke's temporal frame receiving less prominence than in Matthew's version. Other

---

having an adverbial function" (Eugene A. Loos et al., *Glossary of Linguistic Terms* [SIL International, 1997], n.p.). See §3.3.3.

examples of temporal left-dislocations include Matt 13:26; 24:15 (// Mark 13:14; Luke 21:20–21); Luke 13:25; John 7:10; 11:6; 13:27; 15:26; Acts 12:6; 1 Cor 15:28, 54; 16:2; 1 Thess 5:3.

The next example comes from Rom 11, where Paul describes the partial hardening Israel experiences for the benefit of the Gentiles (v. 25). The previous section discussed the salvation of the Gentiles (vv. 17–24). Verse 31 uses a left-dislocation to introduce a basis of comparison between the Gentiles and Israel.

Example 205 :: Romans 11:30–31

30 [LDὥσπερ γὰρ [TPὑμεῖς TP] [TMποτε TM] ἠπειθήσατε τῷ θεῷ,

[TMνῦν TM] δὲ ἠλεήθητε τῇ τούτων ἀπειθείᾳ,LD]

31 [CPοὕτως CP] **καὶ οὗτοι** νῦν ἠπείθησαν τῷ ὑμετέρῳ ἐλέει,

ἵνα [TPκαὶ αὐτοὶ TP] [νῦν] **ἐλεηθῶσιν.**

30 For [LDjust as [TPyou TP] [TMformerly TM] were disobedient to God,

but [TMnow TM] have been shown mercy because of the disobedience of these,LD]

31 [CPso CP] **also these** have now been disobedient for your mercy,

in order that [TPthey also TP] **may** now **be shown mercy.**

The dislocated information has already been discussed in the preceding section. It is repeated here to draw a specific comparison between the similarity of the situations, lest the Gentiles view themselves too highly. The dislocated information is not the most important; the thematically added καὶ οὗτοι is. The dislocation provides the frame of reference for the clause that follows, with the pro-adverb οὕτως signaling the end of the dislocation and highlighting the information.

As was observed with other dislocations, the complexity of the dislocated information likely necessitates a resumptive element to signal the end of the dislocation. There are also several preverbal elements that further complicate the main clause. Two clauses would have been necessary to convey the same information without the dislocation. The construction allows the writer to promote a particular quality of the Jews because of its rhetorical connection to his comment in the main clause. Thematic addition strengthens this connection even more.

Jesus develops an analogy of the vine and the vinedresser in vv. 1–3 of John 15. He has not explicitly tied believers into the analogy, only himself and the Father. He makes reference to the branches bearing fruit and being pruned, but he has not mentioned whom the branches represent. The left-dislocation in v. 4 provides the basis for comparison whereby the vine is correlated to the believer.

Example 206 :: John 15:4

μείνατε ἐν ἐμοί, κἀγὼ ἐν ὑμῖν.	"Remain in me, and I in you.
⟨✖ ⟨✖[LD]καθὼς τὸ κλῆμα οὐ δύναται **καρπὸν** φέρειν ἀφ' ἑαυτοῦ✖⟩ ἐὰν μὴ ⟨✔μένῃ ἐν τῇ ἀμπέλῳ,✔⟩LD]	⟨✖ ⟨✖[LD]Just as the branch is not able to bear **fruit** from itself ✖⟩ unless ⟨✔it remains in the vine,✔⟩ LD]
[CPοὕτωςCP] οὐδὲ **ὑμεῖς**✖⟩ ἐὰν μὴ ⟨✔ἐν ἐμοὶ μένητε.✔⟩	[CPsoCP] neither can **you,**✖⟩ unless ⟨✔you remain **in me.**✔⟩"

The left-dislocation reiterates the relevant information to establish a frame of reference for the clause that follows. This allows for an explicit comparison to be made based on the imagery from the preceding verses. The main clause is so dependent upon the content of the dislocation that the main verb is elided. The syntax of the statements is parallel as well. The pro-adverb καθώς signals the end of the dislocated information, attracting more attention to it for rhetorical purposes.[23]

Emphasis is used to highlight the most important elements, "you" in the main clause, and "me" in the exceptive clause. The inability to bear fruit is presupposed; it is just a matter of who will not be able to bear it. The exceptive clauses in the dislocation and the main clause play a key rhetorical role. The main clause of each negates an entire proposition, but it is not entirely correct. The missing information that makes the main proposition complete is disclosed in the exceptive statement. There actually is a way for a branch to bear fruit: it must remain in the vine. The complete negation of the dislocated main clause ends up attracting extra attention to the one exception, resulting in emphasis. The same holds for the other main clause.

These examples illustrate the use of left-dislocation constructions to introduce new entities that might be too complex to process without some kind of aid. Placing the pronominal trace in a frame of reference can signal the transition from the dislocation to the main clause, making it easier to process. The usage described so far represents the minority of NT usage.

---

23. Other examples of dislocated comparative information that is resumed as a frame of reference include Matt 12:40; Luke 11:30; John 3:14; 5:21, 26; Acts 8:32; Rom 5:12, 15, 18, 19, 21; 6:4, 19; 12:4; 1 Cor 11:12; 12:12; 15:22; 16:1; 2 Cor 1:5; 7:14; 8:6, 11; 10:7; Col 3:13; 2 Tim 3:8; James 2:26.

14.3.3   Discourse-Pragmatic Function

The next section describes the rhetorical use of left-dislocations to highlight entities that are simple enough to be introduced without a resumptive pronoun. Because the pronoun is semantically redundant, it accomplishes the discourse-pragmatic function described in the processing hierarchy. Recall the claim that by the time of the Koiné period, left-dislocations have become a stylized rhetorical device based on the Classical usage. The rhetorical effect is achieved by virtue of the resumptive pronoun's placement in P1/P2. The specific role is determined by the status of the information in the context.

In cases like Rom 8:30, the dislocated topical entity is straightforward enough for a simple topical frame of reference. Use of a left-dislocation represents overkill, which serves the rhetorical function of promoting the topic. In such cases, dislocation and resumption combine to highlight the topic, but they still accomplish the processing function of ensuring that the reader properly tracks the rapid changes. The pronominal trace could easily be omitted without causing confusion. The inclusion provides the reader an explicit break that makes the changes easier to process.

Example 207 :: Romans 8:30

[LDοὓς δὲ προώρισεν,LD] [TPτού-
τους TP] ⟨+καὶ ἐκάλεσεν·+⟩

And [LDthose whom he predes-
tined,LD] [TPthese TP] ⟨+he also
called,+⟩

καὶ [LDοὓς ἐκάλεσεν,LD] [TPτού-
τους TP] ⟨+καὶ ἐδικαίωσεν·+⟩

and [LDthose whom he called,LD]
[TPthese TP] ⟨+he also justified,+⟩

[LDοὓς δὲ ἐδικαίωσεν,LD] [TPτού-
τους TP] ⟨+καὶ ἐδόξασεν.+⟩

and [LDthose whom he justified,LD]
[TPthese TP] ⟨+he also glorified.+⟩

Note that the clauses follow the natural flow of information, whereby the object of one clause becomes the topic of the next. Such changes are easily processed. By virtue of the demonstratives referring to information established in the previous clause, the resumption of the left-dislocation is construed as a topical frame of reference. The + symbols signify *thematic addition*, the adverbial use of καί or other additives to explicitly link discourse entities that would otherwise only be implicitly linked on the basis of content.[24] The pragmatic effect here is to closely link this series of actions to one another using adverbial καί—that is, προώρισεν with ἐκάλεσεν, ἐκάλεσεν with ἐδικαίωσεν, and

---

24. See chapter 16.

ἐδικαίωσεν with ἐδόξασεν. The clauses are parallel not only in their syntax and semantics, but also in the use of an additive to more closely link the actions together.

The next example illustrates the use of dislocation to introduce the most important information of the clause. In the upper room scene just before Jesus is betrayed, the Synoptic Gospels differ in what information is provided about the betrayer. They also differ in the context in which the betrayer is mentioned. In Matthew's version, Jesus declares in 26:21 that he will be betrayed by one of those present. The same holds true in Mark's version, with a statement in 14:18. Luke's version does not contain such a disclosure.

In Matthew and Mark, the disclosure precipitates questions from the disciples about which of them is the betrayer. Matthew provides the answer to this question in 26:23. Since it fills in the blank of the question, it is the most important part of the proposition—that is, focal. The answer is "the one who dips his hand with me in the bowl," which is far too complex to be emphasized in position P2. It would likely be mistaken as a topical frame of reference. The introduction of the answer to the question using a left-dislocation enables Matthew to place the pronominal trace in position P2 for the sake of emphasis.

Example 208 :: Matthew 26:23

ὁ δὲ ἀποκριθεὶς εἶπεν· [LDὁ ἐμβάψας μετ' ἐμοῦ τὴν χεῖρα ἐν τῷ τρυβλίῳLD] **οὗτός** με παραδώσει.	And he answered and said, [LD"The one who dips his hand in the bowl with meLD]—**this one** will betray me."

The effect of using the left-dislocation is to provide a rhetorical buildup. "The one who dips …" is introduced, but it is unclear how this entity relates to the proposition under consideration until it is reiterated in the main clause. The use of emphasis by Matthew says something about the importance that he places on this information.

In Luke's version, Jesus does not state that he will be betrayed, nor is there a question being answered.

Example 209 :: Luke 22:21

Πλὴν ἰδοὺ ἡ χεὶρ τοῦ παραδιδόντος με μετ' ἐμοῦ ἐπὶ τῆς τραπέζης.	"But behold, the hand of the one who is betraying me is with me on the table!"

Luke uses a verbless clause to state that the betrayer is present, but he does not connect the identity to the dipping of the bread. Verse 23 states that the disciples were discussing who the betrayer might be, but there is no identification of the betrayer until Judas arrives in Gethsemane.

The content and structure of Mark's version in 14:20 has the same kind of context as Matthew's, where questions have been asked about the identity of the betrayer. But unlike Matthew's version, the question is answered with a participial clause. There is no main clause that follows.

Example 210 :: Mark 14:20

ὁ δὲ εἶπεν αὐτοῖς· εἷς τῶν δώδεκα, ὁ ἐμβαπτόμενος μετ᾽ ἐμοῦ εἰς τὸ τρύβλιον.	But he said to them, "It is one of the twelve—the one who is dipping bread into the bowl with me."

So while Matthew and Mark both have the same propositional context of a question being asked, Matthew's version uses the left-dislocation and its reiteration to create a dramatic buildup to the answer, emphasizing it by placing the pronominal trace in a marked position. Mark's version simply answers the question without the same rhetorical buildup.

Spatial entities are also introduced using left-dislocations. In most cases, the left-dislocation becomes the basis against which the newly asserted main clause information is highlighted by creating a connection using thematic addition. In this example from James, the dislocated entity was referred to conceptually in v. 14. The dislocation reiterates the concept and creates a specific state of affairs in preparation for the writer to make a comment about it.

Example 211 :: James 3:16

14 But if you have bitter jealousy and selfish ambition in your hearts, do not boast and tell lies against the truth. 15 This is not the wisdom that comes down from above, but is earthly, unspiritual, demonic.

16 [LDὅπου γὰρ ζῆλος καὶ ἐρι-θεία,LD] [SPἐκεῖSP] ἀκαταστασία καὶ πᾶν φαῦλον πρᾶγμα.	16 For [LDwhere there is jealousy and selfish ambition,LD] [SPthereSP] is disorder and every evil practice.

The newly asserted information in the clause is that there will be "disorder" and "every evil practice." The dislocation serves to introduce the location where this assertion holds true; it is not the most important element of the clause. The dislocated information is reiterated by way of a referential pro-adverb. In this instance, ἐκεῖ accomplishes two tasks. First, it signals the end of the dislocation and the beginning of the main clause, although there would be little confusion about this. Second, it has the pragmatic effect of promoting the entity by attracting more attention to it than omitting the resumption. It promotes the location for rhetorical purposes by delaying the comment that is made about it. So the resumptive pro-adverb ἐκεῖ still serves as a processing aid to the reader, even though the dislocated entity is simple enough to introduce using a simple frame of reference (see §10.3). Since it is redundant, it plays the additional rhetorical role of topic promotion, attracting extra attention to the dislocated entity.

In Matt 6:21, the dislocation once again functions as a foil for the new information introduced in the main clause that follows.

Example 212 :: Matthew 6:21

[LDὅπου γάρ ἐστιν ὁ θησαυρός σου,LD] [SPἐκεῖSP] ἔσται ‹+καὶ ἡ καρδία σου.+›	"For [LDwhere your treasure is,LD] [SPthereSP] ‹+also your heart+› will be."

The presupposition is that there will be something where your treasure is; it is just a question of what. This question is answered by the new information of the main clause, further highlighted by thematic addition. The new information of the main clause comes in its default location following the main verb. The only additional highlighting that it receives is the thematic addition.[25]

In the Lukan parallel, the NA[27] reading emphasizes "also your heart" by placing it in marked focus between the spatial frame of reference and the main verb.

Example 213 :: Luke 12:34

[LDὅπου γάρ ἐστιν ὁ θησαυρὸς ὑμῶν,LD] [SPἐκεῖSP] ‹+καὶ ἡ καρδία ὑμῶν+› ἔσται.	"For [LDwhere your treasure is,LD] [SPthereSP] ‹+also your heart+› will be."

In neither case is the focus of the main clause the spatial information, but what is found there: "your heart."[26] The left-dislocation activates a location that is commented on in the main clause. It is not the most important information in the clause, but provides a frame of reference for what follows.

---

25. Codex B and the Boharic manuscripts witness against reading the presence of thematic addition.

26. Codex D and a few other manuscripts and versions read the main clause following the Matthean order, rather than as emphasizing the focal constituent. The thematic addition is undisputed.

Scene-setting *temporal* information typically is introduced in a standard frame of reference, without the use of a resumptive pronominal element in the main clause. Of the more than eight hundred temporal frames of reference identified in the Greek NT, only twenty-one involve a left-dislocation. The following examples illustrate how reiterating the information using a pro-adverb can have the effect of thematically highlighting the information. Temporal information often plays an important theological role by establishing a frame of reference for the main clause. In Col 3:4, the left-dislocation introduces a specific time when believers will be revealed in glory with Jesus. The time is not the most important information in the clause; who is revealed with him is most important.

Example 214 :: Colossians 3:4

[LDὅταν [TPὁ Χριστὸς TP] φανε-
ρωθῇ, ἡ ζωὴ ὑμῶν,LD] [TMτότεTM]
⟨+**καὶ ὑμεῖς**+⟩ σὺν αὐτῷ φανε-
ρωθήσεσθε ἐν δόξῃ.

[LDWhen [TPChrist,TP] who is your
life, is revealed,LD] [TMthenTM]
⟨+**you also**+⟩ will be revealed
with him in glory.

Due to the complexity of the temporal frame (and perhaps because of the fronted subject ὑμεῖς), the resumptive pro-adverb explicitly marks the end of the dislocation and the beginning of the main clause. The semantically redundant subject pronoun is necessary from a syntactic point of view for both emphasis and thematic addition. The pronoun receives emphasis based on it being part of the new information and its placement in a marked position. The adverbial καί creates a thematic connection between "Christ" being revealed and "you" being revealed, strengthening a link that was already present based on the content.

In the next example, the temporal frame has the rhetorical effect of highlighting the information, since it is simple enough not to need the resumptive pro-adverb. It creates a break in the flow, allowing the temporal frame more time to sink in.

Example 215 :: 2 Corinthians 12:10

διὸ εὐδοκῶ ἐν ἀσθενείαις, ἐν
ὕβρεσιν, ἐν ἀνάγκαις, ἐν διωγμοῖς
καὶ στενοχωρίαις, ὑπὲρ Χριστοῦ·

Therefore I delight in weaknesses,
in insults, in calamities, in perse-
cutions and difficulties for the sake
of Christ,

[LDὅταν γὰρ ἀσθενῶ,LD]
[TMτότεTM] **δυνατός** εἰμι.

[LDfor whenever I am weak,LD]
[TMthenTM] I am **strong**.

Because of the contradictory nature of the temporal frame and the comment made about it, promoting the frame with the left-dislocation highlights this contrast even more. The most important part of the comment is placed in a marked position for the sake of emphasis, drawing out the contrast further. It would have been much simpler to omit τότε.

Alternatively, the temporal frame could have been eliminated if Paul had stated, "I am strong whenever I am weak." Wording it like this significantly dampens the rhetorical effect. It also allows ὅταν ἀσθενῶ to be construed as focal information. The use of the temporal frame eliminates this possibility, and the reiteration using τότε promotes temporal information for rhetorical purposes.

More than 180 *comparative* frames of reference can be found in the NT, and forty of these are reiterated using the pro-adverb οὕτως to form a left-dislocation. In Heb 9:27–28, the comparative frame is used to draw a specific correlation between the people destined to die and enter into judgment on the one hand and Jesus on the other.

Example 216 :: Hebrews 9:27–28

^{27} καὶ [LDκαθ' ὅσον ἀπόκειται τοῖς ἀνθρώποις **ἅπαξ** ἀποθανεῖν, [TMμετὰ δὲ τοῦτο$^{TM]}$ κρίσις,$^{LD]}$

^{28} [CPοὕτως$^{CP]}$ [TP‹**+**καὶ ὁ Χριστὸς**+**›$^{TP]}$ **ἅπαξ** προσενεχθεὶς εἰς τὸ πολλῶν ἀνενεγκεῖν ἁμαρτίας **ἐκ δευτέρου χωρὶς ἁμαρτίας** ὀφθήσεται τοῖς αὐτὸν ἀπεκδεχομένοις εἰς σωτηρίαν.

^{27} And [LDjust as it is destined for people to die **once**, and [TMafter this, TM] judgment,$^{LD]}$

^{28} [CPthus$^{CP]}$ [TP‹**+**also Christ,**+**› TP] having been offered **once** in order to bear the sins of many, will appear **for the second time without reference to sin** to those who eagerly await him for salvation.

Christ is portrayed as performing a task comparable to doing one thing followed by another. In the same way that people are destined for death and afterward prepare for judgment, Jesus accomplishes a comparable activity. The first activity is framed as a circumstantial participle, backgrounding it to the main action of "appearing." Being offered up to bear the sins of many enables his second appearance to bring about salvation instead of judgment.

Most all of this information has already been introduced into the discourse, but the comparison of similarities and differences has not been made explicit. Restating the relevant information provides an important frame of reference for the clause that follows. The pro-adverb οὕτως signals the end of the dislocation and rhetorically promotes the information. Stating the information in two clauses would have significantly reduced the rhetorical impact of the comparison. The book of Hebrews contains many such comparisons, but most are executed using simple frames of reference without dislocation.

Left-dislocations may also be used to introduce the most important information of the clause. There comes a point where an entity is too complex to be emphasized in position P2. In such cases, a left-dislocation is used to introduce the entity outside the main clause, with the resumptive pronominal element being simple enough to be placed in position P2 for emphasis. In this way, the "one new thing at a time" constraint is honored, as is the limitation on how complex an entity can be emphasized in position P2. The pronominal trace still serves the same tasks as in other left-dislocations. The only difference is that it refers to the most important information in the main clause.

There are a handful of NT examples where the dislocated spatial information is reiterated with emphasis because it is the most important part of the utterance—for example, it provides the answer to a question. In Matt 18:20, Jesus makes a statement about his presence. The location is the most important part of the utterance. The text of v. 19 is supplied for context.

Example 217 :: Matthew 18:20

19 "Again, truly I say to you that if two of you agree on earth about any matter that they ask, it will be done for them from my Father who is in heaven."

20 [LDοὗ γάρ εἰσιν δύο ἢ τρεῖς συνηγμένοι εἰς τὸ ἐμὸν ὄνομα,LD] ἐκεῖ εἰμι ἐν μέσῳ αὐτῶν.	20 "For [LDwhere two or three are gathered in my name,LD] I am **there** in the midst of them."

Verse 19 introduces the concept of "two or three," and the dislocation of v. 20 builds on this by introducing the location of the "two or three." Jesus has been describing the authority that will be given to followers. The rationale for this authority is provided in v. 20. It is presupposed that Jesus is somewhere; it is just a matter of where. Verse 20 connects the location of the "two or three" with the location of Jesus: they are one and the same. Where they gather, it is "there" that he is (as opposed to some other location).[27] In this instance, the location is not a foil but the point of the utterance. The dislocated clause

---

27. Luz states, "The presence of the risen Lord is promised not only for those who pray but for any two or three who come together for the sake of Jesus. Once again two or three are minimum numbers. In a rhetorically effective way the small number underscores how great is the promise that the risen Lord will be in their midst. Of all the statements in the text v. 20 covers the widest area. Far from being a superfluous addition, therefore, it is the christological center of the entire chapter" (Ulrich Luz, *Matthew: A Commentary*, vol.

element is too complex to be emphasized in position P2. The left-dislocation provides an efficient mechanism for introducing the entity, and the pro-adverb is simple enough to be emphasized. It refers back to the dislocated element, and in this way the dislocated information is both introduced and emphasized based on the status of the information.

In Mark 6 and its Synoptic parallels, Jesus gives instructions to the disciples before sending them out for ministry. Part of the instruction concerns selecting a place to lodge. He intends for them to stay in a particular place that has yet to be mentioned. The dislocated information introduces this location.

Example 218 :: Mark 6:10

καὶ ἔλεγεν αὐτοῖς· [LDὅπου ἐὰν εἰσέλθητε εἰς οἰκίαν,LD] **ἐκεῖ** μένετε ἕως ἂν ἐξέλθητε ἐκεῖθεν.	And he said to them, [LD"Whenever you enter into a house,LD] stay **there** until you depart from there."

It is presupposed that the disciples are to stay somewhere; it is just a matter of where. The left-dislocation provides the answer to this question, but it is too complex to be emphasized. The pro-adverb provides a simplified reference to the dislocated location, and ἐκεῖ can manageably be emphasized.

Luke's version of this saying in 9:4 is quite similar, using a spatial left-dislocation with ἐκεῖ placed in marked focus for the sake of emphasis.[28] Matthew's version in 10:11 has a noteworthy difference. The location still receives emphasis, but it is introduced using the standard "two-clause" activation-then-comment strategy instead of doing both using a left-dislocation.

Example 219 :: Matthew 10:11

[LDεἰς ἣν δ' ἂν πόλιν ἢ κώμην εἰσέλθητε,LD] ἐξετάσατε τίς ἐν αὐτῇ **ἄξιός** ἐστιν·	"And [LDinto whatever town or village you enter,LD] inquire who in it is **worthy**,
κἀκεῖ μείνατε ἕως ἂν ἐξέλθητε.	and stay **there** until you depart."

The "town or village" is introduced in the first clause of the verse, and the comment about it is to "inquire" in it. The embedded clause τίς ἐν αὐτῇ ἄξιός ἐστιν functions as a complement of ἐξετάσατε, and ἄξιος is emphasized. The same location from the first main clause of the verse is reiterated in the second

---

2 [trans. Wilhelm C. Linns; ed. Helmut Koester; Hermeneia; Minneapolis: Fortress, 2001], 458).

28. The left-dislocation differs slightly, reading εἰς ἣν ἂν οἰκίαν εἰσέλθητε.

main clause. Since it is already activated, it may be referred to using the pro-adverb κἀκεῖ. It is placed in marked focus in Matthew's version for the same reason as in Mark's and Luke's: "there" is where they were to stay, as opposed to somewhere else.

These examples illustrate the kind of variation that is possible while at the same time maintaining consistency in the propositional content. Mark and Luke use left-dislocations to introduce an entity and emphasize it in the same clause. Matthew also uses a left-dislocation, but the location is not emphasized until the following clause. The added instruction to inquire about who is worthy in the place solidly grounds the location in the reader's mental representation, allowing it to be referred to using the pro-adverb in the following clause.

As with the other dislocated elements, *temporal* information can be dislocated in order to introduce a complex entity that receives emphasis in the main clause, or simply to highlight the information that is emphasized. Its status as new information and the placement of the resumptive pro-adverb in the marked position bring about the emphasis.

The first example comes from John 8, where Jesus teaches his opponents about who he is, yet they fail to recognize that he is the Messiah. It is presupposed that they will recognize him at some time; it is just a matter of when.

Example 220 :: John 8:28a

εἶπεν οὖν [αὐτοῖς] ὁ Ἰησοῦς· [LDὅταν ὑψώσητε τὸν υἱὸν τοῦ ἀνθρώπου,LD] **τότε** γνώσεσθε ὅτι **ἐγώ** εἰμι,	Then Jesus said to them, [LD"When you lift up the Son of Man,LD] **then** you will recognize that **I** am he,"

The dislocated temporal information introduces this time, but is too complex an entity to be emphasized. The left-dislocation allows the information to be introduced, and the pro-adverb is simple enough to be emphasized. Within the complement of γνώσεσθε ("you will recognize"), the redundant subject pronoun is fronted for the sake of emphasis. It is Jesus who is the Messiah, not someone else.

The left-dislocation in the next example, from John 12, also provides the answer to a presupposed proposition. Verse 16a states that the disciples did not understand these things "at first." This opens the door for them to understand at some later point.

Example 221 :: John 12:16

⟨✗ταῦτα οὐκ ἔγνωσαν αὐτοῦ οἱ   ⟨✗His disciples did not under-
μαθηταὶ τὸ πρῶτον,✗⟩   stand these things at first,✗⟩

ἀλλ' ⟨✓ [LDὅτε ἐδοξάσθη Ἰησοῦς LD]   but ⟨✓ [LDwhen Jesus was
τότε ἐμνήσθησαν ὅτι ταῦτα ἦν ἐπ' glorified, LD] **then** they remem-
αὐτῷ γεγραμμένα καὶ ταῦτα ἐποίη-   bered that these things had been
σαν αὐτῷ.✓⟩   written about him and they did
                                      these things to him.✓⟩

The dislocated temporal information provides the answer to the question of
when they would understand. It is too complex to place in marked focus, as it
could be mistaken to be a temporal frame of reference. The dislocation allows
the information to be introduced and then reiterated in a form simple enough
for emphasis.

The final examples, parallels from Matt 9 and Luke 5, provide the answer
to the Pharisees' disciples when they ask why Jesus' disciples do not fast. Jesus'
answer uses the analogy of the bridegroom and the wedding feast. It presupposes that there will be fasting at some point; it is just a question of when.
The answer to this question is provided in the left-dislocation. Luke 5:34 is
supplied for context.

Example 222 :: Luke 5:35

³⁴ So Jesus said to them, "You are not able to make the bridegroom's
attendants fast as long as the bridegroom is with them, are you?"

³⁵ ἐλεύσονται δὲ ἡμέραι, καὶ   ³⁵ "But days will come, and
[LDὅταν ἀπαρθῇ ἀπ' αὐτῶν ὁ   [LDwhen the bridegroom is taken
νυμφίος, LD] **τότε** νηστεύσουσιν ἐν   away from them, LD] **then** they will
ἐκείναις ταῖς ἡμέραις.   fast in those days."

The temporal dislocation not only is resumed by the pro-adverb τότε, which
receives emphasis; it also is referenced in the prepositional phrase ἐν ἐκείναις
ταῖς ἡμέραις at the end of the clause. Using the far demonstrative ἐκείναις has
the effect of recharacterizing the time as still remote. The content of vv. 34–35
is combined in Matthew's version.

Example 223 :: Matthew 9:15

καὶ εἶπεν αὐτοῖς ὁ Ἰησοῦς· μὴ δύνανται οἱ υἱοὶ τοῦ νυμφῶνος πενθεῖν ἐφ' ὅσον μετ' αὐτῶν ἐστιν ὁ νυμφίος;	And Jesus said to them, "The bridegroom's attendants are not able to mourn as long as the bridegroom is with them.
ἐλεύσονται δὲ ἡμέραι ὅταν ἀπαρθῇ ἀπ' αὐτῶν ὁ νυμφίος,	But days are coming when the bridegroom is taken away from them,
καὶ **τότε** νηστεύσουσιν.	and **then** they will fast."

Matthew's version locates the καί before τότε instead of before ὅταν, creating a meaningful change to the flow. The "days are coming" clause goes on to delineate the more specific time when the bridegroom is taken away. This leaves the main point of "at that time" (τότε) in its own clause, without any preamble. Luke's version develops the time frame more patiently. Matthew's version changes the left-dislocation into a simple subordinate clause.[29] The result is to accomplish in two clauses what Luke accomplishes in one using the dislocation. The parallel in Mark 2:20 also uses two clauses instead of left-dislocation, paralleling Matthew.

Summary

Left-dislocations serve the same basic function in Koiné Greek as they do in other languages. Due to the influence of Classical Greek rhetoric, the placement of the resumptive pronoun in a preverbal position is far more frequent than in Koiné than in other languages, such as biblical Hebrew. Placing the pronoun in a frame of reference often serves a processing function when the dislocated entity is long or complex, marking the transition to the main clause. Where the dislocated entity is simple enough not to need the processing aid, the placement in a frame has the rhetorical effect of thematically highlighting the entity. If the dislocated information is focal, the construction allows a simplified reference to the entity to be placed in marked focus for the sake of emphasis.

Suggested Reading

Andrews, Avery. "The Major Functions of the Noun Phrase."

---

29. The Old Latin witnesses omit καί before v. 35b in Luke.

Blass, F., A. Debrunner, and R. W. Funk. *A Greek Grammar of the New Testament and Other Early Christian Literature.* §466.

Chafe, Wallace L. "Cognitive Constraints on Information Flow."

Givón, Talmy T. *Syntax: A Functional-Typological Introduction.* 1:258–63.

Lambrecht, Knud. *Information Structure and Sentence Form: Topic, Focus, and the Mental Representations of Discourse Referents.* 177–95.

Porter, Stanley E. *Idioms of the Greek New Testament.* 85–86.

Robertson, A. T. A *Grammar of the Greek New Testament in the Light of Historical Research.* 697–98.

Runge, Steven E. "A Discourse-Functional Description of Participant Reference in Biblical Hebrew Narrative," 35–44, 108–20.

Simcox, William Henry. *The Language of the New Testament.* 65–66.

Wallace, Daniel B. *Greek Grammar beyond the Basics: An Exegetical Syntax of the New Testament.* 51–52.

PART 4   THEMATIC HIGHLIGHTING DEVICES

Most of the discourse devices discussed so far are forward-pointing in nature, typically using some element that was either unneeded or out of place in the context. It stuck out by virtue of breaking with the expected norm. Thematic highlighting devices also utilize redundant elements that are not required to know who is doing what to whom. But rather than point forward, these highlighting devices draw attention to the extra information. The information is promoted because of its importance in shaping or informing what follows. Each device serves to make you think about the right thing in the right way at the right time, influencing how you construct and organize your "mental representation" of the discourse (see §9.2.3).

OVERSPECIFICATION AND RIGHT-DISLOCATION

This chapter describes the discourse function of overly specific references to persons or things. In most cases, people tend to use the most succinct reference needed to unambiguously identify the intended person or thing. In spite of this, there are many instances where much longer, overly specific references are used instead in Greek, English, and many other languages. These references go beyond just helping to identify "who is doing what to whom." The information that they provide reiterates thematic information about the entity or provides some elaboration about them that exceeds the minimum needed to "pick them out of a lineup." These constructions are sometimes "corrected" in English translation, as though they represented bad grammar.

Two different constructions are considered in this chapter: overspecification and right-dislocation. They share overlapping functions, with the latter serving a more specialized purpose. *Overspecification* refers to providing more information than is needed to identify a participant. *Right-dislocation* entails referring to a participant in the midst of a clause using a pronoun or generic noun phrase and then adding more information about the same participant at the end of the clause. Both devices serve the common purpose of highlighting particular thematic information that the writer wants the reader to consider at that particular point in the discourse. In most cases, the thematic information has been previously mentioned but is not in the forefront of the reader's memory. Reiterating this known information moves the reader to think about the particular participant in a particular way at that particular point in the discourse.

15.1   Conventional Explanation

There is little systematic treatment of overspecification as a phenomenon in NT studies. Most of the work is largely ad hoc in nature, based upon a commentator's judgment about the usage in a given context. Consider the discussion of the visit by the magi in Matt 2:11, which reads, "And going into the house they saw the child with Mary his mother, and they fell down and worshiped him. Then, opening their treasures, they offered him gifts, gold and frankincense and myrrh" (ESV).

Generally, participants are referred to using only their proper name in contexts where something more than a pronoun is needed. Instead, Mary is overspecified as "his mother." This extra information is not needed to discern which "Mary" is intended. Such nondefault expressions accomplish certain pragmatic effects that commentators notice. However, they often attribute the effects to the order of the participants, not to the expressions used.

Hendriksen comments, "Having entered, the wise men see 'the little child with Mary his mother.' Note that whenever mother and infant are mentioned together (verses 11, 13, 14, 20, and 21) the infant is always mentioned first. It is that little child upon whom the main interest is concentrated."[1] He ascribes what I consider to be a correct observation to the wrong factor. The effect is due not to the ordering of the participants, but to the overspecification of Mary using the redundant information "his mother." Morris arrives at the same conclusion on the same basis: "There they saw the little child and his mother (in each place in this passage where the two are mentioned the child comes first, vv. 13, 14, 20, 21; Matthew's main interest is in Jesus)."[2]

The most detailed comments regarding the actual overspecification are made by Davies and Allison, but they still overlook the role that the over-specification plays even though they arrive at the correct conclusion.

> The phrase, "the child with Mary his mother" recurs (with "and" for "with" and without "Mary") in 2:13, 14, 20, 21. It serves three ends. (1) It puts Joseph out of the picture, thereby reinforcing the impact of 1:16–25: Jesus has no human father. (2) "The child and his mother" probably harks back to Exod 4:20 (τὴν γυναῖκα καὶ τὰ παιδία), for Exod 4:19 is the basis for Mt 2:20.... (3) Because "the child" (see on 2:8–9) is named first, he is shown to be the focus of all the action. Even Mary is in the shadows, for she gains her identity only by being "his mother."[3]

---

1. William Hendriksen, *Exposition of the Gospel According to Matthew* (NTC; Grand Rapids: Baker, 1973), 170.

2. Leon Morris, *The Gospel According to Matthew* (PNTC; Grand Rapids: Eerdmans, 1992), 41.

3. W. D. Davies and Dale C. Allison, *A Critical and Exegetical Commentary on the Gospel According to Saint Matthew*, vol. 2 (ICC; Edinburgh: T & T Clark, 2004), 248.

Reversing the order of the participants in this verse would not have changed the results. Referring to Mary as "his mother" explicitly links her to Jesus; this is how she "gains her identity." Since Mary is the one doing the main action, linking her to Jesus by use of a personal pronoun has the effect of pushing her into the background. It provides an explicit indication that Jesus is the center of attention, not Mary. Omitting the overspecification would have left the center of attention implicit, whereas the overspecification makes it explicit. In chapter 17, on changed reference, I demonstrate that the same effect can be achieved using the simpler expression "his mother" instead of the overspecified "Mary his mother."

More often than not, overspecification is not commented on, perhaps on the assumption that it is stylistic variation or some literary convention. Over-specification is commonly found in the NT Epistles, where often commentators construe it as sign of a "liturgical formula" or a redactional "expansion" by a scribe somewhere in the compositional process. Such explanations sidestep the issue of why it is used, regardless of its origins. It does not describe the function that it plays in the discourse. Consider the overspecification found in Eph 3:9 concerning the reference to God: "and to bring to light for everyone what is the plan of the mystery hidden for ages in God *who created all things*" (ESV [italics added]). This extra information is not needed to pick out which "God" Paul intends. Hendriksen states,

> It is not clear why Paul adds: (God) "who created all things." If I may be per-mitted to add just one more guess to all those that have been made by others, I would say that the expression may, perhaps, rivet the attention on God's sovereignty. He is the God who, by virtue of the very fact that he *created* all things, also proves himself to be the sovereign Disposer of their destinies. In other words, he does not owe it to any one to explain why for a long time the mystery was concealed from the Gentiles, and why it is now revealed to all, regardless of race or nationality.[4]

Hendriksen recognizes that the information is not required to cor-rectly identify which "God" Paul is referring to, and he arrives at an ad hoc conclusion regarding its purpose. O'Brien too sees the redundant informa-tion playing a thematic role, drawing attention to another of God's qualities besides being the one "in whom this secret had previously been hidden from eternity."[5] Lincoln is more specific: "That the mystery had its place from the

---

4. William Hendriksen, *Exposition of Ephesians* (NTC; Grand Rapids: Baker, 1967), 157.

5. Peter T. O'Brien, *The Letter to the Ephesians* (PNTC; Grand Rapids: Eerdmans, 1999), 244.

beginning in God's creative plan is underlined by the following liturgical formula about God as creator of all."[6]

Although there is recognition of the thematic role that these overspecified references play, these observations are far from being the norm. Overspecification may indeed stem from liturgical material. Assigning such a label falls short of describing its present function in the discourse; it provides no rationale for the writer utilizing it. Thus, although there are occasional comments about overspecification and even correct analyses of its contribution to the discourse, such comments are far more ad hoc than systematic, overlooking the much more pervasive usage found throughout the NT and other Greek literature.[7]

We use overspecification in conversational English to accomplish certain effects. If I were to refer to someone as "my best and most faithful friend ever for whom I would do anything" instead of "Bob," he would probably wonder if I was trying to con him into doing some favor for me. This overspecified expression highlights characteristics of faithfulness and dependability. "Bob" would most likely infer intentionality to my reminding him of this information. As native speakers, we use these conventions without consciously thinking about them. We phrase things in such a way as to best accomplish our purposes in the context, and the same holds true for the NT writers. Even if quoting from liturgical formulae, there is still meaning to be derived from the writer's choice to quote the longer expression instead of using a shorter default expression. The attribution of an expression to liturgical origins tells us little about its exegetical function in the text. It also fails to account for the heavy use of overspecification in nonepistolary genres such as narrative proper.

---

6. Andrew T. Lincoln, *Ephesians* (WBC 42; Dallas: Word, 2002), 185.

7. Overspecification is not restricted to the NT. Here are two examples from *1 Clement* (translations, with my emphasis added, from Michael W. Holmes, *The Apostolic Fathers: Greek Texts and English Translations* [2nd ed.; Grand Rapids: Baker, 1999]):

59:3: "Grant us, Lord, to hope on your name, which is the primal source of all creation, and open the eyes of our hearts, that we may know you, **who alone is 'Highest among the high, and remains Holy among the holy.'** "

64:1: "Finally, may the all-seeing God and Master of spirits and Lord of all flesh, who chose the Lord Jesus Christ, and us through him to be his own special people, grant to every soul that has called upon his magnificent and holy name faith, fear, peace, patience, steadfastness, self-control, purity, and sobriety, that they may be pleasing to his name through our high priest and guardian, Jesus Christ, through whom be glory and majesty, might and honor to him, both now and for ever and ever. Amen."

15.2 Discourse Explanation

There are three basic functions of redundant information, and they are not mutually exclusive. Context and good exegesis are keys to making a proper determination. I will start with some background principles of participant reference and then move on to explain the different effects achieved using overspecification and right-dislocations.

- Principle 1: Use the shortest referring expression available.

The primary purpose of references to participants and other discourse entities is to help the reader track "who is doing what to whom." I will call these references *referring expressions*, whether pronouns, proper names, or other noun phrases (e.g., "the man"). Referring expressions always play a semantic function, whether or not they are redundant. Speakers tend to use the most concise expression available to identify participants, whether a pronoun "he" or a simple proper noun such as "Peter." This tendency toward efficiency is what makes overly specific references stand out.[8]

- Principle 2: Use the anchoring relation most relevant to the discourse context.

Another key idea that needs to be considered is the reader's current *mental representation* of the participants.[9] When we read a discourse, we do not just store all of the words in our head. Instead, we build a mental file in which the information is organized and stored. When some new entity is introduced, the introduction inevitably provides some link or "anchor" of the entity to the discourse. For instance, if Mary is introduced into the discourse as Jesus' mother (as opposed to Joseph's wife), the expectation is that Mary's relation to Jesus is her most relevant connection to the discourse. It also indicates that the person to whom she is anchored is a center of attention in the discourse. The anchoring relation instructs the reader how the entity fits into the overall discourse. This anchoring relation becomes the reader's primary basis for relating the entity to the discourse until something changes—that is, another anchor is provided.

We exploit anchoring relations all of the time in English for various purposes. Most of my friends are known to my wife by a first name and an anchoring relation. For example, I know Mike from work, Mike from church, Mike from my old job, Mike from my men's group, and Mike from down the street. It is often easier to use anchoring relations to disambiguate "Mikes"

---

8. See §1.4.
9. See §9.2.3.

than last names, because the relations have built-in hints about which part of my life the intended Mike comes from.

- Principle 3: Use the most relevant anchoring relation available.

Anchoring relations need not remain stagnant. Most participants have a number of potential anchoring relations to the discourse. Mary could be called "Jesus' mother," "Joseph's wife," or "Elizabeth's cousin." All are accurate relations, but not everyone will be relevant in every context. They can be switched as the participant's most relevant relation to the discourse changes.

Similarly, I could be introduced as Glenda's husband, Mike's co-worker, Erwin's son, Mike's friend, or as Logos Bible Software's scholar-in-residence. All of these relations are true, but not all of them are equally relevant in a given context. Speakers tend to choose the most relevant anchoring relation, based on their objectives and the discourse context.

These same principles described above hold true in the NT. John could be accurately anchored as one of the disciples, the brother of James, or as the one whom Jesus loved. All of these relations are true, but the most thematically relevant anchoring relation will be used, based on the context.

- Principle 4: Do not change referring expressions or anchoring relations.

Once a participant has been introduced and anchored to the discourse (and within the reader's mental representation), both the referring expression and anchoring relation typically remain unchanged. If the goal of a referring expression is to help the reader accurately identify the intended referent, it makes little sense to change expressions unless there is some good reason for doing so. Claiming stylistic variation makes no sense because the changes could cause confusion. Nevertheless, there are times when writers will change referring expressions, anchoring relations, or both in order to accomplish certain effects. Understanding what these changes accomplish can really pay off in exegesis. This extra information plays a very important thematic role in the discourse.

There are three basic effects that can be achieved by overspecified references to participants: thematic highlighting, recharacterization, and signaling point-of-view shifts. Each of these will be considered in turn.

15.2.1   Thematic Highlighting

There are contexts where a writer wants you to think about a particular participant in a particular way. This entails reminding you about some aspect or quality that you already knew but might not currently be thinking about. In other words, you knew the information, but you had it on a back burner in your mental representation. The extra information can tell you how the writer wants you to think about something in the particular context.

In the following examples, extra information is added to "the Father." In each case, the information is not needed to disambiguate which "Father" Jesus is talking about. Instead, it highlights a specific quality or characteristic that is important in the context. In Matt 6:1, Jesus warns against doing acts of righteousness in front of people in order to be seen by them.

Example 224 :: Matthew 6:1

Προσέχετε [δὲ] τὴν δικαιοσύνην ὑμῶν μὴ ποιεῖν ἔμπροσθεν τῶν ἀνθρώπων πρὸς τὸ θεαθῆναι αὐτοῖς· εἰ δὲ μή γε, μισθὸν οὐκ ἔχετε παρὰ τῷ πατρὶ ὑμῶν ‹♟τῷ ἐν τοῖς οὐρανοῖς.♟›	"And take care not to practice your righteousness before people to be seen by them; otherwise you have no reward from your Father ‹♟who is in heaven."♟›

Instead of seeking a reward from people, you should seek a reward from the one who really matters. The overspecified information is bracketed by the ♟ symbols. The extra information focuses attention on the one in heaven watching rather than on the people around you.

The referring expression changes in v. 6 to highlight different thematic information. Here Jesus contrasts praying in secret with praying where you can be seen by people. The overspecification of the Father is changed to highlight the themes of *seeing* and *in secret*. The extra information highlights qualities of the Father that are particularly relevant in the context.

Example 225 :: Matthew 6:6

σὺ δὲ ὅταν προσεύχῃ, εἴσελθε εἰς τὸ ταμεῖόν σου καὶ κλείσας τὴν θύραν σου πρόσευξαι τῷ πατρί σου ‹♟τῷ ἐν τῷ κρυπτῷ·♟› καὶ ὁ πατήρ σου ‹♟ὁ βλέπων ἐν τῷ κρυπτῷ♟› ἀποδώσει σοι.	"But whenever you pray, enter into your inner room and shut your door and pray to your Father ‹♟who is in secret,♟› and your Father ‹♟who sees in secret♟› will reward you."

These two overspecified references in v. 6 are not needed to determine which "Father" is intended. In each case, the extra information contributes thematic content that influences how you think about the Father, based on the particular qualities mentioned. You probably already knew that he is omniscient, but this quality may not have been in the forefront of your mind at this particular point in the discourse. The overspecification compels you to recall this particular quality of the Father because of its special relevance to the context.

There are more overspecified references to the Father in this same chapter, highlighting different qualities depending on what is most relevant to the context. In v. 14, there is a shift back to "your heavenly Father" in the discussion of God forgiving our sins according to how we forgive others. In the section about fasting so as not to attract attention from those around you, there is a corresponding shift back to "your Father who sees in secret" in v. 18. These shifts are not stylistic variation. They betray an intentional highlighting of themes or qualities of the participant that are particularly important to the context. There is an exegetical rationale and implication for the change.

15.2.2   Recharacterization

There are times when overspecified information changes the anchoring relation of the participant. In other words, you had been relating the participant to the discourse as X, and the new information compels you to relate that same participant in a new way Y. The anchoring information affects the way you relate the participant to the discourse. This change in anchoring relations—the way you think about them—is referred to as *recharacterization*. A great example of this is found in Luke's parable of the prodigal son, where the older son compares the treatment he has received from his father with that received by his younger brother, who squandered his inheritance.

Example 226 :: Luke 15:30

ὅτε δὲ ὁ υἱός σου οὗτος ‹♟ὁ καταφαγών σου τὸν βίον μετὰ πορνῶν♟› ἦλθεν, ἔθυσας αὐτῷ τὸν σιτευτὸν μόσχον.	"But when this son of yours returned—‹♟who has consumed your assets with prostitutes♟›— you killed the fattened calf for him!"

The older brother could have referred to the younger one by his proper name, as "my brother," or simply as "your son." All are legitimate possibilities. Instead, he calls the younger brother "this son of yours." He anchors the prodigal to his father instead of to himself, effectively creating some degree of distance and unfamiliarity by virtue of not using the closest anchoring relation possible.[10] On top of this, he adds a thematically loaded description that

---

10. See chapter 18.

highlights specific qualities that the older brother sees as particularly relevant to the context. He casts himself as the faithful son in the preceding verse, one who was repaid little for his faithfulness. He contrasts this with his younger, irresponsible counterpart, who seems to be rewarded for his infidelity to the family. Simply calling him "your son" or "my brother" would not have communicated nearly the same amount of emotion and animosity that we find in the biblical text. The overspecified reference has the effect of recharacterizing the younger son in a particular way, based on the older son's communicative goals.

15.2.3   Point-of-View Shifts

In most narratives there is one central participant around whom the story revolves. Such figures are the center of attention—the key participants around whom the action focuses. The other participants typically are anchored to the central character in some way. For instance, if Jesus is the center of attention, the disciples could be referred to as "his disciples," or Mary as "his mother." They are his and not someone else's. The center of attention tends to remain fairly static, but there are times where a writer uses overspecified references to either update or shift the center of attention in a narrative. The extra information contributes little thematically other than identifying the current center of attention.

In the early chapters of the Synoptic Gospels, where Jesus is not yet an active participant, redundant anchoring expressions are added to identify (or possibly even correct) the center of attention. Mary or Joseph performs much of the action, which implies that one of them is the center of attention. In spite of this default expectation, the overspecified references anchor them to Jesus, not Jesus to them. The redundant anchoring expressions provide explicit indications of the current center of attention. This dissonance is likely the source of Davies and Allison's claim that Mary is pushed into the shadows.[11] The main actor typically is expected to be the center of attention, and the other participants are expected to be anchored to him or her. The redundant anchoring expressions indicate that Jesus is the center of attention, even though he is not the one doing the action.

---

11. Davies and Allison, *Saint Matthew*, 248.

Example 227 :: Luke 2:33–34

[33] καὶ ἦν ὁ πατὴρ αὐτοῦ καὶ ἡ μήτηρ θαυμάζοντες ἐπὶ τοῖς λαλουμένοις περὶ αὐτοῦ.	[33] And *his father and mother* were astonished at what was said about him.
[34] καὶ εὐλόγησεν αὐτοὺς Συμεὼν καὶ εἶπεν πρὸς Μαριὰμ ⟨♣τὴν μητέρα αὐτοῦ·♣⟩ ἰδοὺ οὗτος κεῖται εἰς πτῶσιν καὶ ἀνάστασιν πολλῶν ἐν τῷ Ἰσραὴλ καὶ εἰς σημεῖον ἀντιλεγόμενον....	[34] And Simeon blessed them and said to ⟨♣his mother♣⟩ Mary, "Behold, this child is appointed for the fall and rise of many in Israel, and for a sign that is opposed...."

Notice that in v. 33, the ways Joseph and Mary are referred to have changed from proper names to less-specific epithets. This represents a *changed reference*, graphically represented in the example by *italics* (see chapter 17). These epithets achieve the same result as overspecification, anchoring Mary and Joseph to Jesus as the center of attention, even though he is not doing the action.

The same holds for the overspecified reference in v. 34. We were already reminded in the preceding verse that Mary is Jesus' mother. This overspecified reference has the effect of confirming the center of attention, since it contradicts the expectation of the main actor being the center of attention. In this case, we would expect Mary to be the center of attention, not Jesus. Luke uses these devices to correct our mental representation of the discourse. It helps to insure that Jesus is viewed as the center of attention, even though this is somewhat counterintuitive. The use of overspecification for the purposes of shifting the point of view is primarily limited to narrative.

15.3   Application

I begin by considering the specialized uses of right-dislocations in the NT, followed by examples of the various effects achieved using overspecified referring expressions. Both devices have the same basic effect of thematic highlighting.

A right-dislocation is essentially a delayed appositional reference to an entity that was referred to earlier in the clause. This device can be used to explicitly identify the center of attention in ways comparable to overspecification, but through the delay of information to the end of the clause. In this first example, the sentence begins with a singular subject. There is addendum at the end of the clause that indicates that Jesus was not alone: the twelve were with him.

Example 228 :: Luke 8:1

Καὶ ἐγένετο ἐν τῷ καθεξῆς καὶ αὐτὸς διώδευεν κατὰ πόλιν καὶ κώμην κηρύσσων καὶ εὐαγγε- λιζόμενος τὴν βασιλείαν τοῦ θεοῦ καὶ ‹♟οἱ δώδεκα σὺν αὐτῷ....♟›	And it happened that afterward also he was going about from one town and village to another preaching and proclaiming the good news concerning the king- dom of God, and ‹♟the twelve were with him....♟›

Jesus is the main participant in both the current and the preceding pericopes, yet Luke wants to make clear that the disciples are with Jesus. If they are not mentioned, they will drop off the radar, so to speak. If the narration had stated, "Jesus and the disciples went from town to town ... ," it could create the impression that the disciples are of equal importance to Jesus. The right-dislocation construction allows Jesus to be the sole subject of a singular verb, with mention at the end that he was not alone. This allows the writer to keep spotlight on the central participant and at the same time update the narrative state of affairs regarding who was with him. Other examples of this usage are found in Matt 2:3; Luke 6:3; 22:14.

Right-dislocations can also be used to intentionally delay the disclosure of thematic information to highlight it. In most cases, a rather generic term is placed in the main clause, followed by a much more specific reference to the same entity at the end of the clause. The delay tactic makes the dislocated information stand out more than if it were in its normal position within the main clause. Consider the usage in John 1:45, where Philip finds Nathaniel and tells him that he has found the expected Messiah.

Example 229 :: John 1:45

‹⊙εὑρίσκει⊙› Φίλιππος τὸν Ναθαναὴλ καὶ ‹⊙λέγει⊙› αὐτῷ· ὃν ἔγραψεν Μωϋσῆς ἐν τῷ νόμῳ καὶ οἱ προφῆται εὑρήκαμεν, ‹♟Ἰησοῦν υἱὸν τοῦ Ἰωσὴφ τὸν ἀπὸ Ναζαρέτ.♟›	Philip ‹⊙found⊙› Nathanael and ‹⊙said⊙› to him, "We have found the one whom Moses wrote about in the law, and the prophets wrote about—‹♟Jesus son of Joseph from Nazareth!"♟›

The reference in the main clause outlines a description (i.e., "the one whom ...") but lacks an identity. The specific answer is delayed to the end of the clause by dislocation.[12] It probably would have taken two statements to communicate the same propositional content had the writer not used a dislocation.[13] Dislocation constructions are a handy way of introducing participants quickly in one clause instead of two. Other examples of right-dislocations used to intentionally delay the disclosure of information are Matt 2:11; 3:9; Luke 8:21; John 1:45; Acts 9:12; 13:23; 15:22; 19:4; Gal 5:14.

Right-dislocations most often provide additional thematic information about a participant, much like overspecification. Consider this epistolary example in which thematic information is added that is not needed to identify which "invisible attributes" Paul is referring to.

Example 230 :: Romans 1:20

τὰ γὰρ ἀόρατα αὐτοῦ ἀπὸ κτίσεως κόσμου τοῖς ποιήμασιν νοούμενα καθορᾶται, ⟨♣ἥ τε ἀΐδιος αὐτοῦ δύναμις καὶ θειότης,♣⟩ εἰς τὸ εἶναι αὐτοὺς ἀναπολογήτους....	For from the creation of the world, his invisible attributes, ⟨♣both his eternal power and deity,♣⟩ are discerned clearly, being understood in the things created, so that they are without excuse....

God's invisible attributes are first generically mentioned, and then they are spelled out in more detail at the end of the clause in the dislocation. This same content could be phrased as follows, thereby eliminating the need for the generic reference:

ἥ γὰρ ἀΐδιος αὐτοῦ δύναμις καὶ θειότης ἀπὸ κτίσεως κόσμου τοῖς ποιήμασιν νοούμενα καθορᾶται ... (modified)

For his eternal power and divine nature, being understood through what has been made since the creation of the world, have been clearly seen ... (NASB, modified)

Eliminating the generic reference eliminates the rhetorical delay of the more specific information. It communicates the same content, but it lacks the rhetorical effect of the canonical version. The same holds true for the following example from Acts.

---

12. Note the back-to-back use of historical present verbs to highlight the speech that follows (see chapter 6).

13. For example, "We have found the one whom Moses wrote about in the law and the prophets. He is Jesus, the son of Joseph from Nazareth."

Example 231 :: Acts 9:17

Ἀπῆλθεν δὲ Ἁνανίας καὶ εἰσῆλθεν εἰς τὴν οἰκίαν καὶ ἐπιθεὶς ἐπ’ αὐτὸν τὰς χεῖρας εἶπεν· Σαοὺλ ἀδελφέ, ὁ κύριος ἀπέσταλκέν με, ⟨♠Ἰησοῦς ὁ ὀφθείς σοι ἐν τῇ ὁδῷ ᾗ ἤρχου,♠⟩ ὅπως ἀναβλέψῃς καὶ πλησθῇς πνεύματος ἁγίου.	So Ananias departed and entered into the house, and placing his hands on him, he said, "Brother Saul, the Lord has sent me, ⟨♠Jesus who appeared to you on the road by which you came,♠⟩ so that you may regain your sight and be filled with the Holy Spirit." [LEB, modified]

It would have been much simpler to state that "Jesus" or the "Lord Jesus" sent him instead of "the Lord … Jesus." It is one thing for Paul to accept that the Lord met him on the road or sent Ananias; it is quite another to accept that the slain leader of the Christians was responsible. Dislocating "Jesus," in combination with overspecification ("the one who appeared …"), creates a much more dramatic introduction of the information, resulting in more attention being drawn to it than a default construction would bring. Other examples of right-dislocations used for thematic highlighting include Acts 27:10; Rom 2:1; Eph 1:10, 12; Phil 3:9.

Right-dislocations can also be used to (re)characterize participants, often where the subject is second person (i.e., "you") and there is no need for an explicit mention. The overspecification lets the reader know how the writer conceived of the participants at that point in the discourse. The expression characterizes the participant in a particular way, ostensibly to better accomplish the writer's communicative goals.

Example 232 :: Galatians 5:4

κατηργήθητε ἀπὸ Χριστοῦ, ⟨♠οἵτινες ἐν νόμῳ δικαιοῦσθε,♠⟩ τῆς χάριτος ἐξεπέσατε.	You are estranged from Christ, ⟨♠you who are attempting to be justified by the law;♠⟩ you have fallen from grace.

The second person is used throughout Galatians to refer to the addressees as a collective group. Paul uses the dislocated information to characterize his hearers in a particular way. It is not needed to disambiguate whom he is addressing. He could have accomplished much the same task by placing the dislocated information in the vocative case. Doing so may have allowed members of the group to potentially exclude themselves. But by addressing all of them and then characterizing them in a particular way, this possibility is virtually eliminated.

The same kind of recharacterization is found in reported speeches within the Gospels.

Example 233 :: Luke 6:24–25

²⁴ Πλὴν οὐαὶ ὑμῖν ‹▲τοῖς πλου-σίοις,▲› ὅτι ἀπέχετε τὴν παράκλησιν ὑμῶν.	²⁴ "But woe to you ‹▲who are rich,▲› because you have received your comfort.
²⁵ οὐαὶ ὑμῖν, ‹▲οἱ ἐμπεπλησμένοι νῦν,▲› ὅτι πεινάσετε. οὐαί, οἱ γελῶντες νῦν, ὅτι πενθήσετε καὶ κλαύσετε.	²⁵ Woe to you ‹▲who are satis-fied now,▲› because you will be hungry. Woe to those who laugh now, because they will mourn and weep."

Notice that in the first two woe statements there is a second-person pronoun, ὑμῖν. The effect of using both the pronoun and the dislocated element is to recharacterize "you" as the ones "who are rich." If the pronoun had been excluded, Jesus could have been understood to be addressing only those who considered themselves rich. Beginning with the pronoun broadens the audience. The second sentence of v. 25 omits the pronoun, focusing the address only on those who laugh now. Just as in the Gal 5:4 example, the redundant pronoun allows all of the hearers to be included as potential addressees before the additional information is provided.

Example 234 :: Romans 8:28

Οἴδαμεν δὲ ὅτι τοῖς ἀγαπῶσιν τὸν θεὸν πάντα συνεργεῖ εἰς ἀγαθόν, ‹▲τοῖς κατὰ πρόθεσιν κλητοῖς οὖσιν.▲›	And we know that all things work together for good for those who love God, ‹▲for those who are called according to his purpose.▲›

Paul states that God works all things together for good for certain people. These people are first identified as those who love God. The dislocated information refers to the same participants, not a separate group. This additional infor-mation provides another way of looking at them. This new characterization highlights a key theme of the passage: how we are to process circumstances that make it appear as though God has abandoned us. Does God really love us? The verse assures us that God works all these things together for good. The dislocation reminds those who love God that they are called according to his purpose. In other words, the recharacterization links the things that we go through to the calling of his purpose in our lives. Loving God necessitates trusting in his calling and purpose.

I move on now to illustrate the use of overspecification for thematic highlighting, for recharacterization, and for point-of-view shifts. This first example, from Romans, comes from a context where Paul has been talking about the differences between Jews and Gentiles. In 2:14 he uses overspecification to highlight particularly important qualities that the Gentiles possess.

Example 235 :: Romans 2:14

ὅταν γὰρ ἔθνη ⟨♟τὰ μὴ νόμον ἔχοντα♟⟩ φύσει τὰ τοῦ νόμου ποιῶσιν, οὗτοι ⟨♟νόμον μὴ ἔχοντες♟⟩ ἑαυτοῖς εἰσιν νόμος·	For whenever the Gentiles, ⟨♟who do not have the law,♟⟩ do by nature the things of the law, these, ⟨♟although they do not have the law,♟⟩ are a law to themselves,

Paul is not interested just in the Gentiles, but in the fact that they "do not have the law." The overspecification reiterates and highlights this important facet. Knowing that they do not have the law is critical to understanding the irony of them doing the things of the law "by nature" and thus being a law "to themselves." There is nothing spectacular about keeping a law that you have, but keeping a law that you do not have is quite a different matter.

In Paul's defense of his gospel in Galatians he uses overspecification to highlight the pedigree of those who examined it.

Example 236 :: Galatians 2:9

καὶ γνόντες τὴν χάριν τὴν δοθεῖσάν μοι, Ἰάκωβος καὶ Κηφᾶς καὶ Ἰωάννης, ⟨♟οἱ δοκοῦντες στῦλοι εἶναι,♟⟩ δεξιὰς ἔδωκαν ἐμοὶ καὶ Βαρναβᾷ κοινωνίας, ἵνα ἡμεῖς εἰς τὰ ἔθνη, αὐτοὶ δὲ εἰς τὴν περιτομήν·	and when James and Cephas and John—⟨♟those thought to be pillars♟⟩—acknowledged the grace given to me, they gave to me and Barnabas the right hand of fellowship, in order that we should go to the Gentiles and they to the circumcision.

He does not just settle for name-dropping in regard to James, Cephas, and John; he explicitly calls to mind their standing in the Christian community to bolster his claim that follows: they added nothing to his gospel. Later in the letter, Paul again utilizes overspecification to recharacterize the Galatians in a way that expresses his frustration with them for regressing into old patterns of reliance upon the law.

Example 237 :: Galatians 4:19

¹⁸ But it is good to be sought zealously in good at all times, and not only when I am present with you.

¹⁹ τέκνα μου, ‹♟οὓς πάλιν ὠδίνω μέχρις οὗ μορφωθῇ Χριστὸς ἐν ὑμῖν....♟›	¹⁹ My children, ‹♟for whom I am having birth pains again, until Christ is formed in you...!♟›

²⁰ But I could wish to be present with you now, and to change my tone because I am perplexed about you.

Verse 19 serves to punctuate the remarks of v. 18, communicating how Paul views the addressees at that point in time. He expresses warmth, but he also shows frustration regarding the need to be in anguish "again." Such things should happen only once, if at all. This characterization of the Galatians fits with his comment in v. 20 that he is perplexed about them. Verse 19 was not needed to identify whom Paul was addressing. Instead, it allows the writer to communicate his view of the situation by recharacterizing the addressees in a particular way. In this case, Paul repeats something that should need to be done only once.

In Ephesians, Paul uses overspecification to reiterate important thematic information as he compares specific aspects of the old life with the new one. The overspecification provides the information right at the point that it is pertinent.

Example 238 :: Ephesians 4:22–24

²⁰ But you did not learn Christ in this way, ²¹ if indeed you have heard about him, and you were taught by him (just as truth is in Jesus),

²² ἀποθέσθαι ὑμᾶς κατὰ τὴν προτέραν ἀναστροφὴν τὸν παλαιὸν ἄνθρωπον ‹♟τὸν φθειρόμενον κατὰ τὰς ἐπιθυμίας τῆς ἀπάτης,♟›	²² that you take off, according to your former way of life, the old man, ‹♟who is being destroyed according to deceitful desires,♟›
²³ ἀνανεοῦσθαι δὲ τῷ πνεύματι τοῦ νοὸς ὑμῶν	²³ be renewed in the spirit of your mind,
²⁴ καὶ ἐνδύσασθαι τὸν καινὸν ἄνθρωπον ‹♟τὸν κατὰ θεὸν	²⁴ and put on the new man, ‹♟who (in accordance with God)

| κτισθέντα ἐν δικαιοσύνῃ καὶ ὁσιότητι τῆς ἀληθείας.♟› | is created in righteousness and holiness from the truth.♟› |

Paul does not leave the idea of the "old" man without explanation, even though its connection to their former way of life is well established. The overspecification elaborates on exactly what the old life entailed, things that may have faded or been distorted in the Ephesians' memory. The description paints a picture of destruction.

Paul also provides a parallel description of the "new" man, contrasting the deceitful desires with being created in the righteousness and holiness of truth. The picture of what is meant by the "new" man is already clear from the description of the renewing of the mind in v. 23.

Most English translations render the overspecification as a relative "which" clause. An em-dash might better capture the appositional insertion of this information. Here is a modification of the ESV:

> to put off your old self—the one belonging to your former manner of life and is corrupt through deceitful desires—and to be renewed.…

In both v. 22 and v. 24, overspecification contributes significant thematic information to the context by shaping the way the reader thinks about the overspecified entity. The choice to include the extra information is evidence of the writer's intention to have the reader think about a particular thing in a particular way in a particular context, based on his overall communication objectives.

The next example is the transition verse from looking at individual aspects of the human body to looking at the collective implications for the body, an illustration of how members within the body of Christ should work together.

Example 239 :: 1 Corinthians 12:18

| νυνὶ δὲ ὁ θεὸς ἔθετο τὰ μέλη, ‹♟ἐν ἕκαστον αὐτῶν♟› ἐν τῷ σώματι καθὼς ἠθέλησεν. | But now God has placed the members, ‹♟each one of them,♟› in the body just as he wanted. |

Paul maintains a careful balance between considering the collective whole and the individual part throughout the illustration. One of the key points is that each part, no matter how insignificant it may seem, is to be valued and esteemed (see vv. 22–23). Calling them the "members" views things more from the standpoint of the collective whole rather than the individual parts. The overspecification balances this by looking at "each one of them," highlighting the individual side of the issue. Overspecification plays a significant thematic role in Paul's call for unity within the whole, but not at the cost of disrespecting the special role that each part plays.

The next example contains a series of points that spell out what is practically meant by "not at all."

Example 240 :: Matthew 5:34–36

³⁴ ἐγὼ δὲ λέγω ὑμῖν μὴ ὀμόσαι ὅλως·	³⁴ "But I say to you, do not swear at all,
⟨♦μήτε ἐν τῷ οὐρανῷ,♦⟩ ὅτι θρόνος ἐστὶν τοῦ θεοῦ,	⟨♦either by heaven,♦⟩ because it is the throne of God,
³⁵ ⟨♦μήτε ἐν τῇ γῇ,♦⟩ ὅτι ὑποπόδιόν ἐστιν τῶν ποδῶν αὐτοῦ,	³⁵ ⟨♦or by the earth,♦⟩ because it is the footstool of his feet,
⟨♦μήτε εἰς Ἱεροσόλυμα,♦⟩ ὅτι πόλις ἐστὶν τοῦ μεγάλου βασιλέως,	⟨♦or by Jerusalem,♦⟩ because it is the city of the great king.
³⁶ ⟨♦μήτε ἐν τῇ κεφαλῇ σου ὀμόσῃς,♦⟩ ὅτι οὐ δύνασαι μίαν τρίχα λευκὴν ποιῆσαι ἢ μέλαιναν.	³⁶ ⟨♦And do not [swear] by your head,♦⟩ because you are not able to make one hair white or black."

³⁷ "But let your statement be 'Yes, yes; no, no,' and anything beyond these is from the evil one."

The initial command of v. 34 forbids swearing oaths "at all" to confirm testimony. Jesus' solution is that you simply tell the truth and thereby avoid placing yourself in a position where people doubt your testimony. He elaborates on what is intended by ὅλως through a series of right-dislocations in vv. 34b–35. Each one lists a potential object by which one might swear, along with a rationale for not doing so. None of these constructions contains a verb, and thus they are dependent upon v. 34a for the verbal idea. Verse 36 supplies a verb, implying that this clause is not as tightly dependent upon v. 34a as the verbless ones. Verse 36 marks a shift from external physical structures that are not under one's authority to one's own body. Even this, Jesus contends, is beyond our control. Verse 36 also completes the list of negated potential options before the positive alternative is presented in v. 37.

The final example illustrates the role that overspecification can play in understanding the function of seemingly redundant words. They may play only a small role, but it is a role nonetheless.

Example 241 :: Mark 1:20

> [19] And going on a little farther, he saw James the son of Zebedee and his brother John, and they were in the boat mending the nets.

[20] καὶ εὐθὺς ἐκάλεσεν αὐτούς. καὶ ἀφέντες ⟨♣τὸν πατέρα αὐτῶν♣⟩ Ζεβεδαῖον ἐν τῷ πλοίῳ μετὰ τῶν μισθωτῶν ἀπῆλθον ὀπίσω αὐτοῦ.	[20] And immediately he called them, and they left ⟨♣their father♣⟩ Zebedee in the boat with the hired men and went away after him.

When James and John were first introduced in v. 19, they were anchored to the discourse as the "son(s) of Zebedee," even though Zebedee had not previously been mentioned. John is also anchored to James as "his brother." Anchoring the sons to Zebedee leaves open the possibility that Zebedee is the central participant. Instead, his sons are anchored to him rather than the other way around. The overspecification in v. 20 updates the anchoring relations of the participants. We know the relationships that these men have with one another, so "their father" must be accomplishing some other task besides disambiguating which Zebedee is being referred to. The overspecification makes an explicit shift away from the expected center of attention, Zebedee, to James and John, since Zebedee is now anchored to the discourse as "their father." The overspecification directs readers to update their mental representation of the discourse by making this adjustment. The narrative continues by following James and John as they follow Jesus, leaving "their father" behind with the hired men.

Summary

This chapter has discussed the role that redundant information can play in shaping and influencing how we process discourse. Anchoring relations can have the effect of indicating or changing the current center of attention. Thematic information can have the effect of recharacterizing how the reader views the participant.

Suggested Reading

Berlin, Adele. *Poetics and Interpretation of Biblical Narrative.* 23–110.

Runge, Steven E. "A Discourse-Functional Description of Participant Reference in Biblical Hebrew Narrative," 179–218.

———. "Pragmatic Effects of Semantically Redundant Referring Expressions in Biblical Hebrew Narrative."

16 THEMATIC ADDITION

This chapter describes the use of optional adverbial modifiers to attract extra attention to parallel elements in the discourse. Consider the difference that adding "also" or "even" makes in strengthening the connections between the following clauses.

Example 242

> She finished eating her dinner. She ate her vegetables.
> She finished eating her dinner. She *even* ate her vegetables.
>
> Bill worked on his car. Jim worked on his car.
> Bill worked on his car. Jim *also* worked on his car.
>
> I worked in the yard today. I went fishing.
> I worked in the yard today. I *also* went fishing/I went fishing *too*.

Each of these sentences shares a common element. The same subject does a related action in (a), different subjects do the same action in (b), and the same subject does a different action in (c). The sentences with the italicized adverbs share a stronger connection than their counterparts. The adverb constrains the reader to look for some corresponding element from the preceding context that relates to a counterpart in the current clause. The two elements are somehow parallel to one another, and the parallelism is present with or without the adverb.

When a writer wants to strengthen connections between two related elements, particularly if they are separated by one or more clauses, adverbs can provide an explicit link between the two. The "additive" adverb effectively signals the reader to connect what follows to the appropriate counterpart in the preceding context. This addition is generally thematically motivated, explicitly highlighting an important connection that would only have been implicit. This process of connecting thematically related elements I will call *thematic addition*.

16.1   Conventional Explanation

Thematic addition is traditionally identified as the adverbial or ascensive use of conjunctions. Wallace describes these conjunctions as expressing "a *final addition* or *point of focus*. It is often translated *even*."[1] He classifies the use of καί translated as "also" as "adjunctive" or "emphatic," which "*connects an additional element* to a discussion or adds an additional idea to the train of thought."[2] BDF provides a similar description, though apparently correlating the emphasis expressed by καί to the verb as opposed to other clause components.[3] Robertson also refers to this as adjunctive usage—that is, "addition to something already mentioned"[4]—adding that "it may refer to a word or a clause."[5]

BDAG describes the adverbial use of καί as a "marker to indicate an additive relation that is not coordinate to connect clauses and sentences, *also, likewise,* funct[ioning] as an adv."[6] BDAG claims an intensive function associated with the English gloss *even*. Robertson labels this as ascensive use, saying, "The notion of 'even' is an advance on that of mere addition which is due to the context, not to καί. The thing that is added is out of the ordinary and rises to a climax like the crescendo in music."[7]

The traditional explanations rightly recognize the addition quality of adverbial καί. The grammarians also recognize that at times the usage attracts extra attention to the added or intensified element, hence the emphatic appellation.

---

1. Daniel B. Wallace, *Greek Grammar beyond the Basics: An Exegetical Syntax of the New Testament* (Grand Rapids: Zondervan, 1999), 670.

2. Ibid., 671.

3. "Διὰ τοῦτο καί is so fixed a phrase that καί can even be separated from the verb which it emphasizes: 1 Th 2:13 διὰ τ. καὶ ἡμεῖς εὐχαριστοῦμεν, 3:5 διὰ τ. κἀγὼ μηκέτι στέγων ἔπεμψα" (BDF §442[12]).

4. A. T. Robertson, *A Grammar of the Greek New Testament in the Light of Historical Research* (1919; repr., Bellingham, Wash.: Logos, 2006), 1180.

5. Ibid., 1181.

6. BDAG, 495.

7. Robertson, *Grammar*, 1181.

16.2   Discourse Explanation

BDAG's description of καί as an additive marker captures well its basic function and forms the point of departure for the explanation that follows. The traditional classification of adverbial καί largely centers on the two English additives *also* and *even*. Both particles involve addition to something, but they add to different things. From a linguistic standpoint, additives such as *also* or *too* are used "to encourage a search for parallelisms."[8] *Even* serves a distinctly different purpose.

The use of an additive signals the reader to look for some corresponding element in the context. The additive καί precedes the added element in both Greek and English. The parallelism between the two elements would have existed without the additive, but omitting the additive increases the likelihood that the intended relation would be overlooked.

Where one element corresponds to a parallel one in the preceding context, the use of an additive such as *also* makes the parallelism explicit, attracting extra attention to it. The parallels can be between predicates, where different subjects or objects are involved in the same action, as in example 243 (a repeat of example 207).

Example 243 :: Romans 8:30

[LDοὓς δὲ προώρισεν,LD] [TPτού-τους TP] ⟨+καὶ ἐκάλεσεν·+⟩	And [LDthose whom he predestined,LD] [TPthese TP] ⟨+he also called,+⟩
καὶ [LDοὓς ἐκάλεσεν,LD] [TPτού-τους TP] ⟨+καὶ ἐδικαίωσεν·+⟩	and [LDthose whom he called,LD] [TPthese TP] ⟨+he also justified,+⟩
[LDοὓς δὲ ἐδικαίωσεν,LD] [TPτού-τους TP] ⟨+καὶ ἐδόξασεν.+⟩	and [LDthose whom he justified,LD] [TPthese TP] ⟨+he also glorified.+⟩

The subject "God" and the direct objects "those whom he loves/whom he has called according to his purpose" from v. 28 remain the same in v. 30. What changes is the action that God performs: calling, justifying, and glorifying. These same propositions likely would have been correlated without the addi-

---

8. Regina Blass, *Relevance Relations in Discourse: A Study with Special Reference to Sissala* (CSL 55; Cambridge: Cambridge University Press, 1990), 145, cited in Stephen H. Levinsohn, *Self-instruction Materials on Narrative Discourse Analysis* (Dallas: SIL International, 2007), 87.

tive καί. However, omitting the adverb would have significantly weakened the parallelism, leaving it implicit rather than explicit.

The syntax of the clauses in v. 30 is parallel, with each clause using a left-dislocation. The structure alone suggests a parallel relationship, but the additive makes it much more pronounced. The additive also marks which clause element is to be added, the verbs in this case. The emphasis on the verbs is based on the information structure of the clauses, not an emphatic use of καί. Just as frames of reference do not create contrast but simply highlight the contrast already present, the use of the additive attracts extra attention to the parallelism or prominence already present in the context. The verbs are the focal information in each clause.

Additives can also be used to highlight parallelism in contexts where the predicate remains the same, but the subject or object changes.

Example 244 :: John 14:7

[CEἐγνώκατέ με,CE] ⟨+καὶ τὸν πατέρα μου+⟩ γνώσεσθε. καὶ ἀπ᾽ ἄρτι γινώσκετε αὐτὸν καὶ ἑωράκατε αὐτόν.	[CE"If you have known me,CE] you will know ⟨+my Father also.+⟩ And from now on you know him and have seen him."

The predicate "to know" and the subject "you" are the same in the conditional frame and in the main clause of v. 7. The element that changes is the person who is known. The additive here strengthens the connection between Jesus and his Father. The conditional frame provides the basis for the connection by setting the stage for the change in the main clause. "If you have known me, some corresponding thing would also happen." The additive is not required here. It constrains the reader to look for some kind of parallel in the context. These examples illustrate the primary function of additives: constraining readers to search for a parallel element that shares some relation with the added element.

A second function of additives is to confirm some previous proposition or assumption.[9] This is the function associated with the English additives *even* and *indeed*. In Greek, the additive καί signals both constraints: parallelism and confirmation. In the next example, from Gal 2, Paul has been told by the apostles to do the same thing he was eager to do: remember the poor.

---

9. Stephen H. Levinsohn, *Discourse Features of New Testament Greek: A Coursebook on the Information Structure of New Testament Greek* (2nd ed.; Dallas: SIL International), 100.

Example 245 :: Galatians 2:10

[TPμόνον τῶν πτωχῶν^TP] ἵνα μνη-   They asked only that we should
μονεύωμεν, ὃ ⟨**+**καὶ ἐσπούδασα**+**⟩   [TPremember the poor,^TP] **the very**
αὐτὸ τοῦτο ποιῆσαι.   **thing** ⟨**+**I was also eager**+**⟩ to do.

The intensive use of αὐτός is captured in "the very thing," though the demonstrative is not translated. The thematic addition has the effect of confirming what he has been asked to do. He was not just willing to do this very thing, he was even eager to do it. Simply stating that he was eager to do it, without the use of an additive, would significantly weaken Paul's claim.

Another common form of confirmation found in the NT is what Levinsohn calls "confirmation by adding the least likely possibility."[10] The idea here is not just to confirm a concept, but to take the most unlikely extreme of that concept in order to confirm it.

Example 246 :: Philippians 3:8

[7] But whatever things were gain to me, these things I have considered loss because of Christ.

[8] ἀλλὰ μενοῦνγε ⟨**+**καὶ ἡγοῦμαι   [8] More than that, ⟨**+**I even consider
πάντα **ζημίαν** εἶναι**+**⟩ διὰ τὸ   all things to be loss**+**⟩ because of
ὑπερέχον τῆς γνώσεως Χριστοῦ   the surpassing greatness of the
Ἰησοῦ τοῦ κυρίου μου, δι' ὃν τὰ   knowledge of Christ Jesus my Lord,
πάντα ἐζημιώθην, καὶ ἡγοῦμαι   for the sake of whom I have suffered
σκύβαλα, ἵνα Χριστὸν κερδήσω....   the loss of all things, and consider
                                    them dung, in order that I may gain
                                    Christ....

I noted in chapter 4, on point/counterpoint sets, that this section of Phil 3 essentially builds to a crescendo, with thematic addition playing an important role in v. 8. In vv. 4–6, Paul lists things that he could be considered to be of great worth. In v. 7, he states that these potentially noteworthy things he considers to be loss. Thematic addition confirms this by taking a "least likely possibility" to confirm the value he places on knowing Christ. He does not just consider his pedigree to be loss; he even considers "all things" loss. In the final sentence of v. 8, he even goes one step further, considering them "dung" instead of just "loss."

---

10. Levinsohn, *Narrative Discourse Analysis*, 89.

Additives accomplish two primary tasks: they encourage a search for parallels, or they confirm some previous proposition or assumption. The next section provides more examples of these two functions, focusing on the exegetical role that thematic addition plays in the context.

16.3   Application

The first examples in this section focus on the use of thematic addition to highlight existing parallels. John 12:10 uses a standard rhetorical "not only ... but also ..." construction. The additive supplies the "also" part, strengthening the connection of the point back to the counterpoint.

Example 247 :: John 12:9–10

⁹Ἔγνω οὖν [ὁ] ὄχλος πολὺς ἐκ τῶν Ἰουδαίων ὅτι ἐκεῖ ἐστιν καὶ ⟨✗ἦλθον οὐ διὰ τὸν Ἰησοῦν μόνον,✗⟩ ἀλλ'⟨√ἵνα ⟨+καὶ τὸν Λάζαρον+⟩ ἴδωσιν ὃν ἤγειρεν ἐκ νεκρῶν.√⟩

⁹ Now the large crowd of Jews found out that he was there, and ⟨✗they came, not only because of Jesus,✗⟩ but ⟨√so that they could see ⟨+Lazarus also,+⟩ whom he raised from the dead.√⟩

¹⁰ ἐβουλεύσαντο δὲ οἱ ἀρχιερεῖς ἵνα ⟨+καὶ τὸν Λάζαρον+⟩ ἀποκτείνωσιν....

¹⁰ So the chief priests decided that they would kill ⟨+Lazarus also....+⟩

There are two different parallels established in this context, both between Jesus and Lazarus. The first parallel, in v. 9, concerns why the large crowd of Jews came. The subject and the action "came" remains the same. The two reasons why they came are placed in parallel. It was not just because of Jesus, but also to see Lazarus, because of his resurrection from the dead. Establishing this parallel sets the stage for the next parallel, drawn in v. 10. There was mention of a plot by the chief priests to put Jesus to death in John 11:47–52. Verse 10 connects back to this plot, adding Lazarus to the hit list alongside Jesus. Thematic addition constrains the reader to view the decision to kill Lazarus not in isolation, but as parallel to the decision to do the same thing to Jesus. The use of the additives in vv. 9 and 10 provides important thematic linkage between Jesus and Lazarus.

In the next example, the subject and the action again remain the same. The object is changed and placed in parallel with a corresponding element from a different clause.

Example 248 :: Matthew 5:39, 40

³⁹ ἐγὼ δὲ λέγω ὑμῖν ‹✗μὴ ἀντιστῆ-
ναι τῷ πονηρῷ·✗› ἀλλ' ‹✔ὅστις
σε ῥαπίζει εἰς τὴν δεξιὰν σιαγόνα
[σου], στρέψον αὐτῷ ‹✚καὶ τὴν
ἄλλην·✚›✔›

³⁹ "But I say to you, ‹✗do not resist
the evildoer,✗› but ‹✔whoever
strikes you on your right cheek,
turn ‹✚ also the other✚› to him.✔›

⁴⁰ καὶ ‹✔τῷ θέλοντί σοι κριθῆναι
καὶ τὸν χιτῶνά σου λαβεῖν, ἄφες
αὐτῷ ‹✚καὶ τὸ ἱμάτιον·✚›✔›

⁴⁰ And ‹✔the one who wants to go
to court with you and take your
tunic, let him have ‹✚your outer
garment also."✚›✔›

Jesus' instructions involve offering a second parallel element after a first one
has been mentioned. The connection would have existed without the thematic
additive, based on the parallels between "the right cheek/the other" and "your
tunic/the outer garment." The pronoun ἄλλην agrees in case and number
with σιαγόνα, making a very clear connection even without καί. The relation
between the two kinds of garments is not as explicit, yet it is clear enough
to be understood without an additive. Thematic addition has the pragmatic
effect of strengthening the connection that already existed, constraining the
reader to search for a parallel. A similar example usage is found in Matt 18:33.

Romans 5 mentions boasting and rejoicing several times, building one
upon another. The repetition of the verb καυχάομαι creates an implicit connection. The rhetorical use of οὐ μόνον δέ also has the effect of strengthening
the connection back to the previous mentions of boasting in vv. 2 and 3.

Example 249 :: Romans 5:11

¹ Therefore, because we have been declared righteous by faith, we have
peace with God through our Lord Jesus Christ, ² through whom also
we have obtained access by faith into this grace in which we stand, and
we boast in the hope of the glory of God. ³ And not only this, but ‹✚we
also boast✚› in our afflictions, because we know that affliction pro-
duces patient endurance, ⁴ and patient endurance, proven character,
and proven character, hope, ⁵ and hope does not disappoint, because
the love of God has been poured out in our hearts through the Holy
Spirit who was given to us....

¹¹ οὐ μόνον δέ, ἀλλὰ ‹✚καὶ
καυχώμενοι✚› ἐν τῷ θεῷ διὰ τοῦ
κυρίου ἡμῶν Ἰησοῦ Χριστοῦ δι' οὗ

¹¹ And not only this, but ‹✚also
we are boasting✚› in God through
our Lord Jesus Christ, through

νῦν τὴν καταλλαγὴν ἐλάβομεν.   whom we have now received the
                                       reconciliation.

There is a transition in v. 6 away from the development of the argument to
supporting material that strengthens the claims of vv. 3–5. The use of thematic
addition in v. 11 constrains the repetition of the lemma καυχάομαι to be connected to a parallel element in the preceding context, ensuring that the reader
recognizes the return to the main argument. The use of οὐ μόνον δέ also signals a link back to some corresponding element in the preceding context, just
as in v. 3. Thematic addition provides a signpost in v. 11, helping the reader
organize the argument in a manner consistent with Paul's intention.

   Galatians 5 closes with an admonition to walk by the Spirit. Verse 16
states that if we walk by the Spirit, we will not carry out the desires of the
flesh. Verse 25 states that if we live by the Spirit, we must also walk or follow
the Spirit. The implication is that doing so will enable us to avoid becoming
conceited (v. 26), provoking and envying one another. Walking in the Spirit
is the primary way to avoid becoming caught up in sin. Chapter 6 opens by
addressing a "what if" question.

Example 250 :: Galatians 6:1

Ἀδελφοί, [CEἐὰν ‹καὶ +προ-   Brothers, [CEeven if a person ‹+is
λημφθῇ+› ἄνθρωπος ἔν τινι   caught+› in some trespass,CE]
παραπτώματι,CE] ὑμεῖς οἱ πνευ-   you who are spiritual restore such
ματικοὶ καταρτίζετε τὸν τοι-   a person in a spirit of humil-
οῦτον ἐν πνεύματι πραΰτητος,   ity, looking out for yourself, lest
σκοπῶν σεαυτὸν μὴ ‹+καὶ σὺ+›   ‹+you also+› be tempted.
πειρασθῇς.

Thematic addition at the beginning of v. 1 constrains the reader to search for
an intended parallel in the preceding context. Chapter 5 closed by highlighting the strategies for avoiding sin. Chapter 6 opens with what to do if you do
not avoid sin and even are caught in it. The additive here provides a link back
to the previous chapter, even though it begins a new pericope. The parallel is
between the actions of avoiding sin/the flesh and being caught in sin.

   The verse closes with a warning to those doing the restoration, lest they
too be tempted just like the individual caught in the trespass whom they
are trying to restore. The command to restore is in the plural (καταρτίζετε),
addressed to "the spiritual ones" (οἱ πνευματικοὶ). By shifting to the singular
in the exhortation to watch out for being tempted (σκοπῶν σεαυτὸν μὴ καὶ

σὺ πειρασθῇς), the writer personalizes the warning, perhaps suggesting that one is more prone to be tempted when doing the restoring alone versus with other spiritual ones. The connection between the sinner and the one restoring is clear enough from the context. The use of thematic addition makes this implicit connection explicit, as does structuring μὴ καὶ σύ to place emphasis on the element that is already highlighted using the additive.

The next series of examples illustrates the use of thematic addition to confirm a previous proposition. This often involves adding the least likely possibility to the proposition that is highlighted, as in this example from Eph 5.

Example 251 :: Ephesians 5:11–12

¹¹ καὶ ‹✗μὴ συγκοινωνεῖτε τοῖς ἔργοις τοῖς ἀκάρποις τοῦ σκότους,✗› ‹✓μᾶλλον δὲ ‹✚καὶ ἐλέγχετε.✚›✓›	¹¹ And ‹✗do not participate in the unfruitful deeds of darkness,✗› but ‹✓rather ‹✚even expose them.✚›✓›
¹² [ᵀᴾτὰ γὰρ κρυφῇ γινόμενα ὑπ' αὐτῶνᵀᴾ] αἰσχρόν ἐστιν ‹✚καὶ λέγειν.…✚›	¹² For **it is shameful** ‹✚even to speak✚› about [ᵀᴾthe things being done by them in secret.…ᵀᴾ]

Both instances of thematic addition in this passage take the established proposition and confirm it by taking an unlikely possibility as the preferred course of action. Verse 11 forbids participating in the deeds of darkness. Instead of merely avoiding participation, v. 11b confirms this by citing one of the least likely alternatives to participation. The deeds are to be exposed instead of participated in. Another unlikely alternative to participating in these deeds is provided in v. 12. It is shameful not only to do them, but also even to speak of them. Thematic addition here is not constraining the reader to search for a parallel. Instead, it confirms the preceding proposition by highlighting an unlikely extreme of the proposition.

There are two instances in the story recounting Peter's threefold denial of Jesus where thematic addition is used to highlight an established proposition or assumption by describing the least likely form of that action.

Example 252 :: Matthew 26:35

³⁴ Jesus said to him, "Truly I say to you that during this night, before the rooster crows, you will deny me three times!"

³⁵ ‹⊙λέγει⊙› αὐτῷ ὁ Πέτρος· ‹✚κἂν δέῃ με σὺν	³⁵ Peter ‹⊙said⊙› to him, ‹✚"Even if it is necessary for me to die with

σοὶ ἀποθανεῖν,+⟩ οὐ μή σε   you,+⟩ I will never deny you!"
ἀπαρνήσομαι. ὁμοίως καὶ   And ⟨+all the disciples+⟩ said the
⟨+πάντες οἱ μαθηταὶ+⟩ εἶπαν.   same thing.

In Peter's affirmation of his allegiance, he first states in v. 33 that even if everyone else fell away, he would not. Jesus contradicts this claim in v. 34, saying
that Peter will deny him three times before the cock crows. Peter confirms
his previous pledge by creating an even more extreme oath in v. 35: not only
would he stand fast with Jesus, he would even be willing to die with him. Thematic addition at the end of v. 35 draws a parallel between Peter's claim and all
the rest of the disciples.[11] Dying for someone represents what has been called
the ultimate sacrifice. This extreme claim lays the foundation for Peter's tragic
desertion later in the chapter.

As Peter avoids being associated with Jesus, people begin to recognize the
similarities between Peter and Jesus' followers.

Example 253 :: Matthew 26:73

μετὰ μικρὸν δὲ προσελθόντες οἱ   And after a little while those who
ἑστῶτες εἶπον τῷ Πέτρῳ· ἀληθῶς   were standing there came up and
⟨+καὶ σὺ+⟩ ἐξ αὐτῶν εἶ, ⟨+καὶ γὰρ   said to Peter, "⟨+You+⟩ really are
ἡ λαλιά σου+⟩ δῆλόν σε ποιεῖ.   one of them also, because ⟨+even
                                     your accent+⟩ reveals who you are."

In 26:69, 71, slave girls accuse Peter of being a follower of Jesus, which Peter
denies in both cases. The people know that Jesus had followers, and in v .73b
they connect Peter to them. Thematic addition in καὶ σύ constrains the reader
to search for a parallel. The people are so sure that Peter bears the marks of
a follower that they confirm this by describing how even his accent matches
what is expected. This unlikely detail serves as confirmation that Peter is lying
to the people. The correlations move far beyond mere coincidence, and the
thematic addition drives this point home in the form of confirmation.

In the section of his epistle where James questions the value of faith that
is not evidenced by works, he uses the demons as an example of how believing
the right thing without acting on it is not as noble as it sounds.

---

11. Even though "also all the disciples" does not really work in translation, modifiers
such as *rest of* and *other* can create a similar link back to some corresponding element.
Remember, it is the thematic connection that is important, not the specific word used to
reflect it.

Example 254 :: James 2:19

σὺ πιστεύεις ὅτι εἷς ἐστιν ὁ θεός, καλῶς ποιεῖς· ‹+καὶ τὰ δαιμό-νια+› πιστεύουσιν καὶ φρίσσουσιν.	You believe that God is one; you do well. ‹+Even the demons+› believe, and shudder!

After affirming the reader's belief that "God is one" is a good thing, he mini-mizes its goodness by showing who else holds this belief. Even the demons hold this belief, but it will do them little good in the final judgment. James ironically confirms the value of claiming that God is one by showing that even the most unlikely beings also hold to this truth. This confirmation using the-matic addition reinforces James's argument that faith without works is useless (see v. 20).

Sarcastic confirmation achieved through thematic addition is also used by Jesus. He minimizes a potential claim by showing that even those consid-ered unrighteous do as much. By showing that even the most unlikely sinner does the same action, he undercuts any potential claim for self-righteousness.

Example 255 :: Matthew 5:46–47

[46] [CEἐὰν γὰρ ἀγαπήσητε τοὺς ἀγαπῶντας ὑμᾶς,CE] τίνα μισθὸν ἔχετε; οὐχὶ ‹+καὶ οἱ τελῶναι+› τὸ αὐτὸ ποιοῦσιν;	[46] "For [CEif you love those who love you,CE] what reward do you have? Do not the ‹+tax collectors also+› do the same?
[47] καὶ [CEἐὰν ἀσπάσησθε τοὺς ἀδελφοὺς ὑμῶν μόνον,CE] τί περισσὸν ποιεῖτε; οὐχὶ ‹+καὶ οἱ ἐθνικοὶ+› τὸ αὐτὸ ποιοῦσιν;	[47] And [CEif you greet only your brothers,CE] what are you doing that is remarkable? Do not ‹+the Gentiles also+› do the same?"

In v. 44, Jesus commands his listeners to love their enemies and to pray for their persecutors. In vv. 46–47, he addresses potential reasons why some might think that they are already righteous enough. Claiming to love those who love you might sound like a noble thing at first. However, if even tax collectors—the least likely group one might expect to perform acts of righ-teousness—do this action, it significantly waters down the potential value for demonstrating one's own righteousness. The intensive use of αὐτός further strengthens the parallel by highlighting that it is the same activity, not some lesser form of it.

The same holds true for greeting your brothers. If even the Gentiles do the same thing, how special does it make you? Jesus uses a most unlikely can-didate to confirm how little merit these actions really have. This has the effect of bolstering his claim that loving one's enemies is what is truly noteworthy. Praying for your persecutors is what is noble, not just greeting those who are close to you.

Suggested Reading

Blass, F., A. Debrunner, and R. W. Funk. *A Greek Grammar of the New Testament and Other Early Christian Literature.* §442(12).

Blass, Regina. *Relevance Relations in Discourse: A Study with Special Reference to Sissala.* 134–60.

Heckert, Jacob K. *Discourse Function of Conjoiners in the Pastoral Epistles.* 58–70

Levinsohn, Stephen H. *Self-instruction Materials on Narrative Discourse Analysis.* 87–91.

———. "Towards a Typology of Additives."

Robertson, A. T. *A Grammar of the Greek New Testament in the Light of Historical Research.* 1180–81.

Wallace, Daniel B. *Greek Grammar beyond the Basics: An Exegetical Syntax of the New Testament.* 670–71.

CHANGED REFERENCE AND THEMATIC ADDRESS

This chapter considers the discourse function of what amounts to thematically motivated name calling in the NT. The expression used to refer to a participant when he or she is first introduced will typically be used for subsequent references when something more than a pronoun is needed (e.g., a proper name "Paul" or an epithet "his servant"). This consistency in usage helps avoid confusion about to whom the writer is referring.

In spite of this tendency, there are many times in the NT where this basic expectation is violated. Sometimes Jesus is called "Jesus," elsewhere he is referred to as "rabbi," "Lord," "the child," even "son of David." Sometimes Paul addresses the Galatians as "brothers," more often simply as "you," and once as "you foolish Galatians." Vocatives and nominatives of address often play a thematic role in discourse. Changes of reference and thematic forms of address have exegetical significance. Although they are different grammatical phenomena, they rely upon the same principles to achieve comparable pragmatic effects. For this reason, both concepts are covered together in this chapter. Changed references are identified in the examples by *italics*, and thematic forms of address are bracketed by the ✠ symbol.

17.1   Conventional Explanation

The marked use of vocative and nominative expressions of address has not received much attention from Greek grammarians. Conventional wisdom says that these forms of address serve to unambiguously identify the intended addressees. Wallace states, "The vocative is the case used for addressing someone or, on occasion, for uttering exclamations."[1] The marked uses that

---

1. Daniel B. Wallace, *Greek Grammar beyond the Basics: An Exegetical Syntax of the*

are not needed to identify the addressee are often described as an "epistolary convention" to be studied within form criticism. Recall from chapter 5,
on metacomments, that scholars correlated the use of certain NT discourse
devices to their use in letters and epistles. The devices are considered to be
formulas that accomplish specific tasks within a letter. The same kinds of correlations are made regarding thematic address.

Consider the following excerpts from Longenecker's commentary on
Galatians. The description of the literary form is provided in parentheses, followed by the relevant excerpt from the verse.

> A close analysis of Galatians produces the following list of phrases that by
> comparison with those of the nonliterary papyri should probably be judged
> to be based on rather conventional epistolary formulae:

1:1–2	(*salutation*): Παῦλος … ταῖς ἐκκλησίαις τῆς Γαλατίας, "Paul … to the churches of Galatia"
1:3	(*greeting*): Χάρις ὑμῖν καὶ εἰρήνη, "grace and peace to you"
1:6	(*rebuke formula*): θαυμάζω ὅτι, "I am astonished that"
1:9	(*reminder of past teaching*): ὡς προειρήκαμεν, καὶ ἄρτι πάλιν λέγω, "as we have said before, so now I say again"
1:11	(*disclosure formula*): γνωρίζω δὲ ὑμῖν, "I want you to know"
1:13	(*disclosure formula*): ἠκούσατε γάρ, "for you have heard"
3:1	(*vocative-rebuke*): ὦ ἀνόητοι Γαλάται, "you foolish Galatians"
3:2	(*verb of hearing*): τοῦτο μόνον θέλω μαθεῖν ἀφ᾽ ὑμῶν, "only this I want to learn from you"
3:7	(*disclosure formula*): γινώσκετε ἄρα ὅτι, "you know then"
3:15	(*vocative-verb of saying*): ἀδελφοί … λέγω, "brothers, … let me take an example"[2]

Chapter 5 described the function of things like disclosure formulas from
the perspective of discourse and demonstrated that their use is not restricted
to the Epistles. I concluded that they are better viewed as metacomments
based on their function and distribution outside the Epistles.

New Testament (Grand Rapids: Zondervan, 1999), 65. Cf. Stanley E. Porter, *Idioms of the
Greek New Testament* (2nd ed.; Sheffield: Sheffield Academic, 1999), 87–88.

2. Richard N. Longenecker, *Galatians* (WBC 41; Dallas: Word, 1990), cvii.

Chapter 15 showed how overly specific descriptions of participants in texts such as the salutation of Gal 1:1–2 have the effect of characterizing the participants in a particular way, based on the writer's objectives. If more information is provided than is needed to identify "who is doing what to whom," it typically has the effect of (re)shaping how readers think about the participant. It constrains them to make adjustments in their mental representation. The same principles apply to overspecified expressions of address in contexts where the addressee is already clearly identified.

Notice above how the vocative of address in Gal 3:1 is labeled by Longenecker: a "vocative of rebuke." It is well established in the context that Paul is speaking to the Galatians as opposed to some other group. This means that the vocative is not semantically required in this context. It must therefore be doing something other than disambiguating the intended addressees. The phrase ὦ ἀνόητοι Γαλάται, "you foolish Galatians," is a prototypical example of what I call *thematic address*. Comments made about it provide a representative survey of how such phenomena are treated in NT studies.

In Wallace's discussion of the nominative of address, he describes the usage in Gal 3:1: "The pathos of Paul is seen clearly in this text. He is deeply disturbed (or better, outraged) at the Galatians' immediate defection from the gospel."[3] He considers the presence of ὦ to make the address emphatic.

Longenecker says that the use of ἀνόητοι here "highlights the sharpness of Paul's address. It is, indeed, biting and aggressive in tone. Yet more than just a reprimand, it expresses Paul's deep concern, exasperation, and perplexity."[4] This may be a correct interpretation, but he provides no elaboration to support his claim.

Interestingly enough, Martin Luther uses thematic address in his comment about the thematic address in 3:1: "It is as if he were saying, "Alas, what a height you have fallen from, *you miserable Galatians!*"[5] He recharacterizes them as "miserable" to describe what is meant by "foolish," and he does so using a Latin vocative. Barton notes the shift in address compared to the last term used:

In 1:11 Paul had called the believers in Galatia "brothers and sisters" (NRSV); in this verse, he used a much more impersonal *Galatians* to address his con-

---

3. Wallace, *Greek Grammar*, 57.

4. Longenecker, *Galatians*, 99.

5. Martin Luther, *Galatians* (CCC; Wheaton, Ill.: Crossway Books, 1998), 116 (italics added). The original Latin reads, "quasi dicat: 'Heu quo prolapsi estis, o miseri Galatae?'" (D. D. Martini Lutheri, *Commentarium in Epistolam S. Pauli ad Galatas*, vol. 1 [ed. J. C. Irmischer; Erlangen: Sumtibus Caroli Heyderi, 1843], 272).

verts in the region. He preceded it with a strong adjective reprimanding their behavior—they were *foolish*.[6]

The most helpful comment that I found in regard to the specific pragmatic effect achieved by this vocative is made by George:

> Paul not only addressed his readers by name; he also characterized them in a very unflattering way as foolish, stupid, senseless, silly. Or, as J. B. Phillips puts it, "Oh you dear idiots of Galatia ... surely you cannot be so idiotic?"[7]

It is the characterization of the participants in an unexpected way that achieves the effect that the commentators note. Not every vocative would have this effect. Many serve the semantic role of identifying the addressee and thus have no special thematic effects. Others, as Barton notes, exhibit a dissonance against the expected form of address (i.e., the last one used) that achieves the thematic shock value seen in Gal 3:1, making it stand out so starkly. Similarly, Young succinctly states, "The vocative ... can show the speaker's attitude toward the person(s) spoken to."[8] Developing a more complete understanding of why a certain form of address stands out allows the exegete to more accurately determine its significance and function, whether commentators mention it or not.

The other variety of thematic highlighting under consideration in this chapter is *changed reference*. In the account of Jesus' temptation in Matt 4, there are several changes of reference to the devil. Verse 1 states that Jesus was led into the wilderness to be tempted by "the devil."[9] In v. 3, "the tempter" offers his first temptation to Jesus. In v. 5, "the devil" takes Jesus to "the holy city" (not Jerusalem). In v. 8, "the devil" takes Jesus to a high mountain. When Jesus uses a term of address in his speech of v. 10, it is "Satan." Finally, in v. 11, "the devil" departs.

Commentators seem to view "devil," "tempter," and "Satan" as referring to the same participant, essentially as synonyms.[10] Some commentators do

---

6. Bruce B. Barton, *Galatians* (LABC; Wheaton, Ill.: Tyndale House, 1994), 82.

7. Timothy George, *Galatians* (NAC 30; Nashville: Broadman & Holman, 2001), 205.

8. Richard A.Young, *Intermediate New Testament Greek: A Linguistic and Exegetical Approach* (Nashville: Broadman & Holman, 1994), 16.

9. The term διάβολος means "slanderer" or "adversary" and often is understood as a title for this entity (BDAG, 226). The fact that this is the expression used to introduce him to the discourse establishes the expectation that it is his default referring expression.

10. For example, "'The tempter' is another name for the devil (4:1), Satan" (Bruce B. Barton, *Matthew* [LABC; Wheaton, Ill.: Tyndale House, 1996], 58.)

not specifically treat the issue;[11] others see the change as evidence of redaction by an editor rather than as a thematic decision on the part of the writer.[12] Although there is little discussion about the thematic significance of the changes, it is interesting that Keener's changes of terminology in his comments correspond to the changes in the Gospel; for example, he switches from the "devil" to "Satan" in his discussion of vv. 8–10, then back to "devil." Hare likewise switches between "Satan" and "devil." Barton uses "Satan" in his comments without switching. Blomberg,[13] Hagner,[14] and Morris[15] note the changed references, defining each of the terms. Regarding the shift from "devil," Blomberg comments on v. 3, "Matthew now refers to the devil by his function … 'the tempter.'"[16]

As observed with the thematic address of Gal 3:1, some commentators of Matt 4 assign significance to the usage. Others draw conclusions from the data, yet without explicitly explaining what led them there. The thematic use of the vocative is typically described as an epistolary formula, yet this offers little exegetical insight into what the writer meant to accomplish by using it in this nonepistolary context. Similarly, assigning changes of reference to a redactor/editor does not explain why a writer might make or retain such a change.[17]

This brief survey illustrates that comments regarding the purpose and significance of these expressions often hit close to the mark. However, there is no systematic discussion of how these conclusions were reached. Some recognize the pragmatic effect produced by the forms of address, but they give little attention to the principles that led to their conclusions. As a result,

---

11. For example, Douglas R. A. Hare, *Matthew* (IBC; Louisville: John Knox, 1993), 23; Craig S. Keener, *Matthew* (IVPNTC 1; Downers Grove, Ill.: InterVarsity, 1997), 87–95.

12. For example, W. D. Davies and Dale C. Allison, *A Critical and Exegetical Commentary on the Gospel According to Saint Matthew*, vol. 2 (ICC; Edinburgh: T & T Clark, 2004), 360.

13. "'Devil' in Greek means *accuser*, as does 'Satan' in Hebrew (v. 10)" (Craig Blomberg, *Matthew* [NAC 22; Nashville: Broadman & Holman, 1992], 83).

14. Donald A. Hagner, *Matthew 1–13* [WBC 33A; Dallas: Word, 1993], 64–69.

15. Leon Morris, *The Gospel According to Matthew* (PNTC; Grand Rapids: Eerdmans, 1992), 73–76.

16. Blomberg, *Matthew*, 84.

17. The standard redactional explanation is that the redactor was either inept or unwilling to remove elements from different stories that clashed with one another. Neither of these proposals offers a satisfactory explanation. See John Van Seters, *The Edited Bible: The Curious History of the "Editor" in Biblical Criticism* (Winona Lake, Ind.: Eisenbrauns, 2006).

interpretation of thematic address and changed reference tends to be ad hoc, overlooking broader principles governing the usage.

17.2   Discourse Explanation

Thematic address and changes of reference both exploit the same principle of discourse to accomplish the similar pragmatic effect of recharacterizing the participant in a particular way. This effect comes about when the expression used is different from the default or expected referring expression. The characterization stands out because it differs from how readers currently conceive of the participant in their mental representation of the discourse. This dissonance is what brings about the thematic effects.

When a new participant is introduced into a discourse, it is typically assigned two things. The first thing is a *discourse anchor*, which provides a relation or connection point for the reader to know how to relate it to the larger discourse. The second thing is a *referring expression* such as a proper name (e.g., "Peter," "John") or a generic epithet (e.g., "his servant," "the centurion"). The referring expression used at the introduction typically becomes the default expression used to refer to the participant, until there is some reason for it to change.

In chapter 15, on overspecification, I demonstrated that adding more information than is needed to identify a participant can have the effect of changing how you view it. It constrains you to update your current mental representation of the participant based on the extra information. This same effect can be achieved by changing the referring expression, not just by supplementing it. If the writer changes the default referring expression or uses a term of address that is at odds with your current representation, it constrains you to reconcile this by updating your mental representation.

These devices can also update the anchoring relation of the participant to the discourse, indicating a shift in the center of attention. They may simply draw attention to an important thematic quality relating to the participant. In other words, thematic address and changes of reference have the effect of recharacterizing the referent, constraining readers to update how they are thinking about it in their mental representation of the discourse.

17.3   Application

Many of the names or titles assigned to Jesus come in the form of thematic address. In each of the following examples, Jesus has already been established as the intended hearer in the narrative. There is no semantic need for the speaker to use a form of address. Even though it is not semantically required, the expression still performs an important thematic function. The form of address provides an opportunity for the reader to understand how the speaker viewed Jesus, based on the form used. The following figure provides a summary of the expressions used by speakers to refer to Jesus.

Figure 7 :: Forms of address used for Jesus in the Gospels

Reference	Form of address	Speaker/Context
Matt 12:38; 22:36	Διδάσκαλε, Teacher	Scribes and Pharisees; a lawyer
Matt 14:28	Κύριε, Lord	The disciples to Jesus walking on water
Matt 15:22; 20:31	κύριε υἱὸς Δαυίδ, Lord son of David	Canaanite woman with demon-possessed daughter; two blind men
Mat 26:68	Χριστέ, Christ	Those in the Sanhedrin mocking Jesus
Matt 27:29	βασιλεῦ τῶν Ἰουδαίων, King of the Jews	Roman soldiers mocking Jesus
Matt 27:40	ὁ καταλύων τὸν ναὸν καὶ ἐν τρισὶν ἡμέραις οἰκοδομῶν, you who would tear down the temple and in three days build	Onlookers passing by the cross
Mark 5:7 (// Luke 8:28)	Ἰησοῦ υἱὲ τοῦ θεοῦ τοῦ ὑψίστου, Jesus son of the most high God	The Gerasene demoniac
Mark 10:47, 49	υἱὲ Δαυὶδ Ἰησοῦ, Son of David, Jesus	Bartimaeus, the blind man

In each of these instances, the form of address gives insight into how the speakers viewed Jesus at the time of the utterance. This holds true even in contexts where the thematic address is considered to be sarcastic (e.g., Matt 26:68; 27:29, 40). The sarcasm is realized by the apparent mismatch between the form of address and the discourse context. It still provides insight into the speakers, showing that they view Jesus differently than his followers do.

Example 256 :: Luke 12:28 (// Matthew 6:30)

εἰ δὲ ἐν ἀγρῷ τὸν χόρτον ὄντα σήμερον καὶ αὔριον εἰς κλίβα-νον βαλλόμενον ὁ θεὸς οὕτως ἀμφιέζει, πόσῳ μᾶλλον ὑμᾶς, ⟨🔊ὀλιγόπιστοι.🔊⟩	"But if God clothes the grass in the field in this way, although it is here today and tomorrow is thrown into the oven, how much more will he do so for you, ⟨🔊you of little faith?"🔊⟩

Jesus is speaking to his disciples, and he has been since v. 22. It makes no sense to identify them at the end of the speech for semantic reasons. No other information has been provided in the context that identified them as anything other than disciples. Although the address is not semantically required, it serves the pragmatic function of explicitly stating how Jesus views the listeners at this point in the discourse. More specifically, its use here implies that the behavior or attitude that Jesus is describing applies to the hearers, even though there has been no specific mention that they are worrying or lack faith. The same form of thematic address is found in Matt 8:26; 16:28, with the same effect of recharacterizing the participants.

Jesus uses thematic address in another context where it presumably applies to all of the listeners.

Example 257 :: Matthew 11:28

Δεῦτε πρός με ⟨🔊πάντες οἱ κοπιῶντες καὶ πεφορτισμένοι,🔊⟩ κἀγὼ ἀναπαύσω ὑμᾶς.	"Come to me, ⟨🔊all of you who labor and are burdened,🔊⟩ and I will give you rest."

This call to come to him is addressed to the weary and heavy-laden. Rather than just singling out a small group, the implication is that this quality potentially applies more broadly to the listeners. It also serves to characterize those to whom Jesus is appealing in his speech.

Thematic address often is used to negatively characterize participants, especially the religious leaders in the Gospels.

Example 258 :: Matthew 3:7

Ἰδὼν δὲ πολλοὺς τῶν Φαρισαίων καὶ Σαδδουκαίων ἐρχομένους ἐπὶ τὸ βάπτισμα αὐτοῦ εἶπεν αὐτοῖς· ⟨🔊γεννήματα ἐχιδνῶν,🔊⟩ τίς	But when he saw many of the Pharisees and Sadducees coming to his baptism, he said to them, ⟨🔊"Offspring of vipers!🔊⟩ Who

ὑπέδειξεν ὑμῖν φυγεῖν ἀπὸ τῆς   warned you to flee from the
μελλούσης ὀργῆς;   coming wrath?"

The first part of this verse clearly identifies the groups that are approaching John the Baptist. Using this expression does not disambiguate which group of hearers John is addressing. On the contrary, it plays a significant thematic role in letting these approaching hearers know how John views them as introduction for his speech that follows.[18]

Jesus uses thematic address to cast the Pharisees in a similarly unfavorable light later in the Gospel.

Example 259 :: Matthew 23:24

⟨➤ὁδηγοὶ τυφλοί,➤⟩ οἱ διϋλίζο-   ⟨➤"Blind guides➤⟩ who filter out a
ντες τὸν κώνωπα, τὴν δὲ κάμηλον   gnat and swallow a camel!"
καταπίνοντες.

Here we find two clauses performing the function of recharacterizing the addressees according to Jesus' communication objectives in the context. This lengthy expression highlights a character quality that Jesus addresses in his speech.

Thematic address is also found at the end of pronouncements, as seen in Luke 12:28 above. It has the same effect of recharacterizing the listeners based on the preceding pronouncement. The form of address highlights significant themes from the pronouncement.

Example 260 :: Matthew 7:23

καὶ τότε ὁμολογήσω αὐτοῖς ὅτι   "And then I will say to them
οὐδέποτε ἔγνων ὑμᾶς· ἀποχωρεῖτε   plainly, 'I never knew you. Depart
ἀπ' ἐμοῦ ⟨➤οἱ ἐργαζόμενοι τὴν   from me, ⟨➤you who practice
ἀνομίαν.➤⟩   lawlessness!' "➤⟩

This address is used to recharacterize those that claim to have performed exorcisms and miracles in the name of Jesus. This suggests that they view themselves as practitioners of righteousness rather than of lawlessness. The

---

18. Jesus uses the same expression in Matt 12:34 to describe a group of Pharisees who accuse him of casting out demons by Beelzebul, accomplishing much the same effect as in the Baptist's speech.

thematic address takes what is implicit in Jesus' rejection of them "in that day" and provides an explicit reason. He could just as easily have said, "I never knew you because you practice lawlessness." Thematic address highlights the same theme much more powerfully and succinctly.

A similar recharacterization is used in the final pronouncement in the parable of the unmerciful servant and in the parable of the talents.

Example 261 :: Matthew 18:32

τότε προσκαλεσάμενος αὐτὸν ὁ κύριος αὐτοῦ λέγει αὐτῷ· ‹✒δοῦλε πονηρέ,✒› πᾶσαν τὴν ὀφειλὴν ἐκείνην ἀφῆκά σοι, ἐπεὶ παρεκάλεσάς με·	"Then his master summoned him and said to him, ‹✒'Wicked slave!✒› I forgave you all that debt because you implored me!'"

The "wicked slave" was addressed simply as "slave" in the preceding context, without any thematically loaded modifiers. It is only at the point when the master makes his pronouncement against this servant that thematic address is found. It provides an explicit characterization of him as a result of his preceding action. The same holds true with each of the servants as he gives an account of what he did with the entrusted talent(s).

Example 262 :: Matthew 25:21, 23

²¹ ἔφη αὐτῷ ὁ κύριος αὐτοῦ· εὖ, ‹✒δοῦλε ἀγαθὲ καὶ πιστέ,✒› ἐπὶ ὀλίγα ἦς πιστός, ἐπὶ πολλῶν σε καταστήσω· εἴσελθε εἰς τὴν χαρὰν τοῦ κυρίου σου.	²¹ "His master said to him, 'Well done, ‹✒good and faithful slave!✒› You were faithful over a few things; I will put you in charge over many things. Enter into the joy of your master!'"
²³ ἔφη αὐτῷ ὁ κύριος αὐτοῦ· εὖ, ‹✒δοῦλε ἀγαθὲ καὶ πιστέ,✒› ἐπὶ ὀλίγα ἦς πιστός, ἐπὶ πολλῶν σε καταστήσω· εἴσελθε εἰς τὴν χαρὰν τοῦ κυρίου σου.	²³ "His master said to him, 'Well done, ‹✒good and faithful slave!✒› You were faithful over a few things; I will put you in charge over many things. Enter into the joy of your master!'"

Verse 23 reads the same as v. 21. Note the change in address used in v. 26.

Example 263 :: Matthew 25:26

ἀποκριθεὶς δὲ ὁ κύριος αὐτοῦ εἶπεν αὐτῷ· ‹➤πονηρὲ δοῦλε καὶ ὀκνηρέ,➤› ᾔδεις ὅτι θερίζω ὅπου οὐκ ἔσπειρα καὶ συνάγω ὅθεν οὐ διεσκόρπισα;	"But his master answered and said to him, ‹➤'Evil and lazy slave!➤› You knew that I reap where I did not sow and gather from where I did not scatter seed.'"

It is only at the end of the parable that each slave is characterized, after he has given an account of his investment. Had each of them been characterized toward the beginning of the parable, when the talents were distributed, it would have spoiled the dramatic conclusion.

Thematic address is used in the introduction of the prayer from Acts 1 to highlight a quality of the Lord that is particularly relevant to the request that is being made.

Example 264 :: Acts 1:24

καὶ προσευξάμενοι εἶπαν· σὺ κύριε ‹➤καρδιογνῶστα πάντων,➤› ἀνάδειξον ὃν ἐξελέξω ἐκ τούτων τῶν δύο ἕνα....	And they prayed and said, "You, Lord, ‹➤who know the hearts of all,➤› show clearly which one of these two you have chosen...."

There is no need for an expression of address at all since the Lord knows the hearts of all, or "Lord" alone could have been used. The effect of the overly specific expression is to constrain the Lord (and the readers) to recall a thematically important quality.

Paul's use of thematic address in Acts 13 communicates nearly as much about the Jewish false prophet Bar-Jesus as the statement that it introduces.

Example 265 :: Acts 13:10

εἶπεν· ‹➤ὦ πλήρης παντὸς δόλου καὶ πάσης ῥᾳδιουργίας,➤› ‹➤υἱὲ διαβόλου, ἐχθρὲ πάσης δικαιοσύνης,➤› οὐ παύσῃ διαστρέφων τὰς ὁδοὺς [τοῦ] κυρίου τὰς εὐθείας;	and said, ‹➤"O you who are full of all deceit and of all unscrupulousness,➤› ‹➤you son of the devil, you enemy of all righteousness!➤› Will you not stop making crooked the straight paths of the Lord!"

Thematic address sets the stage for the proposition that follows, explicitly communicating Paul's view of Bar-Jesus even before his rhetorical question implies that Bar-Jesus has been making the straight paths of the Lord crooked. This expression plays an important exegetical role in casting Bar-Jesus in a particular light and gives us insight into how Paul viewed him.

The examples above illustrate the widespread use of thematic address to (re)characterize hearers in reported speeches or in epistles. The same kind of recharacterization can be accomplished in narrative proper by changing from the default referring expression used to introduce a participant to one that is more thematically loaded. Consider the changed references in following examples, indicated by italics.

Example 266 :: Matthew 26:46–48

⁴⁶ ἐγείρεσθε ἄγωμεν· ἰδοὺ ἤγγικεν ὁ παραδιδούς με.	⁴⁶ "Get up, let us go! Behold, *the one who is betraying me* is approaching!"
⁴⁷ Καὶ ἔτι αὐτοῦ λαλοῦντος ἰδοὺ Ἰούδας ⟨➤εἷς τῶν δώδεκα➤⟩ ἦλθεν καὶ μετ' αὐτοῦ ὄχλος πολὺς μετὰ μαχαιρῶν καὶ ξύλων ἀπὸ τῶν ἀρχιερέων καὶ πρεσβυτέρων τοῦ λαοῦ.	⁴⁷ And while he was still speaking, behold, *Judas*—⟨➤one of the twelve➤⟩—arrived, and with him a large crowd with swords and clubs, from the chief priests and elders of the people.
⁴⁸ ὁ δὲ παραδιδοὺς αὐτὸν ἔδωκεν αὐτοῖς σημεῖον λέγων· ὃν ἂν φιλήσω αὐτός ἐστιν, κρατήσατε αὐτόν.	⁴⁸ Now *the one who was betraying him* had given them a sign, saying, "The one whom I kiss—he is the one. Arrest him!"

In v. 46, Jesus uses the generic expression "the betrayer" (ὁ παραδιδούς) to refer to Judas, thus avoiding explicitly identifying him to the other disciples. There is no reason to believe that they knew Judas would betray Jesus, and this less descriptive expression keeps them in the dark.[19] In the narrative of v. 47, the proper name "Judas" is used to refer to the same participant. There is a return in the narrative of v. 48 from the default expression "Judas" to the thematically loaded expression used in v. 46. The pragmatic effect is to explicitly identify Judas as the betrayer by using this less expected expression. Its use represents the writer's choice to recharacterize Judas in the narrative in a manner that is consistent with Jesus' assertion in v. 46. From a grammatical standpoint, there is no need for an explicit subject in v. 48, since it is the same

---

19. Cf. John 13:28–29.

as the main clause subject of v. 47. In the Synoptic parallel in Luke 22:47, the writer omits the explicit subject, thereby avoiding a changed reference.

The same kind of recharacterization is observed in Luke regarding the expressions used to refer to Barabbas.

Example 267 :: Luke 23:25

ἀπέλυσεν δὲ τὸν διὰ στάσιν καὶ φόνον βεβλημένον εἰς φυλακὴν ὃν ᾐτοῦντο, τὸν δὲ Ἰησοῦν παρέδωκεν τῷ θελήματι αὐτῶν.	And he released the one who had been thrown into prison because of insurrection and murder, whom they were asking for, but Jesus he handed over to their will.

The expression used here is much longer than the expected proper name "Barabbas." The change may simply be motivated by the fact that he is a new participant, and Luke wants to reinforce his anchoring relation. However, the extent of the thematic description is more likely motivated by a desire to contrast the criminal who was released with the innocent person who was put to death instead.

This same contrast is clearly made between the same participants by Peter changing expressions in his second sermon in Acts.

Example 268 :: Acts 3:14–15

[14] ὑμεῖς δὲ *τὸν ἅγιον καὶ δίκαιον* ἠρνήσασθε καὶ ᾐτήσασθε ἄνδρα *φονέα* χαρισθῆναι ὑμῖν,	[14] "But you denied *the Holy and Righteous One* and demanded that a man—*a murderer*—be granted to you.
[15] *τὸν δὲ ἀρχηγὸν τῆς ζωῆς* ἀπεκτείνατε ‹☛ὃν ὁ θεὸς ἤγειρεν ἐκ νεκρῶν,☚› οὗ ἡμεῖς μάρτυρές ἐσμεν.	[15] And you killed *the originator of life*, ‹☛whom God raised from the dead,☚› of which we are witnesses!"

Jesus is referred to as "the Holy and Righteous One" and "the originator of life," while Barnabas is called "a murderer." Avoiding the use of proper names in these verses introduces a degree of ambiguity that could lead to confusion or miscommunication. However, the changes allow Peter to characterize Jesus in a particular way, as does the characterization of Barabbas as a murderer. Referring to Jesus as "the Holy and Righteous One" and "originator of life" casts the decision to put him to death in a particularly negative light.

In Acts 15:38, a changed reference is used to cast John Mark in a particularly bad light while at the same time recalling important thematic information about his past actions from Acts 13:13.

Example 269 :: Acts 15:38

³⁶ And after some days, Paul said to Barnabas, "Come then, let us return and visit the brothers in every town in which we proclaimed the word of the Lord, to see how they are doing." ³⁷ Now Barnabas wanted to take John who was called Mark along also,

³⁸ Παῦλος δὲ ἠξίου, τὸν ἀποστάντα ἀπ᾽ αὐτῶν ἀπὸ Παμφυλίας καὶ μὴ συνελθόντα αὐτοῖς εἰς τὸ ἔργον μὴ συμπαραλαμβάνειν τοῦτον.	³⁸ but Paul held the opinion they should not take this one along, who departed from them in Pamphylia and did not accompany them in the work.

The reference to John in v. 37 is sufficient to remind the reader which "John" is being referred to. Using the proper name "John Mark" in v. 38 would have made the conflict look more like a simple difference of opinion. Changing the reference to an expression that suggests a lack of faithfulness or commitment on the part of John Mark has the effect of making Paul's opposition much more justifiable from Paul's standpoint. Despite this opposition, it seems as though Barnabas's investment in John Mark paid dividends that Paul did not foresee at the time.[20]

Changes of reference are also used to highlight theological themes relating to God's character or work.

Example 270 :: Philippians 1:6

πεποιθὼς αὐτὸ τοῦτο, ὅτι ὁ ἐναρξάμενος ἐν ὑμῖν ἔργον ἀγαθὸν ἐπιτελέσει ἄχρι ἡμέρας Χριστοῦ Ἰησοῦ....	convinced of this same thing, that *the one who began a good work in you* will finish it until the day of Christ Jesus....

It would have been much simpler and clearer to omit the subject reference in the ὅτι clause, since "God" is the expected subject of the clause. If there were a need for clarity, restating the subject would have sufficed. The expression used

---

20. For more positive description of "the one who left them in Pamphylia," see Col 4:10 and, possibly, 2 Tim 4:11.

holds a much greater possibility for confusion because the intended partici-pant must be inferred from the context. The change of reference has the effect of highlighting a salient characteristic of God as "the one who began the good work" just before the proposition stating that he will finish this work.

Summary

This chapter has demonstrated the effects that can be achieved by referring to a participant with some expression that differs from the expected one, typi-cally that first used to introduce the participant. This kind of change can be accomplished using a vocative or nominative address of some kind in an epis-tle or reported speech. It can also be accomplished in narrative by changing from a default referring expression. Both can have the effect of recharacter-izing the participant in a particular way, based on the writer's or speaker's communication objectives in the context. The change constrains readers to update their mental representation of the participant. These changes often highlight exegetically significant thematic information that shapes our pro-cessing of the discourse.

Suggested Reading

Berlin, Adele. *Poetics and Interpretation of Biblical Narrative*. 33–37, 59–61.

Porter, Stanley E. *Idioms of the Greek New Testament*. 87–88.

Runge, Steven E. "A Discourse-Functional Description of Participant Refer-ence in Biblical Hebrew Narrative," 188–250.

———. "Pragmatic Effects of Semantically Redundant Referring Expressions in Biblical Hebrew Narrative."

Wallace, Daniel B. *Greek Grammar beyond the Basics: An Exegetical Syntax of the New Testament*. 65–71.

NEAR/FAR DISTINCTION

This chapter discusses the use of demonstrative pronouns such as "this" and "that" for thematic purposes. Normally, these pronouns are used to signify a distinction between two different discourse elements based on distance. "This/these" is considered the *near demonstrative* pronoun, represented by the ⬛ symbol; "that/those" is considered the *far demonstrative* and is represented by the ⬛ symbol. These pronouns are also used in contexts where a spatial distinction does not exist. In such cases, the demonstratives express a thematic distinction as though it were a spatial one. This kind of thematic usage is not used much in English but is frequently found in the Greek NT. The mismatch between Greek and English usage has led many to overlook the thematic usage of demonstratives present in the Greek NT.

18.1   Conventional Explanation

Grammarians have proposed a number of different functions for the usage of demonstrative pronouns in Greek, and it is beyond the scope of this chapter to provide a full description of their usage. The goal here is to provide a unified account of their thematic function in discourse. To this end, I will provide a representative overview that covers the issues relevant to the task. Other aspects of their usage have already been covered elsewhere in this volume. Here are the primary functions postulated:

- regular or deictic usage to distinguish between elements that possess a spatial or temporal distinction of some kind;[1]

---

1. Daniel B. Wallace, *Greek Grammar beyond the Basics: An Exegetical Syntax of the New Testament* (Grand Rapids: Zondervan, 1999), 325; A. T. Robertson, *A Grammar of the*

- as a substitute for the personal pronoun αὐτός;[2]
- contemptuous usage, which "is merely one variation of the purely deictic idiom due to the relation of the persons in question";[3]
- emphasis;[4]
- appositional usage, where it refers ahead to some clause element that stands in apposition to the demonstrative;[5]
- pleonastic usage.[6]

I will focus on the first four usages above that have not yet been discussed.

Most grammarians describe the distinction present between οὗτος and ἐκεῖνος in spatial terms, usually as near versus far. For instance, Wallace states that the near/far distinction can be based upon distance in the context (i.e., to the last reference to them), in the writer's mind, or in space or time from the audience's perspective.[7] However, there are caveats to suggest that things are not as simple as they sound: "Sometimes these realms are in conflict: What might be the nearest antecedent contextually might not be the nearest antecedent in the author's mind, etc. A little imagination is sometimes needed to see the reason for the pronoun."[8] The near/far distinction seems to work most of the time; however, the usage found in John 7:45 and Rom 6:21 appears to require a different explanation.

As Wallace moves into his discussion of demonstratives as personal pronouns, the expectation that they convey a near/far distinction is dropped. He describes their demonstrative force as "diminished."[9] He does not attach exegetical significance to their usage; they seem to be viewed as simple substitutes for αὐτός.

Greek New Testament in the Light of Historical Research (1919; repr., Bellingham, Wash.: Logos, 2006), 697; BDF §§290(1), 291(1).

2. Wallace, *Greek Grammar*, 326; BDF §291.6.

3. Robertson, *Grammar*, 697; BDF §291(1).

4. Robertson, *Grammar*, 708; Edwin Abbott, *Johannine Grammar* (London: A. & C. Black, 1906), 283.

5. Robertson, *Grammar*, 698; BDF §§290.3, 291.5; Wallace's "conceptual postcedent" (*Greek Grammar*, 332); see also the discussion in chapter 3 on forward-pointing references.

6. Wallace, *Greek Grammar*, 326; BDF §§209(2), 291(4); see also the discussion in chapter 14 on left-dislocations.

7. Wallace, *Greek Grammar*, 325.

8. Ibid., 325–26.

9. "Although technically οὗτος and ἐκεῖνος are demonstrative pronouns, sometimes their demonstrative force is diminished. In such cases, they act as third person personal pronouns with a simple anaphoric force. This usage is especially frequent in John, occurring more with ἐκεῖνος than with οὗτος" (ibid., 326).

BDF maintains the notion that some kind of distinction is present when a demonstrative is used anaphorically where a personal pronoun might be expected. In the end, however, this claim is downgraded.[10] Regarding the use of ἐκεῖνος, BDF states, "It is used especially in narrative, even imaginary narrative, to designate something previously mentioned together with things associated therewith. Here it is distinguished from οὗτος, in that the latter is used of that which is under immediate consideration, so that confusion rarely arises."[11]

Thus, regarding the regular usage and use as a substitute personal pronoun, there is a general sense that the near/far distinction is somehow semantically present, yet no comment is made regarding the exegetical implications of using a demonstrative over against αὐτός. Those that recognize contemptuous and emphatic usage do see exegetical significance in the usage; however, there is little discussion about how or why this sense comes about. BDF considers Luke 15:30 and John 9:28 to have examples of contemptuous usage but does not elaborate on how this conclusion was reached.[12] Robertson is more specific, stating that "in Mt. 26:61 οὗτος ἔφη we find a 'fling' of reproach as the witnesses testify against Jesus."[13] But what is it about the usage that brings about the "fling of reproach"? He does not provide criteria for making such a determination.

Abbott claims that ἐκεῖνος can be used for emphasis:

> Outside dialogue, when John uses ἐκεῖνος in his own words, or in the words of others reported in the first person, it generally has considerable emphasis as in i. 8 'He was not the Light' (i.e. do not suppose that he, the Baptist, was the Light), i. 18 "The only begotten … he [and no other] hath declared," i. 33 "He that sent me … he [and no other] said to me."[14]

He does not elaborate on how he reaches this conclusion. Robertson affirms Abbott's claim but mitigates this by adding "ἐκεῖνος is not always so emphatic even in John."[15] He cites John 9:11, 25; 10:6; 14:21; 18:17; Mark 16:10ff.; and 2 Timothy 3:9 in support.

As with many of the other devices that we have considered so far, the use of demonstrative pronouns to signal the presence of a near/far distinction is generally recognized. It would seem that the contemptuous and emphatic

---

10. On the equating of ἐκεῖνος with αὐτός, see BDF §292.

11. BDF §291(3).

12. BDF §§290(6), 292(1).

13. Robertson, *Grammar*, 697.

14. Abbott, *Johannine Grammar*, 283.

15. Robertson, *Grammar*, 708.

usages could be attributed to some kind of marked use of the demonstrative, since this is so commonly asserted; yet, the grammarians offer little guidance to the exegete in how to make such a determination. They knew it when they saw it but could say little more. In regard to the apparent use of demonstratives as substitutes for αὐτός, little is said about the meaningful difference between the use of a demonstrative and the use of a personal pronoun. Perhaps it was considered a stylistic convention that needed no explanation. In any case, we now move on to consideration of these issues from the standpoint of discourse grammar.

18.2   Discourse Explanation

The basic premise that demonstratives signal the presence of some distinction provides the foundation upon which my explanation is built. In the case of the Greek demonstratives οὗτος and ἐκεῖνος, the distinction is often spatial in nature. This deictic function represents the default usage of demonstratives. Recall the distinction that I made between semantic meaning and pragmatic effect. Although οὗτος and ἐκεῖνος may have the semantic meaning of spatially "near" and "far" respectively, they can also be used in certain contexts to bring about certain pragmatic effects. This is particularly the case when they are used in contexts where a spatial distinction is not explicitly present. The effect is to highlight a distinction that might otherwise have been overlooked, using the near/far demonstratives to represent the distinction thematically.

The primary function of the demonstrative is to assign a near/far distinction to a discourse entity. This is what has traditionally been called the *regular* or *deictic* usage. As has been noted, οὗτος is used for the near entity, ἐκεῖνος for the far entity, whether that is a literal or a figurative distinction. The distinction can be expressed in a simple generic statement, as in James 4:15.

Example 271 :: James 4:15

ἀντὶ τοῦ λέγειν ὑμᾶς· ἐὰν ὁ κύριος	Instead you should say, "If the
θελήσῃ καὶ ζήσομεν καὶ ποιήσομεν	Lord wills, we will live and do
⟨■τοῦτο■⟩ ἢ ⟨◻ἐκεῖνο.◻⟩	⟨■this■⟩ or ⟨◻that."◻⟩

The only objective in this verse is to differentiate two hypothetical entities, and the default function of the demonstrative is perfectly suited to this.

Similarly, the usage may indicate a deictic pointing, as in the following example where the crowds may be gesturing to Jesus, the referent of οὗτος.

Example 272 :: Matthew 21:10–11

> [9] And the crowds who went ahead of him and the ones who followed were shouting, saying, "Hosanna to the Son of David! Blessed is the one who comes in the name of the Lord! Hosanna in the highest heaven!"

[10] Καὶ εἰσελθόντος αὐτοῦ εἰς Ἱεροσόλυμα ἐσείσθη πᾶσα ἡ πόλις λέγουσα· τίς ἐστιν ‹■οὗτος;■›.	[10] And when he entered into Jerusalem, the whole city was stirred up, saying, "Who is ‹■this?"■›
[11] οἱ δὲ ὄχλοι ἔλεγον· ‹■οὗτός■› ἐστιν ὁ προφήτης Ἰησοῦς ὁ ἀπὸ Ναζαρὲθ τῆς Γαλιλαίας	[11] And the crowds were saying, ‹■"This■› is the prophet Jesus from Nazareth of Galilee!"

Most questions have an expressed subject, and the use of the demonstrative here as a generic reference to Jesus could imply a bodily gesture; hence it is deictic.[16] This deictic representation is carried into the reply to the question in v. 11, further singling out Jesus as the intended referent.

Certain elements in a discourse are thematic, or what "is being talked about."[17] In narrative contexts, it is primarily the events that are thematic. There can also be a thematic participant, which Levinsohn describes as "that participant around whom the paragraph is organized, about whom the paragraph speaks."[18] Levinsohn claims that in the instructional portions of the NT Epistles, by default the exhortations and the addressees are the thematic focus; in the expository portions, such as in the book of Hebrews, the expository theses and the main theme of the exposition are thematic, by default.[19]

When there are other elements in the discourse that potentially compete with the default thematic element, the near and far demonstrative pronouns provide a means for the writer to disambiguate the role that these competing elements play. They provide an efficient way of marking an entity's thematic importance. The near demonstrative marks entities that are *thematic* in the context.

---

16. It is unlikely that αὐτός could be used in v. 10b, since the subject of questions is prototypically specified and not elided (e.g., Matt 7:9; 12:48; 26:68). For a generic reference that omits a subject reference, see Matt 9:13.

17. Kathleen Callow, *Discourse Considerations in Translating the Word of God* (Grand Rapids: Zondervan, 1974), 52–53.

18. Stephen H. Levinsohn, "Participant Reference in Inga Narrative Discourse," in *Anaphora in Discourse* (ed. John Hinds; Edmonton: Linguistic Research, 1978), 75.

19. Stephen H. Levinsohn, "Towards a Unified Linguistic Description of οὗτος and ἐκεῖνος" (paper presented at the annual meeting of the Society of Biblical Literature, Atlanta, Ga., 22–25 November 2003), 2.

In contrast, the far demonstrative ἐκεῖνος marks entities that are not thematic in the context. For instance, if minor participants perform actions in a series of events, one might conclude that they have become the new thematic participants, the center of attention. Use of the far demonstrative as a substitute for a personal pronoun allows the writer the mark them as *athematic*, meaning that the center of attention remains focused on some other thematic participant. The athematic participant is only of passing interest.

It was noted that demonstratives are used to specify that a near/far distinction is present. They can also be used to create a near/far distinction, even in contexts where one does not explicitly exist. The pragmatic effect of using a demonstrative in such a context is to portray the elements as though one is nearer or farther. The near demonstrative has the effect of marking the referent as thematically central to the discourse (i.e., thematic), whereas the far demonstrative marks the referent as of passing thematic interest (i.e., athematic). A good example of this is found in Luke 18:14, in the parable of the Pharisee and the tax collector praying.

Example 273 :: Luke 18:14

⁹ And he also told ⟨∎this parable∎⟩ to some who trusted in themselves that they were righteous, and looked down on everyone else: ¹⁰ "Two men went up to the temple to pray, one a Pharisee and the other a tax collector. ¹¹ The Pharisee stood and prayed ⟨∎these things∎⟩ with reference to himself: 'God, I give thanks to you that I am not like other people—swindlers, unrighteous people, adulterers, or even like this tax collector! ¹² I fast twice a week; I give a tenth of all that I get.' ¹³ But the tax collector, standing far away, did not want even to raise his eyes to heaven, but was beating his breast, saying, 'God, be merciful to me, a sinner!' "

¹⁴ λέγω ὑμῖν, κατέβη ⟨∎οὗτος∎⟩ δεδικαιωμένος εἰς τὸν οἶκον αὐτοῦ παρ' ⟨◻ἐκεῖνον·◻⟩ ὅτι πᾶς ὁ ὑψῶν ἑαυτὸν ταπεινωθήσεται, ὁ δὲ ταπεινῶν ἑαυτὸν ὑψωθήσεται.	¹⁴ "I tell you, ⟨∎this man∎⟩ went down to his house justified rather than ⟨◻that one!◻⟩ For everyone who exalts himself will be humbled, but the one who humbles himself will be exalted."

This usage typically is explained as the near demonstrative being used for the most recently mentioned participant and the far demonstrative for the least recent one. Although this is an appealing explanation, it cannot adequately account for the data. The demonstratives here distinguish the thematic participant from the athematic one. In this case the "most recent mention" explanation can account for the usage.

Consider Rom 6:21, which Wallace cites as an example that cannot be accounted for using the recency explanation.

Example 274 :: Romans 6:21

²⁰ For when you were slaves of sin, you were free with respect to righteousness.

²¹ τίνα οὖν καρπὸν εἴχετε τότε; ἐφ' οἷς νῦν ἐπαισχύνεσθε, τὸ γὰρ τέλος ‹◻ἐκείνων◻› θάνατος.	²¹ Therefore what sort of fruit did you have then, about which you are now ashamed? For the end of ‹◻those things◻› is death.

²² But now, having been set free from sin and having been enslaved to God, you have your fruit leading to sanctification, and its end is eternal life.

Note that the fruit that they used to bear while under sin is only of passing interest, with real interest focusing on the new fruit that leads to sanctification. If we correlate what is thematically central with the near demonstrative (and vice versa), we can consistently explain the apparently anomalous usage of demonstratives.

In this case, Paul, by using the far demonstrative, has signaled that his interest is not in the old fruit. The conventional explanation would predict the near demonstrative here, not the far. The fruit of which they are now ashamed is simply mentioned for the sale of comparison. Paul is more interested in what happens now, not then. The use of the far demonstrative marks the old fruit as athematic, of passing thematic interest. This explanation provides a better and more consistent account of the data observed than does the traditional one.

So far, two of the traditional descriptions of demonstratives have been accounted for: the deictic and the use as a personal pronoun. More examples will be provided in §18.3. Another traditional explanation involves what is called the *contemptuous* use, as found in Luke 15:30.

Example 275 :: Luke 15:30

²⁹ "But he answered and said to his father, 'Behold, so many years I have served you, and have never disobeyed your command! And you never gave me a young goat so that I could celebrate with my friends!'"

³⁰ ὅτε δὲ ⟨■ὁ υἱός σου οὗτος■⟩ ὁ καταφαγών σου τὸν βίον μετὰ πορνῶν ἦλθεν, ἔθυσας αὐτῷ τὸν σιτευτὸν μόσχον.

³⁰ " 'But when ⟨■this son of yours■⟩ returned—who has consumed your assets with prostitutes—you killed the fattened calf for him!' "

Many languages, including English, use the near demonstrative as an adjective to form what is called a "referential indefinite."²⁰ This means that the speaker can identify who is being talked about, but the hearer cannot. The reference is definite enough for the hearer to add the participant to his or her mental representation but not definite enough that the hearer could pick the intended person out of a police lineup. We use referential indefinites all the time in English at the beginning of jokes or stories to provide a quick introduction to the person or thing that we are going to talk about. It takes the form of "this + noun phrase." Consider the following examples.

"This guy walks into a bar wearing a cowboy hat, and this other guy says to him...."

"This guy at work was telling me about a new restaurant that just opened...."

"While we were camping, this truck pulled in around midnight with the radio blasting...."

In each of these instances, some new entity is introduced to the discourse that is unknown to the hearer/reader. The use of the indefinite "this" allows the speaker to make the entity definite enough for hearers to build a mental representation about it even though they do not know exactly who or what it is. It is close enough to get the job done.

The usage in Luke 15 is actually a referential indefinite that is used in a context where the participant is well known. When it is used in contexts where the entity is well known to the hearer, it has the effect of distancing the speaker from the known entity.²¹ The use of the referential indefinite by the older brother expresses a sense of alienation or disgust for his younger brother because he portrays his brother as if the father would not know him. The contemptuous sense of distance is intensified by not using the nearest

---

20. See Jeanette K. Gundel, Nancy Hedberg, and Ron Zacharski, "Cognitive Status and the Form of Referring Expressions in Discourse," *Language* 69 (1993): 275–77.

21. Pamela A. Downing, "Proper Names as a Referential Option in English Conversation," in *Studies in Anaphora* (ed. Barbara Fox; TSL 33; Amsterdam: John Benjamins, 1996), 133.

relational expression available. The younger brother is not just the father's son; he is also the older sibling's own brother. The older brother's disassociation of himself with σου heightens the effect, though the contemptuous sense would still have been present to a lesser degree even with οὗτος alone. This perceived contemptuousness is not a semantic meaning of the demonstrative; it is a pragmatic effect of using the right form in the right context. This explanation accounts for one portion of the data representing contemptuous usage of οὗτος. We now move to the data involving ἐκεῖνος.

Most grammarians have associated the contemptuous usage with ἐκεῖνος rather than οὗτος.[22] As with οὗτος, this usage is not some obscure semantic meaning of the far demonstrative but can be well explained as a pragmatic effect of using ἐκεῖνος in a particular context. Recall the claim that the near demonstrative typically is used for the entity that is thematically central, whereas the far demonstrative is used for one that is athematic. If we look at some of the examples cited as contemptuous usage of ἐκεῖνος, we see that the participant identified is thematic rather than athematic. It is the use of the athematic demonstrative for a thematic participant that achieves this contemptuous effect. BDF cites John 9:28 as such a usage, the interaction of the man born blind with the religious leaders after Jesus has healed him.

Example 276 :: John 9:28

καὶ ἐλοιδόρησαν αὐτὸν καὶ εἶπον· σὺ μαθητὴς εἶ ⟨◻ἐκείνου,◻⟩ ἡμεῖς δὲ τοῦ Μωϋσέως ἐσμὲν μαθηταί·	And they reviled him and said, "You are ⟨◻his disciple!◻⟩ But we are disciples of Moses!"

Jesus is not present in the context. The semantics of the verb ἐλοιδόρησαν may be what lead BDF to interpret the athematic usage in a negative light. Alternatively, a good case could be made that Jesus is indeed thematically central to the context, despite being physically absent. His interaction with the blind man is the focus of the dialogue. The contemptuous sense results from using the athematic demonstrative for a thematic participant. In either case, contemptuousness is not a semantic value of demonstratives, but a pragmatic effect that results from using the incorrect demonstrative.[23]

---

22. Robertson (*Grammar of Greek New Testament*, 697) does cite several examples of supposed contemptuous usage with οὗτος, but these are better explained as marking the participant as being thematically salient, as being in the spotlight (e.g., Matt 26:71; Mark 2:7; Luke 15:2; 18:11; John 6:42; 9:24; 12:34; Acts 5:28; 7:40; 19:26; 28:4).

23. Other possible instances of mismatch in thematicity and the demonstrative used are Matt 27:63; John 19:21.

The final usage claimed by traditional grammarians is *emphasis*. In the introduction to information structure in chapter 9, I noted Levinsohn's claim that *emphasis* is regularly used as a synonym for *prominence* in NT studies. I contend that the thematic/athematic explanation accounts for the claims of this final category, based on the effects that I have described above. Marking participants as thematic is a way of making them more prominent. Flaunting the athematic marker by using it for a thematic participant achieves a similar highlighting effect: contempt. There is no need to create new semantic senses of the demonstratives. The thematic/athematic principle can account for both the default deictic use of demonstratives and the various effects achieved by their marked usage. I also demonstrated in chapter 14, in the discussion of left-dislocations, that demonstratives are virtually the only option for referring to a complex proposition in position P1 or P2. This usage may explain claims of emphasis regarding a different portion of data. Whether because of information structure or thematicity, the demonstrative pronoun may be used to add prominence to the entity to which it refers.

18.3   Application

This section begins with examples in which demonstratives are added as adjectival modifiers in a context where they are not needed to identify the intended referent. Note that the decision to use a demonstrative also requires a choice of which to use, the near or the far. It is not just the presence of a demonstrative, but also a matter of which one. It is important to correlate the thematic value of the demonstrative's referent and the demonstrative used. The demonstratives can be indicators of the participant's thematic significance to the discourse when they are not used deictically.

In this first example, demonstratives are added as modifiers that prioritize the importance of two competing elements.

Example 277 :: Matthew 9:26

καὶ ἐξῆλθεν ⟨◾ᴵἡ φήμη αὕτη◾ᴵ⟩ εἰς   And ⟨◾this report◾⟩ went out
⟨◻ᴵὅλην τὴν γῆν ἐκείνην.◻ᴵ⟩   into ⟨◻that whole region.◻⟩

The report about Jesus' activity is marked as thematically central to the discourse by the use of οὗτος. It is not needed to differentiate it from some other competing report. The far demonstrative, ἐκεῖνος, is added to the geographical description, likely due to it being distant from the writer's point of view. In either case, the demonstrative is not needed; "the whole region" is sufficiently clear to update the location in preparation for the change in v. 27 from "there" to some other place where he meets the two blind men.[24]

The next examples illustrate the use of demonstratives in narrative proper to clarify the current center of attention, identifying which participant is thematically central. As noted above, there are default expectations regarding thematicity. When the writer does something potentially in conflict with these expectations, the option is available of using demonstrative pronouns to mark these entities as either thematic or athematic.

Example 278 :: John 1:7–8

> ⁶ A man came, sent from God, whose name was John.

⁷ ⟨◼οὗτος◨⟩ ἦλθεν εἰς μαρτυρίαν ἵνα μαρτυρήσῃ περὶ τοῦ φωτός, ἵνα πάντες πιστεύσωσιν δι’ αὐτοῦ.	⁷ ⟨◼This one◨⟩ came for a witness, in order that he could testify about the light, so that all would believe through him.
⁸ οὐκ ἦν ⟨◻ἐκεῖνος◨⟩ τὸ φῶς, ἀλλ’ ἵνα μαρτυρήσῃ περὶ τοῦ φωτός.	⁸ ⟨◻That one◨⟩ was not the light, but came in order that he could testify about the light.

> ⁹ The true light, who gives light to every person, was coming into the world.

John the Baptist is only a passing thematic interest in this context. He is marked as thematic in v. 7, but the center of attention quickly changes to the one whom he came to proclaim: Jesus. "The light" in v. 8 becomes the thematic center, and John's athematic role is made clear through the switch to the far demonstrative.

In the next example, there is a shift from Jesus and his family being the center of attention[25] to Simeon and Anna essentially playing significant "cameo" roles.

Example 279 :: Luke 2:25

Καὶ ἰδοὺ ἄνθρωπος ἦν ἐν Ἰερουσαλὴμ ᾧ ὄνομα Συμεὼν καὶ ⟨◼ὁ ἄνθρωπος οὗτος◨⟩ δίκαιος καὶ εὐλαβὴς προσδεχόμενος	And behold, there was a man in Jerusalem whose name was Simeon, and ⟨◼this man◨⟩ was righteous and devout, looking for

---

24. Note there is another comparable shift in v. 31: ἐν ὅλῃ τῇ γῇ ἐκείνῃ.
25. See §15.2.3; also Levinsohn, "Description of οὗτος and ἐκεῖνος," 5.

| παράκλησιν τοῦ Ἰσραήλ, καὶ | ward to the consolation of Israel, |
| πνεῦμα ἦν ἅγιον ἐπ᾽ αὐτόν· | and the Holy Spirit was upon him. |

Simeon is first introduced to the discourse in v. 25a. The second reference to him, rather than employing a simple personal pronoun, uses the near demonstrative modifying a noun phrase.[26] Simeon plays a significant role in the discourse, but it is limited in duration. The application of the near demonstrative marks him as thematic from nearly the outset. Without this, his importance would need to be established by his continued activity in the discourse. This thematic marker draws attention to his role in the discourse, serving as confirmation of Jesus' divine origin and role. Simeon is significant only in this scene, never to be mentioned again.

The same kind of thematic encoding is found again a few verses later at the introduction of Anna, another key but temporary participant.

Example 280 :: Luke 2:36–38

[36] Καὶ ἦν Ἄννα προφῆτις, θυγάτηρ Φανουήλ, ἐκ φυλῆς Ἀσήρ· ⟨◼αὕτη◼⟩ προβεβηκυῖα ἐν ἡμέραις πολλαῖς, ζήσασα μετὰ ἀνδρὸς ἔτη ἑπτὰ ἀπὸ τῆς παρθενίας αὐτῆς	[36] And there was a prophetess, Anna the daughter of Phanuel of the tribe of Asher (⟨◼she◼⟩ was advanced in years, having lived with her husband seven years after her marriage,
[37] καὶ ⟨◼αὐτὴ◼⟩ χήρα ἕως ἐτῶν ὀγδοήκοντα τεσσάρων, ἣ οὐκ ἀφίστατο τοῦ ἱεροῦ νηστείαις καὶ δεήσεσιν λατρεύουσα νύκτα καὶ ἡμέραν.	[37] and ⟨◼herself◼⟩ as a widow up to eighty-four years) who did not depart from the temple with fastings and prayers, serving night and day.
[38] καὶ ⟨◼αὐτῇ τῇ ὥρᾳ◼⟩ ἐπιστᾶσα ἀνθωμολογεῖτο τῷ θεῷ....	[38] And at ⟨◼that same hour◼⟩ she approached and began to give thanks to God....

Just like Simeon, Anna is introduced and then reiterated using the near demonstrative as a substantive. She too plays an important role in affirming Jesus' identity, but only a passing one. Simple personal pronouns could have

---

26. On the significance of overencoded references to active participants, see Stephen H. Levinsohn, *Discourse Features of New Testament Greek: A Coursebook on the Information Structure of New Testament Greek* (2nd ed.; Dallas: SIL International), 135-38.

been used to refer to both Simeon and Anna. Using the near demonstrative establishes the significance of each more quickly than would have happened naturally through their ongoing participation in the discourse. The brevity of their participation necessitates using a thematic device to mark their significance early on.

In the next example, John 18:15, both Peter and John are potential centers of attention as they follow Jesus after his arrest. The information supplied about John in this verse could indicate that attention is shifting from Peter to John, since Peter has been the previous center of attention.

Example 281 :: John 18:15

Ἠκολούθει δὲ τῷ Ἰησοῦ Σίμων Πέτρος καὶ ἄλλος μαθητής. ‹❑ὁ δὲ μαθητὴς ἐκεῖνος❑› ἦν γνωστὸς τῷ ἀρχιερεῖ καὶ συνεισῆλθεν τῷ Ἰησοῦ εἰς τὴν αὐλὴν τοῦ ἀρχιερέως….	So Simon Peter and another disciple followed Jesus. (Now ‹❑that disciple❑› was known to the high priest, and entered with Jesus into the courtyard of the high priest….)

Peter's threefold denial of Jesus is recounted in the following verses, hence Peter is the center of attention. The references to John are intended to provide background information about his presence at these events. Verse 15b could have used a simple pronominal reference or else maintained the same cryptic ἄλλος μαθητής as in v. 15a.[27] The unneeded reference to John with a far demonstrative marks him as athematic, thus avoiding sending mixed signals about the center of attention. The spotlight remains on Peter, regardless of the added attention given to John in v. 15.

This same principle applies in the epistolary literature when authors are referring to participants or other discourse entities. Demonstratives have the unique ability to stand in the place of whole propositions or ideas, not just people or things. This kind of propositional substitution is not possible using personal pronouns. Pronouns such as αὐτός are limited to standing in the place of participants or other noun-like things, not propositional concepts.[28]

---

27. Typically, participants with proper names are central to the story, while those with epithets tend to play secondary roles. One effect of John referring to himself as ἄλλος μαθητής is to avoid using a proper name, thereby making this character appear less important than Peter. See chapter 17, on changed references.

28. Jeanette K. Gundel, Nancy Hedberg, and Ron Zacharski, "Demonstrative Pronouns in Natural Discourse" (paper presented at DAARC-2004, the Fifth Discourse Anaphora and Anaphor Resolution Colloquium, São Miguel, Portugal, 23–24 September 2004), 1.

Demonstrative pronouns are virtually the only available substitute for propositions. So if a demonstrative stands in the place of a proposition or other complex entity, there is really no choice but to use a demonstrative.

Although there is no choice in most cases about using a demonstrative pronoun to refer to a proposition, there is a choice regarding which demonstrative to use: the near or the far. The same thematic and athematic distinctions apply to propositions as to participants, as exemplified in the following examples.

Example 282 :: 2 Corinthians 10:18

Οὐ γὰρ ὁ ἑαυτὸν συνιστάνων, ⟨◨ἐκεῖνός◪⟩ ἐστιν δόκιμος, ἀλλὰ ὃν ὁ κύριος συνίστησιν.	For it is not the one commending himself ⟨◨who◪⟩ is approved, but the one whom the Lord commends.

The counterpoint of v. 18 introduces a hypothetical participant: "the one commending himself." This concept is simple enough to introduce without needing to use a left-dislocation. This implies that the construction was used for rhetorical purposes to promote the topic. Using the far demonstrative for the resumption clearly indicates that "the one commending himself" is not the central thematic interest. The point introduced by ἀλλά provides the positive alternative: "the one whom the Lord commends." The athematic participant functions as a foil for the thematic one, sharpening the contrast between the two. The usage creates a thematic distinction between these two entities by assigning one of them the athematic marker.

Most forward-pointing references utilize demonstrative pronouns to refer to the intended target. This is no surprise, since most of the targets are complex entities or propositions. The status of the forward-pointing demonstrative has exegetical implications, since thematicity is explicitly marked by demonstratives.

Example 283 :: 1 John 1:5

Καὶ ἔστιν ⟨→⟨◧αὕτη◨⟩→⟩ ἡ ἀγγελία ἣν ἀκηκόαμεν ἀπ᾽ αὐτοῦ καὶ ἀναγγέλλομεν ὑμῖν, ὅτι ⟨⊙ὁ θεὸς φῶς ἐστιν καὶ σκοτία ἐν αὐτῷ οὐκ ἔστιν οὐδεμία.⊙⟩	And ⟨→⟨◧this◨⟩→⟩ is the message which we have heard from him and announce to you, that ⟨⊙God is light and there is no darkness in him at all.⊙⟩

The proposition "God is light and there is no darkness in him at all" functions as the topic of the following pericope, focusing on how this affects a person's view of self and of God. Use of the forward-pointing reference affords the opportunity to mark the proposition with an explicit thematic marker. In this case, the near demonstrative marks it as thematic.

Not every highlighted proposition is the thematic point of a passage, as seen in the next example. Some are marked as athematic because they make a secondary point.

Example 284 :: Matthew 24:43

⁴² "Therefore be on the alert, because you do not know what day your Lord is coming!"

⁴³ ‹→‹◻Ἐκεῖνο◻›→› δὲ γινώσκετε ὅτι ‹⊙εἰ ᾔδει ὁ οἰκοδεσπότης ποίᾳ φυλακῇ ὁ κλέπτης ἔρχεται, ἐγρηγόρησεν ἂν καὶ οὐκ ἂν εἴασεν διορυχθῆναι τὴν οἰκίαν αὐτοῦ.⊙›

⁴³ "But understand ‹→‹◻this:◻› →› that ‹⊙if the master of the house had known what watch of the night the thief was coming, he would have stayed awake and would not have let his house be broken into."⊙›

⁴⁴ "For this reason you also must be ready, because the Son of Man is coming at an hour that you do not think he will come."

In vv. 36–41, Jesus exhorted the listeners to be watchful and alert. Verse 42 provides a summary conclusion after a series of illustrations. This verse is the thematic point of the pericope. In v. 43, he provides another illustration to help reinforce the point, but it does not replace the primary point. Jesus is not focused on helping people avoid being burglarized; he is simply illustrating his main point.

This is one of the few forward-pointing references in the NT that uses the far demonstrative. The proposition that it introduces is highlighted by virtue of the forward-pointing reference. However, the use of the far demonstrative indicates that it should not be viewed as supplanting the thematic proposition of v. 42. The same thematic point is reiterated following v. 43 in v. 44, again introduced with an inferential connective διὰ τοῦτο. The use of the athematic demonstrative clearly prioritizes the relative thematic importance of vv. 42–44. It is also consistent with the use of inferential connectives in v. 42 and v. 44 to signal a summary principle or conclusion drawn from the preceding discourse.

In the next example, the thematic concept is reiterated following a left-dislocation by use of the near demonstrative to mark its importance. Left-dislocations serve the basic task of promoting the topic to attract more attention to it. Reiterating it with the near demonstrative marks its centrality to what follows.

Example 285 :: Romans 7:19

[LD‹✖οὐ γὰρ ὃ θέλω ποιῶ ἀγαθόν,✖› ἀλλὰ ‹✔ὃ οὐ θέλω κακὸν✔›LD] ‹🔲τοῦτο🔲› πράσσω.	For [LD‹✖not the good that I want to do, I do,✖› but ‹✔the evil that I do not want to do,✔›LD] ‹🔲this🔲› I do.

Note that the counterpoint is not reiterated, only the point. The same content could have been stated with a left-dislocation in either part of the clause:

οὐ γὰρ πράσσω ὃ θέλω ποιῶ ἀγαθόν, ἀλλὰ ὃ κακὸν.

Alternatively, the left-dislocation could have highlighted the counterpoint concept.

ὃ γὰρ θέλω ποιῶ ἀγαθόν τοῦτο οὐ πράσσω, ἀλλὰ ὃ οὐ θέλω κακὸν.

Changing the clause would change what is marked as thematic, leaving it implicit in the first case, or shifting to "the good that I want to do." Creating the left-dislocation affords the opportunity not only to promote the thematic topic, but also to include an explicit thematic marker.

Note also that both the counterpoint and the point precede the predicate πράσσω. One more often finds the counterpoint following the main predicate, feeding a correction back into the proposition. In this case, we do not know the main verb of the clause until both dislocated elements have been introduced. Their similar wording yet opposite content is naturally contrastive. The use of the dislocations sharpens the contrast that was already present.

In Gal 2, Paul makes the point that nothing was added to his gospel as a result of submitting it to the apostles for approval. There was only one thing that he was urged to do: remember the poor. This proposition is reiterated and emphasized in v. 10b, using the near demonstrative to mark it as thematic, along with the intensive pronoun to reinforce it as the very same thing that he intended to do.

Example 286 :: Galatians 2:10

μόνον τῶν πτωχῶν ἵνα μνημονεύωμεν, ὃ καὶ ἐσπούδασα ‹🔲αὐτὸ τοῦτο🔲› ποιῆσαι.	They asked only that we should remember the poor, ‹🔲the very thing🔲› I was also eager to do.

Restating this proposition with a pronoun allows it to be easily placed in the P2 position for the sake of emphasis. The use of the continuative relative strengthens the connection between vv. 10a and 10b.

Philippians 3 focuses on the theme of being like-minded. Demonstratives are used in v. 15 to contrast thinking alike with thinking differently.

Example 287 :: Philippians 3:15

Ὅσοι οὖν τέλειοι, ⟨◼τοῦτο◼⟩ φρονῶμεν· καὶ εἴ τι ἑτέρως φρονεῖτε, ⟨◼καὶ τοῦτο◼⟩ ὁ θεὸς ὑμῖν ἀποκαλύψει·	Therefore as many as are perfect, let us hold ⟨◼this opinion,◼⟩ and if you think anything differently, God will reveal ⟨◼this also◼⟩ to you.

The near demonstrative in v. 15a provides a summary of at least the content of vv. 13–14. The proposition "you think anything differently" is reiterated with the near demonstrative to contrast with the priorities outlined in vv. 12–13. Τι ἑτέρως refers back to this section as the basis of comparison, whereas τοῦτο refers back to τι ἑτέρως. It is the thinking differently that is thematic in this verse; this is what God will reveal.

Thematic and athematic demonstratives are often used in temporal expressions. Sometimes this usage is contrary to what we might expect. Levinsohn states,

> The "remote" nature of ἐκεῖνος thus manifests itself in two ways in temporal expressions:
>
> • marking past or future times as the **same** as a previously stated remote time
>
> • marking a **discontinuity** of theme, when there is a loose chronological relation between the units so linked …
>
> When οὗτος refers in a temporal expression to a PAST time, the typical pragmatic effect is to imply **continuity in the theme line**, even when the chronological relation between the episodes is vague.[29]

In other words, even if all of the temporal references are past-time and remote from the writer's perspective, the near and far demonstratives can be used to indicate the temporal relationship of these events with respect to one another. The near demonstrative means that the two events are closely related to one another (perhaps even simultaneous); the far demonstrative indicates that they are not closely related from a temporal perspective.

---

29. Levinsohn, "Description of οὗτος and ἐκεῖνος," 9.

Consider, in this example from Eph 2, Paul's use of the far demonstrative to refer to the time when we were apart from Christ, casting it as remote through the use of the far demonstrative.

Example 288 :: Ephesians 2:12

¹² ὅτι ἦτε ⟨◻τῷ καιρῷ ἐκείνῳ◻⟩ χωρὶς Χριστοῦ, ἀπηλλοτριωμένοι τῆς πολιτείας τοῦ Ἰσραὴλ καὶ ξένοι τῶν διαθηκῶν τῆς ἐπαγγελίας, ἐλπίδα μὴ ἔχοντες καὶ ἄθεοι ἐν τῷ κόσμῳ.

¹² that you were ⟨◻at that time◻⟩ apart from Christ, alienated from the citizenship of Israel, and strangers to the covenants of promise, not having hope, and without God in the world.

¹³ But now in Christ Jesus you, the ones who once were far away, have become near by the blood of Christ.

Paul wants to contrast two different points in the believers' lives: the time when they were apart from Christ versus now being in Christ (v. 13). The time when they were apart from Christ is remote or far in comparison to their current state. The far demonstrative typically is used when there is a discontinuity in time with respect to the current time reference. This discontinuity can be either in the past, as in Eph 2:12, or in the future, as in the next example, Mark 13:11.

Example 289 :: Mark 13:11

καὶ ὅταν ἄγωσιν ὑμᾶς παραδιδόν-τες, μὴ προμεριμνᾶτε τί λαλήσητε, ἀλλ᾽ ὃ ἐὰν δοθῇ ὑμῖν ⟨◻ἐν ἐκείνῃ τῇ ὥρᾳ◻⟩ ⟨▪τοῦτο▪⟩ λαλεῖτε· οὐ γάρ ἐστε ὑμεῖς οἱ λαλοῦντες ἀλλὰ τὸ πνεῦμα τὸ ἅγιον.

"And when they arrest you and hand you over, do not be anxious beforehand what you should say, but whatever is given to you ⟨◻at that hour,◻⟩ say ⟨▪this.▪⟩ For you are not the ones who are speaking, but the Holy Spirit."

Jesus is preparing his disciples for the persecution that they will face one day in the future by telling them how to respond to it when it comes. The temporal frame in v. 11a establishes the time: "when they arrest you, handing you over." Jesus clarifies in the next sentence that the reference time is still that future hour, even though there is implicit continuity of time. The far demonstrative makes clear that the time is remote and in the future. The near demonstrative is used to highlight "whatever is given to you" because of its thematic importance. The Holy Spirit is the one giving this, not the speakers themselves.

The near demonstrative is used to indicate temporal continuity with the reference time of the discourse, even in instances where the reference time is in the past (i.e., remote from the writer's standpoint). In other words, if Luke is describing a past event, the reference time of the discourse is that past time period. If another contiguous event occurs in that past reference time, the near demonstrative would be used to signal this continuity, since the reference time of the discourse provides the continuity, not the writer's current time.

Luke 1:5–24 lays out the circumstances surrounding the conception of John the Baptist, describing the angel's visits to Zechariah and Elizabeth. This is followed in vv. 25–38 by the foretelling of Jesus' birth. Mary's visit to Elizabeth begins in v. 39. The writer closely connects this chain of events by using the near demonstrative in v. 39 to signal continuity of time.

Example 290 :: Luke 1:39

Ἀναστᾶσα δὲ Μαριὰμ ‹◼ἐν ταῖς ἡμέραις ταύταις◼› ἐπορεύθη εἰς τὴν ὀρεινὴν μετὰ σπουδῆς εἰς πόλιν Ἰούδα.…	Now ‹◼in those days◼› Mary set out and traveled with haste into the hill country, to a town of Judah.…

Even though the reference time is past and thus far from the writer's perspective, Mary's visit is portrayed as coming right on the heels of the events describing Elizabeth's pregnancy.[30] The foretelling of Jesus' birth begins in v. 26 with a temporal frame of reference, establishing the reference time as the sixth month of Elizabeth's pregnancy. Since there is close continuity of the angel's visit to Mary and Mary's visit to Elizabeth, the near demonstrative is used. Other examples of the near demonstrative being used to establish the reference time include Luke 1:24; 6:12; 19:42; 23:7; 24:18, 21; Acts 1:5, 15; 2:29; 3:24; 11:27; 21:15; 23:1; 26:22; Heb 4:8.

This chapter has presented the use of the near and far demonstratives as markers of thematicity. Several of the highlighting devices mentioned in earlier chapters rely heavily upon demonstratives to accomplish their tasks. When used in such contexts, attention should be given to which demonstrative the writer uses. Particular attention should be given to places where a near or far demonstrative differs from the preferred English counterpart. The near demonstrative is used to attract attention to discourse elements that are thematically important in the context, or that are spatially or temporally near.

---

30. This mismatch of reference time versus time of narration is likely what has led translators to use the far demonstrative "those" rather than the near demonstrative "these."

The far demonstrative is used for elements that are athematic, or that are spatially or temporally remote in the context.

Suggested Reading

Blass, F., A. Debrunner, and R. W. Funk. *A Greek Grammar of the New Testament and Other Early Christian Literature.* DF §§290–92.

Callow, Kathleen. *Discourse Considerations in Translating the Word of God.* 52–53.

Downing, Pamela A. "Proper Names as a Referential Option in English Conversation."

Levinsohn, Stephen H. "Towards a Unified Linguistic Description of οὗτος and ἐκεῖνος."

Robertson, A. T. *A Grammar of the Greek New Testament in the Light of Historical Research.* 697–708.

Wallace, Daniel B. *Greek Grammar beyond the Basics: An Exegetical Syntax of the New Testament.* 325–32.

SUMMARY

This book has discussed a number of different discourse devices, grouped loosely under the headings of forward-pointing devices, information structuring devices, and thematic highlighting devices. Some, like forward-pointing references, can seem quite unrelated to others—for example, right-dislocation. Others seem to accomplish nearly the same discourse task—for example, the historical present and metacomment. The purpose of this chapter is to draw some correlations and conclusions about the relationships of these various devices now that all of them have been introduced and illustrated. Although there is overlap in function, there is far less overlap in distribution when one considers the discourse context for each.

Outline of Discourse Devices

The operating principles governing each different device will be reviewed in preparation for synthesizing a more integrated understanding of their interrelationships. This process will also demonstrate how a relatively small number of discourse principles can be multiplied into such a diverse repertoire of devices.

I. **Forward-Pointing Reference and Target**
   A. *Function:* to attract extra attention to the target by using redundant reference
   B. *Discourse principles*
      - Redundancy: the use of an unneeded pronoun to refer to the target
      - Marked usage: breaks default expectation that pronouns refer backwards rather than forwards

- Delay/interruption: reading the negative postpones the intro-
    duction of the positive alternative
C. *Distribution:* primarily in reported speeches and epistles, rarely in
    narrative proper

II. Point/Counterpoint Sets

A. *Functions*
- To explicitly link two things together that otherwise might not
    have been connected
- To draw more attention to the "point" than it would otherwise
    have received
B. *Discourse principles*
- Redundancy: stating both the positive and negative alternative
    when one or the other would suffice
- Marked usage: often the negative precedes the positive—for
    example, tells you what not to do before telling you what to do
- Delay/interruption: reading the negative postpones the intro-
    duction of the positive alternative
C. *Distribution:* primarily in reported speeches and epistles

III. Metacomments

A. *Function:* to slow down the flow of the text in order to attract atten-
    tion to significant proposition that follows
B. *Discourse principles*
- Redundancy: the comment is not needed to understand the
    proposition that it introduces
- Delay/interruption: interrupts the flow of the discourse by stop-
    ping to comment on what is about to be said; can be used in
    conjunction with attention-getter and thematic address to cause
    further delays
C. *Distribution:* primarily in reported speeches and epistles

IV. Historical Present

A. *Function:* to attract attention to a discourse boundary or important
    event that follows
B. *Discourse principle*
- Marked usage: mismatch of verbal aspect (imperfective aspect
    verb for a perfective action), mismatch of temporal association
    (imperfect associated with past time, present with nonpast)
C. *Distribution:* primarily narrative proper, including narratives
    embedded within reported speeches

V. Redundant Quotative Frames
- A. *Function*
    - to mark the introduction of a new point within the same reported speech
    - to slow down the discourse immediately preceding a key assertion[1]
- B. *Discourse principles*
    - <u>Redundancy</u>: more than one verb of speaking, often as though a question was being answered when none was asked (e.g., "answering, he said....")
    - <u>Marked usage</u>: using the verb ἀποκρίνομαι when no question has been asked
    - <u>Delay/interruption</u>: extra verb of speaking delays the introduction of the speech
- C. *Distribution:* only narrative proper

VI. Tail-Head Linkage
- A. *Function:* to slow down the discourse flow just before something surprising or important
- B. *Discourse principles*
    - <u>Redundancy</u>: repeats verbal action from the previous clause as circumstantial background of the present clause
    - <u>Delay/interruption</u>: extra information delays the introduction of the main clause
- C. *Distribution:* narrative proper, book of Revelation

VII. Frames of Reference
- A. *Function:* to provide an explicit frame of reference for processing the clause that follows, which provides the primary basis for relating what follows to what precedes
- B. *Discourse principle*
    - <u>Marked usage</u>: placing established or knowable information in preverbal position P1 (adverbials follow the expected typological patterns, yet still have the similar effect of creating a frame of reference for the clause that follows)
- C. *Distribution:* narrative proper, reported speeches, and epistles

---

1. Stephen H. Levinsohn, *Discourse Features of New Testament Greek: A Coursebook on the Information Structure of New Testament Greek* (2nd ed.; Dallas: SIL International), 53.

VIII. Emphasis
A. *Function:* to attract extra attention to what was already the most important information of the clause
B. *Discourse principle*
- Marked usage: placing newly asserted information in preverbal position P2 instead of at the end of the clause as predicted by natural information flow
C. *Distribution:* narrative proper, reported speeches, and epistles

IX. Thematic Addition
A. *Function:* to attract extra attention to parallel elements in the discourse
B. *Discourse principle*
- Redundancy: adverbial connective constrains what follows it to be connected back to some corresponding in the preceding context; makes explicit a relationship that was already implicitly present
C. *Distribution:* narrative proper, reported speeches, and epistles

X. Overspecification
A. *Function:* to reiterate thematic information about the entity that constrains readers to think about it in a particular way
B. *Discourse principles*
- Redundancy: provides more information than is needed to know who did what to whom
- Marked usage: use of thematic information that may not currently be active in the readers' mental representation
- Delay/interruption: extra content in constructions such as relative clauses effectively slows the pace of discourse by adding more content
C. *Distribution:* narrative proper, reported speeches, and epistles

XI. Right-Dislocation
A. *Function:* to reiterate thematic information about the entity that constrains readers to think about it in a particular way; also used for delayed introduction
B. *Discourse principles*
- Marked usage: delaying the introduction of information about an entity by separating it from the initial reference in the main clause

- <u>Delay/interruption</u>: separating a portion of the information from the initial reference delays the complete reference; this is especially the case where the reference in the main clause is too underspecified to identify the entity without the dislocated information

C. *Distribution:* narrative proper, reported speeches, and epistles

XII. Changed Reference

A. *Function:* to constrain readers to update their mental representation of the entity based on the new referring expression used

B. *Discourse principle*
- <u>Marked usage</u>: use of a referring expression that differs from the last one used to refer to the same participant

C. *Distribution:* narrative proper, reported speeches, and epistles

XIII. Thematic Address

A. *Function:* "thematic name calling," constraining readers to update their mental representation of the entity based on the new referring expression used

B. *Discourse principles*
- <u>Redundancy</u>: not needed to determine whom the speaker is addressing
- <u>Marked usage</u>: the form of address of differs from how the participants are currently anchored to the discourse (e.g., referring to the Pharisees as "you brood of vipers")
- <u>Delay/interruption</u>: addition of the address interrupts the discourse flow, particularly when it is not at the beginning of the clause (e.g., following a metacomment or temporal frame of reference)

C. *Distribution:* narrative proper, reported speeches, and epistles

XIV. Near/Far Distinction

A. *Function:* to represent a thematic distinction in the discourse using a demonstrative as though it were spatial in nature

B. *Discourse principles*
- <u>Redundancy</u>: unneeded where the demonstrative is added as a nondeictic adjectival modifier
- <u>Marked usage</u>: can break with expected use of personal pronouns where used as a substantive

C. *Distribution:* narrative proper, reported speeches, and epistles

Distribution of Discourse Devices

The table below catalogs the distribution of the different devices, classifying them by type. The distributional classifications are based on the preponderance of the data, acknowledging the inevitable small number of exceptions.

Table 4: Distribution of discourse devices

Discourse Device	Narrative Proper	Reported Speech	Epistles	Forward-pointing	Thematic Device	Structuring Device
Forward-pointing Reference and Target		×	×	×		
Point/Counterpoint Sets		×	×	×		
Metacomments		×	×	×		
Historical Present	×			×		
Redundant Quotative Frames	×			×		
Tail-Head Linkage	×			×		
Frames of Reference	×	×	×			×
Emphasis	×	×	×		×	
Thematic Addition	×	×	×		×	
Overspecification	×	×	×		×	
Right-Dislocation	×	×	×		×	
Changed Reference	×	×	×		×	
Thematic Address		×	×		×	
Near/far Distinction	×	×	×		×	

Genre is a meaningful factor in the distribution of some devices, confirming calls from Longacre and others to respect the different types of texts when analyzing discourse features. Neglecting parameters, such as genre, that meaningfully constrain a device undoubtedly contributes to the notion that discourse is too messy to be described. Most NT scholars make no distinction between narrative proper and reported speech; it is all considered to be narrative.

Note the amount of correlation between reported speech and the Epistles. This data suggests that they bear far more in common than is generally acknowledged. Perhaps in areas such as verbal aspect, a finer gradation of genre than "narrative versus epistles" will bring greater clarification and understanding to the existing descriptions. Reported speeches clearly behave much more like the Epistles than narrative proper and thus should be distinctly treated as such.

Discourse is indeed messy when everything is muddled together in a large heap. However, respecting meaningful differences such as genre, and unifying factors such as redundancy, markedness, and delay/interruption, can bring far greater order to the perceived chaos.

BIBLIOGRAPHY

Abbott, Edwin. *Johannine Grammar*. London: A. & C. Black, 1906.

Achtemeier, Paul J. *Romans*. Interpretation: A Bible Commentary for Teaching and Preaching. Atlanta: John Knox, 1985.

Allen, Willoughby C. *A Critical and Exegetical Commentary on the Gospel According to S. Matthew*. International Critical Commentary. Edinburgh: T & T Clark, 1907.

Andrews, Avery. "The Major Functions of the Noun Phrase." Pages 77–80 in *Clause Structure*. Vol. 1 of *Language Typology and Syntactic Description*. Edited by Timothy Shopen. Cambridge: Cambridge University Press, 1985.

Andrews, Edna. *Markedness Theory: The Union of Asymmetry and Semiosis in Language*. Durham, N.C.: Duke University Press, 1990.

Attridge, Harold W. *The Epistle to the Hebrews: A Commentary on the Epistle to the Hebrews*. Edited by Helmut Koester. Hermeneia. Philadelphia: Fortress, 1989.

Bailey, Nicholas A. "Thetic Constructions in Koiné Greek." Ph.D. diss., Free University of Amsterdam, 2009. Online: http://dare.ubvu.vu.nl/bitstream/1871/15504/4/4727.pdf.

Barton, Bruce B. *Galatians*. Life Application Bible Commentary. Wheaton, Ill.: Tyndale House, 1994.

———. *Matthew*. Life Application Bible Commentary. Wheaton, Ill.: Tyndale House, 1996.

Battle, John A. "The Present Indicative in New Testament Exegesis." Th.D. diss., Grace Theological Seminary, 1975.

Bauckham, Richard J. *Jude, 2 Peter*. Word Biblical Commentary 50. Dallas: Word, 2002.

Beekman, John, and John Callow. *Translating the Word of God*. Grand Rapids: Zondervan, 1974.

Berlin, Adele. *Poetics and Interpretation of Biblical Narrative*. Bible and Literature Series 9. Sheffield: Almond, 1983.

Black, Stephanie L. "The Historic Present in Matthew: Beyond Speech Margins." Pages 120–39 in *Discourse Analysis and the New Testament: Approaches and Results*. Edited by Stanley E. Porter and Jeffrey T. Reed. Journal for the Study of the New Testament: Supplement Series 170. Sheffield: Sheffield Academic, 1999.

———. *Sentence Conjunctions in the Gospel of Matthew*. Journal for the Study of the New Testament: Supplement Series 216. Sheffield: Sheffield Academic, 2002.

Blakemore, Diane. *Relevance and Linguistic Meaning: The Semantics and Pragmatics of Discourse Markers*. Cambridge Studies in Linguistics 99. Cambridge: Cambridge University Press, 2002.

Blass, Friedrich. *Grammar of New Testament Greek*. Translated by Henry St. John Thackeray. New York: Macmillan, 1898.

Blass, Regina. *Relevance Relations in Discourse: A Study with Special Reference to Sissala*. Cambridge Studies in Linguistics 55. Cambridge: Cambridge University Press, 1990.

Blomberg, Craig. *Matthew*. New American Commentary 22. Nashville: Broadman & Holman, 1992.

Brannan, Richard. "The Discourse Function of ALLA." Paper presented at the annual meeting of the Evangelical Theology Society, Providence, R.I., 19–21 November 2008.

Brenier, Jason M., and Laura A. Michaelis. "Optimization via Syntactic Amalgam: Syntax-Prosody Mismatch and Copula Doubling." *Corpus Linguistics and Linguistic Theory* 1 (2005): 45–88.

Brinton, Laurel J. "Historical Discourse Analysis." Pages 138–60 in *The Handbook of Discourse Analysis*. Edited by Deborah Schiffrin, Deborah Tannen, and Heidi Ehernberger Hamilton. Malden, Mass.: Blackwell, 2001.

Bruce, F. F. *1 & 2 Thessalonians*. Word Biblical Commentary 45. Dallas: Word, 1982.

Burton, Ernest De Witt. *A Critical and Exegetical Commentary on the Epistle to the Galatians*. International Critical Commentary. New York: Charles Scribner's Sons, 1920.

Buth, Randall. "Mark's Use of the Historical Present." *Notes on Translation* 65 (1977): 7–13.

———. "Word Order in the Verbless Clause: A Generative-Functional Approach." Pages 79–108 in *The Verbless Clause in Biblical Hebrew:*

Linguistic Approaches. Edited by Cynthia L. Miller. Winona Lake, Ind.: Eisenbrauns, 1999.

Butler, Christopher C. "Focusing on Focus: A Comparison of Functional Grammar, Role and Reference Grammar and Systemic Functional Grammar." *Language Sciences* 27 (2005): 585–618.

Callow, John. "The Historic Present in Mark." Seminar handout, 1996.

Callow, Kathleen. *Discourse Considerations in Translating the Word of God*. Grand Rapids: Zondervan, 1974.

Campbell, Constantine. *Verbal Aspect, the Indicative Mood, and Narrative: Soundings in the Greek of the New Testament*. Studies in Biblical Greek 13. New York: Peter Lang, 2007.

Chafe, Wallace L. "Cognitive Constraints on Information Flow." Pages 21–51 in *Coherence and Grounding in Discourse*. Edited by Russell S. Tomlin. Amsterdam: John Benjamins, 1987.

Comrie, Bernard. *Language Universals and Linguistic Typology: Syntax and Morphology*. Chicago: University of Chicago Press, 1989.

———. *Tense*. Cambridge Textbooks in Linguistics. Cambridge: Cambridge University Press, 1985.

Cox, Steven L. "Are Genitive Absolutes Always Absolute?" Paper presented at the annual meeting of the Society of Biblical Literature, San Antonio, Tex., 20–23 November 2004.

Cranfield, C. E. B. *A Critical and Exegetical Commentary on the Epistle to the Romans*. International Critical Commentary. Edinburgh: T & T Clark, 1979.

Dalman, Gustaf. *The Words of Jesus: Considered in the Light of Post-Biblical Jewish Writings and the Aramaic Language*. Translated by D. M. Kay. Edinburgh, T & T Clark, 1902.

Dana, H. E., and Julius R. Mantey. *A Manual Grammar of the Greek New Testament*. New York: Macmillan, 1968.

Daneš, F. "The Relation of Centre and Periphery as a Language Universal." Pages 9–21 in *Les problèmes du centre et de la périphérie du système de la langue*. Vol. 2 of *Travaux linguistiques de Prague*. Edited by F. Daneš et al. Prague: Librairie Klincksieck; Paris: Academia, Éditions de l'Académie tchécoslovaque des sciences, 1966.

Davies, W. D., and Dale C. Allison. *A Critical and Exegetical Commentary on the Gospel According to Saint Matthew*. Vol. 2. International Critical Commentary. Edinburgh: T & T Clark, 2004.

Decker, Rodney J. *Temporal Deixis of the Greek Verb in the Gospel of Mark in Light of Verbal Aspect*. Studies in Biblical Greek 10. New York: Peter Lang, 2001.

Delin, J. *The Focus Structure of It-Clefts*. Edinburgh: Centre for Cognitive Science, 1989.

Denniston, John Dewar. *The Greek Particles*. 2nd ed. Indianapolis: Hackett, 1996.

Dibelius, Martin, and Heinrich Greeven. *James: A Commentary on the Epistle of James*. Hermeneia. Philadelphia: Fortress, 1976.

Diessel, Holger. "Competing Motivations for the Ordering of Main and Adverbial Clauses." *Linguistics* 43, no. 3 (2005): 449–70.

———. "The Ordering Distribution of Main and Adverbial Clauses: A Typological Study." *Language* 77, no. 2 (2001): 433–55.

Dik, Simon. *The Theory of Functional Grammar: Part I: The Structure of the Clause*. Functional Grammar Series 9. Dordrecht; Providence, R.I.: Foris, 1989.

Dooley, Robert A., and Stephen H. Levinsohn. *Analyzing Discourse: A Manual of Basic Concepts*. Dallas: SIL International, 2001.

Downing, Pamela A. "Proper Names as a Referential Option in English Conversation." Pages 95–144 in *Studies in Anaphora*. Edited by Barbara Fox. Typological Studies in Language 33. Amsterdam: John Benjamins, 1996.

Dunn, James D. G. *Romans 9–16*. Word Biblical Commentary 38B. Dallas: Word, 2002.

Dvorak, James D. "Thematization, Topic, and Information Flow." *Journal of the Linguistics Institute of Ancient and Biblical Greek* 1 (2008): 17–37.

Edwards, James R. *The Gospel According to Mark*. Pillar New Testament Commentary. Grand Rapids: Eerdmans, 2002.

Ellingworth, Paul. *The Epistle to the Hebrews: A Commentary on the Greek Text*. New International Greek Testament Commentary. Grand Rapids: Eerdmans, 1993.

Fanning, Buist. *Verbal Aspect in New Testament Greek*. Oxford Theological Monographs. Oxford: Clarendon, 1990.

Fawcett, Robin. *A Theory of Syntax for Systemic Functional Linguistics*. Amsterdam: John Benjamins, 2000.

Floor, Sebastiaan J. "From Information Structure, Topic and Focus, to Theme in Biblical Hebrew Narrative." D.Litt. diss., University of Stellenbosch, 2004.

Fludernik, Monika. "The Historical Present Tense in English Literature: An Oral Pattern and Its Literary Adaptation." *Language and Literature* 17 (1992): 77–107.

Foley, William A., and Robert D. Van Valin Jr. *Functional Syntax and Universal Grammar*. Cambridge Studies in Linguistics 38. Cambridge: Cambridge University Press, 1984.

―――. "Information Packaging in the Clause." Pages 355–63 in *Clause Structure*. Vol. 1 of *Language Typology and Syntactic Description*. Edited by Timothy Shopen. Cambridge: Cambridge University Press, 1985.

France, R. T. *The Gospel of Mark: A Commentary on the Greek Text*. New International Greek Testament Commentary. Grand Rapids: Eerdmans, 2002.

Funk, Robert W. *A Beginning-Intermediate Grammar of Hellenistic Greek*. 2nd ed. 3 vols. Society of Biblical Literature Sources for Biblical Study 2. Missoula, Mont.: Scholars, 1973.

Fuller, Lois K., "The 'Genitive Absolute' in New Testament/Hellenistic Greek: A Proposal for Clearer Understanding." *Journal of Greco-Roman Christianity and Judaism* 3 (2006): 142–67.

George, Timothy. *Galatians*. New American Commentary 30. Nashville: Broadman & Holman, 2001.

Givón, Talmy. "The Grammar of Referential Coherence as Mental Processing Instructions." *Linguistics* 30 (1992): 5–55.

―――. *Syntax: A Functional-Typological Introduction*. Vol. 1. Amsterdam: John Benjamins, 1984.

Gómez-González, María Ángeles. *The Theme-Topic Interface: Evidence from English*. Amsterdam: John Benjamins, 2001.

Gundel, Jeanette K., Nancy Hedberg, and Ron Zacharski. "Cognitive Status and the Form of Referring Expressions in Discourse." *Language* 69 (1993): 274–307.

―――. "Demonstrative Pronouns in Natural Discourse." Paper presented at DAARC-2004, the Fifth Discourse Anaphora and Anaphor Resolution Colloquium, São Miguel, Portugal, 23–24 September 2004.

Gundry, Robert H., and Russell W. Howell. "The Sense and Syntax of John 3:14–17 with Special Reference to the Use of οὕτως … ὥστε in John 3:16." *Novum Testamentum* 41 (1999): 24–39.

Hadley, James, and Frederic De Forest Allen. *Greek Grammar for Schools and Colleges*. London: Macmillan, 1884.

Hagner, Donald A. *Matthew 1–13*. Word Biblical Commentary 33A. Dallas: Word, 1993.

Halliday, M. A. K. "Notes on Transitivity and Theme in English, Part 2." *Journal of Linguistics* 3 (1967): 199–244.

Halliday, M. A. K., and Christian M. I. M. Matthiessen. *An Introduction to Functional Grammar*. London: Arnold, 2001.

Hare, Douglas R. A. *Matthew*. Interpretation: A Bible Commentary for Teaching and Preaching. Louisville: John Knox, 1993.

Harris, Murray J. *The Second Epistle to the Corinthians: A Commentary on the Greek Text*. New International Greek Testament Commentary. Grand Rapids: Eerdmans, 2005.

Heckert, Jacob K. *Discourse Function of Conjoiners in the Pastoral Epistles.* Dallas: SIL International, 1996.

Heimerdinger, Jean-Marc. *Topic, Focus and Foreground in Ancient Hebrew Narratives.* Journal for the Study of the Old Testament: Supplement Series 295; Sheffield: Sheffield Academic, 1999.

Hendriksen, William. *Exposition of Ephesians.* New Testament Commentary. Grand Rapids: Baker, 1967.

———. *Exposition of the Gospel According to John.* New Testament Commentary. Grand Rapids: Baker, 1953.

———. *Exposition of the Gospel According to Matthew.* New Testament Commentary. Grand Rapids: Baker, 1973.

Heth, William A. "Jesus on Divorce: How My Mind Has Changed." *Southern Baptist Journal of Theology* 6 (1): 4–29.

Holmstedt, Robert D. "The Relative Clause in Biblical Hebrew." Ph.D. diss., University of Wisconsin-Madison, 2002.

———. "Word Order and Information Structure in Ruth and Jonah: A Generative-Typological Analysis." *Journal of Semitic Studies* 54 (2009): 111–39.

Jervis, L. Ann. *The Purpose of Romans: A Comparative Letter Structure Investigation.* Journal for the Study of the New Testament: Supplement Series 55. Sheffield: JSOT, 1991.

Jewett, Robert. *Romans: A Commentary.* Hermeneia. Minneapolis: Fortress, 2006.

Keener, Craig S. *Matthew.* IVP New Testament Commentary. Downers Grove, Ill.: InterVarsity, 1997.

Kiparsky, Paul. "Tense and Mood in Indo-European Syntax." *Foundations of Language* 4 (1968): 30–57.

Kistemaker, Simon J. *Exposition of the Acts of the Apostles.* New Testament Commentary. Grand Rapids: Baker, 1990.

———. *Exposition of the Epistle to the Hebrews.* New Testament Commentary. Grand Rapids: Baker, 1984.

Kumpf, Eric P. "Visual Metadiscourse: Designing the Considerate Text." *Technical Communication Quarterly* 9, no. 4 (2000): 401–24.

Kwong, Ivan Shing Chung. *The Word Order of the Gospel of Luke: Its Foregrounded Messages.* Library of New Testament Studies 298. Studies in New Testament Greek 12. London: T & T Clark, 2005.

Lambrecht, Knud. *Information Structure and Sentence Form: Topic, Focus, and the Mental Representations of Discourse Referents.* Cambridge Studies in Linguistics 71. Cambridge: Cambridge University Press, 1996.

Lane, William L. *Hebrews 9–13.* Word Biblical Commentary 47B. Dallas: Word, 2002.

Leong, Siang-Nuan. "Macro-Structure of Mark in Light of the Historic Present and Other Structural Indicators." M.Th. thesis, Singapore Bible College, 2004.

Levinsohn, Stephen H. "*Also, Too* and *Moreover* in a Novel by Dorothy L. Sayers." *Work Papers of the Summer Institute of Linguistics, University of North Dakota Session* 45 (2001). Online: http://www.und.edu/dept/linguistics/wp/2001Levinsohn.pdf.

———. *Discourse Features of New Testament Greek: A Coursebook on the Information Structure of New Testament Greek.* 2nd ed. Dallas: SIL International, 2000.

———. "Participant Reference in Inga Narrative Discourse." Pages 69–135 in *Anaphora in Discourse.* Edited by John Hinds. Edmonton: Linguistic Research, 1978.

———. "Preposed and Postposed Adverbials in English." *Work Papers of the Summer Institute of Linguistics, University of North Dakota Session* 36 (1992): 19–31. Online: http://www.eric.ed.gov:80/ERICDocs/data/ericdocs2sql/content_storage_01/0000019b/80/12/fc/3c.pdf.

———. "The Relevance of Greek Discourse Studies to Exegesis." *Journal of Translation* 2, no. 2 (2006): 11–21.

———. *Self-instruction Materials on Narrative Discourse Analysis.* Dallas: SIL International, 2007. Online: https://mail.jaars.org/~bt/narr.zip.

———. *Self-instruction Materials on Non-narrative Discourse Analysis.* Dallas: SIL International, 2008. Online: https://mail.jaars.org/~bt/nonnarr.zip.

———. "Towards a Typology of Additives." *Afrikanistische Arbeitspapiere* 69 (2002): 171–88.

———. "Towards a Unified Linguistic Description of οὗτος and ἐκεῖνος." Paper presented at the annual meeting of the Society of Biblical Literature, Atlanta, Ga., 22–25 November 2003.

Lincoln, Andrew T. *Ephesians.* Word Biblical Commentary 42. Dallas: Word, 2002.

Longacre, Robert E. "Discourse Peak as Zone of Turbulence." Pages 81–98 in *Beyond the Sentence: Discourse and Sentential Form.* Edited by Jessica R. Wirth. Ann Arbor, Mich.: Karoma, 1985.

———. *The Grammar of Discourse.* Topics in Language and Linguistics. New York: Plenum, 1996.

Longenecker, Richard N. *Galatians.* Word Biblical Commentary 41. Dallas: Word, 1990.

Loos, Eugene A., et al., *Glossary of Linguistic Terms.* Dallas: SIL International, 1997.

Luther, Martin. *Galatians.* Crossway Classic Commentaries. Wheaton, Ill.: Crossway Books, 1998.

Luz, Ulrich. *Matthew: A Commentary*. Vol. 2. Translated by Wilhelm C. Linns. Edited by Helmut Koester. Hermeneia. Minneapolis: Fortress, 2001.

Mao, Luming R. "I Conclude Not: Toward a Pragmatic Account of Metadiscourse." *Rhetoric Review* 11 (1993): 265–89.

Marshall, I. Howard. *The Gospel of Luke: A Commentary on the Greek Text*. New International Greek Testament Commentary. Grand Rapids: Eerdmans, 1978.

Miller, Cynthia L. 1994. "Introducing Direct Discourse in Biblical Hebrew Narrative." Pages 199–241 in *Biblical Hebrew and Discourse Linguistics*. Edited by Robert D. Bergen. Dallas: Summer Institute of Linguistics, 1994.

———. 2003. *The Representation of Speech in Biblical Hebrew Narrative: A Linguistic Analysis*. Corrected ed. Harvard Semitic Monographs 55. Winona Lake, Ind.: Eisenbrauns.

Moffat, James. *A Critical and Exegetical Commentary on the Epistle to the Hebrews*. International Critical Commentary. Edinburgh: T & T Clark, 1924.

Moo, Douglas J. *The Letter of James*. Pillar New Testament Commentary. Grand Rapids: Eerdmans, 2000.

Morris, Leon. *The Gospel According to Matthew*. Pillar New Testament Commentary. Grand Rapids: Eerdmans, 1992.

Moule, C. F. D. *An Idiom Book of New Testament Greek*. Cambridge: Cambridge University Press, 1959.

Moulton, James Hope, Wilbert Francis Howard, and Nigel Turner. *A Grammar of New Testament Greek*. 4 vols. Edinburgh: T & T Clark, 1908–1976.

Mullins, Terence Y. "Disclosure: A Literary Form in the New Testament." *Novum Testamentum* 7 (1964): 44–50.

———. "Formulas in New Testament Epistles." *Journal of Biblical Literature* 91 (1972): 380–90.

———. "Petition as a Literary Form." *Novum Testamentum* 5 (1962): 46–54.

Nolland, John. *Luke 1:1–9:20*. Word Biblical Commentary 35A. Dallas: Word, 1989.

O'Brien, Peter T. *The Letter to the Ephesians*. Pillar New Testament Commentary. Grand Rapids: Eerdmans, 1999.

Patzia, Arthur G. Review of L. Ann Jervis, *The Purpose of Romans: A Comparative Letter Structure Investigation*. *Journal of Biblical Literature* 111 (1992): 729–30.

Pavey, Emma. "An Analysis of *It*-Clefts within a Role and Reference Grammar Framework." *Work Papers of the Summer Institute of Linguistics, University of North Dakota Session* 47 (2003). Online: http://www.und.edu/dept/linguistics/wp/2003Pavey.pdf.

———. "The English It-Cleft Construction: A Role and Reference Grammar Analysis." Ph.D. diss., University of Sussex, 2004. Online: http://linguistics.buffalo.edu/people/faculty/vanvalin/rrg/PAVEY%202004.pdf.

Plummer, Alfred. *A Critical and Exegetical Commentary on the Gospel According to S. Luke.* International Critical Commentary. Edinburgh: T & T Clark, 1896.

Polyani, Livia. *The Linguistic Structure of Discourse.* Technical Report CSLI-96-200. Stanford, Calif.: CSLI Publications, 1996.

Porter, Stanley E. *Idioms of the Greek New Testament.* 2nd ed. Sheffield: Sheffield Academic, 1999.

Porter, Stanley E., and Matthew Brook O'Donnell. "The Greek Verbal Network Viewed from a Probabilistic Standpoint: An Exercise in Hallidayan Linguistics." *Filología Neotestamentaria* 14 (2001): 3–41.

Powell, Charles E., and John Baima. "Εἰ μή Clauses in the NT: Interpretation and Translation." Online: http://bible.org/article/font-facegreekeij-mhv-font-clauses-nt-interpretation-and-translation.

Reed, Jeffrey T. *A Discourse Analysis of Philippians: Method and Rhetoric in the Debate over Literary Integrity.* Journal for the Study of the New Testament: Supplement Series 136. Sheffield: Sheffield Academic, 1997.

Revell, E. J. "The Repetition of Introductions to Speech as a Feature of Biblical Hebrew." *Vetus Testamentum* 47 (1997): 91–110.

Reynolds, Stephen M. "The Zero Tense in Greek." *Westminster Theological Journal* 32 (1969): 68–72.

Roberts, Craige. "Information Structure: Towards an Integrated Formal Theory of Pragmatics." Pages 91–136 in *Papers in Semantics.* Edited by Jae-Hak Yoon and Andreas Kathol. Working Papers in Linguistics 49. Ohio State University Department of Linguistics, 1996. [Roberts's 1999 revision of this essay is available online: http://www.ling.ohio-state.edu/~croberts/papers-roberts.html.]

Robertson, A. T. *A Grammar of the Greek New Testament in the Light of Historical Research.* 1919. Repr., Bellingham, Wash.: Logos, 2006.

Ropes, James Hardy. *A Critical and Exegetical Commentary on the Epistle of St. James.* International Critical Commentary. Edinburgh: T & T Clark, 1916.

Runge, Steven E. "A Discourse-Functional Description of Participant Reference in Biblical Hebrew Narrative." D.Litt. diss., University of Stellenbosch, 2007.

———. "The Effect of Redundancy on Perceptions of Emphasis and Discontinuity." Paper presented at the annual meeting of the Society of Biblical Literature, New Orleans, La., 21–24 November 2009.

———. "The Exegetical Significance of Prospective Demonstrative Pronouns in Luke's Gospel." Paper presented at the Pacific Northwest regional meeting of the Evangelical Theological Society, Salem, Ore., 24 February 2007. Online: http://www.logos.com/media/academic/runge/cataphoric_pronouns.pdf.

———. "'I Want You to Know …' The Exegetical Significance of Meta-Comments for Identifying Key Propositions." Paper presented at the annual meeting of the Evangelical Theological Society, Providence, R.I., 19–21 November 2008. Online: http://www.ntdiscourse.org/docs/Runge_Metacomments_ETS.pdf.

———. "Joel 3:1–5 in Acts 2:17–21: The Discourse and Text-Critical Implications of Quotation and Variation from the LXX." Pages 103–13 in *Exegetical Studies*. Vol. 2 of *Early Christian Literature and Intertextuality*. Edited by Craig A. Evans and Danny Zacharias. Library of New Testament Studies. New York: T & T Clark, 2009.

———. *The Lexham Discourse Greek New Testament*. Bellingham, Wash.: Logos Bible Software, 2007.

———. "Pragmatic Effects of Semantically Redundant Referring Expressions in Biblical Hebrew Narrative." *Journal of Northwest Semitic Languages* 32, no. 2 (2006): 85–102.

———. "Reconsidering the Aspect of the Historical Present Indicative in Narrative." Paper presented at the annual meeting of the Society of Biblical Literature, New Orleans, La., 21–24 November 2009.

———. "Relative Saliency and Information Structure in Mark's Parable of the Sower." *Journal of the Linguistics Institute of Ancient and Biblical Greek* 1 (2008): 1–16. Online: http://liabg.org/liabg/vol1/JLIABG1-1_Runge.pdf.

———. Review of Ivan Shing Chung Kwong, *The Word Order of the Gospel of Luke: Its Foregrounded Messages*. *Review of Biblical Literature* (26 April 2008). Online: http://www.bookreviews.org/pdf/5903_6264.pdf.

———. "Teaching Them What NOT to Do: The Nuances of Negation in the Greek New Testament." Paper presented at the annual meeting of the Evangelical Theology Society, San Diego, Calif., 13–16 November 2007. Online: http://www.logos.com/media/academic/runge/negation_pragmatics.pdf.

———. "The Verbal Aspect of the Historical Present Indicative in Narrative." Paper presented at the annual meeting of the Society of Biblical Literature, New Orleans, La., 21–24 November 2009. Online: http://www.ntdiscourse.org/docs/ReconsideringHP.pdf.

———. "What Difference Does It Make If NT Greek Has a Default Word Order or Not?" Paper presented at the annual meeting of the Evangelical Theological Society, Washington, D.C., 15–17 November 2006.

———. "Where Three or More Are Gathered, There Is Discontinuity." Paper presented at the international meeting of the Society of Biblical Literature, Edinburgh, 2–6 July 2006.

Runge, Steven E., and Sean Boisen. "'So, Brothers': Pauline Use of the Vocative." Paper presented at the annual meeting of the Society of Biblical Literature, San Diego, Calif., 17–20 November 2007.

Sanday, William, and Arthur C. Headlam. *A Critical and Exegetical Commentary on the Epistle of the Romans.* 3rd ed. International Critical Commentary. Edinburgh: T & T Clark, 1897.

Sanders, J. T. "The Transition from Opening Epistolary Thanksgiving to Body in the Letters of the Pauline Corpus." *Journal of Biblical Literature* 71 (1962): 348–62.

Schwyzer, Eduard. *Griechische Grammatik: Auf der Grundlage von Karl Brugmanns Griechischer Grammatik.* 2 vols. Munich: Beck, 1939–1950.

Seters, John Van. *The Edited Bible: The Curious History of the "Editor" in Biblical Criticism.* Winona Lake, Ind.: Eisenbrauns, 2006.

Simcox, William Henry. *The Language of the New Testament.* New York: T. Whittaker, 1890.

Smith, Michael B. "Cataphoric Pronouns as Mental Space Designators: Their Conceptual Import and Discourse Function." Pages 61–90 in *Cognitive and Communicative Approaches to Linguistic Analysis.* Edited by Ellen Contini-Morava, Robert S. Kirsner, and Betsy Rodríquez-Bachiller. Studies in Functional and Structural Linguistics 51. Amsterdam: John Benjamins, 2004.

Soanes, Catherine, and Angus Stevenson, eds. *Concise Oxford English Dictionary.* Electronic ed. 11th ed. Oxford: Oxford University Press, 2004.

Sperber, Dan, and Deirdre Wilson. *Relevance: Communication and Cognition.* Oxford: Blackwell, 2001.

Thompson, Sandra A. "Subordination and Narrative Event Structure." Pages 435–54 in *Coherence and Grounding in Discourse.* Edited by Russell S. Tomlin. Amsterdam: John Benjamins, 1987.

Thompson, Sandra A., and Robert E. Longacre. "Adverbial Clauses." Pages 171–234. In *Complex Constructions.* Vol. 2 of *Language Typology and Syntactic Description.* Edited by Timothy Shopen. Cambridge: Cambridge University Press, 1985.

Titrud, Kermit. "The Function of καί in the Greek New Testament and an Application to 2 Peter." Pages 239–70 in *Linguistics and New Testament Interpretation: Essays on Discourse Analysis.* Edited by David Alan Black, Katharine Barnwell, and Stephen Levinsohn. Nashville: Broadman, 1992.

Wallace, Daniel B. *Greek Grammar Beyond the Basics: An Exegetical Syntax of the New Testament.* Grand Rapids: Zondervan, 1999.

Wenham, Gordon J. *Genesis 16–50*. Word Biblical Commentary 2. Dallas: Word, 1994.

White, John L. "Introductory Formulae in the Body of the Pauline Letter." *Journal of Biblical Literature* 90 (1971): 91–97.

Winer, G. B. *A Treatise on the Grammar of New Testament Greek*. Translated and revised by W. F. Moulton. 3rd ed. Edinburgh: T & T Clark, 1882.

Young, Richard A. *Intermediate New Testament Greek: A Linguistic and Exegetical Approach*. Nashville: Broadman & Holman, 1994.